Ius Gentium: Comparative Perspectives on Law and Justice

Volume 115

Ius Gentium is a book series which discusses the central questions of law and justice from a comparative perspective. The books in this series collect the contrasting and overlapping perspectives of lawyers, judges, philosophers and scholars of law from the world's many different jurisdictions for the purposes of comparison, harmonisation, and the progressive development of law and legal institutions. Each volume makes a new comparative study of an important area of law. This book series continues the work of the well-known journal of the same name and provides the basis for a better understanding of all areas of legal science.

The *Ius Gentium* series provides a valuable resource for lawyers, judges, legislators, scholars, and both graduate students and researchers in globalisation, comparative law, legal theory and legal practice. The series has a special focus on the development of international legal standards and transnational legal cooperation.

Doron Goldbarsht • Louis de Koker
Editors

Financial Crime and the Law

Identifying and Mitigating Risks

Springer

Editors
Doron Goldbarsht
Macquarie Law School
Macquarie University
Sydney, NSW, Australia

Louis de Koker
La Trobe Law School
Bundoora, VIC, Australia

ISSN 1534-6781 ISSN 2214-9902 (electronic)
Ius Gentium: Comparative Perspectives on Law and Justice
ISBN 978-3-031-59542-4 ISBN 978-3-031-59543-1 (eBook)
https://doi.org/10.1007/978-3-031-59543-1

This Springer imprint is published by the registered company Springer Nature Switzerland AG
The registered company address is: Gewerbestrasse 11, 6330 Cham, Switzerland

To our wives, Erin and Jeanne, and our children, Arielle, Hallel, Allie and Louis. Without their continuing support and their sacrifices, our work would not be possible
Doron and Louis

Contents

Contributors

Louis de Koker La Trobe Law School, Bundoora, VIC, Australia

Jamie Ferrill Australian Graduate School of Policing and Security, Charles Sturt University, Bathurst, NSW, Australia

Doron Goldbarsht Macquarie Law School, Sydney, NSW, Australia

Rhianna Hamilton Queen's University, Kingston, ON, Canada

Hannah Harris Macquarie Law School, Sydney, NSW, Australia

John Langdale Department of Security Studies and Criminology, Macquarie University, Sydney, NSW, Australia

Christian Leuprecht Queen's University, Kingston, ON, Canada
Royal Military College, Kingston, ON, Canada

Michael Levi School of Social Sciences, Cardiff University, Cardiff, UK

Charles Littrell Central Bank of The Bahamas, Nassau, NP, Bahamas

Rachel Southworth Australian Graduate School of Policing and Security, Charles Sturt University, Canberra, Australia

Milind Tiwari Australian Graduate School of Policing and Security, Charles Sturt University, Bathurst, NSW, Australia

Financial Crime and the Law: Identifying and Mitigating Risks

Doron Goldbarsht and Louis de Koker

Abstract In 2012 the Financial Action Task Force, the global intergovernmental standard-setter for anti-money laundering (AML), combating terrorist financing (CTF) and proliferation financing (CPF) standards embedded a mandatory risk-based approach in its standards. This has fundamentally changed AML/CTF/CPF regulatory and compliance approaches globally. This chapter considers the history behind the adoption of this approach and the implications of the approach, framing the papers in this collection.

1 Introduction

Global financial crime measures were rule-based when they originally introduced, especially in United Nations Conventions since the 1980s. Instruments such as the 1988 UN Convention against Illicit Traffic in Narcotic Drugs and Psychotropic Substances (the Vienna Convention),[1] the 1999 UN International Convention for the Suppression of the Financing of Terrorism,[2] the 2000 UN Convention against Transnational Organized Crime (the Palermo Convention)[3] and the 2003 UN Convention against Corruption[4] require countries to adopt laws to criminalise specified conduct. This approach was largely reflected of the rule-based nature of the associated criminal law.

[1] United Nations (1988).

[2] United Nations (1999).

[3] United Nations (2000).

[4] United Nations (2003).

D. Goldbarsht (✉)
Macquarie Law School, Sydney, NSW, Australia
e-mail: doron.goldbarsht@mq.edu.au

L. de Koker
La Trobe Law School, Bundoora, VIC, Australia

D. Goldbarsht, L. de Koker (eds.), *Financial Crime and the Law*, Ius Gentium: Comparative Perspectives on Law and Justice 115,
https://doi.org/10.1007/978-3-031-59543-1_1

The Financial Action Task Force, the global intergovernmental standard-setter for anti-money laundering (AML), combating terrorist financing (CTF) and proliferation financing (CPF) standards adopted a similar approach when it formulated its Forty Recommendations on combating of money laundering in 1990. Over time, that approach of the FATF shifted, in line with changes in financial supervision and financial risk management. By 2012 the FATF adopted a mandatory risk-based approach to AML/CTF and in 2020, it extended risk-based measures to its CPF standards.[5]

How did this come about? This chapter traces the history of that development and some of key motivating factors. It sets the background to the papers in this volume that explores different elements of the risk-based approach to AML/CTF/CPF.

2 Paradigmatic Transition: Rules to Risks

The FATF Recommendations, originally adopted 1990 and subsequently revised, are detailed technical standards that cover regulatory, supervisory, law enforcement, and legal issues. While the 2003 version of the revised Recommendations[6] allowed the adoption of some risk elements by regulated entities, the 2012 version embedded the risk-based approach as mandatory and core to a range of both government and institutional AML/CTF/CPF measures.

Before the introduction of risk measures, the rule-based approach held sway. In the rule-based approach the FATF standards determined the contents of domestic laws and regulations, though countries often went beyond the FATF standards[7] Domestic regulations furthermore specified the due diligence measures that regulated institutions had to employ, for example they prescribed how individuals, companies and trusts had to be identified and their identities verified.[8] Regulatory guidance often provided examples of suspicious conduct and transactions that had to be reported to financial intelligence units. The rule-based approach was not risk-insensitive. The rule-based approach generally incorporated the regulator's views of the relevant risks and appropriate mitigation of those risks.

Under the rule-based model, all participants in specific cohorts or groups were treated similarly. Rigid adherence to transparent and well-defined rules meant that the same standards were applied to all members of such groups or cohorts.

However, alongside this rigidity emerged a certain predictability, enabling malevolent actors to exploit the prescribed regulatory measures by manipulating their transactions to evade detection.

[5] See De Koker (2024), p. X.

[6] FATF (2023).

[7] De Koker (2003), p. 176.

[8] De Koker (2023).

The rule-based approach became increasingly viewed as ineffective at curbing money laundering and terrorist financing activities. For instance, in the realm of money laundering, in which perpetrators are inclined to identify and exploit regulatory gaps, the imposition of rigid rules was viewed as counterproductive. Conversely, within a dynamic regulatory landscape, the risk-based approach seemed to offer a conduit to seamlessly interlink 'detection, prevention and control' with areas that are the focal points of regulatory concern.

The formal rule-based approach also became blamed for over-compliance[9] and for over-reporting of suspicious transactions by regulated institutions. This phenomenon resulted in elevated compliance costs for private sector entities and diminished investigative capacities for financial intelligence units.[10]

Increasingly, therefore, the adoption of the risk-based measures became viewed as a corrective measure to address the bureaucratic and formalistic weaknesses of a rule-based approach. This view was not, however, informed by research and sound evidence. The process of adoption unfolded over a decade.

In 2003 the FATF standards were extensively revised. In this process optional risk-sensitive measures were introduced. For example, the key customer due diligence (CDD) standard stipulated that:[11]

> Financial institutions should apply each of the (prescribed) CDD measures..., but may determine the extent of such measures on a risk sensitive basis depending on the type of customer, business relationship or transaction. The measures that are taken should be consistent with any guidelines issued by competent authorities. For higher risk categories, financial institutions should perform enhanced due diligence. In certain circumstances, where there are low risks, countries may decide that financial institutions can apply reduced or simplified measures.

The 2003 Recommendations also set out a range of examples where simplified CDD measures may be considered[12] and countries were required to regulate and supervise financial institutions and designated non-financial businesses and professions "having regard to the risk of money laundering or terrorist financing in that sector".[13]

The introduction of the new risk elements did not lead to immediate, universal adoption. European regulators, for example, were more reluctant to dilute their rule-based approach as they were concerned about inconsistent approaches in the European Union. In 2007, under the leadership of the United Kingdom, the FATF produced its first high-level guidance of the risk-based approach.[14] This was an important opportunity for the FATF to reach internal consensus on the implications of the risk-based approach and to provide guidance on its implementation and benefits. The core benefit was summarised as follows:

---

[9]De Koker and Casanovas (2024).

[10]Chaikin (2009).

[11]FATF (2003) Rec 5.

[12]FATF (2003) INR5.9.

[13]FATF (2003) Rec 23, read with Rec 24.

[14]FATF (2007).

> By adopting a risk-based approach, competent authorities and financial institutions are able to ensure that measures to prevent or mitigate money laundering and terrorist financing are commensurate to the risks identified. This will allow resources to be allocated in the most efficient ways. The principle is that resources should be directed in accordance with priorities so that the greatest risks receive the highest attention. The alternative approaches are that resources are either applied evenly, so that all financial institutions, customers, products, etc. receive equal attention, or that resources are targeted, but on the basis of factors other than the risk assessed. This can inadvertently lead to a 'tick box' approach with the focus on meeting regulatory needs rather than combating money laundering or terrorist financing.

The FATF at that stage was also aware that the benefits and challenges of the approach should be recognised. The report therefore set these out in more detail and summarised them in a box as follows[15]:

Potential Benefits:

- Better management of risks and cost-benefits.
- Financial institution focus on real and identified threats.
- Flexibility to adapt to risks that change over time.

Potential Challenges:

- Identifying appropriate information to conduct a sound risk analysis.
- Addressing short term transitional costs.
- Greater need for more expert staff capable of making sound judgments;
- Regulatory response to potential diversity of practice.

In 2010 the FATF began to consider the next significant revision of its standards. Its 2010 consultation paper consulted specifically on amendments to the risk-based elements of its standards. At that stage its concern was merely that "the current text on the Risk-Based Approach (RBA) may lack sufficient clarity, and is located in several different parts of the FATF Standards."[16] The solution it explored was to develop "a single comprehensive statement on the RBA, which could be incorporated into the FATF Standards as a new Interpretative Note dedicated to the RBA and applicable to a set of Recommendations."[17] Even though it would be in an interpretative note, the FATF was consulting on a model where with risk assessments and enhanced measures in higher risk cases would be mandatory for countries and institutions. The industry responses received from both developed and developing economies were largely supportive of the proposal, generally noting its improved resource management benefits.[18] They were similarly supportive of risk-based supervision.

The European Banking Federation, for example, supported risk-based supervision "in order to avoid supervisors and legislators applying more prescriptive rule-

---

[15]FATF (2007) par. 1.22.

[16]FATF (2010) par 5.

[17]FATF (2010) par 6.

[18]FATF (2011a, b).

based obligations and supervisory techniques which undermine the principles and benefits of adopting a risk-based approach to manage and mitigate money laundering and terrorist financing risks."[19]

The International Banking Federation pointed to the aftermath of the Global Financial Crises and argued that[20]:

> With the many demands placed on financial institutions around the world following recent economic turmoil, including a host of new regulations and capital requirements, emphasising the risk-based approach in AML/CTF efforts becomes increasingly important to ensure resources are targeted properly and efforts focused where they will be most productive.

In general, the message in the submissions was that financial institutions were already good at implementing the risk-based approach and welcomed a more thoughtful, broader application. The Australian Banking Association, for example, pointed out in response to the proposal on risk-based supervision[21]:

> The risk-based approach is embedded into bank AML programs and operating models. Consideration would need to be given to the impact on operations of any changes to the supervisory model.

Given this broad support expressed by industry, the FATF embedded the risk-based approach as mandatory in its 2012 standards, setting it out in Recommendation 1 and detailing it in further Recommendations and interpretative notes.

Today, the approach serves as a strategic methodology to ensure that the countermeasures implemented for the detection, evaluation, and comprehension of money laundering and terrorist financing activities align with the levels of risk identified.[22] In principle, the risk-based approach empower regulated entities to allocate resources towards sectors with heightened risk profiles that were intrinsic to their geographic location, customer demographics, and operational framework.[23] However, the information and expertise challenges that the FATF recorded in 2007 still remain. These limit the effectiveness and efficiency of the risk-based approach.[24]

3 Empowering Proactive Compliance

The contemporary landscape of AML/CTF initiatives has been fundamentally reshaped by the ascendance of the risk-based approach. Traditional regulatory responsibilities, primarily the identification of money laundering and terrorist

---

[19] FATF (2011b), p. 61.

[20] FATF (2011b), p. 104.

[21] FATF (2011b), p. 23.

[22] FATF (2012–2023) INR 1.

[23] De Koker (2009); Ai and Tang (2011), p. 275; FATF (2023), p. 10.

[24] De Koker and Goldbarsht (2024), p. X.

financing threats and risks and the prescription of appropriate responses, have been redistributed from traditional institutional bodies, such as regulators and supervisors to the reporting entities themselves.[25] Within this framework, reporting entities are tasked with identifying and assessing the risks that necessitate mitigation.[26] They must then devise the most fitting strategies to effectively and proportionally address the relevant risks. This recalibration reflects a shift towards a measure of AML/CTF/CPF-related self-regulation by reporting entities. The landscape now demands that these entities operate as proactive agents, playing pivotal roles in the systematic reduction of money laundering risks. This vigilance ensures the alignment of transactions with the institution's comprehensive understanding of the customer, their operational domain, and their risk propensity. Consequently, entities can no longer rely solely on established procedural norms for compliance with AML/CTF regulations.

It is important to note that the approach is not limited to financial institutions but extends to designated non-financial businesses and professions. Entities in sectors such as real estate, legal, and accounting are required to document transactions or activities earmarked as 'high risk' within those realms.[27]

The risk-based approach demands that reporting entities undertake appropriate risk assessments, tailored to their customer demographics, business frameworks, and geographic locations. This entails deploying enhanced due diligence measures where risks are assessed as higher and potentially—and optionally—simplified measures where risks are assessed as lower. However, the juxtaposition of this approach with the FATF's pre-defined and rule-based categorisation of certain customers (such as politically exposed persons) as higher risk presents a continuing paradox that further complicates the risk-based approach. Importantly, not all aspects of the FATF standards are subject to the risk-based approach. Proliferation financing for example, is for example, not fully subject to risk-based approach as simplified due diligence is not allowed in lower risk scenarios.[28]

The risk-based approach is not exact and accurate and may fail in a range of unforeseeable ways. It cannot work in a context where the regulator sets and enforces standards that in practice translates into a "zero tolerance" or an intolerant approach, i.e. where each prevention failure is viewed as a contravention of AML/CTF/CPF regulation or where negligent prevention failures attract mega fines. Within the framework, asymmetries in threat information can for example lead regulatory agencies and reporting entities to reasonably arrive at divergent views of threat levels. Regulators have to adopt a reasonable position in this regard to prevent entities from adopting overly-conservative responses[29] that limit the efficiency dividend that the risk-based approach is supposed to provide.

---

[25] De Koker (2009), p. 336.

[26] FATF (2012–2023), Rec 10.

[27] Goldbarsht and Benson (2023) and Bello and Harvey (2016).

[28] De Koker (2024).

[29] De Koker and Casanovas (2024).

4 Balancing Profit and Risk

The risk-based approach provides regulated entities with flexibility. Entities are responsible for categorising customers into higher and lower risk groups. The classification hinges on variables such as country or geographic risk, customer risk, and product or service risk. Exact criteria for the categories remain ambiguous, lending complexity to the task of assessing the risk levels of a customer. Customer, product and service risk assessment for each reporting entity is based on a comprehensive evaluation of the information gathered within the framework of their customer due diligence measures through the risk-based approach.[30] This process culminates in the creation of a customer risk profile.[31]

In the domain of AML/CTF, a significant challenge emerges from the fact that certain impacts, though inherently negative, can paradoxically hold financial benefit for the entity. Facilitating transactions with criminal entities seeking to launder illicit funds may yield substantial short-term gains. The act of money laundering itself does not inherently compromise the commercial interests of the facilitating organisation, whether it be a bank or a casino. The risks to the entity rather stems from other dimensions. First, such facilitation intrinsically proves detrimental to the broader society due to its potential repercussions. Second, it constitutes a proscribed activity, thereby inviting associated reputational and legal ramifications. In essence, a comprehensive evaluation of the negative impacts entails considering a range of factors, from regulatory fines to stakeholder concerns and reputational costs.

The spectrum of adverse repercussions includes the following[32]:

(i) *Regulatory sanctions*: The potential negative impact of regulatory fines hinges on the probability of detection and the magnitude of the penalty. Regulators must cultivate credibility in both elements to engender a substantiated threat. In addition to the fines themselves, organisations often incur substantial legal expenses in the immediate aftermath of regulatory intervention.

(ii) *Stakeholder impacts*: The consideration of a broader spectrum of stakeholders aligns with the recent emergence of corporate social responsibility principles. Regrettably, the diffuse repercussions of money laundering and terrorist financing often fail to resonate within organisations. Yet these adverse consequences often reverberate across national borders, affecting victims of criminal activity and terrorism in disparate countries. The more diffused the impact, the lower the likelihood that an organisation will adequately acknowledge and address it.

(iii) *Reputational risk*: Reputational risk is often a key concern but it is very difficult to assess this risk. Should an organisation's involvement in money laundering or terrorist financing become widely known that fact may impact on its stakeholder loyalty (see (ii) above, leading to customer and investor attrition

[30] Goldbarsht and de Koker (2022).

[31] Sinha (2020), p. 54.

[32] Goldbarsht and Sheedy (2024), p. X.

> and complicating recruitment and retention of staff. Costs of equity and debt capital and insurance premiums may increase and there might be a risk of loss of operational licences.[33]

AML/CTF and other risk management lapses frequently materialise due to organisational cultures that undervalue sound risk management. This in turn may result from factors such as overconfidence, a myopic short-term focus, and remuneration structures. These elements collectively hinder the cultivation of a sound risk culture within the organisation, resulting in the insufficient resourcing of risk management systems and functions, coupled with a lax approach to compliance and risk mitigation behaviour. Furthermore, red flags—indicative of potential risk scenarios—are frequently disregarded or neglected in this context. Within such an operational milieu, instances of non-compliance with risk-based methodologies become almost inescapable consequences.

The multifaceted interplay between organisational priorities, cultural attributes, and behavioural incentives underlies the landscape of AML and broader risk management failures.[34] The organisation's proclivity to emphasise goals beyond risk management is exacerbated by cognitive biases such as overconfidence, which can lead to a skewed perception of invulnerability to risks. Moreover, the prevailing culture often exalts short-term gains, leading to the prioritisation of immediate outcomes over long-term risk resilience.

The interconnectedness between cultural drivers and compensation systems should not be overlooked. Remuneration structures that disproportionately reward short-term financial success may inadvertently foster behaviour that disregards or downplays risk concerns, resulting in an imbalanced risk culture. This, in turn, engenders an environment where risk management functions are inadequately supported and risk compliance lapses do not result in appropriate penalties. Consequently, the organisation encounters a compounding deficiency in its ability to detect, address and mitigate risks effectively.

The ramifications of this compromised risk culture are manifest in a lack of resources allocated to risk management systems, leading to their inefficacy. Inadequate resourcing, coupled with a lenient stance on compliance and risk management infractions, creates a feedback loop that perpetuates a subpar risk culture. Moreover, the tendency to overlook or dismiss red flags signifies a breakdown in the organisation's ability to proactively identify and address potential risk scenarios.

Ultimately, the collective culmination of these factors results in an environment where deviations from sound risk-based approaches become almost inevitable. This manifestation of non-compliance and the accompanying ineffectual risk management strategies are a direct outcome of the organisational culture's misalignment with risk-focused imperatives. Thus, the establishment of a robust risk culture is fundamental to sound risk management within organisations.

---

[33] Sheedy (2021), p. 9.

[34] Sheedy (2021), p. 36.

The transition from a rule-based approach to a risk-based paradigm has also lead to important changes in the allocation of responsibilities concerning the identification of suspicious matter reports (SMRs). Much more responsibility was shifted to the wide range of reporting entities to identify what is suspicious given their risk assessments. Divergent views and concepts of 'risk' and 'suspicious" have emerged. The loss of clarity and some consistency regarding what can be viewed as suspicious has not received sufficient attention. SMRs fundamental to money laundering and terrorist financing rest on the subjective premise of 'suspicion'. In essence, an SMR serves as a notification to law enforcement regarding 'suspicious' activities of clients that might indicate potential money laundering or terrorist or proliferation financing. The decision to file an SMR is at the discretion of the reporting officer and contingent on their assessment of the risk presented by the customer or transaction.[35] The risk-based model has therefore led to a more fragmented approach to risk and suspicion, dispersing responsibility among a multitude of actors rather than centralising it within governmental purview. This has inadvertently spawned a range of interpretations of key risk-related concepts and views. Uncertainty has not led to fewer reports being filed. Risk-averse reporting entities may incline towards a conservative stance, opting for over-reporting in order to mitigate the ambiguity surrounding potentially suspect transactions.

Within this scenario, a degree of standardisation in risk discourse could be advantageous. Such standardisation could support a more consistent approach in the identification transactions to be reported. Nevertheless, caution is needed to ensure that the shift towards standardised definitions does not inadvertently lead to a reversion to rule-based regulations. The principles underlying the risk-based approach—emphasising contextual considerations and adaptive strategies—must not be diluted by an overly rigid standardisation process.

In conclusion, the migration from rule-based to risk-based paradigms has redefined the AML/CTF/CPF landscape. Wiht the benefit of experience of the risk-based approach it is opportune to evaluate its success and to consider whether modifications would be beneficial.

5 This Collection

The chapters in this collection—all of which were double peer reviewed—explore various aspects of financial crime risk management, shedding light on emerging challenges and proposing innovative solutions. Each chapter provides the author's perspective on financial crime and the measures required to combat it. Financial crime mitigation is a complex and evolving challenge in today's interconnected world. This collection thoroughly investigates various facets of the challenge, exploring innovative strategies and emerging trends across a range of critical topics.

[35] Sinha (2020), p. 56.

Through a multidisciplinary lens, it investigates the intricate interplay between financial crimes, technology, sustainability, and international cooperation.

Exploring the interplay between financial crime and cryptocurrencies reveals a complex web of connections. In their chapter (*The Crime-Crypto Nexus: Nuancing Risk across Crypto-Crime Transactions*) (Hamilton and Leuprecht 2024), Rhianna Hamilton and Christian Leuprecht critically examine the growing concern about the exploitation of cryptocurrencies for illicit activities. It analyses real-world cases of money laundering, tax evasion, and terrorism financing that utilise the anonymity and borderless nature of digital currencies. The chapter also looks into regulatory responses and the potential role of blockchain analytics in combating crypto-related financial crimes.

In response to escalating deforestation concerns, governments have enacted 'destination country laws' to criminalise the importation of illegally harvested timber. However, these regulations often overlook a significant accomplice in global deforestation: financial institutions. The chapter by Hannah Harris (*Financing Environmental Crime: Financial Sector Complicity in Global Deforestation and Opportunities for Regulatory Intervention*) (Harris 2024) investigates the unexplored territory of the financial sector's involvement in enabling harmful deforestation and facilitating illegal logging. By examining existing regulatory frameworks, it sheds light on the limitations of destination country laws. The chapter then proceeds to map how financial institutions contribute to deforestation incentives and the illicit gains from illegal logging. Ultimately, the chapter argues that conquering deforestation demands the active engagement of the financial sector, heralding a global path towards sustainable economic growth.

In their chapter (*Weeding Out Dirty Money: Cannabis Regulations and Financial Crime*) (Ferrill and Tiwari 2024) Jamie Ferrill and Milind Tiwari examine the potential relationship between cannabis regulations and money laundering. With evolving global cannabis laws and a significant market, they explore how criminal proceeds from this market might require money laundering. Amid changing regulations, the authors analyse how these changes impact the scale of money laundering. Using Australia as a case study, Ferrill and Tiwari employ the rational choice theory and empirical data to assess the influence of cannabis regulations on money laundering potential and to consider policy implications.

As discussed above, the application of a risk-based approach in managing financial crime risk is a fundamental FATF requirement, influencing legislation, regulations, and private-sector practices. In their chapter (*Application of the Risk-Based Approach (RBA) for Financial Crime Risk Management by Banks*) (Southworth and Levi 2024), Rachel Southworth and Michael Levi investigate how banks interpret and implement the risk-based approach. Challenges and variations arise in the conceptualisation and execution of the approach, impacting intelligence gathering and effectiveness measurement. Given the reliance on risk-based approach outcomes by financial intelligence units, the authors argue for a need for greater transparency in methodologies, as understanding these practical challenges is crucial to enhancing private sector participation in the financial crime control landscape.

In 2020 the FATF extended its risk-based measures to its proliferation financing standards. In his chapter (*FATF's Combating of Financing of Proliferation Standards: Private Sector Implementation Challenges*) (De Koker 2024), Louis de Koker addresses the challenges that regulated entities face in complying with 2020 FATF amendments. Drawing on interviews with global experts and the identified challenges, the author identifies elements of appropriate national implementation strategies responding to the new standards.

As terrorists adapt to technological advancements, they employ increasingly covert financing methods. Doron Goldbarsht's chapter (*Dancing in the Dark: Terrorist Financing via the Dark Web*) (Goldbarsht 2024) dives into the underbelly of the internet—the dark web—and its role in facilitating criminal activities, including terrorism financing. It explores the challenges of monitoring and combating illicit transactions within hidden online spaces, calling for heightened technological and collaborative efforts to counteract these threats.

Addressing potential biases in national AML/CTF risk assessments, Charles Littrell's chapter (*Economic and Demographic Biases in FATF Mutual Evaluation Results*) (Littrell 2024) examines how preconceptions can impact the effectiveness of risk management strategies. This chapter empirically examines biases within the FATF's mutual evaluation reports, identifying several biases. It highlights issues such as punitive measures against economically weaker countries and biases against certain regions, including small island states and black-majority countries. The chapter highlights the need for fair and balanced jurisdictional AML/CTF assessments to ensure equity and effectiveness within the global financial ecosystem.

The centrality of casinos within the transnational crime system poses a distinct challenge in the fight against money laundering. An essential quandary surfaces as governments navigate the complex terrain of countering crime and money laundering while concurrently pursuing economic strategies aimed at bolstering employment, international tourism, and revenue generated through casinos. In his chapter (*Combating Money Laundering in Southeast Asian and Australian Casinos*) (Langdale 2024) John Langdale examines the multifaceted dynamics of money laundering within Southeast Asian and Australian casinos, contextualised within the broader framework of the East Asian transnational crime network. The chapter looks at the accelerated growth of transnational crime, particularly in regions—such as the Mekong area—with weaker governance structures. Casinos are critically examined as enablers of this criminal system, unveiling the connectivity between illicit activities and gambling establishments.

The collection concludes with a reflective chapter (*FATF's Risk-Based Approach: Has the Pendulum Swung Too Far?*) (De Koker and Goldbarsht 2024). Louis de Koker and Doron Goldbarsht reflect on some of the challenges that emerged relating to the risk-based approach and identify areas for future research.

Together, these chapters provide a comprehensive overview of the multifaceted landscape of financial crime mitigation. By thoroughly exploring each topic, the collection illuminates the complexity of the challenges at hand and emphasises the need for adaptable, multidisciplinary and collaborative approaches to effectively combat financial crimes.

References

Ai L, Tang J (2011) Risk-based approach for designing enterprise-wide AML information system solution. J Financ Crime 18(3):268–276

Bello A, Harvey J (2016) From a risk-based to an uncertainty-based approach to anti-money laundering compliance. Secur J 30(1):24–38

Chaikin D (2009) How effective are suspicious transaction reporting systems? J Money Laund Control 12(3):238–253

De Koker L (2003) Money laundering control: the south African model. J Money Laund Control 6(2):166–181

De Koker L (2009) Identifying and managing low money laundering risk: perspectives on FATF's risk-based guidance. J Financ Crime 16(4):334–352

De Koker L (2023) South Africa's initial implementation of the financial action task Force's customer identity verification standards: perspectives and reflection on regulatory processes and approaches. In: Chitimira H, Warikandwa T (eds) Financial inclusion regulatory practices in SADC. Routledge, London, 18–45

De Koker L (2024) Chapter 6: The FATF's combating of financing of proliferation standards: private sector implementation challenges. In: Goldbarsht D, de Koker L (eds) Financial crime and the law: identifying and mitigating risks, Ius Gentium: comparative perspectives on law and justice, vol 115. Springer, Cham

De Koker L, Casanovas P (2024) Chapter 3: De-risking, de-banking and denials of bank services: an over-compliance dilemma? In: De Koker L, Goldbarsht D (eds) Financial crime, law and governance, Ius Gentium: comparative perspectives on law and justice. Springer, Cham

De Koker L, Goldbarsht D (2024) Chapter 10: FATF's risk-based approach: has the pendulum swung too far? In: Goldbarsht D, de Koker L (eds) Financial crime and the law: identifying and mitigating risks, Ius Gentium: comparative perspectives on law and justice, vol 115. Springer, Cham

FATF (2003) The forty recommendations. FATF https://www.fatf-gafi.org/content/dam/fatf-gafi/recommendations/FATF%20Recommendations%202003.pdf

FATF (2007) Guidance on the risk-based approach to combatting money laundering and terrorist financing: high level principles and procedures. https://www.fatf-gafi.org/content/dam/fatf-gafi/guidance/High%20Level%20Principles%20and%20Procedures.pdf.coredownload.inline.pdf

FATF (2010) The review of the standards—preparation for the 4th round of mutual evaluations. Consultation paper. https://www.fatf-gafi.org/content/dam/fatf-gafi/public-consultation/First%20public%20consultation%20document.pdf

FATF (2011a) The review of the standards—preparation for the 4th round of mutual evaluations: compilation of responses from the financial sector—Part One. https://www.fatf-gafi.org/content/dam/fatf-gafi/public-consultation/First%20public%20consultation%20document%20responses%20financial%20sector%20part%201.pdf

FATF (2011b) Consultation of proposed changes to the fatf standards: compilation of responses from the financial sector. https://www.fatf-gafi.org/content/dam/fatf-gafi/public-consultation/Second%20public%20consultation%20document%20responses%20financial%20sector.pdf

Ferrill J, Tiwari M (2024) Chapter 4: Weeding out dirty money: cannabis regulations and financial crime. In: Goldbarsht D, de Koker L (eds) Financial crime and the law: identifying and mitigating risks, Ius Gentium: comparative perspectives on law and justice, vol 115. Springer, Cham

Financial Action Task Force (2012–2023) International standards on combating money laundering and the financing of terrorism & proliferation: the FATF recommendations https://www.fatf-gafi.org/en/publications/Fatfrecommendations/Fatf-recommendations.html#:~:text=As%20amended%20February%202023.,of%20weapons%20of%20mass%20destruction

Goldbarsht D (2024) Chapter 7: Dancing in the dark: terrorist financing via the dark web. In: Goldbarsht D, de Koker L (eds) Financial crime and the law: identifying and mitigating risks, Ius Gentium: comparative perspectives on law and justice, vol 115. Springer, Cham

Goldbarsht D, de Koker L (2022) From paper money to digital assets: financial technology and the risks of criminal abuse. In: Goldbarsht D, de Koker L (eds) Financial technology and the law. Law, governance and technology series, vol 47. Springer
Goldbarsht D, Benson K (2023) From later to sooner: exploring compliance with the global regime of anti-money laundering and counter-terrorist financing in the legal profession. J Financ Crime
Goldbarsht D, Sheedy E (2024) Money laundering and the risk in the risk-based approach: the Australian context. Monash Univ Law Rev 50(1)
Hamilton R, Leuprecht C (2024) Chapter 2: The crime-crypto nexus: nuancing risk across crypto-crime transactions. In: Goldbarsht D, de Koker L (eds) Financial crime and the law: identifying and mitigating risks, Ius Gentium: comparative perspectives on law and justice, vol 115. Springer, Cham
Harris H (2024) Chapter 3: Financing environmental crime: financial sector complicity in global deforestation and opportunities for regulatory intervention. In: Goldbarsht D, de Koker L (eds) Financial crime and the law: identifying and mitigating risks, Ius Gentium: comparative perspectives on law and justice, vol 115. Springer, Cham
Littrell C (2024) Chapter 8: Economic and demographic biases in FATF mutual evaluation results. In: Goldbarsht D, de Koker L (eds) Financial crime and the law: identifying and mitigating risks, Ius Gentium: comparative perspectives on law and justice, vol 115. Springer, Cham
Langdale J (2024) Chapter 9: Combatting money laundering in Southeast Asian and Australian casinos. In: Goldbarsht D, de Koker L (eds) Financial crime and the law: identifying and mitigating risks, Ius Gentium: comparative perspectives on law and justice, vol 115. Springer, Cham
Sheedy E (2021) Risk governance: biases, blind spots and bonuses. Taylor & Francis Group, Abingdon
Sinha G (2020) Risk-based approach: is it the answer to effective anti-money laundering compliance? In: Benson K, King C, Walker C (eds) Assets, crimes, and the state: innovation in 21st century legal responses. Routledge, London
Southworth R, Levi M (2024) Chapter 5: Application of the risk-based approach (RBA) for financial crime risk management by banks. In: Goldbarsht D, de Koker L (eds) Financial crime and the law: identifying and mitigating risks, Ius Gentium: comparative perspectives on law and justice, vol 115. Springer, Cham
United Nations (1988) Convention against illicit traffic in narcotic drugs and psychotropic substances. Opened for signature 20 december 1988, 1019 UNTS 175 (entered into force 11 November 1990)
United Nations (1999) International Convention for the Suppression of the Financing of Terrorism. Adopted 9 December 1999, 2178 UNTS 197 (entered into force 10 April 2002)
United Nations (2000) Convention against Transnational Organized Crime. Adopted 15 November 2000, 2225 UNTS 209 (entered into force 29 September 2003)
United Nations (2003) Convention Against Corruption. Adopted 31 October 2003, 2349 UNTS 41 (entered into force 14 December 2005)

Doron Goldbarsht LLB, LLM (HUJI), PhD (UNSW), is the Director of the Financial Integrity Hub (FIH) and an Associate Professor at Macquarie Law School, where he teaches banking and financial crime. He is an authority on anti-money laundering and counter-terrorist financing (AML/CTF) regulations, with expertise in the related fields of compliance and financial innovation, with over 20 years of experience in the field. His recent books *Financial Crime and the Law: Identifying and Mitigating Risks* (Springer 2024, co-edited), *Financial Crime, Law and Governance: Navigating Challenges in Diverse Contexts* (Springer 2024, co-edited), *Financial Technology and the Law: Combating Financial Crime* (Springer, 2022 co-edited), and *Global Counter-Terrorist Financing and Soft Law: Multi-Layered Approaches* (Edward Elgar, 2020), as well as journal and chapter publications, focus on international AML/CTF standards and the mechanisms for their effective implementation and compliance at the national level.

Louis de Koker LLB LLM (UFS) LLM (Cantab) LLD (UFS) FSALS, is a Professor and Associate Dean: Research and Industry Engagement at the La Trobe Law School (Australia), an Extraordinary Professor at the Faculty of Law of the University of the Western Cape (South Africa) and a Board member with the Financial Integrity Hub (FIH) at Macquarie Law School. From 2014 to 2019 he was the national program leader of the Law and Policy research program of the Australian government-funded Data to Decisions Cooperative Research Centre. Louis is an expert on anti-money laundering and counterterrorist and proliferation financing, and especially the relationship between financial integrity and financial inclusion policies and regulations. Louis has worked with the Consultative Group to Assist the Poor, the World Bank, the OECD, the Asian Development Bank regulators and financial service providers on the design and implementation of appropriate integrity and inclusion over the past two decades. He has advised on a range of laws and regulations and his research on integrity laws and their impact on financial inclusion has been cited in publications of various international bodies including the World Bank, IMF, the Financial Action Task Force (FATF) and the Basel Committee on Banking Supervision.

The Crime-Crypto Nexus: Nuancing Risk Across Crypto-Crime Transactions

Rhianna Hamilton and Christian Leuprecht

Abstract Cryptocurrency is supercharging illicit activities by transnational criminal networks, including terrorism, drug trafficking, pornography, sanctions evasion, and ransomware. Yet, mainstream cryptocurrency literature often overlooks this criminal association. The relatively new and transboundary nature of cryptocurrency is restructuring criminal activities. Hacking has emerged as a digital-age bank heist, siphoning off substantial sums from exchange platforms. Crypto crime is dynamic, transitioning from primarily placing and layering the proceeds of precursor crimes into the financial system to a burgeoning trend of stealing virtual currency. While not every online financial crime involves cryptocurrency, the proliferation of crypto-enabled cybercrimes is exponential. Paradoxically, existing literature largely disregards how cryptocurrency-enabled offenses such as Online Child Sexual Exploitation and Abuse (OCSEA), sanctions evasion, and ransomware.

1 Introduction

Cryptocurrency is at the nexus of illicit behaviour by transnational criminal networks involved in terrorism, drug trafficking, pornography, sanctions-evasion, and ransomware. But you would never know it when looking at cryptocurrency literature. By way of example, a recent book on sanctions makes barely two passing

Open Access funding was made possible by the Human-Centric Cybersecurity Partnership, funded by the Social Sciences and Humanities Research Council of Canada, grant #895-2021-1007.

R. Hamilton
University of Adelaide, Adelaide, Australia

C. Leuprecht (✉)
Queen's University, Kingston, ON, Canada

Royal Military College, Kingston, ON, Canada
e-mail: christian.leuprecht@rmc.ca

D. Goldbarsht, L. de Koker (eds.), *Financial Crime and the Law*, Ius Gentium: Comparative Perspectives on Law and Justice 115,
https://doi.org/10.1007/978-3-031-59543-1_2

references to virtual currency.[1] The transboundary, un(der)regulated, and relatively new features of cryptocurrency are having a transformative impact on crime: in 2021 and 2022 a state-sponsored hacking group in North Korea procured billions in crypto coins through ransomware attacks to fund its nuclear arsenal.[2] In addition, North Korea reportedly stole $400 million in cryptocurrency in 2021 alone, which is since estimated to have grown to $1.7 billion, with crypto theft in 2022 estimated to total $3.8 billion.[3] Hacking has emerged as the crypto equivalent of a bank robbery, stealing vast sums from exchange websites: In August of 2016 Bitfinex, a top exchange program for cryptocurrency, was hacked and lost over half its digital assets. Assets valued at US$3.6 billion were traced to a couple who had enriched themselves and laundered proceeds of crime using different cryptocurrencies.[4] In other words, crypto crime is dynamic and changing; whereas virtual currencies had been primarily used to place and layer proceeds of precursor crime into the financial system, theft of actual virtual currency is a rapidly growing crime. Not every financial crime in cyberspace involves cryptocurrency; but the extent of crypto-enabled crimes in cyberspace is growing exponentially.[5] Yet, the current literature on crypto crime largely neglects the crime-crypto nexus as a subset of financial crimes related to Online Child Sexual Exploitation and Abuse (OCSEA), sanctions evasion and ransomware.

This chapter calls into question the prevalent monolithic approach to crypto crime to flag the associated inflexibility of current risk assessment frameworks for financial crime, notably as it pertains to the Financial Action Task Force (FATF), which is the dominant international organization offering guidelines on mitigating financial crimes. The chapter studies the way cryptocurrency is being leveraged to enable OCSEA, sanctions evasion and ransomware to make the case for a more nuanced approach to contain its proliferating use for criminal transactions. The sort of virtual currency in which a business deals, along with shifts in and out of one cryptocurrency or another, for instance, should affect risk scores for particularly businesses. But that is not how the system is set up. The FATF framework currently offers no flexibility for assessments and no real-time assessments. The FATF framework is allegedly over-designed for effect, rather than efficiency. What virtual currency is concerned, however, this chapter concludes that despite global Anti-Money Laundering Counter-Terrorist Financing (AMLCTF) compliance costs upwards of $270 billion a year, the current framework provides neither good traction, nor good results. That is, it is ineffective, in part because it is insufficiently nuanced to capture different types of criminogenic financial risks that emanate from the use of virtual currency. Part of the reason is inherent to the blockchain. While traditional AML is premised on precursor crime where the user is known but the

[1]Jentleson (2022).

[2]NCC Group (2023).

[3]Chainalysis (2022c, 2023b).

[4]Bilton (2022).

[5]Lin et al. (2023), p. 7.

transaction is hidden, virtual currency flips that problem: with Distributed Ledger Technology, the transaction history of the blockchain is transparent to all network nodes and non-repudiable, but the pseudonymity of individual participants is maintained, and the centralised institution replaced with the virtually currency protocol.[6]

In 2022, crypto crime netted at least $20 billion.[7] Other estimates peg profits even higher.[8] This chapter compares three types of transnational crime that stand out for their profits and particularly heinous damage: Online Child Sexual Exploitation and Abuse (OCSEA), sanctions evasion and ransomware. The use cases in this chapter show that cryptocurrency is used differently for each. OCSEA uses cryptocurrency for transactional purposes, choosing coins for pseudonymity. As technology develops to track mainstream coins used in crime, such as Bitcoin, perpetrators are shifting to more anonymous and secure methods of transaction. That partially explains a recent shift in virtual currency out of Bitcoin. For example, Monero offers greater anonymity and security. But is Monero more popular in OCSEA transactions than Bitcoin? Sanctions evasion uses cryptocurrency to transfer value and for rent seeking, when an entity aims to gain wealth without engaging in productivity or reciprocal agreements. Cryptocurrency makes it possible to move large amounts of money without a traditional transactional component. Finally, cryptocurrency is the payment of choice for ransomware attacks because amounts are large. Payments use coins such as Bitcoin but often overlap with other types of coins and mixers because proceeds subsequently need to be laundered from the initial wallet.

The subfield of crypto crime is in its infancy. Researchers are only now starting to gauge the scale of crypto crime and regulatory options to quell it. The Internet Watch Foundation, Interpol, the United Nations Office on Drugs and Crime (UNODC) have all flagged the impact, scale and proliferation of cryptocurrency-based crime on illicit economies. Still, there is little scholarship on the nexus between cryptocurrency and crime.[9] Cryptocurrency regulations remain sector-agnostic with little attention paid to illicit economies. Guidelines lack specificity and largely ignore the way crypto intersects with illicit behaviour. Cryptocurrency is changing network dynamics, geopolitical ramifications, and the dynamic of multiple criminal marketplaces. The discourse on cryptocurrency-based crime remains fairly monolithic: Should it be regulated and if so, how? What is the scale of crypto crime? Has regulation of crypto been effective?[10] Instead of taking up these basic questions, this chapter compares patterns in OCSEA, sanctions evasion and ransomware in the context of cryptocurrency. In doing so, the chapter aims to demonstrate the value of cryptocurrency as an intervening variable in these respective crimes and pivoting mitigation efforts into cryptocurrency-based crimes.

---

[6]Kyles (2022), p. 124.

[7]Chainalysis Team (2022a, b, c).

[8]Chainalysis (2022b), p. 23.

[9]Interpol General Secretariat (2022), UNODC (2022).

[10]Leuprecht et al. (2022), p. 324.

Cryptocurrency is morphing how crimes turn a profit. It has been fuelling the exponential growth of OCSEA.[11] The Internet Watch Foundation reports that cryptocurrency payments for child sexual abuse have been doubling annually.[12] These transactions are peer-to-peer. Sanctions evasion using cryptocurrency has geopolitical implications and threatens regional stability and international security. Russian oligarchs use cryptocurrency to evade sanctions and fund conflict.[13] Ransomware attacks that extort payment using cryptocurrency disproportionately target public infrastructure, incur billions in losses from the public sector due to ransom payments and theft, shut down hospitals, and deprive municipalities of data that is essential to deliver public services.[14] Ransomware can also have geopolitical implications, insofar as it enables proliferation finance of corrupt authoritarian regimes.[15]

The chapter postulates that the underappreciation of nuances in the use of cryptocurrency in crime is hampering efforts to mitigate the nefarious impacts of these crimes. In response, the chapter compares cryptocurrency patterns across these three types of crypto crime. The chapter concludes on ways to mitigate and deter the use of cryptocurrency for crime. The chapter is structured as follows. First, sections on materials and methods outline essential terms and background. Second, the chapter reviews three different crimes and their intersection with cryptocurrency: OCSEA, sanctions evasions, and ransomware attacks. Finally, it discusses the implications of a comparative approach to crypto crime for purposes of mitigation, investigation, and research with specific application to FATF.

2 Materials and Methods

2.1 Key Terms

This section operationalizes key concepts used in crypto laundering scholarship: decentralized coins, centralized coins, stablecoins, state backed coins, NFT's, crypto mixers, cryptocurrency exchanges, and decentralized finance.

Decentralized coins enable peer-to-peer transactions to take place with limited oversight from a central authority.[16] Decentralized currencies aim to disperse financial power beyond reach of any central authority such as a bank or government. Many coins claim to be decentralized to cater to users who are nervous about

---

[11] Interpol General Secretariat (2022), p. 4.

[12] Internet Watch Foundation (2022b).

[13] Będowska-Sójka et al. (2022), p. 2.

[14] Conti et al. (2018), p. 163.

[15] Hayes (2021), p. 11.

[16] Clements (2022), p. 4.

government involvement and bank failure in traditional finance. Still, they tend to have a central authority.

Coins with oversight are *centralized.* These coins are owned or operated by a central authority: a government, company, individual or bank. Rather than being peer-to-peer, like a decentralized network, transactions go through and operate within a central exchange that is monitored by an authority of some capacity.[17]

A *stable coin* can exist in a decentralized or centralized network. Its core characteristic is that its value is tied to a fiat currency such as the US dollar or to assets such as bonds. However, these coins often fall victim to volatility and fail. For example, the Terra stablecoin was marketed as a safe investment because it was tied to an algorithm. Yet, the coin crashed in May 2022.[18] That is an interesting case study in and of itself because it, along with the collapse of FTX that same year: this dynamic environment entails different liquidity requirements because bank runs that used to take days to pick up steam now happen almost instantaneously.

State-backed coins or *central bank digital currencies* (CBDC) are an official response to the growing popularity of digital assets: crypto coins that are held and privately issued by government. There are two types of CBDC's, *retail* which are held and exchanged between individuals and the crypto business, and *wholesale*, which are run by financial institutions.[19] For example, Venezuela's *Petro* or *Petromoneda* coin is issued by the government of Venezuela, backed by the country's oil, gas, gold, and diamond supply.[20] Many crypto users take issue with state-backed coins because they are antithetical to the premise of crypto: to remove financial power from government. Concerns about state-backed currency include cyber security, susceptibility to phishing and ransomware attacks at executive levels of government, and an increase in state surveillance of the population.[21] Although state-backed coins are not always popular, they have been introduced in the Bahamas, China, Jamaica, the Caribbean, and Nigeria. Australia, Thailand, Brazil, India, South Korea, and Russia plan to or are piloting state-backed coins.[22]

Non-fungible tokens, or *NFTs*, are an asset whose value and existence is tied to a blockchain. The NFT contains an identification code that makes it non-interchangeable. A value can be assigned to NFTs, which often popularizes them through images and artwork. NFTs are commonly tied to the Ethereum blockchain.[23]

Crypto mixers are online platforms that are used to distort and redistribute funds to make them more difficult to trace across blockchains used by Bitcoin, Ethereum, and other public blockchains which do not offer criminals the transparency they are

[17] Clements (2022), p. 6.

[18] Rai (2022).

[19] Chainalysis (2023a, b).

[20] Chohan (2018), p. 1.

[21] Atlantic Council (2023).

[22] Atlantic Council (2023).

[23] Clements (2022), p. 43.

seeking.[24] According to Chainalysis, the 30-day moving average of cryptocurrencies sent through crypto mixers reached $US 51.8 million on April 19, 2022, which is twice the amount for the same period in 2021. Nearly 10% of all funds that originate with illicit addresses are sent to mixers—no other service type cracked a 0.3% mixer sending share.[25]

Cryptocurrencies can be traded and sold through *cryptocurrency exchanges*. Exchanges can be centralized in structure and peer-to-peer, but the basic structure is that exchanges provide crypto users opportunities to trade their crypto for other types of cryptocurrencies or for fiat currencies such as the US dollar. Some exchanges specialize in moving crypto for illicit activity while others aim to provide infrastructure to exchange coins legally. Exchanges are susceptible to wash trading, with trading volume appearing higher than is representative of actual trade. In 2019, Bitwise Asset Management claimed that 95% of all reported bitcoin trading volume is faked by users to build the futures market.[26]

*Decentralized finance (*DeFi) is a sector of the financial system that was built on principles of being open source, near anonymous, financially inclusive, and separate to central authority. DeFi takes place on blockchains, for example the Ethereum Blockchain. DeFi technology often does not require verification of identity*; so,* there is little to no traceability when crimes are committed that involve DeFi coins or exchanges.[27] Its focus on limiting transaction traceability and maintaining anonymity makes DeFi difficult to include in AML and CTF initiatives. This has opened an opportunity for criminals who wish to launder money using DeFi with little to no regulatory oversight. One study found that crypto money laundering schemes taking place on Web 3 commonly use DeFi platforms to launder money through token exchanges. Indeed, between 2021 and 2022 DeFi based money laundering is estimated to have increased by 1964 percent![28]

2.2 Literature

This chapter makes two contributions to the literature. First, it posits a systematic nexus between crime and cryptocurrency. Second, it contributes to literature on OCSEA, sanctions evasions, and ransomware attacks by identifying specific cryptocurrency trends. This chapter builds upon scholarly literature on crypto crime by engaging with the nuances of these crimes that use cryptocurrency and discerning differences between them. Specifically, the chapter finds that its anonymous, transnational and digital chapter makes cryptocurrency a particularly heinous

[24] Chainalysis (2022c).

[25] Chainalysis (2022b).

[26] De (2019).

[27] Kirimhan (2023), p. 1; Trozze et al. (2023), p. 1.

[28] Trozze et al. (2023), p. 1.

enabler of OCSEA. In comparison, sanctions evasion requires perpetrators to circumvent regulations, and associated risks are geopolitical rather than local, such as proliferation finance and war.

Scholarship on crypto crime has primarily focused on the regulation of the illicit uses of cryptocurrency,[29] to a lesser extent, theory[30] and investigative techniques to address the illicit use of crypto.[31] As of late there has been a greater focus on the geopolitical risk that is enabled by cryptocurrency, and on transnational crime. The little research that has been done on OCSEA flags cryptocurrency payments in general and their use in paying for illicit materials, but without having collected data on cryptocurrency specifically.[32] The research that does exist suggests that enforcement data is quite limited.[33] Sanctions scholarship focuses on minimizing geopolitical risk and showing that cryptocurrency is used to evade sanctions.[34] Ransomware attacks have attracted the most scholarly attention.[35] This is in keeping with a bigger shift to geopolitical consideration in crypto scholarship.[36] Regardless, data on the use of cryptocurrency in OCSEA, sanctions, and ransomware remains quite limited, which makes the comparative approach in this chapter all the more useful in expanding the scope of available data.

This chapter builds on recent work on money and crypto laundering, especially its role in the Illicit International Political Economy. IIPE gauges political and economic variables of illicit transnational trade. As in the legal economy, there are distinct trends in the networks, geography, and flows of goods in IIPE, which focuses on globalization, financial flows, and the role of the state.[37] Past research on IIPE has focused on the role of digital currency[38]; the intersection between licit and illicit markets and policy[39]; and cross-border cooperation.[40]

---

[29]Ponsford (2015), Pocher and Veneris (2021), Gamble (2017), Towne Morton (2020), Simser (2020), Kethineni and Cao (2020), Jenkins et al. (2023) and Mahdavieh (2022).

[30]Majumder et al. (2019), Desmond et al. (2019), Dupuis et al. (2023), Jenkins et al. 2023 and Lee and Choi (2021).

[31]Maurushat and Halpin (2022), Long et al. (2022) and Europol (2022).

[32]Drejer et al. (2023), Avery (2021), Broadhurst (2019), Noval et al. (2023) and UNICEF Global Insight (2022).

[33]Drejer et al. (2023), p. 10.

[34]Travkina et al. (2022), Theiri et al. (2023), Ungboriboonpisal (2022), Siegmann (2022) and Long et al. (2022).

[35]Hayes (2021), Dupuis et al. (2023).

[36]Lee and Choi (2022).

[37]Andreas (2004).

[38]Leuprecht et al. (2022) and Jenkins et al. (2023).

[39]Legrand and Leuprecht (2021), p. 567.

[40]Leuprecht et al. (2021), p. 360.

2.3 Method

This research is based on data compiled from prosecutions of cases on transnational crypto laundering. Far from providing unfettered access to all nodes and edges, this approach has its limitations because investigators limit themselves to a certain subset of a criminal network, and prosecutors narrow the focus further in deciding who to charge and what charges to lay. That has a funnelling effect on the evidence that eventually becomes publicly available once a case has been prosecuted. However inchoate, our approach thus also draws on other legal documents, news sources, blogs, corporate reporting, and informal interviews to triangulate results and expand the number of data points. The coding instrument comprises variables such as country of origin, sector, type of coin, amount transferred, wallet number, etc. The chapter analyzes the observations in the context of the extant literature, synthesizes findings and identifies priority areas for future research and policy.

3 Online Child Sexual Abuse and Exploitation (OCSEA) and Cryptocurrency

Trigger Warning: This section includes references on how cryptocurrency has been used to pay for the sexual exploitation and abuse of minors.

3.1 Overview of OCSEA Using Cryptocurrency

There is no consensus definition for online child sexual exploitation and abuse. The United Nations Childrens Fund's (UNICEF) includes concerns about child exploitation facilitated by technology: specifically, "technology-facilitated child sexual exploitation and abuse" that is partly or entirely facilitated by technology, either through the internet or other wireless communications channels.[41] OCSEA has been flagged as a rapidly growing crime, which makes it a priority to contain. There is a breadth of pre-existing literature in this area to inform and triangulate findings. Most sources are from cyber safety groups who connected the rise in OCSEA to cryptocurrency payments. Although some literature discusses OCSEA and cryptocurrency transactions, there is little scholarly and policy-based research on the way they are connected. OCSEA networks tend to involve many individuals purchasing content with smaller network nodes that exist within criminal sectors that exploit children for profit. The chapter's findings are then linked to social (such as who is committing these crimes and how they are taking place) and technological

[41] UNICEF Global Insight (2022), p. 7.

Table 1 OCSEA crypto crime reports per year, 2015–2022

Year	Count of report numbers	% per year of total crypto reports	% change from previous year
2015	4	0.15%	
2016	41	1.52%	1%
2017	93	3.44%	2%
2018	81	3.00%	0%
2019	221	8.18%	5%
2020	468	17.31%	9%
2021	1014	37.51%	20%
2022	781	28.89%	−9%
Total	*2703*	*100%*	

attributes (such how the internet is used in investigations and how perpetrators use it to identify and lure victims).[42]

The 2022 Interpol Crime Report ranked OCSEA as a high priority threat. Moreover, 62 percent of Interpol's member states expect OCSEA either to 'increase' or 'significantly' increase over years to come.[43] Yet, top crypto crime analysis groups and scholarly publications do not include materials about OCSEA. That reflects a broader lack of research and reporting on children within the crypto community. Cryptocurrency and blockchain technology increase the risk of child pornography as imagery becomes more readily accessible.[44] The escalating number of websites offering OCSEA content for purchase using cryptocurrency is depicted in Table 1, which also shows the exponential growth in websites year-over-year. In 2022, crypto analysis lab TRM analyzed crypto addresses involved in OSCEA payments, within their sample over two thirds of payments were made to scammers, most of whom advertised their OCSEA 'content' on the dark web.[45] Better analysis of the blockchain and its links to OCSEA payments has potential to minimize this pervasive crime, stop scammers, and better protect children[46]:

In addition, the Internet Watch Foundation has collected raw data on the types of payment being used to pay for child abuse imagery in the UK. In 2022, the Internet Watch Foundation released data reporting that virtual currency was the top form of payment used in 2022 to purchase child sexual abuse imagery. Virtual currency was identified 1366 times in payments, the next highest payment method recorded was credit card purchase, showing up 492 times in total.[47]

[42] Dorotic and Johnsen (2023), Drejer et al. (2023), UNICEF Global Insight (2022) and UNICEF (2021).

[43] Interpol General Secretariat (2022), p. 4.

[44] Broadhurst (2019), p. 28.

[45] TRM (2022), p. 13.

[46] Internet Watch Foundation (2022b).

[47] Internet Watch Foundation (2022a), p. 86.

This data is representative of the concerns that organizations such as Interpol have put forward about increases in OCSEA and crypto as an accelerant.[48] The data put forward by these groups runs counter to other findings that found payment and remittance services are the most common.[49] This change in data points to a rise in crypto payments in 2021 and 2022.

3.2 Case Study: Welcome to Video

In 2019, the US Department of Justice (DOJ) took down the darknet website "Welcome to Video." It specialized in trading content of children being sexually assaulted or exploited.[50] Users purchased content of children as young as 6 months old, with many of the child victims being subjected to ongoing exploitation over many years. The unsealed indictment included a banner warning: "do not upload adult porn", and offered users points and website "perks" for paying in Bitcoin or uploading their own videos.[51] The website used Bitcoin in addition to fiat currency. South Korean Jong Woo Son was eventually arrested as the mastermind behind "Welcome to Video". Authorities were able to trace transactions on the blockchain and use technology linking payments to him.[52] The arrest of Son spawned hundreds of additional arrests based on millions of downloads and the ongoing abuse of at least 23 children located throughout the US, Spain, and the United Kingdom. At least 337 people from over 18 countries have been arrested and charged after inter-agency collaboration among South Korea, the USA, the UK, and Germany. They partnered with agencies in Australia, Brazil, Canada, Czechia, Finland, France, Hungary, Ireland, Italy, Poland, Saudi Arabia, Spain, Sweden, and the United Arab Emirates to apprehend contributors.[53]

At least 7300 transactions reaped over $370,000 worth of Bitcoin between 2015 and 2018.[54] Upon receipt of Bitcoin payments in his wallet, Son would move funds to a Bitcoin account in his own name. Son's approach was unsophisticated. He transferred money to his own personal account from a Bitcoin wallet explicitly tied to a child pornography website. The account to which he transferred funds was linked to him, registered to his name, phone number and email, and his IP address was unblocked.[55] Despite the seemingly obvious financial connection between Son

[48] Interpol General Secretariat (2022).

[49] Napier et al. (2021) and Varrella (2017).

[50] Hollingsworth (2019).

[51] Hollingsworth (2019).

[52] United States District Court for the District of Colombia (2019), p. 8.

[53] The United States Department of Justice (2019), United States District Court for the District of New Jersey (2022) and United States Department of Justice (2021).

[54] 35 United States District Court for the District of New Jersey (2022).

[55] Hollingsworth (2019).

and the illicit website, the website and Bitcoins wallets remained active between 2016 and 2019 and were closed only once Son was indicted in 2019.

Bitcoin was built into the use of the website. "In order to download videos from Welcome to Video, customers redeemed "points." Points could be obtained by: (1) uploading videos depicting child pornography; (2) referring new customers to Welcome To Video; (3) paying 0.03 BTC (approximately $352.59 as of March 5, 2018) for a "VIP" account, which lasted for 6 months and purportedly allowed unlimited downloads; and/or (4) paying for points incrementally (i.e., 0.02 bitcoin for 230 points)."[56] Welcome to Video encouraged customers to make payments through different Bitcoin exchanges registered worldwide; there were over 1.3 million Bitcoin wallets set up through the Welcome to Video platform. In this way, the darknet website was not just moving illicit transactions but also brought in revenue and customers to Bitcoin (Kennedy 2019). The scale of involvement raises concerns about know-your-customer (KYC) requirements for Bitcoin and other cryptocurrencies. A wallet overtly tied to child pornography should have been shut down by administrators.

Investigators were able to secure an indictment and prosecution using a combination of public blockchain information and by tracking the IP address of the website's owner. These tactics were unsophisticated. With software from companies such as Chainalysis and BIG, companies and investigators can track Blockchain transactions and connect contributors to crime.[57] Still, KYC protocols went unheeded for years in this case. These observations suggest that law enforcement and crypto coins that are centralized, such Bitcoin, are ineffective in identifying and addressing crimes like OCSEA.

Son did not use advanced technology, complex money laundering techniques, and did not attempt to hide his location online. Yet for 4 years he ran the world's largest child pornography website, profited from it, and was able to keep and spend much of that money through transfers over a public blockchain. Because it is public, the blockchain holds out tremendous opportunity in principle to identify and mitigate cases in this area; prevention of OCSEA is thus inextricably tied to cryptocurrency.

4 Sanctions Evasion and Cryptocurrency

4.1 Overview

The introduction of cryptocurrency to the global financial system has altered global sanctions regimes. Cryptocurrency has allowed sanctioned entities to evade detection and continue trade that undermines the efficacy of geopolitical aims an

[56] United States District Court for the District of Colombia (2019).

[57] Chainalysis Team (2019).

economic stability. Sanctions have grown more popular as an instrument of international politics. In recent years crypto wallets, coin companies, and mixers have been sanctioned by agencies such as the U.S. Treasury Department's Office of Foreign Assets Control.[58] Under international law sanctions are: "Coercive measures taken [in response to a violation of international law] in execution of a decision of a competent social organ, i.e., an organ legally empowered to act in the name of the society or community that is governed by the legal system."[59]

The logic that informs sanctions evasion payments uses cryptocurrency by means of combination of rent seeking behaviour, moving money and then laundering it, or in political circumstances, for proliferation finance. Sanctions can be implemented at multiple levels and across different trade sectors including oil, food, medicine, and defence. This section focuses on *economic sanctions*: when a state actor leverages economic instruments to control or enforce behaviour by one actor against another. Any entity can impose sanctions on another. However, the power an actor exerts over the international community determines the impact sanctions are likely to have. For purposes of legitimacy or having an economy too small to make an impact unilaterally, many actors choose to enforce sanctions through the United Nations (UN) or through multilateral channels, such as the European Union (EU).

Today, countries that are sanctioned include Russia, Cuba, Iran, Venezuela, and North Korea.[60] Cryptocurrency makes it possible for actors that are subject to sanctions to develop virtual currencies to avoid having to interact with currencies with which they are sanctioned from transacting. In 2022 ten cryptocurrency entities and 400 addresses were sanctioned.[61]

This numbers reflect growing concern about cryptocurrency being used to evade sanctions. The increase in sanctioned addresses and entities corresponds with an increase in sanctions evasions payments using virtual assets. Both 2021 and 2022 saw increases in sanctioned crypto entities, with numbers reaching a record high in 2022. There were nine entities sanctioned in 2021 and ten entities sanctioned in 2022, in addition the wallets sanctioned included 100 addresses in 2021 and 350 addresses in 2022.[62]

The issue became more acute following Russia's invasion of Ukraine in 2022. Russia has been subject to an array of sanctions ever since, notably by the United States and allies. Not only would cryptocurrency enable crime, now it was being used to fund a war. Bitcoin and Ethereum were demonstrably used at greater scale following the period in 2022 of the invasion and subsequent sanctions. Cryptocurrency has made it easier to avoid sanctions imposed by OFAC by moving money without interacting with the US dollar while avoiding Western jurisdictions where wallets may be subject to seizure. Because the world's financial systems are

[58] Office of Foreign Assets Control (OFAC) (2023).

[59] Abi-Saab (2001).

[60] Office of Foreign Assets Control (OFAC) (2023).

[61] Chainalysis Team (2022a, b, c).

[62] Chainalysis Team (2022a, b, c).

interdependent, and the United States' Office of Foreign Assets Control (OFAC) has been able to police bad actors that avail themselves of the U.S. financial system.[63] Global financial flows pass disproportionately through New York for instance. However, with the emergence of cryptocurrency to advance geopolitical agendas, it is now possible to transact without using US territory or the US dollar, which had historically been a comparative strategic advantage for the US.

Transboundary payments, the pseudonymous nature of crypto, and prevalence of technology like mixers and tumblers mean that sanctioned entities can evade sanctions and profit with minimal oversight from traditional regulations. Cryptocurrency is a game changer insofar as it makes it relatively easy to evade sanctions to evade OFAC and its regulations. In many countries, cryptocurrency is not included in sanctions regulations, which making it difficult to prevent the use of cryptocurrency to evade sanctions. OFAC has worked to address the regulatory gap that cryptocurrency has created, imposing economic sanctions on numerous Bitcoin wallet addresses, companies, and individuals, such as the Russian "BitRiver."

Meanwhile, the US DOJ has been bringing criminal charges (United States Department of Justice 2022a). In in response to OFAC sanctioning of numerous crypto entities, in May 2022 Magistrate judge Zia Faruqui approved the first cryptocurrency sanctions complaint. Japan is also reviewing its laws on cryptocurrency to impede Russia from evading sanctions. And the EU has banned high value cryptocurrencies from servicing Russian individuals and entities. Yet, the scale of the impact of virtual currency sanctions evasion remains unclear.

4.2 Case Study: The Lazarus Group

Lazarus is a ransomware attack group affiliated with North Korea's Reconnaissance General Bureau that has been evading sanctions against North Korea, using ransomware to encrypt files and hold them 'hostage.' In 2020, OFAC designated it a "state sponsored malicious cyber group."[64] Lazarus effectively enables proliferation finance by enabling the North Korean regime.[65] Since they are located in North Korea, they do not run the risk of US domestic prosecution. Lazarus thus remains prolific. Victims include healthcare, entertainment, and cryptocurrency, among other sectors. Lazarus uses many different entities to move money, including crypto mixer Tornado Cash.[66] Lazarus can count on support outside of North Korea. In April 2022, a US citizen was indicted for travelling to North Korea to speak at a cryptocurrency conference where he gave advice on blockchain technology and negotiations with the US on nuclear weapons, thereby effectively enabling North

[63] Farrell and Newman (2019) and Drezner et al. (2021).

[64] United States Department of the Treasury (2020).

[65] NCC Group (2023).

[66] Gibbon et al. (2022).

Korean proliferation finance.[67] His intentions were to move money from North Korea to South Korea without being detected by sanctions programs imposed by the USA and South Korea. A year earlier the US Justice Department had named Ghaleb Alaumary, a 36-year-old man from Ontario, and described him as a "prolific money launderer for hackers engaged in ATM cash-out schemes, cyber-enabled bank heists, business email compromise (BEC) schemes, and other online fraud schemes." He was promptly sentenced to 11 years in jail (US Department of Justice 2021).

In 2018 the Lazarus Group hacked into a virtual currency exchange and stole $ USD 250 million in cryptocurrency and laundered the proceeds through multiple wallets and mixers, many through automated accounts. There were 113 cryptocurrency accounts tied to the group. Money came from YouBit, UpBit, and Bithumb, in South Korea. Fake photographs and falsified documentation were used to circumvent KYC requirements.[68]

Online laundering transactions used decentralized currencies including Bitcoin, Ethereum, Dogecoin, Litecoin, Zcash, Ripple and Ethereum Classic, many of which are alt coins of varying value.[69] However, funds also travelled through the traditional financial system. China-based banks were used to launder funds after exchanging crypto for fiat currency. Chian Guangfa, the Agricultural Bank of China, and China Everbright Bank sent $455 million stolen by Lazarus through mixers such as Tornado Cash, which operates on the Ethereum blockchain. It allows users to distort the provenance of funds by putting them through complicated and seemingly random transactions. That makes transactions difficult for law enforcement to track, which makes mixers very popular for sanctions evasion.[70] Tornado Cash has since been sanctioned by the US government for this and numerous other crypto heists.

This case demonstrates complexity of sanctions evasion schemes, especially ones that enjoy the support of a sanctioned government. The Lazarus group partnered with other groups engaged in criminal activity, including mixers and governments. This makes it difficult to shut down and mitigate. In other words, cryptocurrency raises geopolitical risk by opening sanctions gaps that are a function of failure to regulate. Fuelled by cyber profits, in 2022 North Korea's regime tested a record number of nuclear weapons.

[67] United States Department of Justice (2022b, c) and United States Department of Justice (2021).

[68] United States Department of Justice (2020).

[69] Chainalysis Team (2022a), p. 113.

[70] Gibbon et al. (2022).

4.3 Ransomware

4.3.1 Overview

Virtual currency has enabled new crimes, such as crypto theft, to morph. A devastating example of a morphing crime is ransomware: a type of malware designed to encrypt files and make essential information or services (for example healthcare data) inaccessible to the owners. In most cases, the owner must pay a sizeable ransom to have encrypted files unlocked.

Ransomware attacks have been incurring sizeable losses for governments, businesses, and individuals that rise year over year. Ransomware is a form of malware that can encrypt files and hold them as 'hostage'. Criminals require victims to pay a ransom in exchange for a decryption key. Victims include hospital data and healthcare more broadly. In 2022 ransomware attacks ranked as a top crime involving cryptocurrency against federal agencies, at 11.9% of all crimes involving virtual currency.[71] At the state and local level this number is similar with 11.3% of crimes identified as ransomware attacks.[72] Ransomware attacks typically have three stages. The first stage is infection, in this stage a computer receives the malware. The second stage is encryption, in this stage the files, data, or personal information is encrypted, that is, the content is no longer available to the owner. The third stage is demand, when the attacker requests a ransom fee to decrypt infected files. If the ransom is paid, the attacker needs to launder the proceeds, and the files will either be restored or destroyed.

Ransomware technology is a form of malware. Malware is: "hardware, firmware, or software that is intentionally included or inserted in a system for a harmful purpose".[73] These programs are covertly integrated into an operating system to violate a computer's security. While there are many ways to introduce malware to a computer, criminals have several popular techniques including: phishing emails with malware attachments; social engineering; and removable USB devices.[74] The subject matter targeted by ransomware attackers includes threats to financial data, sensitive information, and data necessary to public functionality and wellbeing. The malware attack takes place on a victim's computer as the result of a virus or other code-based entity.[75] After peaking in 2021, the profitability of ransomware attacks declined slightly the following year. There is a notable technological variable in this decline: the average lifespan of ransomware strains has been steadily and rapidly in decline. In 2012 the average lifespan of a strain was 3907 h, and now in 2022 the

[71] Chainalysis (2022b), p. 11.

[72] Ibid, p. 12.

[73] Computer Security Resource Center (2023).

[74] CybSafe (2022).

[75] Computer Security Resource Center (2023).

average lifespan was down to only 70 h.[76] This decline corresponds with more effective, targeted, and aggressive forms of malware.

For the purposes of this chapter, we distinguish between socio-political and financial attributes of ransomware. Socio-political attributes play an important role in varying ransomware attacks, such as state-tolerated bad actors in Russia that combine rent-seeking behaviour with grey-zone adversarial objectives, such as sewing mistrust in public and critical infrastructure. Attacks have increased steadily over the past 20 years. However, this increase stalled in 2022 despite continued advances in the technology. In 2021 ransomware attackers made US$ 765.6 million in profits, but by 2022 that number had dropped to US$ 456.8 million. This steep decline has been attributed to several changes, including a change in law enforcement policy which recommends that victims of attacks not pay up: 59% of individuals did not pay their ransom, the highest number to date.[77] Combined with greater technological resilience, data protections strategies and improved cyber response, these developments are credited for the decline in ransomware profitability.[78]

On the financial side, the publicity of the blockchain has allowed for a trove of data. Recent trends track the movement of funds between the wallet receiving the ransom and its secondary destination: Often funds are initially sent to central exchanges (for example Binance), then on to high-risk exchanges, illicit platforms, and mixers, which are commonly used as secondary points from wallets. Although ransomware attacks use cryptocurrencies to engage in rent-seeking behaviour, ransomware attacks often rely on laundering the proceeds of their illicit gains in combination with the traditional financial system. The scale or ransomware funds tends to necessitate more complex, mixed method laundering techniques, but these often involve Western jurisdictions since that is where targeted entities tend to be located. That gives criminal intelligence a leg up. At the same time, reliance on cryptocurrency to receive ransom payments means that crypto is inextricably linked to ransomware crimes.

The potential risks of ransomware attacks are vast, with the geopolitical implications for proliferation financing being particularly clear. For example, FATF postulates that North Korea's state sponsored ransomware attacks have enabled an "unprecedented number of recent launches of ballistic missiles." These launches have been funded, in large part, by virtual currencies stolen from decentralized exchanges adding up to approximately USD 1.2 billion since 2017 alone.[79] Non-state actors are profiting as well. Illicit groups of many kinds have exploited ransomware attacks and cryptocurrencies to move illicit money. Ransomware attacks can bring billions in profits to nefarious state actors, criminal organizations, and terrorist groups. It is essential to better understand how these different actors occupy ransomware attack spaces within the global economy.

[76]Chainalysis Team (2022a, b, c), p. 45.

[77]Chainalysis (2022b).

[78]Microsoft (2022), p. 14.

[79]FATF (2023), p. 3.

4.3.2 Case Study: The LockBit Gang

In 2022 LockBit, was among the most prolific and profitable criminal ransomware gangs. Their network is global, decentralized, and multinational. Since inception Lockbit has received USD $100 million in payments. In 2022 Lockbit brought in USD $44 million alone.[80] The Canadian Centre for Cyber Security estimated that the LockBit Gang was "responsible for 22 percent of ransomware incidents" in Canada and approximately 44% of global incidents.[81] Mikhail Vasiliev, a Russian-Canadian based in Bradford, Ontario, was charged in the District of New Jersey with "intentionally causing damage to a protected computer" and "knowingly extorting money in relation to damage to a protected computer" between September 2019 and October 2022.[82] The charges were the result of a RCMP investigation lead by the National Cybercrime Coordination Centre (NC3). The investigation uncovered Vasiliev's ownership and stewardship of the LockBit ransomware strain that emerged in January 2020. LockBit is a malware that deploys (hard or soft) ware that can be purchased and deployed to lodge demands for payment. The company is responsible for making over $100 million in ransom demands with tens of millions of these demands resulting in a ransom being paid.[83]

Vasiliev had been coordinating with the rest of the LockBit gang and extorting victims in the USA, Germany, France, and China in 2019.[84] They encrypted companies' entire networks, then reached out to negotiate ransom payments. Upon receiving payment, they provided the decryption key to victims to re-access their files. They requested between one and three Bitcoin as payment and provided the wallet addresses, equivalent to $7000 to $11,000 each, but up to $30,000 USD was paid out in ransom. In 2022 ransom demands increased to multimillion dollar figures.[85] A sample ransom note read as follow (DiMaggio):

ALL YOUR IMPORTANT FILES ARE ENCRYPTED!
There is only one way to get your files back:

1. Contact with us
2. Send us 1 any encrypted your file and your personal key
3. We will decrypt 1 file for test (maximum file size 1 MB), its guarantee what we can decrypt your files
4. Pay
5. We send for you decryptor software

We accept Bitcoin.
Attention!
Do not rename encrypted files.

[80]Petkauskas (2022); TRM (2022), p. 26.

[81]Tunney (2023).

[82]United States District Court for the District of New Jersey (2022) and United States Department of Justice (2021).

[83]United States District Court for the District of New Jersey (2022), p. 3.

[84]DiMaggio (2022).

[85]DiMaggio (2022).

> Do not try to encrypt using third party software, it may cause permanent data loss.
> Do not try to decrypt using third party software, it may cause permanent data loss.
> Decryption of your files with the help of third parties may cause increased price (they add their fee to ours)

By way of example, LockBit targeted St. Mary's, a small town of 7700 residents in Ontario, Canada with limited cybersecurity capacity. It encrypted 67 gigabytes of data; the data belonged to the city and comprised confidential data on citizens and internal financial documents. The group engaged in a double extortion: it demanded a ransom and threatened to release the town's data online if the town did not pay up.[86] In response, the town solicited help from the Canadian Centre for Cyber Security (CCCS), Stratford police, a legal team, and the town council. The CCCS recommended that town council not pay up.[87] CCCS tried to determine the culprit, and whether they could back up the data before deciding on the ransom payment. Whether St Mary's paid up to have its files returned is unclear. The town shut down its servers to prevent exfiltration of data, but that left many of their computer systems unusable. Under similar circumstances Stratford, Ontario paid $75,000 in Bitcoin, while Frederick, Colorado faced a US$200,000 ransom demand for the return of their files.

In addition to the financial losses from ransom payments, ransomware attacks can cause long term damage to digital infrastructure. Regulation and investigations have a hard time keeping up. Victims rely on investigators to track addresses and uncover attackers to recovering funds and data. Failure to reacquire files can damage the public good so hospitals, municipalities, and food providers that have been attacked can resume functioning: they are preferred targets that are vulnerable yet more likely to pay up because they can ill afford lengthy disruptions to their operations.

5 Implications and Recommendations

The aim of this chapter has been to make the case for nuanced policy responses to different types of cryptocurrency-based crime, to which the current FATF framework is ill adapted. This section outlines implications and recommendations for crypto crime covered in this chapter: OCSEA, sanctions evasion, and ransomware attacks.

5.1 OCSEA

To address the rise in OCSEA Interpol has suggested to build out capacity to detect online child luring technology. In addition, Interpol is proposing greater cooperation

[86] Trevithick (2022).

[87] Faife (2022).

among investigating agencies to address the transboundary nature of OCSEA, in support of its broader effort to crack down on crimes that operate on the internet.[88] However, criminal intelligence and other stakeholders could do (much) better at leveraging transparency from blockchains to gauge potential child pornography risks.[89] Wallets are forensic artefacts; their discovery and linking them to a real person can be used as evidence in criminal investigations.[90] As this chapter shows, crypto wallets can indeed provide strong evidence in investigations and prosecutions. In other words, shift strategy to focus more on virtual currency that enables OCSEA, notably privacy-enhancing alt coins such as Monera.

5.2 *Sanctions*

Not all regulation is created equal. Many countries have partial regulation for coins. For example, Canada has an incomplete regulatory framework in development that does not cover all virtual assets. However, crypto laundering is regulated under Canada's anti money laundering and countering terrorism financing legislation after virtual assets were added to Canada's *Proceeds of Crime, Money Laundering and Terrorist Financing Act* (PCMLTFA) (Government of Canada 2000). In contrast, the Bahamas have a full regulatory framework, anti-money laundering procedures, rules on travel, and allowance for stable coin payments in addition to the launch of the Bahamas' own CBDC: The Sand Dollar. FATF enforcing standardized regulation and consensus on a gold standard for crypto regulation would go some way to avoid criminogenic asymmetry whereby criminal exploit crypto exchanges registered in different jurisdictions.

5.3 *Ransomware*

Ransomware is a leading cybersecurity concern for companies, the public sector, and private citizens (Veeam 2022). Ransomware is highly profitable and technology to encrypt or hack files keeps adapting. Cryptocurrency is the payment mechanism of choice for ransomware, with Bitcoin featuring foremost among related financial transactions. Centralized finance is the most common secondary send for ransomware attackers. Preferred targets are smaller entities with large budgets—because they tend to be more vulnerable yet able and willing to pay. With the propensity to pay out ransoms on the wane, ransomware attacks have recently started to decline. A more resilient cybersecurity posture, multisector collaboration, and

[88] Interpol General Secretariat (2022), p. 4.

[89] Chang et al. (2022), p. 1.

[90] Ibid.

more research on the nuances of ransomware and cryptocurrency should offer better insights into the way cryptocurrency is used to launder money. While Bitcoin and Ethereum feature prominently, the role of less mainstream coins such as Monero and ZCash are poorly understood.[91] We also have a poor understanding of the size of ransomware groups and the composition of their networks, which makes it difficult for investigators to "follow the money".

5.4 FATF Cryptocurrency Guidelines

Arm's length from the Organization for Economic Cooperation and Development (OECD), FATF is mandated to set standards for financial crime prevention and assess jurisdictions. At the time of writing FATF's inclusion of virtual currencies within its recommendations are limited and have been active only since 2015.[92] The current standards clarify that entities that offer virtual payment services must be licensed and should comply with pre-existing regulations for money laundering, customer due diligence, record keeping, and must report suspicious transactions. However, this information is vague and does not offer a targeted approach to crypto or specific crypto crimes. Instead, it places virtual assets under a broad category with vague responsibilities. In their 2023 report FATF found that 75 percent of jurisdictions assessed were not or only partially compliant with virtual asset standards.[93] These requirements include FATF's recent update is the so called 'Travel Rule' which applies wire transfer requirements to hold information on both the originators and beneficiaries to virtual assets. This is meant to improve traceability and law enforcement's ability to identify and freeze assets.[94] Failure to implement basic record keeping combined with poor implementation from jurisdictions have made FATF standards for cryptocurrency largely ineffective.

A global standard for crypto regulation by parties to the United Nations and the Financial Action Task Force (FATF) would have a levelling effect. If degrees of regulation vary across countries, implications for cryptocurrency buyers, sellers, or users will differ. Absent an international standard for crypto crime compliance, the global regulatory space is highly diverse and inconsistent, not just in regulation but also in its implementation. While countries such as the Bahamas, France, and Japan have implemented regulations, others have outright banned the development of cryptocurrencies, for example China, Qatar, and Saudi Arabia.[95] Yet, even bans differ. For example, China banned crypto exchanges, initial coin offering's (ICO's), and blocked financial institutions from engaging in cryptocurrency trade. In contrast,

[91] Clements (2022), p. 29.

[92] De Koker et al. (2022), p. 158; FATF (2023).

[93] FATF (2023).

[94] FATF (2023).

[95] PwC (2022), p. 7.

Canadian provinces such as Alberta have encouraged ICO's and Canada has a CBDC ready to launch, if necessary.[96] As countries develop cryptocurrencies and cryptocurrency regulation, collective action holds out promise for setting standards for regulations and opportunities for greater inter-agency collaboration. The criminogenic asymmetry of crypto crime means global standards and cooperation are indispensable to contain crypto crime. Yet, the FATF's framework is not well adapted to addressing trends in the abovementioned spaces, for example peer-to-peer transfers that take place without oversight from central authority.[97] Recommendations to improve FATF's standards have thus far been limited. De Koker et al. recommend that virtual asset service providers be supervised or monitored by a competent authority. Additionally, they recommend that these authorities should take on regulatory measures such as managing and preventing criminal access to virtual assets.[98]

FATF requirements should be updated. However, member states also have a responsibility to ensure that appropriate domestic standards are in place. While FATF is well positioned to take the lead on setting crypto crime standards, FATF cannot do it alone, or without more work. FATF is reliant on its members to implement, regulate, and enforce guidelines, and as of present virtual currency guidelines are simply not being met by member states.[99] FATF is lagging on virtual currencies in general, and on emerging crypto crimes in particular.

6 Conclusion

This chapter compared different types of crypto crime, to make the case for a more nuanced approach to OCSEA, sanctions evasion, and ransomware. The chapter expands the literature by discussing these crimes in the context of cryptocurrency and identifying trends that make the case for more effective mitigation techniques, beyond what is currently on offer by FATF and in many jurisdictions.

The proposition in this chapter, particularly on OCSEA, stands to benefit from more robust data to bridge gaps between literature and criminal intelligence observations on criminogenic trends in virtual currency. OCSEA is quite understudied, and that cryptocurrency is funding this crime on a level disproportionate to the little scholarly and institutional attention it is receiving. For instance, better KYC requirements for crypto are indispensable to contain OCSEA.

The chapter's observations on sanctions evasions suggest that rent seeking and money laundering processes are intertwined. Further work on this section could develop data and aim to understand how different types of sanctioned entities

[96] Alberta Government (2022).

[97] FATF (2023).

[98] De Koker et al. (2022), p. 162.

[99] De Koker et al. (2022).

operate to evade sanctions. To be sure, the crypto economy is too small for an economy as large as Russia to evade sanctions effectively, that is, US dollar liquidity is insufficient to turn billions of dollars in crypto tokens into market value at scale, let alone move it through the crypto exchange system unnoticed. U.S. enforcement agencies have stepped up their game, and cryptocurrency is now mentioned in sanctions packages.[100] The absence of commercial banks and their vulnerability to theft, and the anonymity of non-custodial wallets makes them attractive to evade sanctions: Russians and Russia are using cryptocurrency to evade sanctions, but their modus operandi is different from the North Korean regime: Russia, and Iran, have been using cryptocurrency to pay for imports by avoiding commercial payment systems, whereas North Korea just wants to make up for lost revenue. FATF's cryptocurrency recommendations need to reflect a better and more nuanced understanding of sanctioning crypto wallets and entities to match this growing form of evasion. The current literature on the effectiveness of sanctions would benefit from including crypto sanctions evasion. Sanctions evasion has geopolitical implications, from the potential to fund wars of aggression, to their role in proliferation finance.

This chapter expands the literature on ransomware attacks by discussing how money is laundered and crypto payments are used: Ransomware attackers launder funds at scale because of the amounts involved and extensive attention from law enforcement. Akin to sanctions evasion, ransomware has geopolitical and social implications. If attackers can profit from their crimes, public data will be at risk. Illicit actors have been bankrolling aggressive authoritarian regimes at minimal overhead costs.

The crime-crypto nexus is much more nuanced than commonly presumed, and FATF is inflexibly postured to address it. Investigators can enhance capabilities to keep up with criminal adaptation. Blockchain-based investigations, continuous content monitoring, and other methods allow for the analysis of wallets as forensic evidence. Stringent regulations on enablers of dangerous content and greater penalties for companies that are complicit in the sale of illicit content such as child pornography or ransomware soft- and hardware could help draw red lines. Criminals are rent seekers; cryptocurrency has made crime more profitable and easier to perpetrate. Technology, its adoption by enforcement and a better understanding of the human and socio-economic drivers of crypto crime highlight the risks of untethered crypto as geopolitical actors and nefarious actors look to exploit cryptocurrency for illicit gain. FATF's failure to provide jurisdictions with timely, nuanced information on alternative financial ecosystems such as cryptocurrency poses vast financial, social, and political risk. As this chapter has shown, even with limited open-source information it is possible to make the case for the nuanced characteristics of crypto-enabled crime and cryptocurrency as an accelerant.

[100] Reinsch and Palazzi (2022).

Acknowledgements Research for this article was supported by the Social Sciences and Humanities Research Council of Canada, Insight Grants 435-2022-0862 and 435-2019-1333 and Partnership Grant 895-2021-1007.

References

Abi-Saab G (2001) Keynote address the concept of sanction in international law. In: United Nations sanctions and international law. Brill, Leiden. https://doi.org/10.1163/9789004502871_005

Alberta Government (2022) Financial Innovation Act. https://open.alberta.ca/publications/f13p2

Andreas P (2004) Review: illicit international political economy: the clandestine side of globalization. Rev Int Polit Econ 11(3):641–652. https://doi.org/10.1080/0969229042000252936

Atlantic Council (2023) Central digital currency tracker. https://www.atlanticcouncil.org/cbdctracker/. Accessed 26 Apr 2023

Avery F (2021) Prosecuting the live streaming of sexual abuse involving children abroad. SSRN. https://papers.ssrn.com/sol3/papers.cfm?abstract_id=3773367. Accessed 26 Apr 2023

Będowska-Sójka B, Demir E, Zaremba A (2022) Hedging geopolitical risks with different asset classes: a focus on the Russian Invasion of Ukraine. Financ Res Lett 50:1–8. https://doi.org/10.1016/j.frl.2022.103192

Bilton N (2022) The Ballad of Razzlekhan and Dutch, Bitcoin's Bonnie and Clyde. https://www.vanityfair.com/news/2022/08/the-ballad-of-razzlekhan-and-dutch-bitcoins-bonnie-and-clyde. Accessed 26 Apr 2023

Broadhurst R (2019) Child sex abuse images and exploitation materials, SSRN. https://papers.ssrn.com/sol3/papers.cfm?abstract_id=3384499. Accessed 26 Apr. 2023

Chainalysis (2023a) The current state of Central Bank Digital Currencies (CBDCs) in 2023. https://blog.chainalysis.com/reports/central-bank-digital-currencies-cbdc/#:~:text=The%20Current%20State%20of%20Central%20Bank%20Digital%20Currencies%20(CBDCs)%20in%202023&text=Blockchain%20technology%20has%20made%20digital,immutability%2C%20pseudonymity%2C%20and%20more. Accessed 26 Apr 2023

Chainalysis (2023b) 2022 Biggest Year Ever for Crypto Hacking with $3.8 Billion Stolen, Primarily from DeFi Protocols and North Korea-linked Attackers. https://blog.chainalysis.com/reports/2022-biggest-year-ever-for-crypto-hacking/. Accessed 2 July 2023

Chainalysis Team (2019) DOJ announces shutdown of largest child pornography website. https://blog.chainalysis.com/reports/chainalysis-doj-welcome-to-video-shutdown/. Accessed 26 Apr 2023

Chainalysis Team (2022a) Crypto crime trends for 2022: illicit transaction activity reaches all time high in value, all-time low in share of all cryptocurrency activity. https://blog.chainalysis.com/reports/2022-crypto-crime-report-introduction/. Accessed 26 Apr 2023

Chainalysis Team (2022b) Ransomware revenue down as more victims refuse to pay. https://blog.chainalysis.com/reports/crypto-ransomware-revenue-down-as-victims-refuse-to-pay/. Accessed 26 Apr 2023

Chainalysis Team (2022c) Crypto mixers and AML compliance. https://blog.chainalysis.com/reports/crypto-money-laundering-2022/. Accessed 14 June 2023

Chang E, Darcy P, Raymond K, Le-Khac N (2022) Forensic artefact discovery and attribution from android cryptocurrency wallet applications. ArXiv. https://arxiv.org/ftp/arxiv/papers/2205/2205.14611.pdfcles(arxiv.org)

Chohan UW (2018) Cryptocurrencies as asset-backed instruments: the Venezuelan Petro. SSRN. https://ssrn.com/abstract=3119606

Clements R (2022) Commissioned paper: cryptocurrency: challenges to conventional governance of financial transactions. Public Order Emergency Commission, Ottawa. https://

publicorderemergencycommission.ca/files/documents/Policy-Papers/Cryptocurrency. Accessed 26 Apr 2023

Computer Security Resource Center (2023) Malware. https://csrc.nist.gov/glossary/term/malware#:~:text=Definition(s)%3A,system%20for%20a%20harmful%20purpose. Accessed 26 Apr 2023

Conti M, Gangwal A, Ruj S (2018) On the economic significance of ransomware campaigns: a bitcoin transactions perspective. Comput Secur 79:162–189. https://doi.org/10.1016/j.cose.2018.08.008

CybSafe (2022) What is ransomware in 2023: detection, prevention, recovery. https://www.cybsafe.com/blog/what-is-ransomware/. Accessed 26 Apr 2023

De N (2019) Bitcoin futures volume is more significant than you think, Bitwise Says. www.coindesk.com/markets/2019/03/22/bitcoin-futures-volume-is-more-significant-than-you-think-bitwise-says/

De Koker L, Ocal T, Casanovas P (2022) Where's Wally? FATF, virtual asset service providers, and the regulatory jurisdictional challenge. In: Financial technology and the law, law, governance and technology series, vol 47. Springer, Cham. https://doi.org/10.1007/978-3-030-88036-1_7

Desmond DB, Lacey D, Salmon P (2019) Evaluating cryptocurrency laundering as a complex socio-technical system: a systematic literature review. J Money Laund Control 22(3):480–497. https://doi.org/10.1108/JMLC-10-2018-00633

DiMaggio J (2022) Ransomware diaries: Volume 1. Analyst1. https://analyst1.com/ransomware-diaries-volume-1/. Accessed 26 Apr 2023

Dorotic M, Johnsen J (2023) Child sexual abuse on the internet. BI Norwegian Business School. https://biopen.bi.no/bi-xmlui/bitstream/handle/11250/3055430/SOBIrapport_finalversion_BIOpen.pdf?sequence=1xmlui/bitstream/handle/11250/3055430/SOBIrapport_finalversion_BIOpen.pdf?sequence=1. Accessed 26 Apr 2023

Drejer C, Riegler MA, Halvorsen P, Johnson MS, Baugerud GA (2023) Livestreaming technology and online child sexual exploitation and abuse: a scoping review. Trauma Violence Abuse. https://doi.org/10.1177/15248380221147564

Drezner WD, Farrell H, Newman AL (2021) The uses and abuses of weaponized interdependence. Brookings, Washington, DC

Dupuis D, Smith D, Gleason K (2023) Old frauds with a new sauce: digital assets and space transition. J Financ Crime 30(1):205–220. https://doi.org/10.1108/JFC-11-2021-0242

Europol (2022) Seizing the opportunity: 5 recommendations for crypto assets-related crime and money laundering. Institute of Governance, Basel. https://www.europol.europa.eu/cms/sites/default/files/documents/2022_Recommendations_Joint_Working_Group_on_Criminal_Finances_and_Cryptocurrencies_pdf. Accessed 26 Apr 2023

Faife C (2022) A small canadian town is being extorted by a global ransomware gang. The Verge. https://www.theverge.com/2022/7/22/23274372/st-marys-canada-lockbit-ransomware-cyber-incident. Accessed 26 Apr 2023

Farrell H, Newman AL (2019) Weaponized interdependence: how global economic network shape state coercion. Int Secur 44(1):42–79. https://doi.org/10.1162/isec_a_00351

FATF (2023) Targeted update on implementation of the FATF standards on virtual assets/VASPs. FATF, Paris. https://www.fatf-gafi.org/en/publications/Fatfrecommendations/targeted-update-virtual-assets-vasps-2023.html

Gamble C (2017) The legality and regulatory challenges of decentralised crypto-currency: a Western perspective. Int Trade Bus Law Rev 20:346–336

Gibbon R, Bayyari S, Klauder A, Profaci E (2022) OFAC Sanctions Virtual Currency Mixer "Tornado Cash". Squire Patton Boggs. https://www.globalinvestigations.blog/uncategorized/ofac-sanctions-virtual-currency-mixer. Accessed 26 Apr 2023

Government of Canada (2000) Proceeds of crime (Money Laundering) and terrorist financing act. Justice Laws. https://laws-lois.justice.gc.ca/eng/acts/P-24.501/FullText.html. Accessed 26 Apr 2023

Hayes K (2021) Ransomware: a growing geopolitical threat. Netw Secur 8:11–13. https://doi.org/10.1016/S1353-4858(21)00089-1

Hollingsworth J (2019) How Bitcoin transactions were used to track down the 23-year-old South Korean operating a global exploitation site from his bedroom. CNN. https://edition.cnn.com/2019/10/19/asia/south-korea-child-exploitation-international-police. Accessed 26 Apr 2023

Internet Watch Foundation (2022a) Annual Report 2022. https://www.iwf.org.uk/about-us/who-we-are/annual-report-2022/. Accessed 26 Apr 2023

Internet Watch Foundation (2022b) Websites offering cryptocurrency payment for child sexual abuse images 'Doubling Every Year.' https://www.iwf.org.uk/news-media/news/websites. Accessed 26 Apr 2023

Interpol General Secretariat (2022) Interpol Global Trend Summary Report. https://www.interpol.int/en/content/download/18350/file/Global%20Crime%20Trend%20Summary%20Report%20EN.pdf. Accessed 26 Apr 2023

Jenkins C, Hamilton R, Leuprecht C (2023) Canadian cryptocurrency conundrums: a socio-technical systems analysis of crypto laundering in Canada. In: Leuprecht C, Ferrill J (eds) Dirty money: financial crime in Canada. McGill Queen's University Press, Montreal, pp 322–341

Jentleson BW (2022) Sanctions: what everyone needs to know. Oxford University Press, Oxford

Kennedy M (2019) One of the worst forms of evil: more than 330 arrested in child porn site bust. NPR. https://www.npr.org/2019/10/16/770628069/one-of-the-worst-forms-of-evil-more. Accessed 26 Apr 2023

Kethineni S, Cao Y (2020) The rise in popularity of cryptocurrency and associated criminal activity. Int Criminal Justice Rev 30(3):325–344. https://doi.org/10.1177/1057567719827051

Kirimhan D (2023) Importance of anti-money laundering regulations among prosumers for a cybersecure decentralized finance. J Bus Res 157:1–10. https://doi.org/10.1016/j.jbusres.2022.113558

Kyles D (2022) Centralised control over decentralised structures: AML and CTF regulation of blockchains and distributed ledgers. In: Goldbarsht D, de Koker L (eds) Financial technology and the law. Springer, Cham, pp 121–150

Lee H, Choi K (2021) Interrelationship between bitcoin, ransomware, and terrorist activities: criminal opportunity assessment via cyber-routine activities theoretical framework. Vict Offenders 16(3):363–384. https://doi.org/10.1080/15564886.2020.1835764

Legrand T, Leuprecht C (2021) Securing cross-border collaboration: transgovernmental enforcement networks, organized crime and illicit international political economy. Polic Soc 40(4):565–586. https://doi.org/10.1080/14494035.2021.1975216

Leuprecht C, Brunet-Jailly E, Hataley T, Legrand T (2021) Patterns in nascent, ascendant and mature border security: regional comparisons in transgovernmental coordination, cooperation, and collaboration. Commonwealth Comp Politics 59(4):349–375. https://doi.org/10.1080/14662043.2021.1997192

Leuprecht C, Jenkins C, Hamilton R (2022) Virtual money laundering: policy implications of the proliferation in the illicit use of cryptocurrency. J Financ Crime. https://doi.org/10.1108/JFC-07-2022-0161

Lin D, Wu J, Fu Q, Yu Y, Lin K, Zheng Z, Yang S (2023) Towards understanding crypto money laundering in web3 through the lenses of ethereum heists. Proceedings of the ACM SIGMETRICS Conference 2023 (SIGMETRICS'23), June 19–23, 2023, Orlando, Florida, USA. ACM, New York, NY, USA. https://arxiv.org/pdf/2305.14748.pdf

Long H, Demir E, Sojka B, Zaremba A, Shahzad S (2022) Is geopolitical risk priced in the cross-section of cryptocurrency returns? Financ Res Lett. https://doi.org/10.1016/j.frl.2022.103131

Mahdavieh R (2022) State adoption of cryptocurrency: a case study analysis of Iran, Russia, and Venezuela. Am J Undergraduate Res 19(1):13–22. https://doi.org/10.33697/ajur.2022.055

Majumder A, Routh M, Singha D (2019) A conceptual study on the emergence of cryptocurrency economy and its nexus with terrorism financing. In: Das RC (ed) The impact of global terrorism on economic and political development, pp 125–138. https://doi.org/10.1108/978-1-78769-919-920191012

Maurushat A, Halpin D (2022) Investigation of cryptocurrency enabled and dependent crimes. In: Goldbarsht D, de Koker L (eds) Financial technology and the law: combating financial crime. Springer, Cham, pp 235–267. https://doi.org/10.1007/978-3-030-88036-1_10

Microsoft (2022) Microsoft digital defense report 2022: illuminating the threat landscape and empowering a digital defense, Microsoft. https://query.prod.cms.rt.microsoft.com/cms/api/am/binary/RE5bUvv?culture=en-us&country=us

Napier S, Teunissen C, Boxall H (2021) How do child sexual abuse live streaming offenders access victims? Trends Iss Crime Criminal Justice 642:1–18. https://search.informit.org/doi/abs/10.3316/agispt.20220310063199

NCC Group (2023) The Lazarus Group: North Korean Scourge for +10 years responsible for some of the largest cyber attacks worldwide. https://www.nccgroup.com/us/the-lazarus-group-north-korean-scourge-for-plus10-years/group-north-korean-scourge-for-plus10-years/. Accessed 26 Apr. 2023

Noval SMR, Soecipto JA, Saputra DD, Munifah NF, Nurhasanah RRS, Lestia SN (2023) The fusion of blockchain, pornography and human trafficking in a global digital dragnet that forms the online child sex trafficking. Russian Law J 11(5):50–68

Office of Foreign Assets Control (OFAC) (2023) Sanctions programs and country information. https://doi.org/10.33697/ajur.2022.055iceofForeignAssetsControl(treasury.gov). Accessed 26 Apr 2023

Petkauskas V (2022) Why individual arrests will not shut down lockbit. Cybernews. https://cybernews.com/editorial/arrests-wont-shut-down-lockbit/. Accessed 26 Apr 2023

Pocher N, Veneris A (2021) Privacy and transparency in CBDCs: a regulation-by-design AML/CFT scheme, 2021 IEEE International Conference on Blockchain and Cryptocurrency, pp. 1–9. https://doi.org/10.1109/ICBC51069.2021.9461090

Ponsford M (2015) A comparative analysis of bitcoin and other decentralised virtual currencies: legal regulation in the People's Republic of China, Canada, and the United States, Hong Kong. J Leg Stud 9:29–50. https://doi.org/10.2139/ssrn.2554186

PwC (2022) PwC Annual Crypto Tax Report. global https://www.pwc.com/gx/en/financial-services/pdf/global-crypto-tax-report-2022.pdf-crypto-tax-report-2022.pdf(pwc.com)

Rai R (2022) The death spiral: how terra's algorithmic stablecoin came crashing down. Forbes. https://www.forbes.com/sites/rahulrai/2022/05/17/the-death-spiral-how-terras-algorithmic-stablecoin-came-crashing-down/?sh=1386c85471a2. Accessed 26 Apr 2023

Reinsch WA, Palazzi AL (2022) Cryptocurrency and U.S. sanctions evasion: implications for Russia. Centre for International and Strategic Studies, Washington, DC. https://www.csis.org/analysis/cryptocurrencies-and-us-sanctions-evasion-implications-russia. Accessed 3 July 2023

Savage C (2020) U.S. seizes bitcoin said to be used to finance terrorist groups. https://www.nytimes.com/2020/08/13/us/politics/bitcoin-terrorism.html#:~:text=WASHINGTON%20%E2%80%94%20The%20United%20States%20government,paramilitary%20arm%2C%20the%20Al%20Qassam

Siegmann S (2022) Crypto evasion: the new frontier of sanctions enforcement. Hinckley Allen International Trade & Global Security. https://www.hinckleyallen.com/publications/crypto-evasion-the-new-frontier-of-sanctions-enforcement/evasion-the-new-frontier-of-sanctions-enforcement/. Accessed 26 Apr. 2023

Simser JR (2020) Canada's financial intelligence unit: FINTRAC. J Money Laundering Control 23(2):297–307. https://doi.org/10.1108/JMLC-10-2019-0079

Theiri S, Nekhili R, Sultan J (2023) Cryptocurrency liquidity during the Russia–Ukraine war: the case of bitcoin and Ethereum. J Risk Financ 24(1):59–71. https://doi.org/10.1108/JRF-05-2022-0103

Towne Morton D (2020) The future of cryptocurrency: an unregulated instrument in an increasingly regulated global economy. Loyola Univ Chicago Int Law Rev 16(1):129-[ii]

Travkina EV, Fiapshev AB, Belova MT (2022) Stablecoin-based digital trading and investment platforms and their potential in overcoming sanctions restrictions. Economies 10(10):246. https://doi.org/10.3390/economies10100246

Trevithick M (2022) St. Marys, Ont. grapples with cyberattack as ransomware group threatens to publish stolen data. global news. https://globalnews.ca/news/9009347/st-marys-ont

TRM (2022) Illicit crypto ecosystem report: page 2 A comprehensive guide to illicit finance risks in crypto, TRM. Illicit Crypto Ecosystem Report. https://www.trmlabs.com/illicit-crypto-ecosystem-report-2023. Accessed 8 July 2023

Trozze A, Davies T, Kleinberg B (2023) Of degens and defrauders: using open-source investigative tools to investigate decentralized finance frauds and money laundering. Forensic science international. Digit Investig 46:1–18. https://doi.org/10.1016/j.fsidi.2023.301575

Tunney C (2023) Intelligence agency says ransomware group with russian ties poses 'an enduring threat' to Canada. CBC News. https://www.cbc.ca/news/politics/cse-lockbit-threat

Ungboriboonpisal T (2022) Efficacy of economic sanctions in the face of cryptocurrency. New York Univ J Int Law Politics 55(1):221–235

UNICEF (2021) Ending online child sexual abuse and abuse: lessons learned and promising practices in low and middle income countries. https://search.informit.org/doi/abs/10.3316/agispt.20220310063199SexualExploitationandAbuse.pdf (unicef.org)

UNICEF Global Insight (2022) Prospects for children in 2022: a global outlook. https://www.unicef.org/globalinsight/media/2471/file/UNICEF-Global-Insight-Prospects-for-Children-Global-Outlook-2022.pdf

United States Department of Justice (2019) "Welcome to Video" THIS HIDDEN SITE HAS BEEN SIEZED. https://www.justice.gov/opa/press-release/file/1210446/download

United States Department of Justice (2020) Two chinese nationals charged with laundering over $100 million in cryptocurrency from exchange hack. https://www.justice.gov/opa/pr/two-chinese-nationals-charged-laundering-over-100-million

United States Department of Justice (2021) Department of justice seizes $2.3 million in cryptocurrency paid to the ransomware extortionists darkside. https://www.justice.gov/opa/pr/department-justice-seizes-23-million-cryptocurrency-paid

United States Department of Justice (2022a) U.S. Citizen who conspired to assist North Korea in evading sanctions sentenced to over five years and fined $100,000. https://www.justice.gov/opa/pr/us-citizen-who-conspired-assist-north-korea

United States Department of Justice (2022b) Russian and Canadian national charged for participation in lockbit global ransomware campaign. https://www.justice.gov/usao-nj/pr/russian-and-canadian-national-charged-participation-lockbit-global-ransomware-campaign

United States Department of Justice (2022c) International money launderer sentence to over 11 years in federal prison for laundering millions in cyber crime schemes. https://www.justice.gov/usao-cdca/pr/international-money-launderer-sentenced-over-11-years-federal-prison-laundering

United States Department of the Treasury (2020) Treasury sanctions individuals laundering cryptocurrency for Lazarus group. https://home.treasury.gov/news/press-releases/sm924

United States District Court for the District of Colombia (2019) United States of America v twenty-four cryptocurrency accounts, civil action No. 19-cv-3098. https://www.dcd.uscourts.gov/sites/dcd/files/22mj00067CriminalOpinion.pdf

United States District Court for the District of New Jersey (2022) United States of America v Mikhail Vasiliev, Mag. No. 22-12370. https://www.justice.gov/usao-nj/press-release/file/1551116/download

UNODC (2022) UNODC opens the first cryptocurrency analysis laboratory in the Southeast Asia. https://www.unodc.org/roseap/en/malaysia/2022/05/cryptocurrency-analysis-laboratory/story.html

Varrella A (2017) Live streaming of child sexual abuse: background, legislative frameworks and the experience of The Philippines. ECPAT Int J 12:47–61. https://ecpat.org/wp-content/uploads/2021/05/ECPAT-Summary-paper-on-Online-Child-Sexual-Exploitation-2020.pdf

Veeam (2022) 2022 Ransomware Trends Report, Veeam. https://go.veeam.com/ransomware-trends. Accessed 16 July 2023

Rhianna Hamilton is a PhD student at the University of Adelaide and a research coordinator working out of Queen's University's Institute of Intergovernmental Relations. Her research interests include the study of illicit networks, with a specific focus on transnational environmental crimes like wildlife trafficking, money laundering, crypto crime, and the structures of networks engaging in crime.

Christian Leuprecht is Class of 1965 Distinguished Professor at the Royal Military College of Canada and Editor-in-Chief of the *Canadian Military Journal*. He also directs the Institute of Intergovernmental Relations in the School of Policy Studies and is an Adjunct Research Professor in the Australian Graduate School of Policing and Security at Charles Sturt University. A former Bicentennial Professor in Canadian Studies at Yale University (2009–2010), Matthew Flinders Fellow at Flinders University of South Australia (2017–2018), Eisenhower Fellow at the NATO Defence College (2019), and Fulbright Research Chair in Canada–US Relations at John Hopkins University's School for Advanced International Studies (2020), he is an elected member of the College of New Scholars of the Royal Society of Canada, recipient of the Cowan Prize for Excellence in Research at the Royal Military College of Canada and past president of the International Sociological Association's Research Committee 01: Armed Forces and Conflict Resolution.

Financing Environmental Crime: Financial Sector Complicity in Global Deforestation and Opportunities for Regulatory Intervention

Hannah Harris

Abstract In recent years, governments around the world have passed laws that criminalise the importation of illegally harvested timber in an effort to combat harmful deforestation and protect vital forest ecosystems. These 'destination country laws' focus on one important aspect of this substantial challenge, but they ignore the role of financial institutions in enabling harmful deforestation and facilitating illegal logging practices on a global scale. This chapter summarises the existing regulatory landscape and limits of destination country laws, before exploring financial sector complicity in global deforestation, mapping the ways that finance contributes to deforestation incentives and facilitates the transfer of wealth from illegal logging practices. The chapter goes on to present several regulatory interventions that could incentivise shifts in governance practices within the financial sector, leveraging the power and influence of these important stakeholders to support, rather than undermine, the goals of environmental protection and sustainable development. Due to the complexity of the global financial system and the numerous avenues for engagement and intervention, this chapter establishes the foundation for ongoing research and analysis on this important topic. It is argued that the challenge of illegal logging and harmful deforestation cannot be overcome without support from the financial sector, and furthermore, that such support will facilitate enhanced opportunities for sustainable and regenerative economic development on a global scale.

1 The Deforestation Challenge

Forests are essential to our planet's ability to sustain life. Forests cover nearly one third of all land on earth. They provide the infrastructure essential to the survival of millions of species, including our own. Unfortunately, we are experiencing a deforestation and land clearing crisis. The area of primary forest worldwide has

H. Harris (✉)
Macquarie Law School, Sydney, NSW, Australia

Research Fellow, Financial Integrity Hub, Sydney, Australia
e-mail: Hannah.harris@mq.edu.au

D. Goldbarsht, L. de Koker (eds.), *Financial Crime and the Law*, Ius Gentium: Comparative Perspectives on Law and Justice 115,
https://doi.org/10.1007/978-3-031-59543-1_3

decreased by over 80 million hectares since 1990.[1] Deforestation results in loss of vital ecosystems and biodiversity,[2] and increased carbon dioxide in the atmosphere, accelerating climate change and undermining our planet's resilience. According to National Geographic: 'The Amazon rain forest absorbs one-fourth of the CO2 absorbed by all the land on Earth. However, due to deforestation, the amount of CO2 absorbed by the Amazon today is 30% less than it was in the 1990s.[3] Furthermore, green criminology scholarship has long emphasised the importance of addressing and responding to environmental crimes;[4] crimes that, given the current era of impending ecosystem collapse, 'produce more harm and victimization than street crime.'[5]

Illegal logging is an environmental crime that generates substantial harm and represents a significant barrier to ending global deforestation. Illegal logging refers to the harvest of timber in contravention of laws in place in the country where that timber originated.[6] It can include harvesting timber without a license for the purpose of selling that timber on the global market, or logging in protected areas to clear land for other activities, such as crop farming or livestock production. Illegal logging accounts for up to 90% of tropical deforestation in some countries[7] and costs the global community up to $206 billion each year.[8] The cost of illegal logging is more than just financial. Illegal logging has significant environmental, social, and political implications.[9] Goncalves et al. (2012) cite the International Organization for Migration, who estimate that there are some 33,000 forced laborers in Peruvian logging.[10] In addition to issues of forced labour, Reboredo notes the interaction between illegal logging and organised crime, asserting that 'between 50 and 90% of logging in key tropical countries of the Amazon basin, Central Africa, and Southeast Asia is being carried out by organized crime, leading to the increase of murder, violence, and atrocities against indigenous forest dwellers.'[11]

Recognising the magnitude of the challenge pose by global deforestation, The New York Declaration on Forests was agreed by world leaders at the 2014 Climate Summit. The goals set by the New York Declaration were to halve the rate of deforestation by 2020 and end it by 2030, in addition to restoring millions of hectares of degraded land. Unfortunately, in the period between 2014 and 2020, deforestation rates have increased, rather than reversing. Data from the United Nations Food and

---

[1] FOA (2020), p. xvi.

[2] Tracewski et al. (2016), p. 1071.

[3] National Geographic (2023).

[4] South (2014).

[5] Lynch (2020), p. 50.

[6] Harris (2019a).

[7] Interpol (2020).

[8] Department of Agriculture, Forestry and Fisheries (DAFF) (2022).

[9] Goncalves et al. (2012) and Reboredo (2013).

[10] Goncalves et al. (2012).

[11] Reboredo (2013), p. 297.

Agriculture Organization (UN FAO) shows that over the decade since 2010, the net loss in forests globally was 4.7 million hectares per year, with actual deforestation rates being significantly higher still.[12] At COP26, on the second of November 2021, leaders of 141 countries reaffirmed their commitment to 'working collectively to halt and reverse forest loss and land degradation by 2030 while delivering sustainable development and promoting an inclusive rural transformation.'[13] This commitment was labelled the Glasgow Leaders' Declaration on Forests and Land Use.[14] One year later, at COP27, the Forests and Climate Leaders Partnership (FCLP) was launched, 'to enhance cooperation on delivery of pledges made in Glasgow'.[15] These commitments demonstrate a need to move beyond the legality of logging operations and to ensure that global forest ecosystems are adequately protected, for the environmental, social and economic prosperity of current and future generations. However, ending illegal logging is an essential component of this goal.

The drivers of illegal logging include global demand for timber and other commodities that require forest clearing, increased regulation of timber in some jurisdictions driving shifts in logging practices to less well-regulated environments, reliance on agriculture and forestry industries for economic opportunities in source countries, and corrupt incentives for profit between landholders and foreign corporations.[16] For example, in the Pacific, the cultural, social, and physical value of forestry resources is undermined by corruption and prioritisation of the economic value of timber, which is driven by demand in developed western economies. In Papua New Guinea, Special Agricultural Business Leases have been found to lack accountability and consistent implementation, resulting in perpetuation of illegal logging practices with harmful impacts for customary landowners.[17] In the Solomon Islands, the nation's heavy reliance on revenue generated by logging operations complicates efforts to overcome illegal activity,[18] despite ongoing issues around customary land ownership, corruption, and lack of transparency.[19] Further afield, Brazil continues to struggle with enforcement of laws to protect the Amazon rainforest. Efforts are undermined by lack of political will,[20] and by fraudulent and corrupt schemes driven by strong economic incentives for deforestation to make way for agriculture and livestock operations.[21] Even in developed countries like Australia, a failure to recognise the importance of sustainable land management in corporate policies and practices has led to illegal logging by domestic companies

---

[12] Ritchie and Roser (2021).

[13] United Nations Climate Change Conference (2021).

[14] ibid.

[15] World Resource Institute (2022).

[16] Harris (2019a).

[17] Act Now PNG (2016) and Harris (2019b).

[18] Organized Crime and Corruption Reporting Project (OCCRP) (2018).

[19] Harris (2019a).

[20] National Geographic (2019).

[21] Schmidt and McDermott (2015).

including Vic Forests, with a number of other Australian corporations complicit in the purchase of timber from this illegal source.[22] These examples demonstrate the different drivers of illegal logging and the diversity of contexts in which illegal logging occurs. They also reveal the challenge of enforcement presented by activities that occur as part of complex global supply chains.

Due to the transnational nature of the challenge, it has been established that 'importing countries need to expand cooperation with source countries' to eliminate illegal logging.[23] In response to this call to action, destination country laws have proliferated across many jurisdictions where timber is imported and sold, including the United Kingdom, United States, Australia and the European Union. More recently, Japan, Korea and China have also passed similar laws.[24] Destination country laws require importing entities (corporations) to conduct due-diligence to prevent illegally harvested timber from entering their supply chains. This approach reflects a broader trend towards the use of corporate due-diligence obligations in domestic law, to manage social and environmental harms resulting from transnational business operations.[25] It has been established that these laws represent part of 'a joined-up transnational regime' to combat illegal logging.[26] Other components of the transnational regulatory framework or 'regime' include laws in source countries, certification schemes, and the policies and practices of a range of stakeholders including corporate actors, government bodies and regulators, forest reliant communities, civil society groups, and consumers and investors.

Destination country laws are an important component of the framework to overcome illegal logging and harmful deforestation. However, several limitations have constrained their effectiveness and thus necessitate revision and adaption. The four fundamental limitations that can be identified as follows: (1) reliance on source country definitions of legality; (2) failure to address harms that result from legal deforestation; (3) application only to the importation of timber products; (4) a narrow focus on commodity importers (ignoring the role of finance in contributing to harmful deforestation and illegal logging). Before discussing the fourth limitation in detail, as well as the legal innovations that are being developed to overcome it, a brief summary of the former three limitations is warranted. This summary provides useful context for understanding the full extent of the deforestation challenge, and for explaining recent regulatory innovations that have been developed or proposed in key jurisdictions including the United Kingdom and European Union. These innovations demonstrate a path forward for a more robust transnational legal framework to end deforestation, inspiring continued legal adaption to protect vital forest ecosystems.

---

[22] Carvalho et al. (2019), p. 126.

[23] Guan et al. (2018), p. 37.

[24] Forest Stewardship Council (FSC) (2018).

[25] Schilling-Vacaflor and Lenschow (2021), Quijano and Lopez (2021) and Partzsch and Vlaskamp (2016).

[26] Zeitlin and Overdevest (2021).

2 The Limits of Current Illegal Logging Laws

2.1 Reliance on Source Country Definitions of Legality

All existing destination country laws rely on source country definitions of legality to establish an offence. In Australia, under the Illegal Logging Prohibition Act ('*ILPA*'), the definition of illegal logged is: 'harvested in contravention of laws in force in the place (whether or not in Australia) where the timber was harvested'.[27] In Europe, the EU Timber Regulation ('*EUTR*') establishes the definition of illegal harvested under Article 2(d) as 'harvested in contravention of the applicable legislation in the country of harvest'.[28] In the United States, the 2008 Amendments to the US Lacey Act of 1900 16 USC §§ 3371–3378 ('Lacey Act') were the first attempt to criminalise the importation of illegally harvested timber. The wording of the Lacey Act is slightly more complicated than the EU and Australian laws, but the effect is largely the same. The Lacey Act makes it an offence to 'import, export, transport, sell, receive, acquire, or purchase any...plant taken, possessed, transported, or sold in violation of any law, treaty, or regulation of the United States or in violation of any Indian tribal law'.[29] However, as Lee (2014) notes, 'congress limited the Lacey Act when defining the reach of these foreign and domestic laws by requiring that the underlying law be one that regulates any or all of six different areas.'[30] The areas include: laws governing theft of plants, taking of plants from protected or otherwise designated areas, taking plants without relevant authorisation, payment of relevant taxes or fees, and export or trans-shipment requirements.[31] Thus, the Lacey Act can be interpreted as more constrained in scope than the Australian and European laws.

A final example of the reliance of destination country laws on source country definitions of legality is usefully found in the United Kingdom Environment Act 2021, Schedule 17, titled 'Use of Forest Risk Commodities in Commercial Activity'. This Act will be explored further in Sect. 3 below, as this law was the first to expand the scope of destination country laws beyond timber products, to include other commodities linked to deforestation. While the law is innovative regarding the scope of commodities covered, it is consistent in its reliance on source country laws for establishing legality. Schedule 17(2)(1) and (2) assert that a person must not use a forest risk commodity or derivative product in their UK commercial activities 'unless relevant local laws were complied with in relation to that commodity.' Schedule 17(2)(4) limits the scope of relevant local law to those relating to the ownership or use of the land on which the commodity was grown, raised or cultivated.

[27] ILPA (2012), S7.

[28] EUTR (2010) Art 2(d)).

[29] Lacey Act, §3372 a(1).

[30] Lee (2014), p. 191.

[31] Lacey Act, §3372 a(2)&(3).

Ultimately, all destination country laws prohibit importation of illegally harvested timber, but they rely on definitions of legality established by the laws in operation in the source country where the timber is harvested. The problem here is that it is very difficult to guarantee the legality of timber (or other commodities) harvested in far flung jurisdictions, where legal frameworks are often complex, law enforcement is weak, and incentives for fraud and corruption abound.[32] As Rose highlights, using the case study of Indonesia, 'bribery remains pervasive among forestry officers, police and customs officials, politicians, court officials and judges'.[33] This creates an evaluation challenge for importers, and a detection and enforcement challenge for regulators.[34] For example, the United States enforcement of the Lacey Act against company Lumber Liquidators revealed that a Chinese company marketing to the United States had offered to provide fraudulent Forest Stewardship Council Certification on illegal wood flooring for a 10% mark up.[35] The department responsible for enforcement of Australia's ILPA has flagged that fraudulent certification is a concern for validating timber legality.[36] The guidance note for the regulations that accompany the ILPA and establish the due-diligence requirements for importers states: 'some countries/regions have issues with governance and enforcement over forestry activities or issues with corruption that result in illegal logging'.[37] Thus, destination country laws are limited in terms of both compliance and enforcement, by their reliance on source country definitions of legality. This, in turn, produces corrupt incentives to fraudulently obtain documents that provide the appearance of legality but do not guarantee legal acquisition.

It should be noted that innovations in tracking, monitoring and traceability are helping to alleviate some of the challenges related to verifying timber legality. For example, He and Turner (2022) identify a range of blockchain-based applications that have been designed to trace timber and validate legality, including several built on the well-known crypto-currency platform, Ethereum.[38] The Forest Stewardship Council and Preferred by Nature, two major global providers of sustainable forestry certifications, have both recently developed their own blockchain based traceability platforms.[39] While such technological innovations are unlikely to solve all of the problems that result from the reliance on source country definitions of legality and the corrupt incentives they produce, they do demonstrate the ongoing commitment to innovation in this area. Considering that the alternative would be to establish a legally binding and internationally agreed definition of harmful deforestation,

[32] Rose (2017), p. 138.
[33] Rose (2017), p. 134.
[34] dos Reis et al. (2021).
[35] Conniff (2018).
[36] Harris (2019a), p. 77.
[37] Department of Agriculture, Water and the Environment (DAWE) (2019).
[38] He and Turner (2022), p. 9.
[39] Ledger Insights (2021).

technological solutions and awareness of corrupt incentives by importers and regulators may be the most pragmatic approach in the short to medium term.

2.2 The Connection Between 'Legal' Logging and Harmful Deforestation

The second limitation of destination country illegal logging laws is linked to the first. Because illegal logging legislation focuses on source country definitions of legality, it fails to recognise the connection between *legally justified* logging and harmful deforestation. In some countries, where the forestry or agricultural industries are a major contributor to the economy, laws to protect natural forests are weak and subject to fickle shifts in political will.

Brazil is an excellent example of how shifts in political will can impact laws that protect forests, enabling felling of the Amazon, despite globally recognised need to preserve this essential resource. Although Brazil was able to reduce deforestation by 80% from 2005 to 2014, Moraes et al. (2021) note that changes in the legal framework in Brazil 'threaten public forests in the Amazon'.[40] The authors cite lobbying by local and national agribusiness elites, political financing by private companies, and a shifting political agenda as contributors to the changing legal environment in Brazil. These forces led to weakening of environmental protections with the passage of the 2012 Forestry Act, resulting in reductions of the area required for legal reserves on rural private properties and establishment of an amnesty on illegal deforestation prior to 2008.[41] Both changes have been flagged as significant setbacks in the fight against harmful deforestation[42] and the continually changing regulatory environment represented by such legal change complicates effective due-diligence efforts by importers and increases the regulatory and enforcement burden in destination countries. A 2020 study notes that 'since 2013, official deforestation rates have been on an upward trend'[43] in Brazil. 'The 2020 deforestation rate is 182% higher than the established target of 3925 km^2 and represents a reduction of only 44% instead of the 80% established in law.'[44]

Historically, logging concessions were often seen by developing countries as a means to generate income and elevate debt. Even today, Butler (2012) notes that 'debt payments are still an important factor in the need for governments to pursue and exploit natural resources in an unsustainable manner'.[45] Thus, the legality of logging is shaped by economic interests and does not guarantee strong

[40] Moraes et al. (2021).

[41] Sant'Anna and Costa (2021) and Freitas et al. (2018).

[42] Asher (2019).

[43] Silva Jr et al. (2021), p. 144.

[44] Ibid.

[45] Butler (2012).

environmental governance or protection of vital forest ecosystems. Here, we begin to see the strong link between market economics, finance, and deforestation. This link will be further explored in subsequent sections of this chapter.

2.3 *Limited Scope: A Focus on Timber and Timber Products*

The third limitation of illegal logging laws has been partially mitigated by recent regulatory innovations in the United Kingdom and proposed regulatory changes in the European Union, which expand the scope of existing regulation to cover "forest risk commodities" beyond timber. Such adaptions are new and have not been finalised in either the UK or Europe, nor yet contemplated in other jurisdictions such as Australia or the United States.

By focusing exclusively on the importation and harvest of *timber products*, current laws often fail to acknowledge the interconnections between illegal logging, deforestation, and economic activities *unrelated to the forestry industry*. Deforestation and subsequent export of timber may be a by-product of other industries. A recent study by Pendrill et al. (2022) established that 'agricultural expansion is a primary cause of tropical deforestation and therefore a key driver of greenhouse gas emissions, biodiversity loss, and the degradation of ecosystem services vital to the livelihoods of forest-dependent and rural people.'[46] To re-use the Brazilian example, a report by Forest Trends from 2021 cites that 'the major agricultural commodities responsible for deforestation in Brazil are beef and soy', with clearing for livestock pasture representing more than 80% of the deforestation in the Brazilian amazon.[47] Other industries are also complicit in large scale deforestation, including the mining sector.[48] In East Asia and the Pacific, deforestation has occurred to make way for oil palm plantations—with well documented and devastating impacts on local communities and ecosystems.[49]

While discussion of the impacts of 'legal' deforestation above have already mentioned these industries and their impact on global forests, it is important to recognise that the logging that occurs to make way for other industrial activities is often illegal—in breach of source country laws. For example, 'Indonesia's Supreme Audit Agency found less than 20% of palm oil operations in compliance with national laws and regulations.'[50] In these cases, destination country laws that focus exclusively on timber and timber products do not expose companies importing the resulting commodities (Brazilian soy for cattle feed or Palm oil in food and cosmetic products) to due-diligence requirements—despite the risk that these

[46] Pendrill et al. (2022).

[47] Dummett and Blundell (2021), p. 27.

[48] Sonter et al. (2017).

[49] Human Rights Watch (2019) and Friends of the Earth (2005).

[50] Dummett and Blundell (2021), p. 3.

products contributed to illegal deforestation. As noted above, this significant gap has been recognised in some jurisdictions, including the United Kingdom and the European Union. In both the UK and Europe cases, laws now include due-diligence requirements for "forest risk commodities", not just for timber products. However, the full scope of these laws remains to be determined by secondary legislation and regulatory guidance.

On 17 November 2021 the European Commission published its Proposal for a Regulation on Deforestation-Free Products, with the stated objective: 'to curb deforestation and forest degradation that is provoked by EU consumption and production.'[51] As originally proposed, the regulation would require companies (with an exclusion for Small and Medium Sized Enterprises) The proposal would require 'operators' placing 'relevant commodities' on the EU market to conduct due-diligence and ensure that they are 'deforestation free' and 'produced in accordance with the relevant legislation of the country of production'.[52] The commodities covered by the proposal include wood, beef, palm oil, soy, cocoa and coffee, with the possible addition of rubber.[53] The proposal is currently in the legislative process of the European Parliament and is awaiting formal adoption by the council and parliament.[54]

The UK is slightly further along in the legislative process, having enacted the UK Environment Act 2021 which includes the previously mentioned Schedule 17 on 'Use of Forest Risk Commodities in Commercial Activity', prohibiting the importation of forest risk commodities acquired in contravention of local laws. Ongoing consultations have provided some guidance on the scope of the obligations, which will apply to (at minimum) the importation of products containing cattle (beef and leather), cocoa, rubber, palm oil, soy, coffee and corn.[55] The importation of timber will remain under the governance of the already established UK Timber Products Regulations, which have continued to operate in line with the EU Timber Regulations since the UK left the European Union.

Interestingly, both the EU and UK have also discussed expansion of the scope of destination country laws in another way, to include due-diligence not only for other "forest risk commodities" but to include financial service entities in the due-diligence obligations.[56] The importance of this additional expansion of regulatory scope will be explored further below and then discussed in more detail for the remainder of this chapter.

[51] European Commission (2021).

[52] ibid.

[53] Sarmiento and Oeschger (2022).

[54] European Parliament (EP) (2023).

[55] CMS (2022).

[56] Global Resource Initiative (GRI) (2022), Tridos Bank (2022) and Fern (2023).

2.4 *Limited Scope: Due-Diligence Obligations Apply Only to Importers (Ignoring the Role of the Financial Sector)*

The proliferation of destination country laws targeting illegal logging and the expansion of due-diligence obligations to forest risk commodities, as discussed above, has been celebrated as a positive step in combating illegal logging and harmful deforestation.[57] However, a narrow focus on commodity importers—ignoring the role of the finance sector in contributing to harmful deforestation and illegal logging, has been noted by many stakeholders as a substantial limitation of the current transnational legal framework. For example, an open letter to the European Parliament signed by a group of banks and financial institutions with more than EUR 177 billion in assets under management argued that: 'despite voluntary commitments and policies to tackle deforestation, financial institutions are continuing to provide investments linked to deforestation practices.'[58] The letter urged the EU to support the inclusion of the financial sector in due-diligence obligations related to forest risk commodities.

Despite such calls, existing destination country laws already mentioned above, as well as the emerging regulatory frameworks targeting forest risk commodities, are all limited in their scope to importers. For example, the Lacey Act prohibitions apply to 'a person' generally, but the offences are structured such that they apply only to physical acts of acquisition or trade, rather than financing. The Australian ILPA adopts the same approach as the Lacey Act, prohibiting 'importation' by a 'person' and therefore excluding any related financing activities. The due-diligence requirements under the ILPA are also limited to importation. The EU Timber Regulations as well as the contemplated Regulation on Forest Risk Commodities requires due-diligence by 'operators' who are 'placing on the market' timber or forest risk commodities. 'Placing on the market' under the Timber Regulations is defined as 'the supply. . .of timber or timber products for the first time on the internal market for distribution or use in the course of a commercial activity'. The UK Timber Regulation and UK Environment Act are similarly constrained. However, as the Global Resource Initiative (GRI) notes in its 2022 report, finance plays a substantial role in driving global deforestation and incentivising illegal logging.[59] The mechanisms through which the financial sector facilitates deforestation will be documented further in the following section, before exploring possible regulatory solutions that could enhance the existing legal framework and bring the financial sector into the fold.

---

[57] Durán and Scott (2022).

[58] Tridos Bank (2022).

[59] Global Resource Initiative (GRI) (2022), p. ii.

3 Financial Sector Complicity

Having demonstrate the devastating impact of deforestation on climate, ecology and society, and given the limits of existing regulatory interventions, it is necessary to analyse the role played by global finance in contributing to this harmful activity. This analysis helps to justify an expansion of the legal focus to explicitly include financial firms and investment actors in due-diligence obligations, and to include financial institutions as stakeholders in the development of a more robust global legal framework to combat harmful deforestation and end illegal logging. While such a goal may be ambitions, there exists established precedent for expanded financial sector participation in (and accountability for) environmental risks and harms. This chapter builds on such precedent and provide a starting point for further expansion of existing stakeholder engagement and regulation.

3.1 Lending and Forest Risk Commodities

The NGO Global Canopy has been monitoring the top 500 companies and financial institutions with exposure to deforestation since 2014. In its 2023 annual report, it highlights that the 150 financial institutions covered in its assessment provide US $6.1 trillion in finance to companies in forest-risk supply chains.[60] That same report also found that 61% of the financial institutions that are most exposed to deforestation do not have a deforestation policy covering their lending and investments.[61] This is a significant barrier to eliminating illegal logging and ending harmful deforestation. Several studies have demonstrated that the trillions of dollars being invested by these financial institutions in companies in forest-risk supply chains have been funding illegal and harmful deforestation practices with large scale impacts on local ecosystems and forest reliant communities. Reports by Jubilee Australia illustrate how commercial bank lending practices have enabled decades of illegal logging in Papua New Guinea.[62] Furthermore, Rose notes that the nexus between illegality in the forestry sector and the provision of financial services by banks and other lending institutions exposes these enterprises to the risk of money laundering and the enforcement of legal regimes designed to combat such

[60] Global Canopy (2023), p. 6.

[61] Ibid, p. 8.

[62] Jubilee Australia, *The Money Behind the Chainsaws: how commercial banks support destructive logging in Papua New Guinea* (2021) available at: https://www.jubileeaustralia.org/storage/app/uploads/public/61a/5d9/ce1/61a5d9ce16130650682639.pdf; Jubilee Australia, *Lending to the Loggers: how the non-bank sector is financing forest destruction in Papua New Guinea* (2023) available at: https://www.jubileeaustralia.org/storage/app/uploads/public/645/9f2/3de/6459f23de6ba0785084450.pdf.

offences.[63] A recent report detailing the connection between forest crime and financial crime in Papua New Guinea demonstrates the extent of the connection between forest crime and financial crime, as well as opportunities for enhanced regulation and law enforcement efforts that bridge the divide between poorly enforced forestry law frameworks and stronger and more effective enforcement strategies that target money-laundering, tax evasion, corruption and bribery.[64] Acknowledging the nexus between illegal logging and financial crime, suggestions have been made that Indonesian financial service providers should suspect all logging transactions in their jurisdiction to be high risk, from the perspective of potential illegality, and should conduct appropriate due-diligence following domestic anti-money laundering laws and the Recommendations of the Financial Action Task Force (FATF).[65]

It is important to recognise that investment can take different forms, with implications for the nature and extend of potential regulatory interventions to be discussed in the following section. Due to the complexity of the financial system further research is warranted to explore additional mechanisms through which the financial sector may contribute to illegal logging and deforestation. However, the below examples provide a starting point for understanding how different business practices by financial institutions have been linked to illegal and destructive practices, through their interaction with high-risk commodities.

The most obvious interaction between financial institutions and forest risk commodities is through direct investment, either by means of share equity or debt. A lack of transparency limits the ability of third parties to accurately assess the full extent of financial institution investment in forest risk commodities. However, NGO Global Witness provided an insightful report in 2021 titled "Deforestation Dividends", which claims that 'financial institutions made an estimated $1.74 billion in deforestation-adjusted proceeds from deals with some of the world's most harmful deforesters in the five years following the Paris Climate Agreement's adoption in December 2015'.[66]

Not all examples documented in the report are directly linked to illegality, although the challenges discussed earlier in this chapter around verification of legality in the complex operating environments where forest risk commodities are sourced raises significant concerns for the legitimacy of such business operations. This concern is exacerbated by the statistics referenced by the GRI, which states:

> Deforestation has been driven predominantly through the expansion and development of commercial agriculture in particular the production of commodities such as soy, palm oil, timber and beef…The majority, at least 69%, of this land conversion over the last decade has

[63] Rose (2017), p. 131.

[64] Hannah Harris, *Illegal Logging and the Criminal Law Context in Papua New Guinea* (2024) available at: https://actnowpng.org/sites/default/files/publications/IllegalLogging_CriminalLaw_Report_Final_Apr24.pdf.

[65] Goldbarsht and Harris (2020).

[66] Global Witness (2021a), p. 7.

> been conducted in violation of national laws and regulations, equivalent to an area roughly the size of Norway. In Brazil, over the same time period, at least 95% of all deforestation was illegal.[67]

This demonstrates the strong correlation between agricultural deforestation and illegality. Furthermore, the Global Witness report provides specific examples of direct investment by global banks in companies linked to illegal deforestation and human rights abuses. On such example is the direct equity holdings of HSBC, Barclays Bank, Deutsche Bank, JP Morgan, Santander and Black Rock in the meat packing company JBS. The meat packing company was fined more than USD eight million by Brazilian authorities in 2017 for purchasing livestock raised in illegally deforested areas in the state of Para.[68] However, Global Witness has documented continued misconduct by the company, asserting that 'JBS bought cattle from Rafael Saldanha, a rancher accused of human rights abuses, murder and land-grabbing by Brazilian prosecutors.'[69] Another example is the lucrative relationship between BNP Paribas and Cargill, estimated at over 16 million since 2016. The report found that the bank has provided Cargill with credit facilities and bond underwriting worth almost $4 billion in the last 5 years.[70] This is concerning considering that Cargill has been implicated in a wide range of environmental and human rights abuses and has been fined millions of USD for activities linked to illegal deforestation.[71] The Financial Times cites JP Morgan Chase's provision of USD 730 million to Olam International via revolving credit facilities, despite the company being under investigation by the Forest Stewardship Council for allegedly destroying rainforest in the African state of Gabon.[72]

In addition to direct shareholding and provision of retail financial services to commodity companies complicit in illegal logging and deforestation, global financial institutions may also hold shares in other financial entities which directly invest in high-risk commodities and supply chains. This form of indirect investment has been documented in the case of palm oil from Papua New Guinea. Illegal logging and deforestation related to palm oil production in Papua New Guinea is well documented.[73] A sector specific investigation, again by Global Witness, links three major palm oil producers in PNG to 'tax avoidance, corruption and abuses of both local communities and their environment.'[74] Relevant to the investment discussion, the investigation found that these palm oil companies were financed by large loans (in the hundreds of millions of USD) provided by major Malaysian

---

[67] Global Resource Initiative (GRI) (2022), p. 1.

[68] Earthsight (2017).

[69] Global Witness (2021a), p. 22.

[70] Ibid, p. 14.

[71] Spring (2018).

[72] Hodgson and Morris (2021).

[73] Harris (2019a), Lawson (2014) and Gabriel and Wood (2015).

[74] Global Witness (2021b), p. 8.

banks.[75] Furthermore, 'these banks count among their major shareholders some of the biggest names in global finance. . .such as BlackRock, Norges Bank Investment Management (NBIM), and the Vanguard Group.'[76] Thus, we see that financial sector complicity in illegal logging and harmful deforestation extends beyond direct investment to indirect forms of finance too. This is a relevant consideration for the scope of regulatory interventions to follow.

3.2 ETFs and Other Fund Portfolios

There is an additional dimension of the financial sector that also deserves mention: the global funds market, and in particular the market for Exchange Traded Funds (ETFs). An ETF is a listed investment vehicle that invests in a basket of stocks, bonds and other assets including commodities and currencies. These baskets of assets can, and often do, contain companies linked to deforestation and illegal logging.[77] As of the end of December 2022, total ETF assets under management have reached $6.7 trillion across the US and Europe, growing at approximately 15% compound annual growth rate since 2010.[78] This growth has seen ETFs gain significant market share over more traditional mutual funds. This presents both an opportunity and a risk for investment in forest risk sectors.

Planet Tracker provides an excellent overview of the relationship between ETFs and forest risk in their 2020 report "Exchange Traded Deforestation". In that report, Planet Tracker points out that ETF sponsors (including major financial institutions such as BlackRock, Vanguard and State Street) have often been less active in their stewardship efforts than more traditional mutual funds, despite making public commitments to end deforestation.[79] The report provides one impactful example drawn from research by Profundo and Friends of the Earth which found that 'since 2012. . .BlackRock, Vanguard and State Street have voted against or abstained from all 16 shareholder resolutions calling for action on deforestation, effectively taking a stance against industry change'.[80]

Following this analysis of the complicity of ETFs and their sponsors in deforestation, the report calls on these financial institutions 'to issue a public pledge committing to reduce deforestation risk in their holdings or indices.'[81] As part of its recommendations, the report emphasises the value of disclosure of forest risk commodities in indexes and funds, as well as promoting stewardship by ETF

[75] ibid., p. 26.

[76] ibid., p. 27.

[77] Cannon (2021).

[78] Kaczmarski et al. (2023).

[79] Planet Tracker (2020), p. 7.

[80] ibid.

[81] ibid., p. 18.

sponsors (as shareholders in companies with forest risk in their supply chains) to guide those companies towards eliminating such risks. These recommendations present some interesting opportunities for regulatory intervention in line with broader Responsible Investment (RI) principles. While it is beyond the scope of this chapter to explore these interventions in detail, this presents a valuable opportunity for further investigation and analysis.

3.3 Central Banks and Corporate Bonds

Before concluding this exploration of the role of financial institutions in contributing to harmful deforestation and illegal logging, it is important to be aware of the role played by public finance. Recently, Central Bank purchases of corporate bonds came under fire for contributing financial support to companies with high levels of deforestation risk.[82] It has been established that 'the Bank of England, European Central Bank, and the US Federal Reserve System have purchased large volumes of debt issued by companies linked to deforestation and forest destruction.'[83] A Global Witness investigation found that the US Federal Reserve purchased USD 16 million of bonds issued by Archer-Daniels-Midland, Bunge and Cargill. The Bank of England also invested in an undisclosed fraction of a 150 million Europe Cargill bond and the European Central Bank also bough debt issued by Bunge. Cargill's poor record of involvement in deforestation of the Amazon has already been noted. The report also cites a finding by Greenpeace that all three companies 'were found to have lobbied the EU to weaken its anti-deforestation plans in the final days of the COP26 climate conference.'[84] Investment by Central Banks is an important dimension of financial sector involvement in harmful deforestation and illegal logging, but it also represents an opportunity for positive and transformative action. A report by UCL asserts that government bond portfolios have 'considerable signalling power to financial markets and could have a material impact on the uptake of prudent risk management practices by the private sector relating to nature degradation.'[85] On this basis, it has been emphasised that central bank policies should consider deforestation as prudential risks, signalling, both through policy and investment practice, that global capital should be focused on creating resilience to nature related financial risks (rather than contributing to them).[86]

To summarise, there is substantial evidence of investment institution complicity in illegal logging and harmful deforestation. This complicity is often in direct conflict with voluntary commitments made by such institutions, including those

[82] Downie (2022).

[83] Global Witness (2022), p. 2.

[84] Ibid, p. 3.

[85] Kedward et al. (2021).

[86] ibid.; Jun and Robins (2022).

related to Net Zero objectives and combating climate change. The breadth of this complicity and the failure of the existing legal framework to hold financial institutions accountable for their role in illegal logging and harmful deforestation justify the exploration of regulatory interventions. The potential tools for such intervention are introduced in the following section, before concluding remarks that suggest pathways for further research and analysis.

4 Regulatory Interventions

The earlier summary of the existing transnational law framework against illegal logging and harmful deforestation emphasised four core limitations. The above analysis of the role of global finance in contributing to harmful deforestation has made clear the need to include financial regulation as part of the solution. However, there are several avenues to pursue this objective. The first, and most immediate, is to include financial actors in the due-diligence requirements of existing destination country laws (documented above). This is an intervention that has been contemplated in Europe and the United Kingdom and will be discussed further below.

An additional legal intervention to consider is the enforcement of ESG accountability for companies generally, and the financial sector in particular. Beyond hard law interventions, there is also potential for softer policy-based approaches to enhance the role of finance and investment in combating illegal logging and overcoming harmful deforestation. These softer approaches could include contemplating sovereign debt relief as a mechanism for environmental protection,[87] as well as the scaling up investment in sustainable and regenerative agriculture.[88] The following sections of this chapter will focus on the hard law interventions, with exploration of softer policy options left for subsequent research and development.

4.1 Expanding Due-Diligence Requirements

The most obvious entry point for regulatory intervention is expansion of existing due-diligence requirements under destination country laws targeting importation of timber and other forest risk commodities. These laws could easily be expanded to include financial institutions within the scope of due-diligence obligations. Both the European Union and the United Kingdom have been considering such expansion, after several consultation responses emphasised that existing destination country laws do not go far enough to have meaningful impact on illegal logging and deforestation.

---

[87] Georgieva et al. (2022) and Simmons and Ray (2021).

[88] Romijn et al. (2019) and Niles et al. (2002).

A submission to the UK Environment Bill Committee by Greener UK and the Wildlife and Countryside Link asserted that the law as originally drafted was insufficient without establishing equivalent due-diligence obligations for financial institutions.[89] This mirrors the recommendations of the Global Resource Initiative (GRI) which have been calling for mandatory due-diligence obligations to be placed on financial institutions to address harmful deforestation since the Environment Bill was first proposed. The GRI have recommended that the UK establish a legal duty on Financial Institutions to prohibit lending and investment in illegally produced forest risk commodities.[90] Unfortunately, such recommendations have not been heeded, although a currently proposed amendment to the Financial Services and Markets Bill in the UK may be poised to address this issue.[91] In support of this proposed amendment, Sir Ian Cheshire of GRI asserted that 'financial institutions should be required to assess and identify environmental and human rights risks and impacts within their portfolios and take action to prevent or mitigate those risks and publicly report on progress.'[92] In his letter to the house of lords, the GRI representative further notes that 'reporting mechanisms such as the Taskforce on Nature-related Financial Disclosures (TNFD) and voluntary net zero pledges are insufficient to prevent deforestation financing.'[93] The current framework of nature-related disclosures and net zero pledges will be explored further in the context of ESG reporting and accountability below.

Two limiting factors should be considered with regard to this regulatory intervention. First, there is the challenge of ensuring the effectiveness of due-diligence policies in practice. As noted by Partiti, 'non-financial due diligence enrols the regulatory capacity of private firms.'[94] It is therefore essential that clear procedural guidelines are established to ensure due-diligence policies are up to standard and are actioned in practice, not just drafted on paper.[95] A second limiting factor relates to the earlier discussion of destination country law reliance on source country definitions of legality fundamentally. Such reliance constrains the effectiveness of this legal mechanism to combat harmful deforestation, because it creates incentives for fraud and corruption in the supply chains for forest risk commodities, and does not account for the political, social and economic factors in source countries that shape the regulatory landscape. Therefore, further research is needed to explore the possibility of establishing an internationally agreed definition of harmful deforestation. Such a definition would supplement and enhance destination country laws and contribute to a more wholistic approach to ending harmful deforestation. Because such agreement is unlikely in the short term, alternative regulatory interventions

[89] Greener UK and Wildlife and Countryside Link (2021).

[90] Global Resource Initiative (GRI) (2022).

[91] Fern (2023).

[92] Global Witness (2023).

[93] ibid.

[94] Partiti (2021), p. 163.

[95] Sarfaty (2015).

should also be considered. Establishing legal accountability for existing ESG reporting practices and enhancing mandatory disclosure obligations for non-financial risks are two related mechanisms through which the financial sector could be supported to combat illegal logging and deforestation.

4.2 Enforcing ESG Accountability and Enhanced Disclosures

An important point to note is the overlap between existing due-diligence obligations for commodity importers and the investment landscape. The already established due-diligence requirements for companies engaged in the production and importation of forest risk commodities under UK and EU laws provides important information to the market that can and should be used in the formulation of investment decisions by financial institutions. These obligations 'provide businesses and financiers with the certainty they need to invest and adapt their supply chains or portfolios, particularly in lagging commodity sectors.'[96] Enhancing Environmental Social and Governance (ESG) reporting and accountability frameworks provides an opportunity to further leverage these market dynamics.

Currently, some financial institutions such as HSBC disclose their customers in the palm oil industry,[97] but there are no legal requirements to disclose banking customers in any particular sector and this limits the transparency of the financial system in terms of the scope of exposure to forest risk commodities. Disclosures should also go beyond assessment of banking customers and include all material investment in companies and activities that could contribute to illegal logging and harmful deforestation. This recommendation is effectively an expansion and hardening of the evolving ESG disclosure framework, which would provide legal certainty for companies and investors, as well as ensuring accountability for greenwashing of business practices and mislabelling of financial products such as ESG funds and ETFs.

In response to the GRI letter discussed above, the House of Lords asserted that the UK has 'supported the Taskforce on Nature Related Financial Disclosures (TNFD) which is developing a framework for reporting on nature-related dependencies, impacts, and risks for corporates, investors and lenders'.[98] This framework is set to be published in September 2023 and will align with and enhance the established recommendations of the Taskforce on Climate Related Financial Disclosures (TCFD).

While it is beyond the scope of this chapter to document the full gambit of voluntary disclosure regimes in detail, a brief summary is helpful, particularly

---

[96] WWF (2022).

[97] Global Witness (2021a), p. 12.

[98] Global Witness (2023).

Action on Aid (2023) The vicious cycle: connections between the debt crisis and the climate crisis. https://actionaid.org/sites/default/files/publications/The_vicious_cycle.pdf

Asher C (2019) Brazil's New Forest Code puts vast areas of protected Amazon forest at risk. Mongabay. https://news.mongabay.com/2019/03/brazils-new-forest-code-puts-vast-areas-of-protected-amazon-forest-at-risk/

ASIC (2022a) 22-124MR: ASIC highlights focus areas for 30 June 2022 reporting. https://asic.gov.au/about-asic/news-centre/find-a-media-release/2022-releases/22-124mr-asic-highlights-focus-areas-for-30-june-2022-reporting/

ASIC (2022b) Info Sheet 271. https://asic.gov.au/regulatory-resources/financial-services/how-to-avoid-greenwashing-when-offering-or-promoting-sustainability-related-products/

Australian Treasury (2022) Climate-related financial disclosure consultation. https://treasury.gov.au/consultation/c2022-314397

Beehive (2021) NZ becomes first in world for climate reporting. https://www.beehive.govt.nz/release/nz-becomes-first-world-climate-reporting

Butler R (2012) Debt and deforestation. Mongabay. https://rainforests.mongabay.com/0815.htm

Cannon J (2021) Seven financial firms key to rooting out deforestation, report finds. Mongabay. https://news.mongabay.com/2021/01/seven-financial-firms-key-to-rooting-out-deforestation-report-finds/

Carvalho W, Mustin K, Hilario R et al (2019) Deforestation control in the Brazilian Amazon: a conservation struggle being lost as agreements and regulations are subverted and bypassed. Perspect Ecol Conserv 17:122

CMS (2022) Forest risk commodities consultation outcome published. https://cms-lawnow.com/en/ealerts/2022/06/forest-risk-commodities-consultation-outcome-published

Conniff R (2018) Greenwashed timber: how sustainable forest certification has failed. Yale Environ 360. https://e360.yale.edu/features/greenwashed-timber-how-sustainable-forest-certification-has-failed

Corrs (2021) Mandatory ESG reporting gains momentum. https://www.corrs.com.au/insights/mandatory-esg-reporting-gains-momentum

Department of Agriculture, Forestry and Fisheries (DAFF) (2022) Illegal logging. https://www.agriculture.gov.au/agriculture-land/forestry/policies/illegal-logging#:~:text=The%20United%20Nations%20and%20Interpol,by%20value%20in%20the%20world.&text=We%20have%20also%20seen%20isolated,Australian%20timber%20being%20illegally%20logged

Department of Agriculture, Water and the Environment (DAWE) (2019) Due diligence for importers. https://www.agriculture.gov.au/agriculture-land/forestry/policies/illegal-logging/importers/due-diligence#step-1%2D%2Destablish-and-maintain-a-due-diligence-system

dos Reis TNP, de Faria VG, Lopes GR et al (2021) Trading deforestation - why the legality of forest-risk commodities is insufficient. Environmental Research Letters

Downie A (2022) World's central banks financing destruction of the rainforest. The Guardian. https://www.theguardian.com/environment/2022/sep/28/worlds-central-banks-financing-destruction-of-the-rainforest

Dummett C, Blundell A (2021) Illicit harvest, complicit goods: the state of illegal deforestation for agriculture. Forest Policy Trade and Finance Initiative Report. https://www.forest-trends.org/wp-content/uploads/2021/05/Illicit-Harvest-Complicit-Goods.pdf

Durán GM, Scott J (2022) Regulating Trade in Forest-Risk Commodities: Two Cheers for the European Union. Journal of Environmental Law 34(2):245–267. https://doi.org/10.1093/jel/eqac002

Earthsight (2017) World's largest beef producer fined after buying cattle raised on illegally deforested land in Brazil. https://www.earthsight.org.uk/news/idm/worlds-largest-beef-producer-fined-buying-cattle-raised-illegally-deforested-land-brazil

Economist (2023) Invest in our planet: the business case for biodiversity. https://impact.economist.com/sustainability/ecosystems-resources/invest-in-our-planet-the-business-case-for-biodiversity

European Commission, Proposal for a Regulation on Forest Risk Commodities, 2021/0366 (COD) https://environment.ec.europa.eu/system/files/2021-11/COM_2021_706_1_EN_ACT_part1_v6.pdf

European Parliament (EP) (2023) Towards deforestation-free commodities and products in the EU. https://www.europarl.europa.eu/RegData/etudes/BRIE/2022/698925/EPRS_BRI(2022)698925_EN.pdf

Fern (2023) The UK may introduce mandatory due diligence for financing forest-risk sectors. https://www.fern.org/publications-insight/the-uk-may-introduce-mandatory-due-diligence-for-financing-forest-risk-sectors-2652/

Food and Agricultural Organization of the United Nations (FOA) (2020) The state of the world's forests: forests, biodiverse and people. https://www.fao.org/documents/card/en/c/ca8642en

Forest Stewardship Council (FSC) (2018) Legislation to prevent illegal imports into Asian countries. https://fsc.org/sites/default/files/2019-04/Legality%20Legislation %20in%20Asia%20-%20FSC%20briefing%20May%202018%20EN.pdf

Forests and Finance (2022) The taskforce on nature-related financial disclosures. https://forestsandfinance.org/tnfd/

Freitas FLM, Englund O, Sparovek G et al (2018) Who owns the Brazilian carbon? Glob Chang Biol 24(5):2129

Friends of the Earth (2005) Greasy palms: the social and ecological impacts of large-scale oil palm plantation development in Southeast Asia. https://socialvalueuk.org/wp-content/uploads/2016/04/greasy_palms_impacts.pdf

FSB (2022) TCFD Status Report: task force on climate-related financial disclosures. https://www.fsb.org/2022/10/2022-tcfd-status-report-task-force-on-climate-related-financial-disclosures/#:~:text=Just%20over%2060%25%20of%20companies,to%20the%20other%20recommended%20disclosures

Gabriel J, Wood M (2015) The Rimbunan Hijau Group in the Forests of Papua New Guinea. J Pac Hist 50(3):322

Georgieva K, Chamon M, Thakoor V (2022) Swapping debt for climate or nature pledges can help fund resilience. IMF Blog. https://www.imf.org/en/Blogs/Articles/2022/12/14/swapping-debt-for-climate-or-nature-pledges-can-help-fund-resilience

Global Canopy (2023) Forest 500 Annual Report - a watershed year for action on deforestation. https://forest500.org/sites/default/files/forest_500-2023_annual_report.pdf

Global Resource Initiative (GRI) (2022) Finance report. https://assets.publishing.service.gov.uk/government/uploads/system/uploads/attachment_data/file/1087635/global-resource-initiative-finance-report-may-2022.pdf

Global Witness (2021a) Deforestation dividends: how global banks profit from rainforest destruction and human rights abuses. https://www.globalwitness.org/en/campaigns/forests/deforestation-dividends/

Global Witness (2021b) The true price of Palm Oil - how global finance and household brands are fuelling deforestation, violence and human rights abuses in Papua New Guinea. https://www.globalwitness.org/en/campaigns/forests/true-price-palm-oil/

Global Witness (2022) Bankrolling destruction. https://www.globalwitness.org/en/campaigns/forests/bankrolling-deforestation/

Global Witness (2023) Former Barclays Chair and Head of government-backed taskforce on deforestation calls for new financial regulations to protect forests, as Financial Service and Markets Bill debated in Parliament. https://www.globalwitness.org/en/press-releases/former-barclays-chair-and-head-government-backed-taskforce-deforestation-calls-new-financial-regulations-protect-forests-financial-service-and-markets-bill-debated-parliament/

Goldbarsht D, Harris H (2020) Transnational regulatory networks: a study in compliance and legitimacy in counter-terrorist financing. J Financ Crime

Goncalves M, Panjer M, Greenberg T, Magrath W (2012) Justice for forests: improving criminal justice efforts to combat illegal logging. The World Bank. https://www.worldbank.org/en/topic/

financialsector/publication/justice-for-forests-improving-criminal-justice-efforts-to-combat-illegal-logging-report
Greener UK and Wildlife and Countryside Link (2021) Environment bill committee briefing: due diligence on forest risk commodities and global footprint. https://greeneruk.org/sites/default/files/download/2021-07/Environment_Bill_Greener_UK_Link_briefing_Lords_Committee_deforestation_and_global_footprint.pdf
Guan Z, Xu Y, Gong P, Cao J (2018) The impact of international efforts to reduce illegal logging on the global trade in wood products. Int Wood Prod J 9(1):28
Harris H (2019a) Illegal logging, corruption and the limits of destination country laws in the Pacific. New Zealand Yearb Int Law 17:64
Harris H (2019b) Corruption and the forestry industry in Papua New Guinea: transnational actors, local dynamics and environmental impact. Asia Pacific J Environ Law 22(1):48
Harris H, Nolan J (2022) Outsourcing the enforcement of modern slavery: overcoming the limitations of a market-based disclosure model. J Ind Relat 64(2):223
He Z, Turner P (2022) Blockchain applications in forestry: a systematic literature review. Appl Sci 12(8):3723
Hodgson C, Morris S (2021) Global finance industry sinks $199bn into companies linked to deforestation. Financial Times. https://www.ft.com/content/ff1eccc8-645a-497b-a02d-6eb38efe6219
Human Rights Watch (2019) "When we Lost the Forest, We Lost Everything"—Oil palm plantations and rights violations in Indonesia. https://www.hrw.org/report/2019/09/23/when-we-lost-forest-we-lost-everything/oil-palm-plantations-and-rights-violations
Interpol (2020) Forestry crime: targeting the most lucrative of environmental crimes. https://www.interpol.int/en/News-and-Events/News/2020/Forestry-crime-targeting-the-most-lucrative-of-environmental-crimes
Jun MA, Robins N (2022) Central banking and supervision in the biosphere. NGFS Occasional Paper. https://www.lse.ac.uk/granthaminstitute/wp-content/uploads/2022/03/Central-banking-and-supervision-in-the-biosphere_NGFS-INSPIRE-Final-Report.pdf
Kaczmarski K, Farrar S, Zelter P, van der Zee M (2023) The renaissance of ETFs - exchange-traded funds are fueling market opportunities. Oliver Wyman. https://www.oliverwyman.com/our-expertise/insights/2023/may/exchange-traded-funds-are-fueling-market-opportunities.html#:~:text=As%20of%20the%20end%20of,faster%20than%20traditional%20mutual%20funds
Kedward K, Buller A, Ryan-Collins J (2021) Quantitative easing and nature loss: exploring the nature-related financial risks and impacts in the European Central Bank's corporate bond portfolio. UCL Policy Report. https://www.ucl.ac.uk/bartlett/public-purpose/sites/bartlett_public_purpose/files/quantitative_easing_and_nature_loss_23_july.pdf
Lashitew AA (2021) Corporate uptake of the sustainable development goals: mere greenwashing or an advent of institutional change? J Int Bus Policy 4:184
Lawson S (2014) Illegal logging in Papua New Guinea. Energy, Environment and Resources
Ledger Insights (2021) Two blockchain solutions target timber supply chain sustainability. https://www.ledgerinsights.com/two-blockchain-solutions-target-timber-supply-chain-sustainability/
Lee YJ (2014) The Lacey Act Amendments of 2008: the world's first ban on illegal logging combats deforestation but gets stumped by foreign laws. San Diego J Climate Energy Law 5:187
Lynch MJ (2020) Green criminology and environmental crime: criminology that matters in the age of global ecological collapse. J White Collar Corporate Crime 1(1):50
McCarthy N (2022) Deforestation's role in financial disclosures. Climate Advisers. https://www.climateadvisers.org/insightsfeed/deforestations-role-in-financial-disclosures/
Moraes I, Azevedo-Ramos C, Pacheco J (2021) Public forests under threat in the Brazilian Amazon: strategies for coping shifts in environmental policies and regulations. Front Global Change 4(631756):1
National Geographic (2019) Inside the faltering fight against illegal Amazon logging. https://www.nationalgeographic.com/environment/article/brazil-logging

National Geographic (2023) Amazon deforestation and climate change. https://education.nationalgeographic.org/resource/amazon-deforestation-and-climate-change/

Niles JO, Brown S, Pretty J, Ball AS, Fay J (2002) Potential carbon mitigation and income in developing countries from changes in use and management of agricultural and forest lands. Philos Trans R Soc 360:1621

Nisanci DA (2021) Chapter 1: FSB task force on climate-related financial disclosures. World Scientific Encyclopedia of Climate Change 3

Organized Crime and Corruption Reporting Project (OCCRP) (2018) Current logging rate will strip Solomon Islands by 2036. https://www.occrp.org/en/daily/8764-current-logging-rate-will-strip-solomon-islands-by-2036

Partiti E (2021) Private processes and public values: disciplining trade in forest and ecosystem risk commodities via non-financial due diligence. Transnational Environ Law 11(1):141

Partzsch L, Vlaskamp M (2016) Mandatory due diligence for 'conflict minerals' and illegally logged timber: emergence and cascade of a new norm on foreign accountability. Extractive Indus Soc 3(4):978

Pendrill F, Gardner TA, Meyfroidt P et al (2022) Disentangling the numbers behind agriculture-driven tropical deforestation. Science 377:6611

Planet Tracker (2020) Exchange-traded deforestation - seven companies can reduce rising deforestation risk hidden within ETFs. https://planet-tracker.org/wp-content/uploads/2021/07/Exchange-Traded-Deforestation.pdf

Quijano G, Lopez C (2021) Rise of mandatory human rights due diligence: a beacon of hope or a double-edged sword? Bus Human Rights J 6(2):241

Reboredo F (2013) Socio-economic, environmental, and governance impacts of illegal logging. Environ Systems Decisions 33(2):295

Ritchie H, Roser M (2021) Forests and deforestation. https://ourworldindata.org/forests-and-deforestation

Romijn E, Coppus R, De Sy V, Herold M, Roman-Cuesta RM, Verchot L (2019) Land restoration in Latin America and the Caribbean: an overview of recent, ongoing and planned restoration initiatives and their potential for climate change mitigation. Forests 10(6):510

Rose G (2017) Australian law to combat illegal logging in Indonesia: a gossamer chain for transnational enforcement of environmental law. Rev Eur Comp Int Environ Law 26(2):128

Sant'Anna AA, Costa L (2021) Environmental regulation and bail outs under weak state capacity: deforestation in the Brazilian Amazon. Ecol Econ 186(107071):1

Sarfaty GA (2015) Shining light on global supply chains. Harv Int Law J 56(2):419

Sarmiento F, Oeschger A (2022) Due diligence requirements to tackle deforestation: an overview of the EU and British proposals. ISDD. https://www.iisd.org/articles/policy-analysis/deforestation-overview-eu-british-proposals

Schilling-Vacaflor A, Lenschow A (2021) Hardening foreign corporate accountability through mandatory due diligence in the European Union? New trends and persisting challenges. Regul Gov:1

Schmidt C, McDermott C (2015) Deforestation in the Brazilian Amazon: local explanations for forestry law compliance. Soc Leg Stud 24(1):3

Silva CHL Jr, Pessôa ACM, Carvalho NS et al (2021) The Brazilian Amazon deforestation rate in 2020 is the greatest of the decade. Nat Ecol Evol 5:144

Simmons BA, Ray R (2021) Financing forest protection without fueling the debt crisis. Global Development Policy Center. https://www.bu.edu/gdp/2021/11/29/financing-forest-protection-without-fueling-the-debt-crisis/

Sonter LJ, Herrera D, Barett DJ et al (2017) Mining drives extensive deforestation in the Brazilian Amazon. Nat Commun 8:1013

South N (2014) Green criminology: reflections, connections, horizons. Int J Crime Just Soc Democr 3(2):5

Spring J (2018) Brazil fines five grain trading firms, farmers connected to deforestation. Reuters. https://www.reuters.com/article/us-brazil-deforestation-bunge-carg-idUSKCN1IO1NV

Steinweg T, Rijk AG, Piotrowski M (2021) Chain reaction research applies TCFD-aligned framework to assess deforestation risks. Chain Reaction Research. https://chainreactionresearch.com/wp-content/uploads/2021/01/Chain-Reaction-Research-Applies-TCFD-aligned-Framework-to-Assess-Deforestation-Risks.pdf

TCFD (2017) Recommendations of the task force on climate-related financial disclosures. https://www.fsb-tcfd.org/recommendations/

TNFD (2023) The TNFD nature-related risk and opportunity management and disclosure framework beta V0.4—summary. https://framework.tnfd.global/wp-content/uploads/2023/03/23-23882-TNFD_v0.4_Short_Summary_v5.pdf

Tracewski L, Butchart S, Di Marco M et al (2016) Toward quantification of the impact of 21st-century deforestation on the extinction risk of terrestrial vertebrates. Conserv Biol 30(5):1070

Tridos Bank (2022) Open letter on proposal for an EU-deforestation regulation. https://www.triodos.com/en/articles/2022/triodos-bank-supports-call-to-include-the-financial-sector-in-the-eu-deforestation-regulation

United Nations Climate Change Conference (2021) Glasgow leaders' declaration on forests and land use. https://ukcop26.org/glasgow-leaders-declaration-on-forests-and-land-use/

World Resource Institute (2022) Forest and climate leaders' partnership and forest-related funding at COP27. https://www.wri.org/news/statement-forest-and-climate-leaders-partnership-and-forest-related-funding-cop27

WWF (2022) Due diligence on forest-risk commodities. Policy briefing. https://www.wwf.org.uk/sites/default/files/2022-03/WWF-UK-Due-Diligence-Secondary-Legislation-External-Policy%20Briefing-V2.pdf

Yang Z, Nguyen TTH, Nyuyen HN et al (2020) Greenwashing behaviours: causes, taxonomy and consequences based on a systematic literature review. J Bus Econ Manag 221(5):1486

Zeitlin J, Overdevest C (2021) Experimentalist interaction: joining up the transnational timber legality regime. Regul Gov 15:686

Hannah Harris is a scholar, Senior Lecturer at Macquarie Law School and a Research Fellow with the Financial Integrity Hub. Her research area is transnational law and corporate regulation. Her current work analyses legal responses to transnational challenges, including illegal logging and forest degradation, modern slavery, foreign bribery and financial crime. She is also engaged in research that seeks to understand the interaction between law and technology, focusing on the challenges and opportunities presented by Artificial Intelligence for policing, law enforcement, and regulatory compliance. Dr. Harris' research is concerned with development of optimal regulatory incentives and sanctions, as well as optimal internal governance practices within key organisations and institutions that shape the way the law is practiced and experienced by stakeholders and regulatory targets.

Weeding Out Dirty Money: Cannabis Regulations and Financial Crime

Jamie Ferrill and Milind Tiwari

Abstract This chapter wades into the contentious waters of cannabis regulations, specifically to interrogate potential links between them and money laundering. The legal status of cannabis continues to evolve globally; at the same time, its market remains enormous. Much of this market represents dirty money from criminal acts, which often requires laundering. In the context of changing cannabis regulations, legislation, and policies, we address the possible implications of such changes on the extent of money laundering. The chapter interrogates the implications of the evolution of cannabis regulations on money laundering activities, using the theoretical underpinning of rational choice. Using Australia as a replicable critical case study, we employ Walker's Gravity model and use UNODC-reported prices of cannabis from 2003–2017 along with Australian Criminal Intelligence Commission reports to empirically validate the effects of cannabis regulations on the potential proceeds available for laundering. Several policy considerations are discussed in tandem.

1 Introduction

The illicit drug trade provides organized crime with one of its most financially lucrative criminal markets. It should go without saying that a key motivator for illicit actors, namely serious and organized criminals involved in the drug market, is money. Estimating the exact value of the global illicit drug trade is difficult due to its illegal nature, but some estimates suggest that it is worth hundreds of billions of dollars per year. According to the United Nations Office on Drugs and Crime (UNODC), the global illicit drug market was estimated to be worth $450 billion in

J. Ferrill (✉) · M. Tiwari
Australian Graduate School of Policing and Security, Charles Sturt University, Canberra, ACT, Australia
e-mail: jferrill@csu.edu.au

D. Goldbarsht, L. de Koker (eds.), *Financial Crime and the Law*, Ius Gentium: Comparative Perspectives on Law and Justice 115,
https://doi.org/10.1007/978-3-031-59543-1_4

2021.[1] In the same vein, the illicit drug trade would probably not exist if it weren't for money laundering to manage the large capital accumulated from these illicit activities.[2] Organized crime groups (OCGs) leverage money laundering as a business to obfuscate financial flows.[3] By cleaning the dirty money generated from the illicit drug trade, it can then not only be used in the legitimate economy, but OCGs can use the proceeds to expand their criminal enterprises, bribe officials, purchase weapons and other equipment, and otherwise continue their illegal activities without attracting attention from authorities. This makes it more difficult for law enforcement agencies to investigate and prosecute drug crime and ultimately undermines efforts to combat drug trafficking and related criminal activity. It is in the best interest of States to question what they can do to dampen this vicious cycle.

One part of this vicious cycle is the cannabis market, being part of the overall global drug market. It is also perhaps the most contentious when it comes to legal status and regulation: its legality exists on a spectrum around the world. From criminal to legal, illegal but not enforced, and from decriminalized to prohibited, countries think of cannabis in different ways. What's more, the reasons for usage can be recreational or medicinal. Regardless, what makes the cannabis market different to other drugs or substances is how large the market is and so the sums generated. It has been estimated that the global cannabis industry could grow to be worth US $1 trillion.[4] Due to its varied status around the world, much of this dollar value represents dirty money; that is, money generated from criminal acts such as smuggling, trafficking, or black-market sales. This dirty money usually needs to be laundered, especially in the case of organized crime. This paper addresses the questions: if we change the legal status of a substance, does it affect money laundering? If so, how, and to what extent? Both are critical questions for countries, for the sake of public health and safety, economic stability, international relations, and national security.

It is vital to examine the implications of such regulatory and legislative changes on OCGs, specifically in terms of money laundering, since the latter costs economies profoundly; from interest rates, to exchange rates, to inflation—among other serious social effects. This has implications for a financial system's stability, as it can distort the quality of economic data used in public policy and commercial decision-making.[5] Still, regulating drugs and illicit finance on a transnational level often involves asymmetrical power dynamics as much as legal considerations.[6] With that in mind,

[1] See the 2021 UNODC World Drug Report for the most recent estimate. In this report, the global drug market was estimated to be worth around $450 billion per year in 2019, with a range of $320 billion to $640 billion, depending on the assumptions and methodologies used.

[2] See Compin (2008).

[3] See Ferrill et al. (2023).

[4] See Yeoh (2020).

[5] See further explanations in Bajada (2017), Barone and Schneider (2018) and Crime and Misconduct Commission [CMC] (2005).

[6] See Clarke (2022).

we consider the role of countries, in this case, Australia, in consolidating legal and policy frameworks on cannabis control and suppressing drug-related money laundering.[7]

This chapter aims to evaluate the *potential* for the legal status of cannabis to influence money laundering activity. The word potential is used intentionally for a number of reasons. First, as mentioned, it is difficult to ascertain the actual value of the illicit drug market due to a lack of transparency around transactions, variable drug prices, differences in currency, and a lack of reporting. Second, we utilize pricing information based on information provided by covert police units and informants, which lacks reporting standardization. This led to using a quantity discount factor to acquire uniform prices. Third, for ease of calculation, aspects such as the purity levels of cannabis, different cannabis variants, and the purpose usage (i.e., either recreational or medicinal) were not considered. Fourth, due to a lack of information on annual cannabis production, we relied on the weight of cannabis seized annually to project the proceeds of trafficking. Fifth, there are different methods of quantifying illicit financial flows; the effect of changes in cannabis policies on the potential amount of funds laundered can be ascertained through alternative methods.[8] We identified Walker's Gravity model as most suitable for our critical case study. Finally, and importantly, we do not propose that legalizing cannabis will eliminate the illicit market. Rather, with a combination of factors, legalization or to a lesser extent decriminalization cuts into profitability for OCGs.

Nevertheless, the mixed-method approach employed[9] attempts to evaluate the implication of regulatory changes on the amount of money laundered using Walker's Gravity model.[10] We found that, based on the available information, there was a notable trend between shifting regulations/the legal status of cannabis and the amount of money generated in need of laundering. The theoretical rigor and broad applicability of Walker's Gravity model encouraged us to use it to estimate the relationship between estimates of drug proceeds, in this case, cannabis, and money laundering. The rationale is that since the prohibition makes illegal the revenue generated from cannabis consumption, a need to launder the proceeds arises. The

[7] Ibid [6].

[8] Another model is the multiple indicators, multiple causes (MIMIC) approach. MIMIC tests the influence of a set of exogenous causal variables on the latent variable, and the effect of the latent variable on indicator variables. The effect of changes in cannabis regulation, being an exogenous causal variable, on the shadow economy, a latent variable, and its effect on the amount of funds laundered, an indicator variable, can be examined.

[9] As developed in Lamprecht and Guetterman (2019).

[10] Walker (1999) is regarded as a pioneer in the domain of estimating the extent of money laundering, and his proposed framework has often been used to estimate the magnitude of money laundering (Collin 2020). Over time, there have been efforts to improve the Walker Gravity model and one such improvement is the method proposed by Walker and Unger (2009). The proposed method is not only supported by the ease of data availability from publicly available sources and its use in past academic works (Ferwerda et al. 2013 and Khan et al. 2018), but also has a more robust theoretical foundation than other money laundering measures.

perspectives considered provide an argument on the possible results of changes in regulations from prohibition to decriminalization and legalization, and the amount of funds laundered.

The chapter is organized as follows. The next section provides a brief background on the state of cannabis in Australia given it is the site of the critical case study. Then, it explains the links between money laundering, serious organized crime, and cannabis. The chapter then presents a model based on empirical data to illustrate the effects of cannabis regulations on money laundering, using Australia as a replicable case study. Following this, it presents a proposition that draws on this model to explain the implications of cannabis regulations on price and degree of money laundering. Next, the policy considerations are proposed. Finally, conclusions and various suggestions for future research are provided. The perspectives considered in this chapter address the possible consequences of changes in regulations from those focusing on prohibition to ones focusing on decriminalization and legalization on the amount of funds being laundered.

2 Cannabis in Australia and the State of Regulations

Cannabis has been a subject of evolving legislation and regulation around the world, which can be grouped into a range of categories including (i) full prohibition (ii) depenalization, (iii) decriminalization, and (iv) legalization.[11] Discrepancies exist in cannabis regulations between countries within close geographical proximity. For instance, in Sweden, cannabis is not treated as less harmful than any other drug and the Swedes criminalize its possession and consumption. In the Netherlands, retail sales take place through coffee shops while cannabis production is prohibited. In Spain, cultivation and possession of cannabis are not criminalized, but the sale is. The procurement takes place through cannabis clubs which are private and non-profit organizations. The decriminalization of cannabis in Europe was initiated by Portugal in 2001, followed by Estonia in 2002, Belgium in 2003, and later, by the Czech Republic and Poland in 2010 and 2011, respectively. On the other end of the spectrum, cannabis production and its use for recreational purposes have been legalized in numerous jurisdictions such as Canada, Uruguay, and at a sub-national level in the United States. Germany is set to follow suit in 2023.

Similar to the United States, legislation in Australia is state-based with different penalties surrounding different drugs. It is a notable setting for further analysis as a critical case study considering factors such as the high rate of drug consumption,[12]

[11] As described by Lee and Ritter (2020) and Wang et al. (2017).

[12] The rate of drug consumption is the focus in Degenhardt et al. (2013), UNODC (2015) and AIHW (2020b).

prominence of cannabis,[13] geographical isolation, and a lack of attitudinal shifts considering regulatory changes.[14] Cannabis was decriminalized in three Australian states before 2001; namely, South Australia (1987), the ACT (1992), and the Northern Territory (1996). Similar to what has been observed in other countries, decriminalization and depenalization did not objectively increase cannabis use.[15] However, after 2001, the policy changes adopted a more prohibitive approach up until 2015.[16] In 2016, the Australian Federal Government passed legislation allowing registered healthcare professionals to prescribe a range of cannabis-based products to patients.[17] The regulatory changes related to cannabis until 2019 across various states and territories in Australia are documented in Appendix 1.[18]

There has been a shift from a prohibitionist approach toward a more harm-reduction approach concerning cannabis policies surrounding its cultivation for scientific or medical purposes, which was legalized in 2016, with further measures toward the legalization of cannabis for recreational use being enacted in the ACT in 2020. The literature has generally focused on understanding the introduction or reformation of drug policies. Such an understanding allows us to observe the interactions between actors, processes, knowledge, and power dynamics in policy formulation. Additionally, the deeply entrenched belief in prohibition overwhelmingly shared by policymakers, government-backed investment agencies, and a variety of advocates such as Drug Free Australia, Family Voice Australia, and to an extent, the National Cannabis Prevention and Information Centre makes it challenging to transition to a truly harm-reduction focused model.

Cannabis is readily available and the most widely used drug in Australia[19] and internationally.[20] The National Drug Strategy Household Survey conducted by the AIHW in 2019 reported that 43% of people aged 14 years and over in Australia had used illicit drugs at least once, an increase from 38% in 2007.[21] Among the various drugs used, cannabis was found to be the most popular one both in Australia and internationally.[22] A 2020 survey of cannabis users in Australia found that 62.4% of users obtain it illicitly, with an additional 24.3% of respondents using both illicit and

[13]The prominence of cannabis is the focus in AIHW (2014), Cunliffe et al. (2017) and Hughes et al. (2016).

[14]Ritter and Sotade (2017) address attitudinal shifts about regulatory changes.

[15]As explored in Baker and Goh (2004) and Lenton et al. (2000).

[16]Explained by Lancaster and Ritter (2014).

[17]See Lintzeris et al. (2020).

[18]The regulatory changes are developed by drawing on Ritter and Sotade (2017) and Hughes (2020).

[19]See the Australian Institute of Health and Welfare [AIHW] (AIHW 2017, 2020a) and Broadhurst et al. (2014) for the domestic statistics.

[20]See the UNODC 2021 for the international statistics.

[21]As in the 2019 AIHW National Drug Strategy Household Survey report, published in 2020.

[22]According to the ACIC [2019] and AIHW (2020a).

prescribed cannabis.[23] This gives rise to the idea that illicit sales are still prevalent and generate large sums of dirty money.

Current research on cannabis, in terms of its consumption, medical benefits and harms, and regulatory changes, has been a source of immense debate among policymakers, medical practitioners, and academics.[24] However, the primary focus of much debate has been on health, crime, taxation, and education. The possible effects of regulatory changes on the cannabis market and the extent of money laundering associated with it have been under-examined in the current literature.[25]

3 Money Laundering, Organized Crime, and Cannabis

Money is a driving force for illegal actors, particularly OCGs, operating in the drug market. These actors generally prioritize financial gain over the safety and security of individuals and communities, given the sheer profitability of the market. The relationship between money and drug crime is thereby significant.[26] OCGs accumulate large amounts of capital that would be relatively easily traced back to them if it weren't for money laundering. Hence the motivation to explore the effects of evolving cannabis regulations on the level of funds needing laundering.

Money laundering is the process of giving "dirty" money a more legitimate appearance. The UNODC defines money laundering as the process of converting or transferring an asset originating from a criminal source to conceal its origin or to aid the person involved in committing a criminal offense.[27] Several methods are used for estimating the prevalence of global money laundering activities.[28] They have commonly resulted in varying estimates from 2–5% of global GDP to between USD 800 billion and USD 2 trillion.[29]

Money laundering facilitates the use of illegal proceeds obtained from activities, including the drugs and weapons trades, cybercrime, corruption, and human and

[23] Ibid [17].

[24] For examples, see Weatherburn and Jones (2001), Bogdanoski (2010), Ritter et al. (2011), Pacula et al. (2015), McGinty et al. (2016), Chang and Jacobson (2017), Ritter and Sotade (2017), Wang et al. (2017), Chan et al. (2018), Chu and Gershenson (2018), Wang et al. (2018), Bresin and Mekawi (2019), Chu and Townsend (2019), Chan and Hall (2020), Lintzeris et al. (2020), Siklos-Whillans et al. (2020) and Zahra et al. (2020).

[25] Tiwari and Ferrill (2023) identified this gap in the literature and attempt to empirically validate the links between cannabis regulations and money laundering.

[26] See Canhoto (2020).

[27] See the UNODC overview of money laundering at https://www.unodc.org/unodc/en/money-laundering/overview.html#:~:text=%E2%80%9Cthe%20conversion%20or%20transfer%20of,legal%20consequences%20of%20his%20actions%E2%80%9D.

[28] As explored in Bajada (2017).

[29] See the FATF (2012) and UNODC (2016).

wildlife trafficking.[30] These criminal activities are collectively called predicate crimes, with money laundering subsequently aiding criminals in drawing benefits from them. According to the Crime and Corruption Commission (formerly Crime and Misconduct Commission), Australia's most common predicate crimes include drug trafficking, bribery, corruption, terrorism, and white- and blue-collar crimes.[31] Money laundering is a characteristic element of these illicit activities, including illegal drug sales and corruption.[32] The financial magnitude of these illicit activities, collectively called Serious Organized Crime (SOC), is substantial.[33]

The money made from high-level drug trafficking is the one in most need of immediate laundering.[34] Drug trafficking is the most profitable activity undertaken by criminals around the world.[35] It is also arguably the leading driver of other SOC, including money laundering.[36] Moreover, it is safe to assume that while most street-level or small-scale cannabis trafficking will not necessitate money laundering due to its scale, SOC-level trafficking will. This illuminates the need to better understand the linkages between illicit drug markets, SOC, and money laundering and the impact legal initiatives can have.

We can turn to traditional economic explanations to understand why the illicit cannabis market is dominated by SOC[37] and why regulatory changes may affect SOC. Markets, specifically the drug market, can be understood as "socially constructed arenas where repeated exchanges occur between buyers and sellers under a set of formal rules and informal understandings that govern relations among competitors, suppliers, and customers".[38] These markets react to prices and incentives under competition.[39] Consequently, it has been proposed that by legalizing drugs, we can reduce further crimes like money laundering as this would remove the need to hide the proceeds from these activities.[40] It's simple: eliminate the predicate crime and reduce the need for money laundering. The word *reduce* here is deliberate; an illicit market will likely remain due to pricing, access, and selection.[41] Further, the displacement of crimes happens; for example, in Canada

[30] See Barone and Schneider (2018).

[31] See CMC (2005).

[32] As supported by the studies including Mitchell et al. (1998) and Lyman (2011).

[33] See Barone et al. (2018), Barone and Masciandaro (2011), Barone and Schneider (2018) and Reuter and Truman (2004).

[34] As supported by Paoli (2014), UNODC (2011) and Hughes et al. (2017).

[35] See UNODC (2011).

[36] See Hughes et al. (2017).

[37] See Wilkins and Casswell (2003) for further analysis.

[38] See Fligstein and Dioun (2015, p. 67).

[39] See Moeller (2018).

[40] See Barone and Schneider (2018).

[41] After Canada legalized marijuana in 2018, a black market remained, albeit displaced. Public Safety Canada cited several reasons for this, including price disparity between licit and illicit, availability, and selection. https://www.publicsafety.gc.ca/cnt/trnsprnc/brfng-mtrls/prlmntry-bndrs/20200930/026/index-en.aspx?wbdisable=true.

following the legalization of cannabis, a man was sentenced to 6 years in prison for operating an illegal cannabis dispensary and laundering the proceeds through his legitimate businesses. Still, as an ascendant industry, there are bound to be growing pains. Rightfully so, considerable legislative attention on the use of drugs has gone into decriminalizing and even legalizing cannabis for medical and recreational purposes.

For several reasons, the first being the relatively high rate of illicit drug use, it has become critical to consider the regulations around cannabis use in countries like Australia. In 2019, 43% of Australians admitted to using illicit drugs at least once in their lifetime.[42] According to the Australian Crime Commission, the illicit supply of drugs is the most significant source of income for SOC operating in the country and is generally associated with crimes such as money laundering.[43] Second, cannabis is one of the most consumed drugs in Australia, with inelastic price variation occurring between online and conventional sales routes.[44] This consumption prominence creates a need to investigate the relevant cannabis regulations in Australia, particularly given the extensive international debate on this drug and the existing research evaluating its effects.[45] Third, the lack of any shifts in the public attitude in Australia toward cannabis consumption despite regulatory changes provides an opportunity to focus on the other possible implications of these changes.[46] The adoption of a prohibitionist approach makes it difficult to supply and procure cannabis for consumption, thereby creating an environment where there is a need to launder the proceeds generated as a result of its sale. Consequently, it is necessary to consider the effects of changes in cannabis regulations on the prominence of money laundering in Australia, considering this lack of attitudinal shifts.

The pro- and anti-legalization arguments concerning cannabis have both focused on the criminal justice element and the factors of costs, tax revenues, education, public health consequences, and crime rates. Its link to money laundering activity is, however, still in its infancy. Given the tremendous negative effects money laundering has on a State's economic security and the safety and security of citizens, it is an important area for exploration.

[42] See Degenhardt et al. (2013), UNODC (2015) and AIHW (2020b).

[43] See ACC (2015).

[44] See AIHW (2014), Hughes et al. (2016) and Cunliffe et al. (2017).

[45] See Chang and Jacobson (2017), Ghosh et al. (2017), Chan et al. (2018), Wang et al. (2018), Chu and Townsend (2019), Dragone et al. (2019) and Zahra et al. (2020).

[46] The approach to public opinion is addressed by Ritter and Sotade (2017).

4 Evaluating Cannabis Regulations and Amount of Funds Potentially Laundered

To empirically evaluate the consequences of changes to cannabis regulations on the potential amount of funds laundered in Australia, we consider the prices of cannabis from 2003 to 2017[47] to determine the illicit proceeds that would have been *available* for laundering due to undetected cannabis sales. This does not imply that all the proceeds are laundered; indeed, we consider those laundering activities to be primarily linked to SOC-related cannabis trafficking. The per-gram prices of cannabis were obtained from illicit drug data reports and the UNODC database.[48] It is important to note that the price information provided in these reports was collected from all police jurisdictions in Australia and is based on the information provided by covert police units and informants. A lack of standardization exists herein as some reports contain price information per ounce while others measure prices per gram. Hence, a quantity discount factor is used to derive the prices if the information per ounce is unavailable (which is the case in 2007). To simplify the calculation, the purity levels of the cannabis, the different variants found, and the purpose of its usage (i.e., either recreational or medicinal) were not considered.

Once the price information is made available, the amount of cannabis seized annually[49] is used to determine the amount of illicit proceeds generated by cannabis trafficking if sales had not been detected. This is summarized in the formula below:

$$\text{Proceeds of cannabis trafficking} = \text{Price per gram of cannabis} \times \text{Weight of cannabis seized (in grams)}$$

This paper considers the weight of cannabis seized annually as it is difficult to ascertain the actual quantity of annual cannabis production. Deriving the illicit proceeds generated using a measurable commodity, like cannabis (in this case, the proceeds that would have been generated if not detected), based on weight and price per unit, is in line with past research.[50] This existing research states that the illicit proceeds generated for a measurable commodity can be ascertained by multiplying the weight of the commodity with its respective per-unit price.

Once the illicit funds through cannabis trafficking are known, the next step involves computing the subsequent proceeds available for laundering. Not all illicit proceeds are available for laundering, and it is essential to compute the percentage of these proceeds that are usable herein.[51] Using case studies to examine the behavior

[47] As in the UNODC (2020) report.

[48] The prices were drawn from ACIC (2016, 2017, 2018, 2019) and UNODC (2020) reports.

[49] As found in the ACIC (2016, 2017, 2018, 2019) reports.

[50] As supported by Unger et al. (2006).

[51] As done in Walker (1999), Smekens and Verbruggen (2004), Unger et al. (2006), Unger (2007) and Meloen et al. (2003).

of money launderers who police have caught found that those involved in drug-related crimes generally laundered 80% of their criminal proceeds.[52] It has also been suggested that less than half and no more than a quarter of revenues from established drug markets need laundering and are influenced by various parameters.[53] For the current work, based on past literature, to derive the potential amount of funds available for laundering, we used an aggressive approach and estimated it to be around 80% of the total illicit proceeds generated. This estimate can be summarized using the formula below:

$$\text{Amount available for laundering} = \text{Proceeds of crime from cannabis trafficking} \times 0.80$$

Once the quantity of illicit proceeds (i.e., cannabis trafficking) available for money laundering is ascertained, the next step involves determining the proportion of funds that would have been laundered in Australia specifically. Using Walker's Gravity model,[54] the proportion of funds laundered domestically can be ascertained. The model's equation is as follows:

$$P(A, y_i) = \frac{\frac{\text{attractiveness}(y_i)}{\text{dist}(A, y_i)}}{\sum_{i=1}^{n} \frac{\text{attractiveness}(y_i)}{\text{dist}(A, y_i)}}.$$

Wherein P is the proportion of funds flowing from country A (Australia) to country y_i, which is also Australia in this case. The attractiveness and distance components are as follows:

$$\text{Attractiveness} = \text{GDP}^* \ (3^*\text{BS} + \text{GA} + \text{SWIFT} + \text{FD} - 3^*\text{CF} - \text{CR} - \text{EG} + 10)$$

Wherein GDP is Gross Domestic Product, BS is banking secrecy, GA is governmental attitude, SWIFT is the Society for Worldwide Interbank Financial Telecommunication member, FD is financial deposits, CF is conflict, CR is corruption, and EG is Egmont Group member.

$$\text{Distance} = \text{Language} + \text{Trade} + \text{Colonial Background} + \text{Distance}$$

To compute the proportion of funds laundered within a given country, the distance component for Australia is computed using the great circle formula.[55]

[52] These observations are in line with Walker (1999) and Unger (2007).

[53] Found by Caulkins and Reuter (2022).

[54] In line with Walker (1999), Walker and Unger (2009), Ferwerda et al. (2013), Ene (2014) and Khan et al. (2018).

[55] In line with Mayer and Zignago (2011).

Once the proportion of funds laundered in Australia is computed, the findings can be used in combination with the proceeds available for laundering to determine the amount of funds that would have been laundered, annually, through undetected cannabis trafficking.[56] This can be summarized using the formula below:

$$\begin{aligned}&\text{Amount of cannabis laundering in Australia}\\&\quad = \text{Proceeds available for laundering}\\&\quad \times \text{Proportion of funds laundered in Australia}\end{aligned}$$

The annual prices of cannabis (per gram), weight seized (in kilograms), illicit proceeds available for laundering, the proportion of funds laundered in Australia, and the amount that would have been laundered through undetected cannabis trafficking are provided in Table 1.

5 Implications of Cannabis Regulations on Its Prices and the Degree of Money Laundering

The highest prices per gram of cannabis were observed in 2006, 2010, and 2011, in increasing order. The regulations in these respective years were likely influential in terms of cannabis prices. For example, the price increase in 2006 could be attributed to policy changes, such as increased penalties for hydroponic cannabis in New South Wales, as shown in Appendix 1.

The price increases in 2010 and 2011 coincided with further prohibitory measures toward cannabis, taken in the ACT, South Australia, New South Wales, the Northern Territory, and Tasmania. The relatively low prices in 2015 and 2016 may be attributed to federal government policies introduced at the time to facilitate the medicinal use of cannabis in 2016.[57] This relationship directs our attention toward the need for empirically evaluating the extent to which these regulations have influenced the price of cannabis in Australia.

There are various data constraints around determining the amount of cannabis produced and consumed; as a result, this paper focuses on the amount of cannabis seized annually. Once again, it is important to note that the quantity of cannabis seized does not directly reflect the amount produced and consumed annually. Consideration is required of other factors in the variations of cannabis seizures, as this is not an accurate indicator of the actual regulatory effects. Still, this does need to be considered due to the absence of other reliable indicators. A substantial number of cannabis seizures were observed in 2003 and 2012. Before 2001, cannabis usage was decriminalized in three Australian states (ACT, South Australia, and the Northern

[56] The annual cannabis laundering proceeds have been computed up until 2017 because the World Bank's financial deposits data is currently only published up to this year.

[57] See Lintzeris et al. (2020).

Table 1 Annual estimates of money laundered through cannabis in Australia[a]

Year	Weight Seized (in kilograms)	Price Estimates (Average prices from ounces to per gram given in IDDR report	Proceeds of Crime Detected	Amount Available for Money Laundering	Proportion Laundered in Australia as per Walker Gravity Model	Estimate of Amount Laundered
2003	9900	$ 9.05	$ 89,571,428.57	$ 71,657,142.86	20.49%	$14,681,832.00
2004	7600	$ 8.33	$ 63,333,333.33	$ 50,666,666.67	23.42%	$11,866,133.33
2005	4482.626	$ 11.07	$ 49,629,073.57	$ 39,703,258.86	23.79%	$9,445,405.28
2006	4781.9	$ 20.54	$ 98,199,732.14	$ 78,559,785.71	23.38%	$18,367,277.90
2007	5409	$ 9.31	$ 50,365,461.58	$ 40,292,369.26	26.53%	$10,689,565.57
2008	5573	$ 12.50	$ 69,662,500.00	$ 55,730,000.00	30.19%	$16,823,772.40
2009	5989	$ 12.14	$ 72,723,571.43	$ 58,178,857.14	21.25%	$12,363,007.14
2010	5452.4	$ 16.96	$ 92,496,071.43	$ 73,996,857.14	23.38%	$17,301,945.14
2011	7349.2	$ 16.07	$ 118,112,142.86	$ 94,489,714.29	26.71%	$25,238,202.69
2012	9344	$ 12.50	$ 116,800,000.00	$ 93,440,000.00	30.92%	$28,891,648.00
2013	7074	$ 11.79	$ 83,372,142.86	$ 66,697,714.29	32.98%	$21,996,906.17
2014	6004.7	$ 11.61	$ 69,697,410.71	$ 55,757,928.57	31.59%	$17,613,929.64

2015	6081.5	$ 10.89	$ 66,244,910.71	$ 52,995,928.57	24.62%	$13,047,597.61
2016	7547.8	$ 11.61	$ 87,608,392.86	$ 70,086,714.29	21.95%	$15,384,033.79
2017	8665.9	$ 11.61	$ 100,586,339.29	$ 80,469,071.43	21.29%	$17,131,865.31

[a]Based on Meloen et al. (2003), Smekens and Verbruggen (2004), Unger (2007), Unger et al. (2006) and Walker (1999)

Territory); however, since 2001, cannabis policy changes in Australia have taken a more prohibitive and stricter turn.[58] One outcome of this prohibitory approach is the higher rate of seizures documented in 2003 and 2012. As shown in Appendix 1, in 2003, the Cannabis Control Act was introduced in Western Australia, while 2012 was marked by a ban on the sale of drug equipment in both South Australia and Victoria, following a series of prohibitive measures enacted in 2010 and 2011.

This study uses Walker's Gravity model to estimate the proportion of funds that could have been laundered in Australia using the profits of cannabis sales.[59] This model uses the prices of cannabis available from the ACIC illicit drug data reports as well as the UNODC database.[60] The prices and quantity of cannabis seized annually are then combined to determine a lower estimate of the illicit proceeds that would have been available for laundering if the cannabis sales had remained undetected. Once the proceeds available for laundering are known, the gravity model is used to determine the proportion of funds that would have been laundered in Australia. Finally, changes in cannabis regulations can be used to gauge the effects on the amount of funds laundered.

The specific regulations affecting cannabis prices and seizures did affect the extent of illicit proceeds generated from trafficking. The years 2011 and 2012 witnessed the highest amount of illicit proceeds generated and, consequently, funds available for money laundering. Furthermore, an estimate for potential money laundering resulting from cannabis sales within Australia between 2003 and 2017 is provided in Fig. 1, wherein 2006 and 2012 witnessed a sharp rise, followed by a sharp decline in 2015.

Regulatory changes, among other factors, often influence the weight and price per unit of cannabis sold, in turn influencing the illicit profits generated. It is important to note that the estimated amount of money laundering annually depends on the proceeds generated by criminal activities like cannabis trafficking, influenced by the per-unit cost of cannabis and the weight sold. Using rational choice theory to examine the need to launder funds, empirical validation of the resulting estimates is documented in Table 1.[61] The need to launder funds becomes critical notably when a prohibitory approach toward cannabis is implemented. This is evident from the highest amount estimated in 2012 (AUD 28.8 million). Consequently, the effects of regulatory changes on the amount of funds being laundered, or made available for laundering, needs careful consideration in future research.

---

[58] See Ritter and Sotade (2017).

[59] For more on Walker's Gravity model, see Walker and Unger (2009) and Khan et al. (2018).

[60] As earlier noted, these values were drawn from ACIC (2016, 2017, 2018, 2019) and UNODC (2020) reports.

[61] Rational choice theory guides this approach, with the underlying principle of *Ceteris paribus;* the primary thrust predicts that given a prohibitory approach to cannabis, the expected utility of mobilizing channels to launder funds will be higher for illicit dealers (Gilmour, 2016). Similarly, the need to launder funds might decline with a regulatory change towards decriminalization.

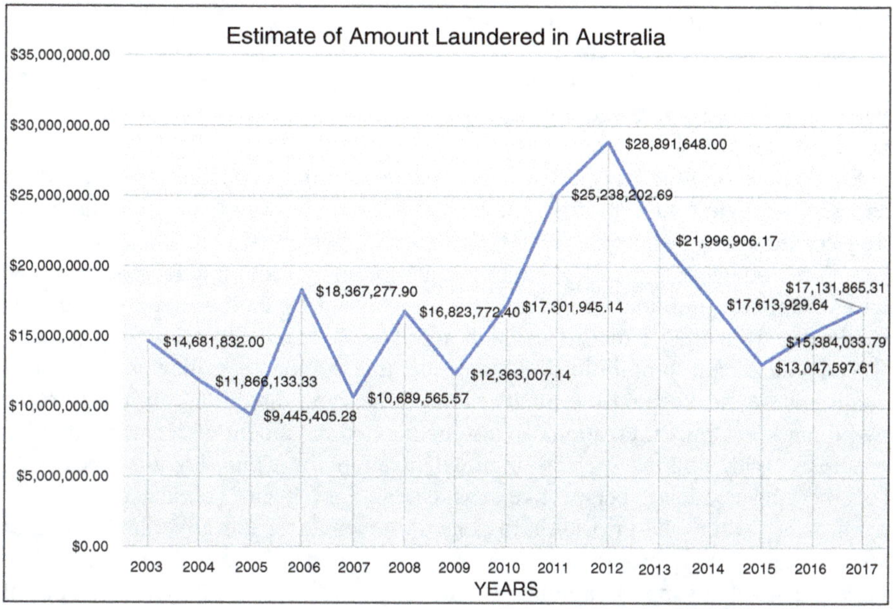

Fig. 1 Annual estimates of potential money laundering as a result of cannabis sales in Australia

6 Policy Perspectives Associated with Cannabis Regulations and Money Laundering

At this point, we have highlighted the implications—and potential implications—of regulatory shifts regarding cannabis. The perspectives illuminated in this chapter can be used alongside others to help inform policymakers when they broach the contentious issue of cannabis regulations. As we have alluded to, policymakers have a number of options when it comes to cannabis: they can regulate it as a legal product and in some cases commercialize it, depenalize it, prohibit it, or adopt the middle ground of decriminalization. We also consider that the framing or focus on specific aspects of an issue can influence its appeal to the audiences and subsequently influence public policy support.[62] For instance, on one hand, anti-legalization arguments often emphasize adverse public health effects, while on the other hand, the pro-legalization arguments direct attention toward criminal justice and economic issues, such as a reduction in prison overcrowding, a decline in racial disparities in cannabis arrests, an increase in tax revenue, and the creation of new jobs.[63] As earlier alluded to, it is a contentious issue for good reason. Our view is that displacing the illicit market is an important consideration given the OCG activity that ensues within

[62] See Scheufele and Tewksbury (2007).

[63] See McGinty et al. (2016).

it. We are also mindful of and advocate for a holistic approach; one that considers various approaches, including the economic model, criminal justice model, social justice model, personal freedom model, medical model, and international model—to name a few. Still, there are key approaches that can help to inform our money laundering reduction model.

From an economic perspective, the debates around cannabis regulations are centered on trade-offs.[64] That is, there are trade-offs between perceived harms of drug consumption (physical, mental, and social), perceived benefits of drug consumption, and harms from illegal markets: all driven by economic factors. Here, the harms from consumption, in general, are outweighed by the consumption benefits and harms from illegal markets, which supports the need for behavioral policies instead of blanket prohibition.[65] Alongside this notion, a policy with optimal taxation is key to keeping the illicit market at bay and directing consumers to the lawful market. Optimal taxation can also be applied in tandem with harm-reduction principles, with options such as minimal taxation for *Cannabis 2.0* products.[66] Together, this economic perspective can advocate for a legal,[67] regulated, optimally taxed policy where the priority is to generate revenue for the government, reduce costs that accompany prohibition, support industry, and ultimately displace the illicit market. This also supports a public health model, where the safety and quality of regulated products can also lead to reducing health risks. It can also reduce the stigma associated with drug use and the reluctance of users to seek out health services.[68]

From the social and criminal justice perspective, reducing the harm associated with prohibition or criminalization is the key focus. Again, with a regulated or decriminalized approach, there is the potential to not only reduce cannabis-related arrests and costs associated with criminalization, but we can also reduce OCG activity by reducing the demand for and profitability of the illicit cannabis market. While we acknowledge the relationship between cannabis regulations and crime is contested,[69] this approach can also be used to protect the lawful market through enforced regulations, which then feed the economic approach. Money that was once in the hands of OCGs and destined to be laundered can instead be put to good use, such as social programs funded by the government, transportation, or education.

[64] See Rogeberg (2018).

[65] Ibid [65].

[66] Cannabis 2.0 products include cannabis-based edibles, vapes, beverages, oils, and topicals. These were found to be important products from a harm-reduction viewpoint in a Canadian study by Sen (2023).

[67] A legal, commercialized market has the greatest economic influence, but the decriminalized market could also have a modest influence.

[68] See *The Lancet* (2016).

[69] As summarized by Neill Harris and Martin (2019). *The Case For Marijuana Decriminalization.*

From an international approach, regulatory measures will of course be disparate. The key UN conventions that act to regulate drug control[70] have prohibitive characteristics.[71] However, cannabis trafficking and other associated OCG activity is largely an international or cross-border crime. Therefore, any domestic policy needs to consider its effect on the international markets while also considering the international context and role of transnational actors. For instance, Uruguay was the first country, in 2013, to legally regulate cannabis. While a growing body of research addresses drug policy reform in the country, the international dimension of this process is often ignored, treating it as a domestic issue.[72] Still, a reformation of the international drug convention is required to provide opportunities for policy experimentation.[73] The efforts concentrated on striving for uniformity in drug policy reforms have been ineffective, nor are they seemingly too effective. Therefore, efforts to reform the UN international convention should direct attention on loosening the terms of the treaties to prohibit them from impeding drug policy innovation and diversity.

Underlying all these approaches and those we have not developed is public opinion; this is of course an important issue for any policy debate. The framing of an issue or its presentation can impact its appeal to the public and therefore influence support for public policy.[74] For instance, opponents of cannabis legalization will focus on the potential negative impact on public health, whereas proponents will focus on its potential benefits.[75] Such strategic emphasis influences public perception and consequently influences the policy debate. It is not the goal of this chapter to definitively say which pathway is better for the greater good. Rather, it adds an additional viewpoint; that the illicit cannabis market might be reduced in size if different regulatory approaches were adopted. These regulatory changes play a role in how illicit markets take shape. More so, they will inherently change how sellers and suppliers operate and how they make decisions about the need to launder their proceeds.[76] Finally, the role of regulatory changes in evaluating the need to launder funds serves as a critical outcome measure for evaluating policy effectiveness.[77]

---

[70] The three main UN conventions for drug control are the 1961 Single Convention on Narcotic Drugs (United Nations, 1961), as amended by the 1972 Protocol, the 1971 Convention on Psychotropic Substances (United Nations, 1971) and the 1988 Convention against Illicit Traffic in Narcotic Drugs and Psychotropic Substances.

[71] As reviewed by Bewley-Taylor (2003).

[72] See von Hoffman (2015) as an exception. Here, the international dimension is considered.

[73] See Roadmaps to reforming the UN drug conventions: A Beckley foundation report—Room and Mackay (2012). See also Chatwin (2017) for an analysis of global drug policy reform.

[74] See Scheufele and Tewksbury (2007).

[75] See McGinty et al. (2016) for a discussion on both sides.

[76] See Clarke and Cornish (1985), Piquero et al. (2002) and Tibbetts and Gibson (2002).

[77] See Bewley-Taylor (2016).

7 Conclusion

As documented in financial crime scholarship, money laundering is a typical element that follows illicit activities committed by OCGs. Consequently, the rise in revenue generated from organized crime increases the significance and likelihood of money laundering. Furthermore, among a range of illicit activities, drug trafficking has been identified as the main contributor to the proceeds of organized crime.[78] Finally, among the various drugs available, cannabis is the most widely consumed (albeit not the most expensive) illicit drug worldwide and in Australia.[79] An implication more often than not ignored in public policy debate is around the effectiveness that decriminalization or legalization could have regarding cannabis policies on the quantum of money laundering: we propose that it will act to displace the illicit market.

This chapter expands on the current understanding of cannabis policy reforms and their implications for money laundering using Australia as a critical case study. It also provides an empirical grounding in terms of the implications that these policies have on criminals' need to launder funds.[80] In turn, we propose the use of outcome measures relevant to both individuals and communities when evaluating the effectiveness of a given policy. In other words, we need to develop metrics that focus on outcomes that matter; in this case, reducing money laundering activity. Usefully, the model used can be replicated in other countries. However, when considering alternative metrics for measuring policy effectiveness, such as the illicit income generated from drug trafficking as a proportion of national GDP,[81] establishing a sense of uniformity in a nation's cannabis regulations at the national level is appropriate. It is essential to address these legislative disparities when examining effective policy implementation.

Changes in regulations and legislation can either deter money laundering activities, enable them, or encourage them.[82] This chapter, through our empirical validation, found some supporting evidence for the argument that prohibitive measures toward cannabis use actually contribute to an increase in the need to launder the proceeds generated.[83] Such a finding plays a vital role in adding to the debate about cannabis legalization by providing a more detailed depiction of the harm arising from these illegal markets. This has implications for economies attempting to tackle

[78] See Paoli (2014) and UNODC (2011).

[79] See AIHW (2020a) and UNODC (2019) for the values.

[80] Bewley-Taylor (2016) asserts that traditional drug policy metrics, such as the number of drug arrests or the quantity of drugs seized, do not adequately measure the effectiveness of drug policies in achieving their intended outcomes.

[81] As in Werb et al. (2016).

[82] See Bajada (2017).

[83] A similar relationship between illicit activities and money laundering has also been identified in a study in Colombia by Loayza et al. (2019).

the problem of money laundering by providing an avenue through which to consider the issues surrounding cannabis.

Our approach does have limitations in calculating the lower estimates of the illicit proceeds that would have been laundered through undetected cannabis sales, as earlier covered. That is, the price information used is based on information provided by covert police units and informants, which lacks reporting standardization. This led to using a quantity discount factor to acquire uniform prices. Second, for ease of calculation, aspects such as the purity levels of cannabis, different cannabis variants, and the purpose usage (i.e., either recreational or medicinal) were not considered. Finally, due to a lack of information on annual cannabis production, this study considered the weight of cannabis seized annually when ascertaining the proceeds of trafficking.

Nevertheless, this study contributes to the overall debates about cannabis regulations by evaluating the implication of regulatory changes on the amount of money laundered using Walker's Gravity model. We found that the years with a stricter approach toward cannabis, stemming from regulations and annual seizures (including 2006, 2008, and 2012), experienced an increase in the potential amount of money laundered. Furthermore, the years with a more tolerant approach toward cannabis consumption (including 2015 and 2016) witnessed a decline in the potential amount of money being laundered. It is important to note that small price variations can be ignored because of a lack of accurate price estimates; however, the observed variations in this study that were of significant magnitude contribute to our understanding of the effects of regulatory changes on money laundering.

As a result, the prices obtained from consumers through survey responses are paramount for researching fluctuating consumption based on changes in drug costs. It is possible to obtain information about these transactions from those producing, selling, and purchasing cannabis in the legal market.[84] The effects of cannabis regulations on its price through the resulting changes in its production costs and taxes have crucial implications for its consumption, government budgets, and the size of illicit markets.[85] There is however a need for better data to analyze cannabis policy changes—for example, better indices for measuring its consumption, such as by examining the total grams consumed or typical potency per dose or by using self-report surveys and market transaction data.[86]

Further, there are several important opportunities for future research, practice, and policy. First, there is a need for a more advanced empirical assessment of the influence of cannabis regulations on the amount of funds being laundered or available for laundering in illicit drug markets. More attempts to quantify this relationship would help better inform policymakers in their decision-making processes as well as law enforcement in their OCG and SOC mitigation strategies. The

[84] See Kilmer and Pacula (2017).

[85] As in Kilmer et al. (2010) and Caulkins et al. (2015).

[86] As supported by Kilmer and Pacula (2017).

changes occurring annually in response to developments in cannabis regulations can be measured by controlling for other factors using various existing models.[87]

Second, it would benefit public policymakers to consider several approaches in tandem including economic, criminal justice, social justice, personal freedom, medical, international, and money laundering models, the latter of which is advocated for in this chapter. Public perceptions are of course central to employing these models; that is, the factors responsible for changes in public attitudes toward cannabis. Apart from regulatory movements, changes in cannabis usage can be attributed to factors like the purpose of usage, decreased stigmatization toward its use, availability of alternatives, and its portrayal in the media.[88] As a result, a detailed analysis of factors responsible for changes in cannabis use also needs to be conducted in future research.

Third, it would be valuable for researchers to empirically evaluate the effects of different regulations in a given country on their policies' effectiveness. That is, it can provide insight into how illicit cannabis can be mitigated through regulations, and how regulations can be mitigated by the status of cannabis. It is mutually co-constructed in this sense. The diversity in drug policies should be viewed as a strength if they contain scope for flexibility. In the presence of international conventions, policy innovations and diversity have thrived, as seen in various European countries.[89] Cross-national policy diversity has also been encouraged: however, policy consistency at the national and sub-national levels is essential for its effectiveness considering metrics like the amount of funds laundered. For instance, the diversity in tax rates for cannabis products within states in Canada not only increases price differentials between legal and illegal alternatives but also between different states, thus providing an incentive to fuel the underground economy.[90] Uniformity in policy formulation and implementation would also allow for macroeconomic monitoring of the illicit economy, allowing for appropriate changes to be made to cannabis policies. In sum, the implications of any future policy changes must be monitored and analyzed to better inform policymakers.

[87] Such as in Schneider and Enste (2000), Reuter and Greenfield (2001), Argentiero et al. (2008), Ferwerda et al. (2013), Ardizzi et al. (2014) and Hendriyetty and Grewal (2017).

[88] See Hughes et al. (2011), AIHW (2014) and Bresin and Mekawi (2019).

[89] See Chatwin (2017).

[90] As explored by Sen (2023) in his analysis of optimal taxation policies to mitigate the underground economy.

Appendix 1: Cannabis Policy Changes at the State/Territory Level in Australia

Year	Jurisdiction	Policy and legislative changes
2001	South Australia	Amendment to Cannabis Expiation Notice (CEN) resulting in a reduction of the number of cannabis plants attracting a fine from three to one
2002	South Australia	Further amendment of CEN resulting in a ban on the cultivation of hydroponic plants
2003	Western Australia	Introduction of Cannabis Control Act 2003 to facilitate the issuance of cannabis infringement notices
2004	Western Australia	Introduction of Cannabis Infringement Notice Scheme to facilitate personal use (decriminalization)
	Victoria	Trial for roadside drug saliva testing for amphetamines and cannabis
2005	Australian Capital Territory	Simple Cannabis Offence Notice expiation scheme amended to reduce the eligibility criteria for the number of plants allowed and exclusion of hydroponically grown cannabis
	Tasmania	Introduction of roadside drug testing
2006	New South Wales	Increment in penalties for hydroponic cannabis
	South Australia	Commencement of random roadside drug testing
2007	New South Wales, Queensland, and Western Australia	Introduction of random drug driving testing
	Western Australia	Review of Cannabis Infringement Notice resulting in expansion of scope to juveniles, reduction in the quantity of cannabis, and increased fines for noncompliance
2008	Northern Territory	Adoption of roadside drug testing for amphetamines, cannabis, and ecstasy
	South Australia	Increment in penalties against the cultivation of hydroponic cannabis
2009	South Australia	Adoption of strict regulation on the sale of equipment for hydroponic growth of cannabis
	Western Australia	Introduction of unlicensed driving vehicle sanctions affecting people who had their license suspended under the Cannabis Infringement Notice Scheme
2010	Australian Capital Territory	Random Drug Testing Amendment Bill 2009 for testing of amphetamines, cannabis, and ecstasy

(continued)

Year	Jurisdiction	Policy and legislative changes
	Western Australia	Previous cannabis legislation replaced by stricter Cannabis Intervention Requirement (CIR) Scheme
2011	Australian Capital Territory, New South Wales, Northern Territory, South Australia, and Tasmania	Imposition of a ban on the sale and use of synthetic cannabinoids
	Western Australia	Making use, possession, or cultivation of cannabis a criminal offense
2012	South Australia and Victoria	Banning the sale of drug equipment such as bongs and cannabis pipes
2013	Western Australia	Introduction of offenses concerning the sale and display of drug equipment incorporating anything that could be made or modified for smoking cannabis
2014	Australian Capital Territory	Introduction of Drugs of Dependence (Cannabis Use for Medical Purposes) Amendment Bill 2014 to allow use, possession, and cultivation of cannabis for medical purposes
	New South Wales	Introduction of Terminal Illness Cannabis Scheme to facilitate police in not enforcing the law against registered adults and carers
	Northern Territory	Introduction of the Misuse of Drugs Amendment Act 2014 allowing police to charge a person with supply to the indigenous community of drugs such as amphetamines and cannabis
	Victoria	Introduction of Drugs, Poisons and Controlled Substances Amendment (Clinical Trials) Bill facilitating clinical trials of medical cannabis
2015	Australian Capital Territory	Passing of Crimes Legislation Amendment Bill 2014 to prohibit display but not the sale of drug pipes
	New South Wales	Regulatory changes to facilitate doctors' applications for prescriptions of cannabis-based medicines
	Northern Territory	Adoption of Traffic and Other Legislation Amendment Act 2015 to allow for random drug testing for methamphetamines, cannabis, and ecstasy
	Victoria	Announcement to legalize access to medical cannabis in exceptional circumstances from 2017
	Western Australia	Adoption of Misuse of Drugs Amendment (Psychoactive Substances) Act 2015 banning the sale, supply, manufacturing, advertising, and promotion of psychoactive substances unless approved through existing regulation or legislation

(continued)

Year	Jurisdiction	Policy and legislative changes
2016	Australian Capital Territory	Announcement to establish a medical cannabis scheme as a priority
	New South Wales	Renaming of Terminal Illness Cannabis Scheme as Medical Cannabis Compassionate Use Scheme to evaluate its extension to non-terminal patients; authorization to conduct medical cannabis cultivation research
	Queensland	Adoption of Public Health (Medicinal Cannabis) Act 2016 allowing medicinal cannabis products to be prescribed and dispensed to patients in Queensland
	Tasmania	Announcement to facilitate medical practitioners to prescribe medicinal cannabis for patients with severe illnesses through a Controlled Access Scheme (CAS)
	Victoria	Adoption of Access to Medicinal Cannabis Act 2016 to allow for lawful cultivation and manufacturing of medicinal cannabis products by patients with certain conditions and symptoms
	Western Australia	The Narcotic Drugs Amendment Act 2016 legalizing the cultivation of medical cannabis, prescription by a doctor or dispensation by a pharmacist
2017	Victoria	An inquiry into drug law reform to monitor the effectiveness of laws, procedures, and regulations concerning synthetic and illicit drugs and the misuse of prescription medication in minimizing drug-related harm
2018	Australian Capital Territory	Proposition to legalize cannabis for personal use by removing possession of less than 50 grams of dried cannabis as a criminal offense
	South Australia	Issuance of Statutes Amendment (Drug Offences) Bill 2018 to increase penalties for cannabis possession
	Victoria	Proposition to legalize, regulate and tax recreational cannabis for people aged 18 and over
2019	Australian Capital Territory	Passing of The Drugs of Dependence (Personal Cannabis Use) Act 2019 to legalize personal cultivation, use, and possession of cannabis for recreational purposes
	Northern Territory	Recommendation to amend the misuse of drugs act to allow for uniform decriminalization of cannabis use to address inconsistencies that exist in police discretion

Source: Hughes (2020) and Ritter and Sotade (2017)

References

ACC (2015) Organised crime in Australia 2015. A. C. Commission. https://apo.org.au/sites/default/files/resource-files/2015-05/apo-nid54772.pdf

ACIC (2016) Illicit drug data report 2014–15. https://www.acic.gov.au/sites/default/files/2016/08/acic-iddr-2014-15.pdf?v=1561619004

ACIC (2017) Illicit Drug Data Report 2015–16. https://www.acic.gov.au/sites/default/files/2017/06/illicit_drug_data_report_2015-16_full_report.pdf?v=1561618955

ACIC (2018) Illicit Drug Data Report 2016–17. https://www.acic.gov.au/sites/default/files/iddr_2016-17_050718.pdf?v=1561090189

ACIC (2019) Illicit drug data report 2017–18. https://www.acic.gov.au/sites/default/files/illicit_drug_data_report_2017-18.pdf?v=1564727746

AIHW (2014) National drug strategy household survey detailed report 2013 (Drug Statistics Issue). https://www.aihw.gov.au/reports/illicit-use-of-drugs/2013-ndshs-detailed/summary

AIHW (2017) National drug strategy household survey detailed report 2016 (Drug Statistics Issue). https://www.aihw.gov.au/about-our-data/our-data-collections/national-drug-strategy-household-survey/2016-national-drug-strategy-household-survey

AIHW (2020a) Alcohol, tobacco & other drugs in Australia. https://www.aihw.gov.au/reports/alcohol/alcohol-tobacco-other-drugs-australia

AIHW (2020b) Illicit drug use. https://www.aihw.gov.au/reports/australias-health/illicit-drug-use

Ardizzi G, Petraglia C, Piacenza M, Schneider F, Turati G (2014) Money laundering as a crime in the financial sector: a new approach to quantitative assessment, with an application to Italy. J Money Credit Bank 46(8):1555–1590. https://doi.org/10.1111/jmcb.12159

Argentiero A, Bagella M, Busato F (2008) Money laundering in a two-sector model: using theory for measurement. Eur J Law Econ 26(3):341–359. https://doi.org/10.1007/s10657-008-9074-6

Bajada C (2017) Money laundering activities in Australia—an examination of the push and pull factors driving money flows. In: dela Rama M, Rowley C (eds) The changing face of corruption in the Asia Pacific. Elsevier, Berkeley, pp 127–147. https://doi.org/10.1016/B978-0-08-101109-6.00009-5

Baker J, Goh D (2004) The cannabis cautioning scheme three years on: an implementation and outcome evaluation. New South Wales Bureau of Crime Statistics and Research Sydney, Sydney

Barone R, Masciandaro D (2011) Organized crime, money laundering and legal economy: theory and simulations. Eur J Law Econ 32(1):115–142. https://doi.org/10.1007/s10657-010-9203-x

Barone R, Schneider FG (2018) Shedding light on money laundering. Is it a damping wave? SSRN Journal. https://doi.org/10.2139/ssrn.3204289

Barone R, Delle Side D, Masciandaro D (2018) Drug trafficking, money laundering and the business cycle: does secular stagnation include crime? Metroeconomica 69(2):409–426. https://doi.org/10.1111/meca.12193

Bewley-Taylor D (2003) Challenging UN drug control conventions: problems and possibilities. Int J Drug Policy 14(2):171–179

Bewley-Taylor D (2016) Towards metrics that measure outcomes that matter. Policy Brief 10

Bogdanoski T (2010) Accommodating the medical use of marijuana: surveying the differing legal approaches in Australia, the United States and Canada. J Law Med 17(4):508–531

Bresin K, Mekawi Y (2019) Do marijuana use motives matter? Meta-analytic associations with marijuana use frequency and problems. Addict Behav 99:106102. https://doi.org/10.1016/j.addbeh.2019.106102

Broadhurst R, Lauchs M, Lohrisch S (2014) Transnational organized crime in Oceania. In: Reichel P, Albanese J (eds) Transnational organized crime: an overview from six continents. Sage, Thousand Oaks, pp 141–162

Canhoto AI (2020) Leveraging machine learning in the global fight against money laundering and terrorism financing: an affordances perspective. J Bus Res. https://doi.org/10.1016/j.jbusres.2020.10.012

Caulkins JP, Reuter P (2022) How much demand for money laundering services does drug selling create? Identifying the key parameters. Int J Drug Policy 103:103652. https://doi.org/10.1016/j.drugpo.2022.103652

Caulkins JP, Kilmer B, Kleiman M, MacCoun RJ, Midgette G, Oglesby P, Pacula RL, Reuter PH (2015) Considering marijuana legalization: insights for Vermont and other jurisdictions. Rand Corporation, Santa Monica

Chan GCK, Hall W (2020) Estimation of the proportion of population cannabis consumption in Australia that is accounted for by daily users using Monte Carlo simulation. Addiction. https://doi.org/10.1111/add.14909

Chan GCK, Leung J, Quinn C, Weier M, Hall W (2018) Socio-economic differentials in cannabis use trends in Australia. Addiction 113(3):454–461. https://doi.org/10.1111/add.14010

Chang TY, Jacobson M (2017) Going to pot? The impact of dispensary closures on crime. J Urban Econ 100:120–136. https://doi.org/10.1016/j.jue.2017.04.001

Chatwin C (2017) UNGASS 2016: insights from Europe on the development of global cannabis policy and the need for reform of the global drug policy regime. Int J Drug Policy 49:80–85. https://doi.org/10.1016/j.drugpo.2015.12.017

Chu Y-WL, Gershenson S (2018) High times: the effect of medical marijuana laws on student time use. Econ Educ Rev 66:142–153. https://doi.org/10.1016/j.econedurev.2018.08.003

Chu Y-WL, Townsend W (2019) Joint culpability: the effects of medical marijuana laws on crime. J Econ Behav Organ 159:502–525. https://doi.org/10.1016/j.jebo.2018.07.003

Clarke R (2022) Navigating the US "green rush": anti-money laundering and de-risking implications for banking cannabis-related businesses in Jamaica. J Financ Crime 29(2):564–575. https://doi.org/10.1108/JFC-10-2021-0235

Clarke RV, Cornish DB (1985) Modeling Offenders' decisions: a framework for research and policy. Crime Justice 6:147–185

CMC (2005) Money laundering, background intelligence briefing

Collin M (2020) Illicit financial flows: concepts, measurement and evidence. World Bank Res Obs 35(1):44–86

Compin F (2008) The role of accounting in money laundering and money dirtying. Crit Perspect Account 19(5):591–602. https://doi.org/10.1016/j.cpa.2007.01.001

Cunliffe J, Martin J, Décary-Hétu D, Aldridge J (2017) An Island apart? Risks and prices in the Australian cryptomarket drug trade. Int J Drug Policy 50:64–73. https://doi.org/10.1016/j.drugpo.2017.09.005

Degenhardt L, Whiteford HA, Ferrari AJ, Baxter AJ, Charlson FJ, Hall WD, Freedman G, Burstein R, Johns N, Engell RE, Flaxman A, Murray CJL, Vos T (2013) Global burden of disease attributable to illicit drug use and dependence: findings from the global burden of disease study 2010. Lancet 382(9904):1564–1574. https://doi.org/10.1016/S0140-6736(13)61530-5

Dragone D, Prarolo G, Vanin P, Zanella G (2019) Crime and the legalization of recreational marijuana. J Econ Behav Organ 159:488–501. https://doi.org/10.1016/j.jebo.2018.02.005

Ene CM (2014) Measuring money laundering using "the Walker gravity model". Ann Univ Apulensis Series Oeconomica 2(16):1–13

FATF (2012) The FATF recommendations: international standards on combating money laundering and the financing of terrorism & proliferation. https://www.fatf-gafi.org/en/topics/fatf-recommendations.html#:~:text=The%20FATF%20Recommendations%20are%20the,measures%20in%20their%20national%20systems. Accessed 15 Jan

Ferrill J, Leuprecht C, Simser J (2023) Introduction. In: Leuprecht C, Ferrill J (eds) Dirty money: financial crime in Canada. McGill-Queens University Press, Quebec

Ferwerda J, Kattenberg M, Chang HH, Unger B, Groot L, Bikker JA (2013) Gravity models of trade-based money laundering [article]. Appl Econ 45(22):3170–3182. https://doi.org/10.1080/00036846.2012.699190

Fligstein N, Dioun C (2015) Economic sociology. In: Wright JD (ed) International encyclopedia of the social and Behavioral sciences. Elsevier, Amsterdam, pp 67–72

Ghosh TS, Vigil DI, Maffey A, Tolliver R, Van Dyke M, Kattari L, Krug H, Reed JK, Wolk L (2017) Lessons learned after three years of legalized, recreational marijuana: the Colorado experience. Prev Med 104:4–6. https://doi.org/10.1016/j.ypmed.2017.02.021

Gilmour N (2016) Understanding the practices behind money laundering—a rational choice interpretation. Int J Law Crime Justice 44:1–13. https://doi.org/10.1016/j.ijlcj.2015.03.002

Hendriyetty N, Grewal BS (2017) Macroeconomics of money laundering: effects and measurements [conference paper]. J Financ Crime 24(1):65–81. https://doi.org/10.1108/JFC-01-2016-0004

Hoffman V (2015) The international dimension of drug policy reform in Uruguay. Int J Drug Policy 34:27–33

Hughes C (2020) The Australian (illicit) drug policy timeline: 1985–2019. https://ndarc.med.unsw.edu.au/sites/default/files/ndarc/resources/Australian%20Illicit%20Drug%20Policy%20Timeline%20-%201985-2019%20-%20FINAL.pdf

Hughes CE, Lancaster K, Spicer B (2011) How do Australian news media depict illicit drug issues? An analysis of print media reporting across and between illicit drugs, 2003–2008. Int J Drug Policy 22(4):285–291. https://doi.org/10.1016/j.drugpo.2011.05.008

Hughes CE, Chalmers J, Bright DA, McFadden M (2016) Poly-drug trafficking: estimating the scale, trends and harms at the Australian border [article]. Int J Drug Policy 31:80–89. https://doi.org/10.1016/j.drugpo.2016.01.005

Hughes CE, Ritter A, Lancaster K, Hoppe R (2017) Understanding policy persistence—the case of police drug detection dog policy in NSW, Australia. Int J Drug Policy 44:58–68. https://doi.org/10.1016/j.drugpo.2017.03.007

Khan WA, Jawaid ST, Arif I (2018) Where does a nation's wealth go? Evidence from a third world country [article]. J Money Laundering Control 21(3):426–476. https://doi.org/10.1108/JMLC-01-2017-0005

Kilmer B, Pacula RL (2017) Understanding and learning from the diversification of cannabis supply laws. Addiction 112(7):1128–1135. https://doi.org/10.1111/add.13623

Kilmer B, Caulkins JP, Pacula RL, MacCoun RJ, Reuter P (2010) Altered state? Assessing how marijuana legalization in California could influence marijuana consumption and public budgets. RAND, Santa Monica

Lamprecht C, Guetterman TC (2019) Mixed methods in accounting: a field based analysis. Meditari Accountancy Res 27(6):921–938. https://doi.org/10.1108/MEDAR-11-2018-0403

Lancaster K, Ritter A (2014) Making change happen: a case study of the successful establishment of a peer-administered naloxone program in one Australian jurisdiction. Int J Drug Policy 25(5): 985–991. https://doi.org/10.1016/j.drugpo.2014.02.003

Lee N, Ritter A (2020) Australia's recreational drug policies aren't working, so what are the options for reform? The Conversation. https://theconversation.com/australias-recreational-drug-policies-arent-working-so-what-are-the-options-for-reform-55493

Lenton S, Humeniuk R, Heale P, Christie P (2000) Infringement versus conviction: the social impact of a minor cannabis offence in South Australia and Western Australia. Drug Alcohol Rev 19(3):257–264

Lintzeris N, Mills L, Suraev A, Bravo M, Arkell T, Arnold JC, Melissa J (2020) Medical cannabis use in the Australian community following introduction of legal access: the 2018-2019 online cross-sectional cannabis as medicine survey (CAMS-18). Harm Reduct J

Loayza N, Villa E, Misas M (2019) Illicit activity and money laundering from an economic growth perspective: a model and an application to Colombia. J Econ Behav Organ 159:442–487. https://doi.org/10.1016/j.jebo.2017.10.002

Lyman MD (2011) Drugs and crime. In: Lyman MD (ed) Drugs in society, 6th edn. Anderson Publishing, Ltd., Scotch Plains, pp 197–230. https://doi.org/10.1016/B978-1-4377-4450-7.00006-0

Mayer T, Zignago S (2011) Notes on CEPII's distances measures: The GeoDist database

McGinty EE, Samples H, Bandara SN, Saloner B, Bachhuber MA, Barry CL (2016) The emerging public discourse on state legalifzation of marijuana for recreational use in the US: analysis of news media coverage, 2010–2014. Prev Med 90:114–120. https://doi.org/10.1016/j.ypmed.2016.06.040

Meloen J, Landman R, De Miranda H, Van Eekelen J, Van Soest S, Van Duyne P, Tilburg V, Wagner D (2003) Buit en besteding: Een empirisch onderzoek naar de omvang, de kenmerken en de besteding van misdaadgeld. Den Haag Reed Bus Information 186:380–396

Mitchell A, Sikka P, Willmott H (1998) Sweeping it under the carpet: the role of accountancy firms in moneylaundering. Account Organ Soc 23(5–6):589–607. https://doi.org/10.1016/S0361-3682(98)00010-5

Moeller K (2018) Drug market criminology: combining economic and criminological research on illicit drug markets. Int Criminal Justice Rev 28(3):191–205. https://doi.org/10.1177/1057567717746215

Neill Harris K, Martin W (2019) The case for Marijuana decriminalization

Pacula RL, Powell D, Heaton P, Sevigny EL (2015) Assessing the effects of medical marijuana laws on marijuana use: the devil is in the details. J Policy Anal Manage 34(1):7–31

Paoli L (2014) Types of organized crime. In: Bruinsma G, Weisburd D (eds) Encyclopedia of criminology and criminal justice. Springer, New York, pp 3376–3387. https://doi.org/10.1007/978-1-4614-5690-2_628

Piquero AR, Gibson CL, Tibbetts SG (2002) Does self-control account for the relationship between binge drinking and alcohol-related behaviours? Crim Behav Ment Health 12(2):135–154. https://doi.org/10.1002/cbm.492

Reuter P, Greenfield V (2001) Measuring global drug markets. World Econ 2(4):159–173

Reuter P, Truman E (2004) Chasing dirty money: the fight against anti-money laundering. Peterson Institute for International Economics, Washington, DC

Ritter A, Sotade O (2017) Explaining the declining rates of past year cannabis use in Australia: a first pass. Drug Alcohol Rev 36(5):602–608. https://doi.org/10.1111/dar.12553

Ritter A, Lancaster K, Grech K, Reuter P (2011) An assessment of illicit drug policy in Australia (1985 to 2010): themes and trends. National Drug and Alcohol Research Centre, New South Wales

Rogeberg O (2018) Prohibition, regulation or laissez faire: the policy trade-offs of cannabis policy. Int J Drug Policy 56:153–161. https://doi.org/10.1016/j.drugpo.2018.03.024

Room R, MacKay S (2012) Roadmaps to reforming the UN drug conventions. A Beckley Foundation report. https://www.tni.org/files/publication-downloads/roadmaps_to_reform.pdf

Scheufele DA, Tewksbury D (2007) Framing, agenda setting, and priming: the evolution of three media effects models. J Commun 57(1):9–20. https://doi.org/10.1111/j.0021-9916.2007.00326.x

Schneider F, Enste DH (2000) Shadow economies: size, causes, and consequences. J Econ Lit 38(1):77–114. https://doi.org/10.1257/jel.38.1.77

Sen A (2023) Optimal taxation, the underground economy and government policy: recommendations for tobacco, Vaping, Marijuana and Gaming. Canadian Chamber of Commerce. https://chamber.ca/wp-content/uploads/2023/02/FEB-14-Chamber-of-Commerce-Recommendations-for-Tobacco_-Vaping_-Marijuana_-and-Gaming.pdf

Siklos-Whillans J, Bacchus A, Manwell LA (2020) A scoping review of the use of cannabis and its extracts as potential harm reduction strategies: insights from preclinical and clinical research. Int J Ment Heal Addict. https://doi.org/10.1007/s11469-020-00244-w

Smekens M, Verbruggen M (2004) De illegale economie in nederland

The Lancet (2016) Reforming international drug policy. Lancet 387(10026):1347. https://doi.org/10.1016/S0140-6736(16)30115-5

Tibbetts SG, Gibson CL (2002) Individual propensities and rational decision-making: recent findings and promising approaches. In: Piquero AR, Tibbetts SG (eds) Rational choice and criminal behavior: recent research and future challenges. Routledge, Oxford, pp 3–24

Tiwari M, Ferrill J (2023) Evolution of cannabis regulations and their overlooked link with money laundering: Australia as a critical case study. J Money Laund Control., (ahead-of-print). https://doi.org/10.1108/JMLC-11-2022-0158

Unger B (2007) The scale and impacts of money laundering. Edward Elgar, Cheltenham

Unger B, Siegel M, Ferwerda J, de Kruijf W, Busuioic M, Wokke K, Rawlings G (2006) The amounts and the effects of money laundering. Report for the Ministry of Finance, 16

UNODC (2011) Estimating illicit financial flows resulting from drug trafficking and other transnational organized crimes. https://www.unodc.org/unodc/en/data-and-analysis/WDR-2011.html

UNODC (2015) World Drug Report 2015. https://www.unodc.org/wdr2015/

UNODC (2016) Outcome document of the 2016 United Nations general assembly special session on the world drug problem. United Nations Office on Drugs and Crime, New York

UNODC (2019) World Drug Report 2019. https://wdr.unodc.org/wdr2019/

UNODC (2020) World Drug Report 2020. https://wdr.unodc.org/wdr2020/index2020.html

UNODC (2021) World Drug Report 2021. https://www.unodc.org/unodc/en/data-and-analysis/wdr2021.html

Walker J (1999) How big is global money laundering? J Money Laund Control 3(1):25–37. https://doi.org/10.1108/eb027208

Walker J, Unger B (2009) Measuring global money laundering. Rev Law Economics 5(2):821–853. https://doi.org/10.2202/1555-5879.1418

Wang GS, Heard K, Roosevelt G (2017) The unintended consequences of marijuana legalization. J Pediatr 190:12–13. https://doi.org/10.1016/j.jpeds.2017.08.023

Wang GS, Davies SD, Halmo LS, Sass A, Mistry RD (2018) Marijuana legalization and adolescent health. J Adolesc Health 63(3):367. https://doi.org/10.1016/j.jadohealth.2018.06.018

Weatherburn D, Jones C (2001) Does prohibition deter cannabis use? (BOCSAR NSW Crime and Justice Bulletins, Issue). https://www.bocsar.nsw.gov.au/Publications/CJB/cjb58.pdf

Werb D, Wood E, Strathdee S, Kazatchkine M, Des Jarlais D, Hankins C (2016) Open letter to the United Nations: A call for a reprioritisation of metrics to evaluate illicit drug policy. In: Toronto, Canada: International Centre for Science in Drugs Policy

Wilkins C, Casswell S (2003) Organized crime in cannabis cultivation in New Zealand: an economic analysis. Contemp Drug Probl 30(4):757–777. https://doi.org/10.1177/009145090303000403

Yeoh P (2020) Legal challenges for the cannabis industry. J Money Laundering Control 23(2):327–340

Zahra E, Darke S, Degenhardt L, Campbell G (2020) Rates, characteristics and manner of cannabis-related deaths in Australia 2000–2018. Drug Alcohol Depend 108028. https://doi.org/10.1016/j.drugalcdep.2020.108028

Jamie Ferrill is the Head of Financial Crime Studies and Lecturer in the same at the Australian Graduate School of Policing and Security, Charles Sturt University, and a Research Fellow with the Financial Integrity Hub (FIH) at Macquarie Law School. She has nearly a decade of law enforcement experience, having worked for the Canadian federal government prior to commencing an academic career. Jamie holds a PhD from Loughborough University (UK), a Master's in Homeland Security Leadership from the University of Connecticut (US), and a Bachelor's in Criminal Justice from Mount Royal University (Canada). Jamie research threats to national and economic security; her current focus is on the nexus of money laundering with border governance, transnational cooperation and collaboration, and organizational processes. Her latest book is titled Dirty Money: Financial Crime in Canada (McGill-Queen's University Press).

Milind Tiwari is a Researcher and Lecturer in Financial Crime Studies at the Australian Graduate School of Policing and Security, Charles Sturt University. Milind has extensive experience in AML investigations pertaining to customer due diligence, enhanced customer due diligence, and transaction monitoring, among others, and has worked for Big 4, namely, KPMG, EY, and Deloitte, in India and Australia. Milind holds a PhD in money laundering from Bond University (Australia), a

Master of Science in Finance from the University of Manchester (UK), and a Bachelor of Business Administration from Christ University (India). Additionally, he is a Certified Fraud Examiner (CFE) and a Certified Anti-Money Laundering Specialist (CAMS). As a financial crime academic and researcher, Milind's work focuses on various facets associated with money laundering, including its detection.

Application of the Risk-Based Approach (RBA) for Financial Crime Risk Management by Banks

Rachel Southworth and Michael Levi

Abstract The application of a risk-based approach (RBA) to managing financial crime risk has been a long-standing requirement and rhetoric of the Financial Action Task Force (FATF), filtering into national legislative requirements, regulatory expectations, and the private sector management of financial crime risk. The RBA concept can be deconstructed at a micro level by analysing how banks—a subset of regulated firms—define, manage, and attempt to mitigate financial crime(s) risk(s) in practice. The authors conclude that there are some serious challenges for the conceptualisation, and variations in the application, of the RBA from an operational perspective. There are also limitations for intelligence gathering and of the measurement of 'effectiveness' for financial crime control, where risk assessment methodologies informing the RBA differ between organisations. Given that the outputs of these RBAs are relied upon so heavily by national Financial Intelligence Units (FIUs) and by Regulatory Supervisors, there is a need for increased transparency in such methodologies. An understanding of the practical challenges and limitations faced by regulated entities in their interpretation and application of the RBA is critical if there is a legitimate desire to improve, and to make more consistent, private sector participation within the financial crime control landscape.

R. Southworth (✉)
Australian Graduate School of Policing and Security, Charles Sturt University, Canberra, ACT, Australia
e-mail: rsouthworth@csu.edu.au

M. Levi
School of Social Sciences, Cardiff University, Cardiff, UK
e-mail: levi@cardiff.ac.uk

D. Goldbarsht, L. de Koker (eds.), *Financial Crime and the Law*, Ius Gentium: Comparative Perspectives on Law and Justice 115,
https://doi.org/10.1007/978-3-031-59543-1_5

1 Introduction

Banks are a subset of regulated firms, but the role that they play in the financial crime control landscape has been the subject of growing academic attention. They are part of what Verhage terms the 'Anti-Money Laundering (AML) Complex' (2009, 2011, 2017): a network of international actors united in the fight against money laundering.[1] The heterogenous nature of banks, and how organisational diversity impacts the conceptualisation and management of financial crime(s) risk(s), however, is not widely documented. Banks are socially significant institutions, yet their role in what Power (2009) terms 'absorbing', 'collectivising' and redistributing' risks, in particular the array of financial crime risks, beyond money laundering, remains understudied: as does their role in 'risk policing' and 'responsibilisation' in relation to crime control functions (Levi 2010). To meet regulatory obligations, which involves identifying customers and reporting suspicious activity, banks are required to implement a risk-based approach (RBA) to manage ill-defined 'financial crime risk' (Levi 2022). In the public domain, very little is known about the internal workings of banks and how organisations go about defining and responding to risk (s); yet banks operate with significant autonomy and discretion in their application of a RBA, which in turn informs (or at times misinforms or even disinforms) societal conception(s) of financial crime(s) risk(s) (Southworth 2013). This chapter deconstructs the concept of the RBA at a micro level, by assessing the different types of risk assessment that banks undertake and the contributing factors that impact risk output. Once we begin to understand how complex and heterogenous banks can be, with multiple actors and competing motivations, involved in defining 'risk' (directly and indirectly) and the RBA applied to managing that risk, we gain insight into the powerful role that even a single bank can play as an agent in the financial crime control landscape. We also gain insight into challenges for Regulatory Supervisors and/or Financial Intelligence Units (FIUs)[2] (where they are separate entities), in managing the output of financial crime 'risk' definitions, where banks individually, and as a collective industry sector, dictate and, to an extent limit the law enforcement agenda, by means of the intelligence they are providing and not providing, whether as explicit or, more commonly, implicit policy and practice.[3]

This chapter provides an insight into how banks go about identifying and defining financial crime risk(s) as the basis for a risk-based approach (RBA): an 'innovative paradigm' in itself, according to Savona and Riccardi (2019). Drawing upon one of the authors' experience and Ph.D. research (Southworth 2013), and focusing

[1]The extent to which banks are willingly rather than compulsorily 'united' is a topic for further debate.

[2]Whether they are cognisant of such challenges or not.

[3]The role FIUs then play in dictating and driving the law enforcement agenda by filtering intelligence and distributing suspicious matter/activity and transaction reports to law enforcement agencies (LEAs) is also worthy of further research, although outside the scope of this chapter. It would be foolish to expect this to be consistent.

primarily on Australia, some practical challenges and limitations in the conceptualisation and application of the RBA are discussed. This includes: (1) risk identification challenges; (2) the diverse application of risk appetite and risk tolerance parameter settings; (3) challenges with data dependencies including customer data integrity and readiness; (4) the multiple actors and business decision makers involved in maintaining the infrastructure of systems and controls that represent application of the RBA[4]; and (5) the ability to measure or indeed to conceptualise 'effectiveness' meaningfully.

2 The Conceptualisation of 'Financial Crime(s) Risk(s)'

The risk-based approach (RBA) for regulatory compliance and for effective financial crime risk management relies on the expectation that financial institutions can *identify, assess, and understand the money laundering and terrorist financing (ML/TF) risks to which they are exposed, and implement the most appropriate mitigation measures'* (FATF 2014, p. 6). In Australia, it is a requirement of the Anti-Money Laundering and Counter-Terrorism Financing Act 2006 (AML/CTF Act) that regulated entities offering designated services identify, mitigate, and manage their financial crime risks via a documented risk assessment. The premise of the RBA is that it enables risk prevention and response prioritisation, as firms identify the risks posed to their organisations and invest in systems and controls, and adequate resources, to manage the 'highest' posed risks. Risk assessments, therefore, are a critical element in determining who, what and in which places, is deemed higher risk, and subjected to enhanced controls. They ultimately inform organisational risk mitigation strategies (including de-risking or, less politely, de-banking). In practice, banks (and other organisations) will do things differently to identify and respond to risk(s), from the way they implement organisational structures; operate within a certain culture; hire different leaders and teams; use different technological systems; maintain control processes and make business decisions. Likewise, risk assessment methodologies will vary between and within organisations. This chapter highlights the impact that different risk assessments and methodologies can have upon the definition of 'high, medium and low risk' and upon the consistent forming of 'suspicion'. In theory, there should be a causal relationship between risk ratings and suspicious matter/activity reporting, as it seems more likely that a high-risk customer will be reported for suspicious activity

[4]Acknowledging the organisational factors and human elements that play a role in framing risk response is important not just for our review of the banking sector but in all agents and actors that perform a role within the financial crime control landscape. There is a diversity of risk rhetoric and application of meaning both within and between different regulated entities, Financial Intelligence Units (FIUs), Regulators (where they are not also acting in an FIU capacity), police forces and other specific law enforcement agencies (LEAs).

where they are subject to enhanced customer due diligence (ECDD) and heightened transaction monitoring controls.[5] This is, however, affected by the reliability and validity of the data used to inform the customer risk assessment, transaction monitoring parameters and investigations.

In practice, the denotation of those financial crime(s) requiring appropriate mitigation measures extends beyond Money Laundering (ML) and Terrorist Financing (TF) to include International Financial Sanctions, Bribery and Corruption, Tax Non-Compliance and Proliferation Finance as well as Fraud, Market Abuse and Insider Dealing (Southworth 2013).[6] It is important to appreciate how challenging a task this is. Different financial crime types warrant different financial crime subject matter experts to review and interpret relevant global, legislative and regulatory requirements in order to (i) identify the applicable legal and regulatory obligations, and (ii) determine the risk(s) posed to the bank, in order to ensure regulatory compliance. Subject matter experts are required to ensure the legislation issued by different countries and (in Federal ones such as the US and Australia) States in which the firm operates, are fully mapped and understood (including any conflicts between them).[7] Identifying, interpreting, assessing, and understanding the full range of financial crime risks across multiple geographies, and implementing mitigation measures to manage them, thus can be a dynamic and complex process, involving many different internal and external actors.

To comply with regulatory requirements, banks (a conglomerate of different actors within multiple departmental functions) must evidence that they have completed their risk assessment(s); implemented financial crime compliance (FCC) policy (or the AML Program as it is known in Australia); completed appropriate customer due diligence (CDD) including identification and verification (ID&V) measures where applicable; and designed and implemented robust systems and controls to prevent, detect, monitor and report incidents of financial crime(s). Operational controls will include 'know your customer' (KYC) and risk rating processes; enhanced customer due diligence (ECDD) for high-risk customers; sanctions, politically exposed person (PEP) and negative news screening; transaction

---

[5] Although using the same argument, if a low or medium risk customer triggers an unusual alert and there is less due diligence available for the investigations team, they may be more likely to be reported as suspicious from a less informed, defensive position.

[6] The number and type of predicate offences to Money Laundering where the proceeds of crime can be handled have also expanded (and vary by jurisdiction) but can also now include environmental crimes such as wild-life trafficking and modern slavery including orphanage trafficking. This is in addition to traditional offences such as drug trafficking, human trafficking, arms trafficking, tax evasion, theft, counterfeit and piracy, corrupt practices and fraud. In some jurisdictions kidnap and ransom and smuggling would also be predicate offences. See also Comply Advantage (2020) on the topic of predicate offences and their expansion under the European Union's sixth Money Laundering Directive (6AMLD).

[7] Non-financial crime legislation may also impact the mapping of obligations and the interpretation of risk.

monitoring; employee due diligence (EDD); regulatory reporting processes (the filing of Suspicious Matter Reports (SMRs) or equivalent[8]); staff training and awareness; and compliance monitoring.[9]

As part of the overarching risk framework and application of the RBA, there is a requirement for firms to set 'risk appetite', a term that refers to the amount of risk an organisation is willing to take, whilst pursuing its strategic objectives.[10] Risk tolerance levels for financial crime types will also be established, i.e., designating certain customer types, industries, or jurisdictions they are not willing to do business with. Senior Management and the Board of Directors are required to establish and approve the financial crime risk appetite framework (RAF), in the form of a risk appetite statement (RAS) (Financial Stability Board 2013). Whether this is done before, during or after the risk assessment is completed may vary between banks, but in theory it should be an ongoing process.[11] Compliance monitoring and/or assurance testing is required to provide Senior Management with some form of evidence and confidence that the systems and controls are working 'effectively' to (i) manage the risk identified; and (ii) conduct business within risk appetite. Figure 1 provides a visual example of the basic steps required in the application of the RBA for financial crime risk management.[12]

Regulated entities in Australia, including banks, are required by their regulator the Australian Transaction Reports and Analysis Centre (AUSTRAC) to document their risk assessment method and process (AUSTRAC 2021a). There is, however, very little, if any, information available publicly about their methodologies and how they inform risk mitigation strategies and internal financial crime policy. At the national level, Ferwerda and Reuter (2019, p. 5) found there was substantial variation in terms of the analytical methods and data used to conduct National Risk Assessments (NRAs), as well as a lack of guidance on how NRAs should be conducted. Unlike NRAs, we cannot review and dissect the individual banking

---

[8]SMRs are referred to as Suspicious Activity Reports (SARs) in other jurisdictions. Dependent upon the jurisdiction, there may be multiple controls in relation to reporting requirements. In Australia, for example, there is a requirement to report any cash transaction over $10,000, known as a Threshold Transaction Report (TTR) and any international transfer instruction of *any* amount known as an International Fund Transfer Instruction (IFTI).

[9]In the training guide for 'Combating Money Laundering and the Financing of Terrorism', The World Bank (2009) provides a similar list of operational controls, although as Turkington (2019, p. 137) points out in his research on 'the effectiveness of private sector engagement in international financial crime countermeasures', this is not comprehensive, and some 'operational' controls may not be accepted as 'compliance' controls.

[10]Definitions of risk appetite and risk tolerance can be accessed via the Institute of Risk Management webpage, available at 'Risk appetite and tolerance (theirm.org)'.

[11]Trigger events that require an update to risk assessments and impact risk output i.e., risk ratings, may require a review of risk appetite and/or risk tolerance levels. Although if Board approval is required this time is very difficult to get in calendars (especially in advance), when there are limited annual meetings and already packed agendas.

[12]N.B. these are not necessarily presented in strict order, as many of the steps are interconnected and will inform each other.

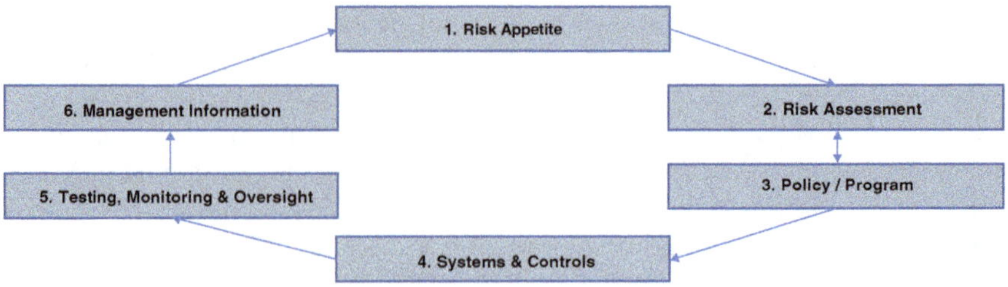

1. Risk Appetite – define risk appetite i.e. who you will and won't do business with.
2. Complete Risk Assessments – to determine the highest risk and controls required.
3. Maintain an up to data program/Policy – for the organisation to comply with obligations and risk appetite.
4. Implement and maintain adequate systems and controls- to meet the regulatory obligations and manage risk.
5. Test controls to ensure effectiveness – regular compliance monitoring, assurance and/ or audit for example.
6. Provide Management with regular reporting on the adequacy of systems and controls in place via Committee structures and formal/informal reports.

Fig. 1 Application of a Risk-Based Approach (RBA)

risk assessments. We also know very little about the actors responsible for designing and completing risk assessments. Reassessing risk and constantly updating controls based on the risk definition for different financial crime types is usually the job of Legal, Risk, Compliance and Financial Crime Operations teams within banks, sitting across the first and second line of defence.[13] Knowing who within and outside the bank is overseeing the risk assessment process from a governance perspective, and which if any 'qualified' persons are checking for accuracy (if indeed that is an appropriate term for an RBA), are important if we are to understand (i) the impacts of different methodologies in existence; (ii) the impact a variation in methodology may have upon the risk output; and (iii) the impact such differentiation has upon the definitions of financial crime risk(s) used by external parties.

3 Identifying, Assessing and Understanding Financial Crime Risk(s): Risk Assessments

Banks complete financial crime risk assessments in the form of an enterprise-wide risk assessment (often referred to as EWRA or ERA). The completion of an EWRA is usually an annual process but should also be subject to trigger review and refreshed if any material changes arise, i.e., if new international sanctions on a particular country or sector are imposed; a new money laundering typology is issued by the regulator; or the organisation changes its business model and intends to offer new products in a new country. The EWRA should be reviewed and approved by Senior Management and presented to the Board. How sophisticated and mature the

[13]This is dependent on the organisational structure of the bank, whether Risk and Compliance are a combined function for example, or Legal and Compliance are separate or combined functions, or whether there is a first line risk team dedicated to financial crime risk management.

Fig. 2 Enterprise-wide financial crime risk assessment framework

EWRA model is, often depends on factors including the size, nature, and complexity of the organisation; management focus and tone from the top; how evolved risk and compliance culture is intra-organisationally; the experience, capability and capacity of staff completing the risk assessment, and overseeing it; and how much money the organisation has invested in financial crime risk and compliance.

In Australia, the EWRA should include all legal entities that fall within a designated business group (DBG) if there is one, constituting 'the reporting entity'[14]; and all 'designated services' (products and services that are regulated by the AML/CTF Act 2006). To calculate the EWRA's overall 'inherent risk' (the natural, untreated risk) and 'residual risk' (inherent risk minus the impact of existing risk controls) ratings, the risk assessment will consider several risk categories as visualised in Fig. 2. This includes the customer base; the jurisdictions in which the organisation operates (and where customers reside or are nationals); transaction types; the products and services offered; the channels through which those products and services are offered; and in some organisations, employee, and third-party risk. Individual risk assessments are often performed on these risk categories to feed into the overarching EWRA. Two of the key categories informing the EWRA are the individual and detailed product and channel risk assessments. From an academic and practical perspective, we know very little about how the inherent and residual risk ratings are calculated by banks for these individual product and channel risk assessments, as well as the overarching EWRA. The methodologies used to calculate risk may differ between organisations according to the type of organisation, risk category, risk assessment template design and the vendor or tool being used. Some vendors offer an 'off the shelf' template that can also be tweaked to suit organisational requirements; others tailor a bespoke risk assessment template for the firm, ranging from lengthy questionnaires and a manual methodological calculation to a more sophisticated system generated tool. Whilst regulators such as AUSTRAC provide guidance on risk assessments, there is no defined methodology,

[14] Although some organisations will complete separate risk assessments per legal entity if the nature of business is starkly different between entities.

nor is there a portal to review or in any sense to 'validate' different methods and vendors offering solutions in the market.[15] There is a growing market for technological solutions for regulation and compliance, referred to as 'regtech'; and a vast body of firms offering Know Your Customer ('KYC') solutions, customer risk rating systems and Transaction Monitoring capabilities.[16] There are fewer firms, however, that specialise in technological solutions for the completion of enterprise-wide risk assessments.[17] So it is not clear that this constitutes 'market failure', but it is also not clear what counts as market success in choosing 'solutions'. The absence of a global template for very good or indeed very poor technological assistance may contribute to herding behaviour among regulated bodies, which may at least generate more consistency, but this is not the same as 'effectiveness'.

Most large banking organisations will have multiple EWRAs, and for financial crime(s), this is often divided into three main streams of financial crime risk (i) money laundering and terrorist financing; (ii) sanctions; and (iii) bribery and corruption, as outlined in Fig. 2.[18] How the EWRA is completed, and by whom, will depend upon the organisational structure. The amount of effort required to pull together an EWRA for a global banking organisation is huge. To complete the EWRA, each banking division may complete a divisional risk assessment, or three if organised as above, by providing information relating to risk category, i.e., product, channel, customer, and geography. This is gathered from the many different departments and actors and systems within the bank, of which there can be hundreds, for large institutions with multiple legal entities within their DBG. For example, the bank may be separated into different banking arms that have different divisions within them, including Retail Banking (this may include day-to-day Retail Banking, Credit, Lending including Home Loans, Insurance, Shares and Investments, and Superannuation for example); Private Banking (offering high net-worth banking facilities); Business Banking (including Business Banking facilities and Trade Finance); and Investment/Corporate Banking (this may include Financial Markets, Corporate and Structured Finance and Transaction Banking for example). Each banking arm/division will then have their own consolidated risk assessment with inherent and residual risk ratings that may vary to the overarching EWRA risk rating (s). The results from the overarching EWRA may conclude that the bank is medium risk, but there can be high risk and low risk banking divisions within it. The way in which EWRAs' results are summarised and reported has the potential to present a misleading narrative for Senior Management and regulators, who are not immersed

[15]That the authors are aware of.

[16]Including firms such as SAS, BAE Systems, Oracle, Lexis Nexis, Accuity, Fiserv, Nice Actimize and Refinitiv.

[17]There are smaller firms such as Arctic Solutions, for example, in Australia or Elucidate in Germany.

[18]It is plausible that all three EWRAs will have different inherent and residual risk ratings. Fraud risk also tends to sit separately in most banks, and may be subject to a separate EWRA, although this may be a changing future trend.

in the day-to-day detail, nor have read the full accompanying document (which can be hundreds of pages).

4 Practical Challenges and Limitations in the Application of the Risk-Based Approach (RBA)

4.1 Risk Identification

Risk definition has a dependency on the actors involved in the absorbance of risk information, as well as the methodology applied to calculate inherent and residual risks. The cartography of banking structures (including first line business risk and operations as well as second line risk, compliance, and legal teams) provides a basis to measure the internal workings of a bank and the multiple actors involved in financial crime risk absorbance, collectivisation, and redistribution (Southworth 2013). Actors within banks draw an understanding of the financial crime(s) risk (s)—including legal, operational, and reputational risk—from legislation, the vast array of information and documentation relating to risk(s), and typologies available from a wide range of global organisations and industry bodies. To name but a few, this includes the Financial Action Task Force (FATF); the United Nations (UN); the International Monetary Fund (IMF); the World Bank; the Bank for International Settlements (BIS) and the Basel Committee on Banking Supervision (BCBS); the Wolfsberg Group; the Egmont Group; international and local charities and think tanks; international and local Law Enforcement Agencies (LEAs) and respective Regulators and Industry Associations. The more advanced firms will also use their own data and information derived from the output of their systems and controls for managing financial crime risk, including investigations data.[19] The extent to which banks will use the breadth of material available to them is dependent upon the approved procedures and processes within each bank and the actors performing this task. There is sometimes a reliance on in-house staff within banks (whether they are experts or not) to collate and digest the information that is required to conceptualise risk. Other banks will outsource this task and rely upon consultants or 'expert' firms to do this on their behalf. The identification and conceptualisation of risk will therefore differ according to an actor's own knowledge, preference and capability to extract what is regarded as relevant information. How actors interpret information may also be impacted by the department that they sit in—whether they are from a legal team, for example, from risk and/or compliance, the front-line business, or from a combination—and this will ultimately determine how the collective organisation defines 'risk'.

[19]This is a product of the initial definition of risk and may therefore be diverse across organisations where their identification, assessment and understanding of risk differs.

Whilst there is a wealth of guidance material published by multiple 'official' sources, some of this will be outdated, and the lack of a centralised source document plus human factors relating to interpretation, increases the likelihood that banks will interpret risk differently. For banks to reliably assess the risk(s) they are exposed to (or at least validly according to their own conceptualisation of risk), there is also a reliance upon *national* risk or threat assessments. According to FATF, countries and competent authorities have a responsibility to determine how the threat of money laundering and terrorist financing activities will affect them (FATF 2014). One initial setback for reporting entities in Australia is the fact that the Australian national threat assessment (NTA) was originally classified, and the last published version by AUSTRAC was in 2011. On 27th June 2023, AUSTRAC announced they are working on two new national risk assessments, one for Money Laundering (due early 2024) and one for Terrorist Financing (due late 2023), presumably as a prelude to the long delayed FATF Mutual Evaluation Report.[20] An up-to-date threat assessment is pivotal to a firm's ability to interpret the financial crime(s) risk(s) specific to Australia. As Transparency International noted in their submission to the Parliamentary review on the adequacy and efficacy of Australia's anti-money laundering and counter terrorist financing (AML/CTF) regime, '*one of the key methods of identifying emerging ML/TF problems is to conduct a National Risk Assessment (NRA). Australia does not have a national policy which sets out what the overall AML/CTF system is meant to achieve, and how success would be monitored or measured. This makes it challenging to determine how well the ML/TF risks are being addressed*' (2021, p. 2).

Between 2016 and 2021, AUSTRAC published 16 national risk assessments, but these are specific to certain products or sectors, such as Stored Value Cards and Traveller's cheques; and Superannuation and Securities and derivatives sectors. In 2017 AUSTRAC also published a Pacific remittance corridor risk assessment. Between 2016 and 2018 AUSTRAC co-authored four regional risk assessments, but three out of the four were specific to terrorism financing and the other on cross-border movement of funds (AUSTRAC 2021c). In 2021 AUSTRAC released four money laundering and terrorist financing (ML/TF) risk assessments covering Australia's four major banks, other domestic banks, foreign subsidiary banks, and foreign bank branches, '*to help the banking sector identify, understand and disrupt serious financial crime*' (AUSTRAC 2021b, p. 1). The first national proliferation financing risk assessment was then released in December 2022 (AUSTRAC 2022).[21] AUSTRAC openly states that risk profiles are '*impacted by the maturity of*

[20] See the AUSTRAC website New national risk assessments in development | AUSTRAC. Last accessed 16 December 2023.

[21] Whilst this is the first NRA on proliferation finance produced by AUSTRAC, it is not a new category of financial crime risk for banks. It has been intertwined in the practical response to AML and sanctions obligations for years with customer due diligence, screening and monitoring controls in place to manage this risk (albeit the quality of these controls will vary amongst institutions). The impact that the introduction of the Australian NRA will have on the application of the RBA by regulated entities is worthy of future attention.

individual entities' anti-money laundering/counter terrorist financing (AML/CTF) programs in place, which are implemented with varying degrees of effectiveness across the sector' (AUSTRAC 2021b, p. 1). If the maturity of the AML Program impacts effectiveness, then the maturity of the banks' ability to define risk would impact risk output, i.e., the definition of high-risk (and low-risk) customers, products and services and the controls put in place to manage identified risk(s). Ironically, the risk assessments issued by AUSTRAC are often constructed with the information obtained by the regulated sector, from suspicious matter reports (SMRs), threshold transaction reports (TTRs), and international funds transfer information (IFTI). This information is analysed by the regulator alongside partner agency intelligence reporting (AUSTRAC 2021c). The risk assessments being issued by the regulator are therefore dependent on banks' operationalisation of their own risk definitions.

4.2 The Diverse Application of Risk Appetite and Risk Tolerance Parameter Setting

The setting of risk appetite is integral to the lifecycle of the RBA as the organisation's Management delegates authority to designated individual executives to manage the risk and compliance functions and to conduct the risk assessment. In practice, risk assessments completed at the enterprise level are often retrospective, completed with data from the previous calendar or financial year. The consequence for suspicious matter/activity reporting is that the risk appetite and/or risk tolerance levels, are also retrospective and certain high-risk customers will not be reported or could be reported and/or exited later than they would have if the process was 'real time'.[22]

Setting risk appetite can be challenging when translated into practice, where appetite may differ according to the different types of financial crime, notwithstanding the FATF 'all crimes' approach. There is usually a zero tolerance for sanctions and terrorist financing, especially where there is extra-territorial reach of foreign legislation and civil liability such as from the U.S., and a bank can be fined large amounts or risk losing their banking licence. There will usually be a zero tolerance for facilitating money laundering, but that requires evidence and knowledge that money laundering has taken place. For the most part, banks are managing the risk and likelihood of money laundering occurring and making decisions about whether to bank persons or entities they suspect of being involved with money laundering i.e., a subset of high-risk clients (often referred to as 'restricted and/or prohibited customers'). This may result in identifying high risk sectors that they choose not to bank, historically remittance sectors, some gaming operators (especially those subject to 'adverse media'), and tattoo and sex industries have been on the radar of larger

[22]This is potentially one of the key factors leading to enforcement action on banks, where their systems and controls are not up to date, and they are using out-of-date information to feed into the risk assessment and generate risk ratings.

institutions for de-risking and de-banking.[23] The number of high-risk customers will usually be a small percentage of the total customer population. It could be as small as 1%, although some firms have now started sub categorising 'very high' risk as the 1%, and 'high risk' will be a larger percentage of clients. Again, the numbers are dependent on the methodology applied to determine risk and whether there is a cap on the number of high-risk customers that a firm is willing to bank, which means either 'downgrading' other customers that have generated a high-risk rating to medium risk or exiting them from the bank altogether. The topic of de-banking customers, whilst not the focus of this chapter, is an important component of how banks manage expectations of the RBA from multiple standard setters and regulators, amidst the practical, operational backdrop of 'doing business'.[24] Such de-banking includes implicitly or explicitly issues such as human rights, financial inclusion (of at least basic banking), and the likelihood of greater critical scrutiny from onboarding or continuing to bank individual and corporate customers who have attracted 'adverse media' or are predicted to do so in future.

4.3 Data Dependencies: Customer Data Integrity and Readiness

Customer risk information is a key set of data to feed into an EWRA. The customer risk rating methodology that informs the customer risk assessment will be dependent on 'know your customer' (KYC) information and data, referred to as customer due diligence (CDD) and, for those customers categorised as 'high risk' from a financial crime risk perspective, ECDD.[25] Sometimes this methodology will differ according to the type of banking division. Historically, except where banks have real time screening and risk rating technology in place, this risk rating may not occur for days, weeks or even months after the client is onboarded. Reforms to the Anti-Money Laundering and Counter-Terrorism Financing Act 2006 (AML/CTF Act) in

[23] Although de-risking has faced criticism in recent years from a financial inclusion standpoint, the risk of regulatory penalty has historically driven this approach where control costs to manage the high-risk population outweigh the risk and reward of maintaining that client base. This may also be a factor behind the business view in some firms that a high-risk client means bad news from a compliance perspective and is to be avoided at all costs. See attempts by The Wolfsberg Group (2022, 2023) to push EU regulators into a more subtle approach.

[24] In June 2023, AUSTRAC published new guidance on de-banking Financial services for customers that financial institutions assess to be higher risk | AUSTRAC. Note also the 2022 Opinion from the European Banking Authority (EBA Opinion and annexed report on de-risking.pdf (europa.eu)) and the 2023 work from the US Treasury Department (Treasury Department Announces 2023 De-Risking Strategy | U.S. Department of the Treasury) on the topic of de-risking (all last accessed 16 December 2023).

[25] Note that ECDD is Australian terminology, however, in other jurisdictions it may be referred to as Enhanced Due Diligence (EDD), not to be confused with Employee Due Diligence (EDD) that uses the same acronym.

Australia came into effect on 17 June 2021, however, clarifying customer due diligence obligations *before* providing a designated service.

Different banks (and areas within them) may collect more KYC and CDD information than others to inform their customer risk ratings, risk assessment (s) and RBA. In Australia, simplified due diligence (SDD) can be applied to customers determined to be low risk, but if one bank collects 50 data fields and another bank only five, whilst both may be compliant with ID&V and KYC regulatory requirements, the variance in detail could dramatically affect their risk coding even if they use the same methodology. Many banks face challenges with the collection and storage and updating of data. There will usually be multiple customer systems within banking organisations holding varying degrees of customer data. It is not unusual for large, global banks without a single customer view to have hundreds of systems within their systems architecture, holding different (and duplicate) customer data sets. Challenges with upgrading systems, inheriting systems (e.g., post-merger) and transitioning to new systems all impact how customer data is stored. This can impact the risk assessment output if not all customer data is being fed into the overarching assessment (including the number of customers and customer types as well as the data fields being captured for each customer as a due diligence requirement). This affects screening for sanctions as well as risk assessment.

A difference in risk rating due to different customer data collection means banks will have different controls in place over different segments of that same customer base type. A 'high risk' customer in Bank A could be categorised as a 'medium risk' customer in Bank B, and therefore whilst subject to ECDD and heightened transaction monitoring controls in Bank A, they would not be subject to these additional controls in Bank B, impacting the likelihood of reporting a suspicious matter report (SMR).[26] The risk starting point may be unknown and whilst banks are required to document their risk assessment method, little is known about how the regulator uses this information to inform supervision and enforcement measures.

In Australia, firms are required to identify politically exposed persons (PEPs) either before the provision of a designated service to the customer or as soon as practicable after the designated service has been provided (AML/CTF Rules 2007, 4.13.1).[27] The size, nature and complexity of the business dictates what would be deemed as soon as practicable, so there is room for firms to justify a delayed identification if justifiable in their RBA. This could be due to lack of system capability at on-boarding, or a reliance on manual processes, reflecting historical business priorities for investment. Whilst section 4.13.3 (2) of the AML/CTF Rules 2007 states that senior management approval is required before establishing or

[26]That is for SMRs generated by systems, not for suspicious activity that is manually raised by bank staff for example, the risk rating would not be a consideration or even known by the staff member raising the internal suspicious activity/unusual activity report.

[27]Anti-Money Laundering and Counter-Terrorism Financing Rules Instrument 2007 (No. 1) - 'AML/CTF Rules 2007'.

continuing a business relationship with a high risk domestic or foreign PEP, if identification has occurred post on-boarding it is plausible that the high risk PEP could have been carrying out business with the bank for a number of days, weeks or indeed months before the appropriate ECDD is carried out and senior management approval is obtained to retain the business. The challenge banks and ultimately law enforcement agencies (LEAs) face here, however, is that if a high-risk customer is not identified immediately and subject to enhanced controls then behaviour that ought to be suspected is less likely to be picked up through screening and transaction monitoring alerts and sent across to the Financial Intelligence Unit (FIU) as a suspicious matter/activity report (SMR/SAR). It may be less likely that unusual / suspicious activity will be identified by the first line of defence (the business acting as front office, customer facing staff) as well, if there is no flag on the customer database categorising the client as high risk. But not all firms will allow the first line to see the risk categorisation of clients, for fear that this can lead to tipping off. Whilst prior suspicion can be a trigger for high-risk ratings, however, not all high-risk customers will have a suspicious matter/activity report filed against them to the FIU. Some individuals within firms (especially front-line business) may not understand the premise of the RBA and are under the impression that if a customer is high risk or a PEP that they can no longer be a customer: hence a business reluctance to have their customers rated as high.

There are multiple vendors that offer 'off the shelf' operational definitions of risk types, which places reliance on third parties, for setting Politically Exposed Person ('PEP') rules or transaction monitoring rules for example. For country risk, banks have the option to create their own internal risk index based on documentation in the public domain, or they may rely upon external indexes such as the Transparency International Corruption Perception Index (CPI), the Basel Institute Index, FATF peer reviews, or a combination thereof. New products to the market to measure country risk also include those provided by specialist firms formed by ex-financial crime compliance personnel (the financialcrimenews.com for example) in the form of Financial Crime Country Dashboards. Sanctions and PEP screening vendors will also often include a pre-set country risk rating functionality within their platform, as well as Sanctions and PEP screening lists, and in some cases negative news lists. The country risk rating can have a dramatic impact on the output of the RBA, by categorising sub-sets of the customer population as high-risk, dependent on residency and/or visa status. If a potentially high-risk country (as seen through the eyes of the regulator or law enforcement) is categorised as medium risk at a bank, then hundreds or even thousands of customers may be 'wrongly' risk rated, resulting in no ECDD measures being taken on that population and potentially fewer suspicious matter/activity reports being filed. Unless a regulator is micro supervising, however, country risk categorisation and the impact this has upon the overarching risk assessment will remain known only to that organisation (unless this was disclosed voluntarily to the Regulator).

4.4 Multiple Actors and Business Decision Makers Involved in Completing the Risk Assessment and Maintaining the Infrastructure of Systems and Controls

Many large banking organisations operate across multiple jurisdictions and have acquired different entities and undergone mergers over time. There are therefore often technological limitations and system legacy issues surrounding the housing and extraction of data that is required to inform a risk assessment. Coupled with the myriad of actors involved in larger organisations, in the risk assessment end-to-end process, it can be quite a complex and long-drawn-out process. As highlighted by The Wolfsberg Group (2015, p. 1), *'other departments across a FI [Financial Institution], including business risk management, compliance monitoring or audit, may also undertake forms of risk assessment and therefore both the undertaking and the results of all risk assessments should be coordinated, to the extent that this is possible'*. The fact that most EWRAs are made on the basis of data from the previous year reduces their utility to a rational risk management approach: but no-one may ever know.

The involvement of different teams in risk assessment processes will depend upon the structure of the bank and the compliance function, the direction of the leadership team and the maturity of the risk and compliance culture across the organisation. In large banking organisations, there is usually a financial crime governance team or role within Financial Crime Compliance (FCC), that oversees the completion of the risk assessment process. It can take many months to initiate and complete the risk assessment process, or longer if new approaches are being trialled. Some banks hire temporary consultants to help gather information or even outsource the risk assessment process. This can cause friction within organisations where the persons collecting information do not know intricate details about the business and act as 'post boxes' requesting large amounts of information from front line staff, duplicating obligations and control assessment processes, and the annual AUSTRAC compliance assessment, for example. If organisations are not coordinated in gathering governance related information, it can become particularly tiresome for front line staff having to speak with multiple contacts from different teams, as well as external consultants, to provide different versions of the same information at different times.

In some cases, the inherent financial crime risk for a bank will be calculated as high, but the residual risk will be calculated as low because of their own judgments about the quality of the controls in place (that in principle are subject to monitoring and assurance and independent testing/internal audit). There may be various iterations of the Risk Assessment document and the (legitimate or not) overriding or steering of results, dependent on the methodology adopted, the persons responsible for completing the risk assessment and the quality of governance and oversight overseeing the process. Without 'appropriate' compliance oversight, challenge and subject matter expertise, conflict between internal actors can influence the final risk ratings. The actors choosing and/or defining and approving the methodologies adopted for risk assessments will impact the outputs. Some firms, often smaller, less complex firms may choose to design their own risk assessment methodology. If external vendors are contracted to provide off-the-shelf technologies, then there may be a level of consistency in approach across the firms that use that same vendor, but there is still the ability to manually override a risk rating. Products of a similar nature sometimes are grouped into broader product types to avoid there being hundreds of product risk assessments of a repetitive nature. In Retail banking alone, each type of mortgage lending product, each transaction account type, and each credit lending facility may require a separate risk assessment. One of the difficulties a bank faces is the Financial Crime Compliance (FCC) team that often coordinates the risk assessment process is rarely expert in all the different types of products and channels and is therefore heavily reliant on the information provided by, and expertise sitting within, the front-line business.

4.5 *Measuring Effectiveness*

Being able to measure the effectiveness of a bank's ability to prevent, detect, and monitor incidents of financial crime(s), including money laundering, is challenging. How the effectiveness of the Anti-Money Laundering (AML) regime can be measured as a whole, has been a debated topic by FATF, governments, regulators, the Wolfsberg Group and academics, and the lack of credible evidence of the effectiveness of the system, and its constituent parts, has been well noted, if seldom acted upon, SWIFT Institute (2021), Halliday et al. (2020), Turkington (2019), Levi et al. (2017)[28], de Koker and Turkington (2015) and Sharman (2011). The ultra-sceptic Pol (2020) summarises that anti-money laundering policy intervention has a less than 0.1% impact on criminal finances, and that compliance costs exceed recovered criminal funds more than a hundred times over. The FATF guidance (2014, p. 6)—updated since for particular sectors only—recognises that application of the RBA is not a 'zero failure' approach and even where banks do have a robust risk assessment that does not mean they could never be used for money laundering or terrorist financing purposes. Arguably, the systems and controls in place within a bank do not tell us very much about the practical value of the RBA, unless it can be proven that they are inextricably and tangibly linked to the output of the risk assessment. It is plausible that banks that implement standard processes and systems without an adequate risk assessment may do just as well in managing financial crime risk

[28] As Levi et al. (2017, p. 324) stated, the UK-led efforts to share suspected transaction data between banks and enforcement agencies via the Joint Money Laundering Intelligence Taskforce (JMLIT) reflected a frustration that the cost of compliance, which itself is inadequately measured, has little observable effect and is seemingly cost-inefficient. This 'public-private partnership' approach has subsequently been adopted more widely, but is too large an issue for this chapter. A more recent study has been carried out by RUSI, commissioned by the SWIFT Institute (2021) in relation to transaction monitoring.

(s) as the banks that have excelled in their risk assessment documentation. Without a standard metric to measure the relationship with effectiveness it is difficult to judge whether fine tuning suspicious typologies according to the risk of a particular customer type will increase the overall effectiveness of the bank in managing its overall risk. It may at that time provide more intelligence reports on a particular subsection of risk that the authorities (Regulators and/or Law Enforcement) are interested in (if law enforcement notices have been issued that trigger suspicious reporting), but had the bank not focused primarily on that area, they may have 'freed' up resources to focus on other areas that could also be just as worthy of reporting.

The questions thus remain, what is (and what will be regarded post-exposé as) an 'acceptable' failure rate for the RBA, how do different actors within the financial crime control landscape measure banks, and how do they measure their own effectiveness? What the regulator views as a sound risk assessment and robust framework of systems and controls may in practice not provide law enforcement agencies (LEAs) with proactive and targeted intelligence (which they anyway in a target-rich environment may not have the motivation or resources to act upon). The banks that invest in proactive internal intelligence hubs in addition to traditional systems and controls may be viewed by law enforcement as more effective, if those intelligence hubs produce what they deem to be better quality suspicious matter reports (SMRs), as opposed to defensive reporting triggered by existing bank practices such as the processing of law enforcement notices.

In practice, some banks fail to complete a risk assessment at all, let alone an adequate risk assessment, and this absence *per se* may provoke regulatory enforcement action. The Commonwealth Bank of Australia (CBA) reportedly '*failed to conduct a proper risk assessment before the [Intelligent Deposit Machines] IDMs were launched, or in the years that followed, which led to... 14 admissions to breaches of the [AML/CTF] act*' (Australian Financial Review 2018). Other banks may have incomplete and/or inaccurate datasets, skewing the risk assessment output and influencing the approach taken to managing perceived risk. Different banks have different ways of identifying 'high risk' customers that are then subject to ECDD processes and increased likelihood of internal investigation. Subsets of high-risk populations will differ according to each bank's definition of 'high risk', and this can impact the risk output in the form of the unusual/suspicious transaction alerts raised for investigation, and the SMRs that are disclosed to the Financial Intelligence Unit (FIU)—in Australia, being AUSTRAC. The somewhat subjective nature of the RBA, and lack of risk assessment standardisation, increases the likelihood that banks will report differently (if they report at all) on subsets of their customer populations to the relevant FIU.[29] Where a risk assessment was deemed inaccurate (noting banks' risk ratings may not always correspond to a published regulatory

[29] Other factors are more likely to increase the chance of collective reporting, such as intelligence received directly from law enforcement agencies (LEAs) or regulators by way of typology reports, or law enforcement notices for example, that may trigger a high-risk customer flag and trigger an investigation.

view), or non-existent, this could impact alerts generated for investigating suspicious activity. There is no space here to examine the actual or potential impact of that reporting on actual investigation or criminal justice, and the impacts of the process as a whole on the reduction of any form of crime or its organisation remain largely unanalysed.

5 Conclusion

Banks are often large, complex institutions with multiple departments and actors involved in policy and standards development, implementation, and ongoing management. Money laundering and other financial crime risk interpretation and application can vary between organisations, as well as between different banking divisions (retail, business, private and investment) within organisations.[30] Whilst this chapter did not explore the RBA applied by regulators for supervision purposes,[31] it has provided an insight into the risk assessments completed by banks, including the risk categories informing the overarching EWRA, and other factors influencing the identification, interpretation, assessment and understanding of 'financial crime risk(s)'. More information on the differences between organisational risk assessments, both in terms of the actors influencing them and the methodologies used to evaluate risk, would be useful, given their output can influence and dictate decision making around the appropriate risk response. Variety may be an accepted and advantageous outcome of the RBA by Regulators, Law Enforcement Agencies (LEAs), Governments and FATF. However, it is not self-evident that any particular approach generates a better outcome, especially when so few reports of suspicions lead to new or enhanced investigations or to financial crime prevention.[32] The RBA is an attractive concept compared with the rigidity of its predecessor Rules-Based Assessment, but its practice and quality evaluation remain underdeveloped by banks, by regulators and by law enforcement, and even—in the context of Grand Corruption and environmental crimes—by NGOs, especially those committed to zero tolerance, which in our view is incompatible with a risk-based approach.

This chapter has highlighted the practical tensions firms face in the operationalisation of financial crime risk management and mitigation, from defining risk(s); measuring risk(s); responding to risk(s) and documenting the response to risk (s). Tsingou (2018, p. 195) refers to compliance professionals in financial institutions as 'foot soldiers' in the fight against money laundering. This chapter concludes

---

[30] If there is this much variation within banks alone, the variation between other regulated industries and sectors is also worthy of research and greater attention.

[31] We know very little about how regulators obtain and manage information; store and feed data into chosen models; apply methodologies to assess risk, and manage the enforcement agenda, to maintain supervisory oversight and to ensure that the management of financial crime risk is appropriate by banks.

[32] Although regulatory enforcement could be seen as one measure for this.

that banks (individually and collectively) and the financial crime control practitioners that work within them[33] are much more than foot soldiers: as actors in the financial crime control landscape, they have the potential to drive and dictate a powerful policing agenda, whether they and other participants are cognisant of it or not. The heterogenous nature of banking practices impacts the definitions of financial crime risk(s) which ultimately impacts the intelligence that is used to determine and drive aspects of the policing (including regulatory) agenda and responses. Through their own implicit or explicit conceptualisation of risk(s), banks can influence how members of society view and respond to financial crime risk (s) including the banking sector more broadly: regulators, LEAs, the general public and media, and politicians. The outputs of the conceptualisation and application of the RBA applied by regulated firms are heavily relied upon by other agents, including regulators. Therefore, an understanding of the challenges and limitations surrounding the operationalisation of the RBA is critical to increase awareness and improve private sector participation within the financial crime control landscape.

On the basis of their major international review of national risk assessments, Ferwerda and Reuter (2022) suggest the need for increased clarity about the conceptualisation of risk, transparency about data and methods so that each country can learn from others, and the adoption of more formal and standardized methods of eliciting expert opinion. We conclude that this also applies at the micro level within and between regulated firms. We hope that this chapter has given readers some insight into the convoluted process that lies behind the formation of firms' risk assessments which in turn may be examined (usually with a light touch) by their regulators in a social, economic and media climate that may be quite different from that when the process was begun.

References

AUSTRAC (2021a) AUSTRAC Insights. Assessing ML/TF Risk. Available online at https://www.austrac.gov.au/sites/default/files/2020-08/AUSTRAC%20Insights%20-%20Assessing%20ML-TF%20Risk.pdf. Last Accessed 16 Dec 2023

AUSTRAC (2021b) Key findings overview: Australian banking sector money laundering and terrorism financing risk assessments. Available online at https://www.austrac.gov.au/sites/default/files/2021-09/Overview_Australian%20Banking%20Sector%20ML_TF%20risk%20assessments%202021.pdf. Last Accessed 16 Dec 2023

AUSTRAC (2021c) AUSTRAC Submission. Inquiry into the adequacy and efficacy of Australia's anti-money laundering and counter-terrorism financing (AML/CTF) regime. Submission 33. August 2021. file:///C:/Users/south/OneDrive/Desktop/Submissions%20-%20Parliamentary%20Enquiry/Submission%2033%20-%20AUSTRAC.pdf Last Accessed 16 Dec 2023

[33] Including Financial Crime Compliance (FCC) professionals, but also first- and second-line risk teams, operations teams, audit functions, Human Resources (HR) and other front line business staff.

AUSTRAC (2022) Proliferation financing in Australia. National risk assessment. Available online at proliferation financing in Australia - National Risk Assessment (austrac.gov.au). Last Accessed 16 Dec 2023

Australian Financial Review (2018) Money laundering scandal: what CBA admitted to, and why it happened. *James Eyers. June 4, 2018.* Available online at https://www.afr.com/companies/financial-services/money-laundering-scandal-what-cba-admitted-to-and-why-it-happened-20180604-h10xm3. Last Accessed 16 Dec 2023

Comply Advantage (2020) Website article: https://complyadvantage.com/knowledgebase/adverse-media/6amld-22-predicate-offenses-money-laundering/. Last accessed 16 December 2023

De Koker L, Turkington M (2015) Anti-money laundering measures and the effectiveness question. In: Rider B (ed) Research handbook on international financial crime. Edward Elgar Publishing, Cheltenham

FATF (2014) Guidance for a risk-based approach. The Banking Sector

Ferwerda J, Reuter P (2019) Learning from money laundering National Risk Assessments: the case of Italy and Switzerland. Eur J Crim Policy Res 25:5–20. https://doi.org/10.1007/s10610-018-9395-0

Ferwerda J, Reuter P (2022) National Risk Assessments of money laundering risks: learning from eight advanced countries' NRAs. World Bank, Washington DC. https://doi.org/10.1596/37305

Financial Stability Board (FSB) (2013) Principles for an effective risk appetite framework. Available online at 'FSB consultative document'. Last accessed 16 Dec 2023

Halliday T, Levi M, Reuter P (2020) Why do transnational legal orders persist? The curious case of anti-money laundering. In: Shaffer G, Aaronson E (eds) Transnational legal ordering of criminal justice. Cambridge University Press, Cambridge, pp 51–83. ISBN 978-1-108-83658-6

Levi M (2010) Combating the financing of terrorism: a history and assessment of the control of 'threat finance'. Br J Criminol Special Issue Terrorism Criminol Perspect 50(4):650–669

Levi M (2022) Financial crimes—a criminological research perspective. In: Rider B (ed) A research agenda for financial crime. Edward Elgar, Ch3, Cheltenham, pp 49–68

Levi M, Reuter P, Halliday T (2017) Can the AML system be evaluated without better data? Crime Law Soc Change 69:307–328. https://doi.org/10.1007/s10611-017-9757-4

Pol RF (2020) Anti-money laundering: the world's least effective policy experiment? Together, we can fix it. Policy Design Practice 3(1):73–94. https://doi.org/10.1080/25741292.2020.1725366

Power M (2009) The risk management of nothing. Account Organ Soc 34(6–7):849–855

Savona EU, Riccardi M (2019) Assessing the risk of money laundering: research challenges and implications for practitioners. Eur J Crim Policy Res 25:1–4

Sharman JC (2011) The Money Laundry: Regulating Criminal Finance in the Global Economy (Ithaca, NY, 2011; online edn, Cornell Scholarship Online, 18 Aug. 2016). https://doi.org/10.7591/cornell/9780801450181.001.0001. Accessed 23 May 2024

Southworth R (2013) Financial crime control: risk, regulation and the role(s) of the UK banking sector, PhD thesis, Cardiff University

SWIFT Institute (2021) The future of transaction monitoring: better ways to detect and disrupt financial crime. Available online at The Future of Transaction Monitoring: Better Ways to Detect and Disrupt Financial Crime by Matthew Redhead: SSRN. Last Accessed 16 Dec 2023

The Wolfsberg Group (2015) The Wolfsberg frequently asked questions on risk assessments for money laundering, sanctions and bribery & corruption. https://www.wolfsberg-principles.com/sites/default/files/wb/pdfs/faqs/17.%20Wolfsberg-Risk-Assessment-FAQs-2015.pdf. Last Accessed 16 Dec 2023

The Wolfsberg Group (2022) Wolfsberg group comment letter on the EU AML/CFT legislative package, https://db.wolfsberg-group.org/assets/cdadc063-1c94-42f6-8419-0892522596ae/Wolfsberg%20Joint%20Letter%20to%20EU%20Regulator_0.pdf. Last Accessed 16 Dec 2023

The Wolfsberg Group (2023) Consultation on effective management of ML/TF risks when providing access to financial services (EBA/CP/2022/13), https://db.wolfsberg-group.org/assets/6226de08-ef43-4839-815b-e0ff6157a02d/Wolfsberg%20IIF%20Comment%20letter%20to%20EBA%20on%20derisking.pdf. Last Accessed 16 Dec 2023

The World Bank (2009) Combating money laundering and the financing of terrorism: a comprehensive training guide

Transparency International (2021) TI Australia submission to the legal and constitutional affairs reference committee inquiry into the adequacy and efficacy of Australia's anti-money laundering and counter-terrorism financing (AML/CTF) regime. Submission 17. file:///C:/Users/south/Downloads/Submission%2017.pdf Last Accessed 16 Dec 2023

Tsingou E (2018) New governors on the block: the rise of anti-money laundering professionals. Crime Law Soc Chang 69(2):191–205. https://doi.org/10.1007/s10611-017-9751-x

Turkington M (2019) The effectiveness of private sector engagement in International Financial Crime Countermeasures, PhD thesis, La Trobe University

Verhage A (2009) Corporations as a blind spot in research: explanations for a criminological tunnel vision. In: Cools M, De Kimpe S, De Ruyver B, Easton M, Pauwels L, Ponsaers P, Vande Walle G, Vander Beken T, Vander Laenen F, Vermeulen G (eds) Governance of security research papers series I, contemporary issues in the empirical study of crime. Maklu, Antwerp, pp 80–108

Verhage A (2011) The anti money laundering complex and the compliance industry. Routledge, London

Verhage A (2017) Great expectations but little evidence: policing money laundering. Int J Soc Soc Policy 37(7/8):477–490

Rachel Southworth Adjunct Lecturer, Australian Graduate School of Policing and Security, Charles Sturt University, Canberra, Australia. Rachel has a Ph.D. in 'Financial Crime Control: Risk, Regulation and the Role of the UK Banking Sector' from Cardiff University, Wales. Rachel specialises in leadership and strategic thinking in financial crime control. Rachel has worked internationally in a range of Financial Crime Compliance, Risk and Operations positions for major financial institutions in Australia, Hong Kong and the UK. Prior to working in the banking sector, Rachel has also worked in various policy roles, with the UK Regulator, the Financial Services Authority (now Financial Conduct Authority); the UK Treasury in Financial Crime Policy; and Surrey Police in Policing Policy. Rachel is alumni of the London School of Economics and Political Science (LSE) where she was awarded her MSc in Criminal Justice Policy and BSc in Sociology.

Michael Levi has been Professor of Criminology at Cardiff since 1991. His main work has been making sense of the linkages and differences between white-collar and organised crime and their public and private sector controls, intersecting with fraud, corruption, money laundering and terrorism locally and transnationally. He has major lifetime and other research prizes from the British, European and American Societies of Criminology, the Tackling Economic Crime Award in the UK 2019, and the UNODC/Al Thani Corruption Research and Education prize 2020. His external roles include membership of the Law Society's Money Laundering Task Force, of the Global Coalition to Fight Financial Crime and of the Global Initiative Against Transnational Organized Crime. His current and recent projects include A Public Health Approach to Fraud (https://www.westmidlands-pcc.gov.uk/fraud/); Fraud and its relationship to Pandemics and Economic Crises from 1850 to the Present; the Impact of technologies on criminal markets and transnational organised crime; and cyber-enabled fraud and money laundering projects. He is a Senior Associate Fellow of the Royal United Services Institute and of RAND Europe. See further, http://www.cardiff.ac.uk/people/view/38041-levi-michael.

The FATF's Combating of Financing of Proliferation Standards: Private Sector Implementation Challenges

Louis de Koker

Abstract The financial integrity standards of the Financial Action Task Force (FATF) create a framework that enlists financial institutions and designated businesses and professions. The effectiveness of the standards is highly dependent on the effectiveness of the measures employed by these regulated institutions. This chapter considers the challenges faced by regulated institutions to comply with the 2020 amendments to the FATF's standards aimed at combating the financing of the proliferation of weapons of mass destruction. The FATF first adopted proliferation financing (PF) measures in 2012. These support the targeted financial sanctions (TFS) measures of the United Nations Security Council (UNSC), i.e. the UNSC's sanctions against named individuals and entities linked to proliferation programs of Iran and the Democratic People's Republic of Korea. The discussion reflects initial perspectives gained in interviews with 46 experts globally. The challenges identified in this study can be clustered in four broad groups: navigating different definitions of PF; assessing and mitigating PF risk with limited information about PF threats and with a limited geopolitical and geo-economic capacity to identify and mitigate threats; monitoring trade-related transactions effectively to prevent PF-TFS while having limited or no information about the goods involved; and efficiently and effectively combating PF-TFS without being allowed to simplify compliance measures where risks are lower. An overarching challenge is, however, a surprising lack of considered policy about the purpose and strategic objectives of the new measures to be implemented.

Given the identified challenges the chapter proposes the following as elements of a national PF-TFS strategy: adopting a meaningful definition of PF that fits with the country's general proliferation policy; implementing a phased approach that first focuses on a select group of higher risk institutions with capacity; embracing a collaborative approach bringing that select group together with the range of government authorities that address aspects of PF-TFS to explore best practice approaches to supporting effective and efficient compliance; making appropriate use of the

L. de Koker (✉)
La Trobe Law School, Bundoora, VIC, Australia
e-mail: l.dekoker@latrobe.edu.au

D. Goldbarsht, L. de Koker (eds.), *Financial Crime and the Law*, Ius Gentium: Comparative Perspectives on Law and Justice 115,
https://doi.org/10.1007/978-3-031-59543-1_6

FATF's low risk exemption to exclude low risk institutions from PF-TFS risk management obligations; facilitating PF-TFS compliance by supporting sectoral risk assessments and the development of appropriate compliance technologies; tailoring compliance expectations given the limited information that institutions may have; and monitoring implementation for intended and unintended consequences and reporting on impact and progress.

Though ambitious, FATF standards are minimum standards. Countries and regulated institutions may therefore elect to go beyond the standards and adopt policies, regulations and compliance practices that serve broader non-proliferation and disarmament objectives. Given the current increase in WMD risks globally that approach deserves serious consideration. Increased compliance with global non-proliferation obligations is required and the FATF's financial surveillance framework can provided a helpful additional layer of controls.

1 Introduction

In 2012 the Financial Action Task Force (FATF), the intergovernmental global standard-setting body for anti-money laundering and combating of financing of terrorism (AML/CTF), broadened the scope of its standards to aspects of financing of proliferation of weapons of mass destruction (WMD). In 2020 it revisited its proliferation financing (PF) standards to require countries and regulated institutions to undertake risk assessments and to enhance their risk control measures where risks were assessed as higher. The FATF's combating of PF (CPF) measures support the targeted financial sanctions (TFS) measures of the United Nations Security Council (UNSC), i.e. the UNSC's sanctions against named individuals and entities linked to proliferation programs of Iran and the Democratic People's Republic of Korea.

This chapter considers key challenges that regulated institutions face when complying with these standards.

The chapter reflects initial perspectives on these challenges gained in a study of the implementation of the FATF's PF standards. The study included semi-structured interviews by video link. These were conducted from August 2022 to February 2023 with 46 FATF, proliferation and PF experts, compliance consultants, development experts, representatives of civil society and compliance officers representing global, larger, and smaller banks.

Interviewees included representatives from two FATF member delegations; three FATF-Style Regional Body (FSRB) secretariats, PF and WMD experts from two nuclear weapon states and compliance experts in both developed and developing countries. Participants were based in the UK, US, EU, Africa, and the Asia-Pacific.

The study was conducted in accordance with human research ethics approval given by La Trobe University (application number HEC22146) and consent obtained from interviewees. The interviews were conducted on the basis of anonymity. Given the small size of the PF community, information about the interviewees and the institutions they work for is deliberately limited in this chapter to avoid deidentification. Where cited, each participant (P) is identified with a unique number and classification indicating whether the participant is a government official (O), private sector expert (P), or FATF or FSRB secretariat official (S).

2 The FATF: From Money Laundering to Proliferation Financing

On 24 January 2023 the Science and Security Board of the Bulletin of the Atomic Scientists placed the hands of the Doomsday Clock at 90 seconds to midnight. This is the closest to midnight—the nightmare hour of global catastrophe—in its 75-year existence. The increasing nuclear risk linked to the war in Ukraine, the continuing investment of the Democratic the Democratic People's Republic of North Korea (DPRK) in its nuclear program, and the increasing fragility of international non-proliferation agreements added to this assessment.[1]

Due to global security risks posed by WMD, proliferation measures—broadly defined as measures aimed at combating the acquisition and use WMD—have been increasing over the past two decades. As a result, the FATF, the intergovernmental global standard-setting body for AML/CTF, was given the mandate in 2008 to also combat PF, i.e. financial or economic support for the proliferation of WMD.[2] This chapter considers private sector challenges relating to the implementation of risk-based elements that were linked to the FATF's PF standards in 2020. Brief background information about the FATF, non-proliferation and the FATF's PF mandate will be helpful to frame the 2020 amendments.

2.1 *The FATF and Its Standards*

In 1989 the G7 established a task force to advise on how the large economies can best protect their financial systems against drug-related money laundering abuse. In 1990 the task force, known as the FATF, formulated 40 recommendations.[3] These recommendations developed into global standards with more than 200 jurisdictions

[1] Science and Security Board (2023). Also see NATO (2023), par 45: "NATO will take all necessary steps to ensure the credibility, effectiveness, safety and security of the nuclear deterrent mission. This includes continuing to modernise NATO's nuclear capability and updating planning to increase flexibility and adaptability of the Alliance's nuclear forces, while exercising strong political control at all times. The Alliance reaffirms the imperative to ensure the broadest possible participation by Allies concerned in NATO's nuclear burden-sharing arrangements to demonstrate Alliance unity and resolve." The start of this new nuclear race comes at a time when nuclear war and deterrence expertise is limited. See Bender 2023.

[2] Financial Action Task Force (2012-2023).

[3] Financial Action Task Force (1991), De Koker and Turkington (2016).

politically committing to the implementation of these standards in domestic law, law enforcement and financial regulation. In 1996 the FATF framework was extended to proceeds of all serious offences,[4] and in 2001 to financing of terrorism.[5]

The FATF standards create a framework where financial institutions and designated non-financial businesses and professions must identify and verify the official identities of their customers. They must also profile their customers and use these profiles to identify unusual and suspicious transactions that may involve proceeds of crime. Collectively these measures comprise so-called customer due diligence measures.[6] Should concerns remain after internal investigations, these transactions must be reported to national financial intelligence units that must support law enforcement agencies with appropriate financial intelligence. Certain standard transactions, for example large cash transactions, may also be made reportable by countries regardless of whether they are suspicious.

Since 2012 the FATF standards require countries and institutions to assess their money laundering and terrorist financing crime risk exposure and to tailor their control measures accordingly. This is known as the FATF's risk-based approach. Regulated institutions therefore maintain different customer due diligence processes for customers depending on their risk profiles. Continuing risk assessment processes assess changes in customer profiles and result in appropriate changes in the customer due diligence measures as well.

The FATF standards therefore determine aspects of national regulations, law enforcement and of compliance programs of regulated financial institutions (e.g., banks, insurance companies, etc.) and designated businesses and professions (lawyers, accountants, real estate agents, etc.) worldwide.

Country-level compliance with the standards is closely monitored. The FATF and FSRBs assess countries for their level of technical compliance with the standards and, since 2013, also for the effectiveness of their measures. Countries that are deemed to fall short may be grey- or blacklisted. Risk management requirements that apply in relation to listed countries and their institutions hold negative economic impacts, and listed countries generally work hard to reach the required compliance levels in order to be delisted.[7] Institutional compliance is also monitored at a domestic level by regulators. Banks and other regulated institutions that fail to comply with AML/CTF laws face penalties that may run into billions of dollars.

Before considering the obligations of regulated institutions it is important to distinguish more clearly between PF and PF-TFS as governments and regulated institutions will have to navigate the conceptual complexities that this differentiation introduced.

[4]Financial Action Task Force (1996).

[5]Financial Action Task Force (2001).

[6]Lyman et al. (2019); Cooper et al. (2020).

[7]De Koker et al. (2023).

2.2 *Non-Proliferation*

The concept of non-proliferation focuses on preventing the spread of nuclear weapons and nuclear weapons technology and the banning of biological and chemical weapons. This is a complex field where several international, regional, and bilateral instruments provide the global non-proliferation framework and national laws and regimes detail these at a domestic level. Key global instruments are:

- the Non-Proliferation Treaty (NPT);[8]
- the Biological and Toxin Weapons Convention (BTWC);[9] and
- the Chemical Weapons Convention (CWC).[10]

While the BTWC and CWC prohibit the development or use of biological and chemical weapons,[11] the NPT prohibits the proliferation of nuclear weapons. The NPT also obliges all parties, including nuclear weapon States, to negotiate towards nuclear disarmament. The non-proliferation obligation of the NPT is subject to compliance and enforcement procedures but not the disarmament obligation.[12] Concern about the lack of progress in this regard led to the adoption of the 2017 Treaty on the Prohibition of Nuclear Weapons (TPNW)[13] that aims to ultimately eliminate nuclear weapons. To date the TPNW has mostly been signed by smaller, non-nuclear weapon States.[14]

---

[8]The Treaty on the Non-Proliferation of Nuclear Weapons, opened for signature on 1 July 1968, 729 UNTS 161 (entered into force 5 March 1970).

[9]The Convention on the Prohibition of the Development, Production and Stockpiling of Bacteriological (Biological) and Toxin Weapons and on Their Destruction, opened for signature 10 April 1972, 1015 UNTS 163) (entered into force 3 March 1975).

[10]The Convention on the Prohibition of the Development, Production, Stockpiling and Use of Chemical Weapons and on their Destruction, opened for signature 13 January 1993, 1974 UNTS 45 (entered into force 13 April 1997).

[11]The USA, the last possessor State of chemical weapons, completed the destruction of its declared chemical weapons stockpile on 7 July 2023. See Organisation for the Prohibition of Chemical Weapons (2023).

[12]In 1995, following the end the Cold War, 173 States reaffirmed their renunciation of nuclear weapons in return for the explicitly reaffirmed commitment by China, France, Russia, the UK and the US, to eventually eliminate their nuclear arsenals. Cirincione (2005). Little resulted from that promise and in 2023 the global nuclear arsenal increased again. Stockholm International Peace Research Institute (2023).

[13]The Treaty on the Prohibition of Nuclear Weapons opened for signature at the United Nations in New York on 20 September 2017 (entered into force on 22 January 2021).

[14]Tensions are evident in relation to the TPNW. See e.g., NATO Heads of State and Government (2023), par 54: "We reiterate that the Treaty on the Prohibition of Nuclear Weapons (TPNW) stands in opposition to and is inconsistent and incompatible with the Alliance's nuclear deterrence policy, is at odds with the existing non-proliferation and disarmament architecture, risks undermining the NPT, and does not take into account the current security environment. The TPNW does not change the legal obligations on our countries with respect to nuclear weapons. We do not accept any argument that the TPNW reflects or in any way contributes to the development of customary international law. We call on our partners and all other countries to reflect realistically on the ban

The NPT has more than 190 signatories, including five nuclear weapon States: China, France, the Russian Federation, the UK, and the US.[15] The treaty empowers for example, the International Atomic Energy Agency (IAEA) to inspect countries for compliance with identified safeguards. These powers extend to countries that are not parties to the treaty but that agreed to implement certain safeguards and be inspected for compliance by the IAEA.[16]

Ensuring compliance with non-proliferation obligations is challenging and generally involves physical inspections as well as automated monitoring, for example for evidence of nuclear tests.[17] As became clear after the invasion of Iraq, concerns about alleged breaches do not necessarily reflect reality.[18] The invasion was predicated on intelligence that Iraq held WMDs in breach of its international obligations. This intelligence was later found to be false.[19]

In addition to the three key treaties, there are test ban treaties, where states agreed to not carry out (certain) nuclear weapon tests; and US-Russia nuclear arms limitation and reduction treaties, relating generally to the numbers or types of their deployed nuclear delivery vehicles and nuclear warheads.[20] President Putin, however, suspended Russia's participation in the last remaining US-Russia arms control treaty in February 2023.[21]

Importantly, non-proliferation sanctions have been adopted by the United Nations Security Council (UNSC). The UNSC has been acting under Chapter VII of the United Nations Charter, a chapter that enables the UNSC to address threats to the peace, breach of the peace, or an act of aggression. These resolutions bind all UN members. The UNSC currently has 15 sanctions regimes which focus on supporting political settlement of conflicts, non-proliferation, and counter-terrorism. The UNSC for example adopted Resolution 1540 in 2004, aimed at preventing non-state actors from acquiring nuclear, biological, and chemical weapons, their means of delivery, and related materials and adopted focused sanctions against Iran and the DPRK.

In 2015, in terms of the Joint Comprehensive Plan of Action (JCPOA), the UN lifted nuclear sanctions against Iran while retaining restrictions on Iran's missile

---

treaty's impact on international peace and security, including on the NPT, and join us in working to improve collective security through tangible and verifiable measures that can reduce strategic risks and enable lasting progress on nuclear disarmament."

[15] Suseanu (2021) Russia and the US hold about 90% of the global nuclear arsenal. See Stockholm International Peace Research Institute (2023).

[16] Suseanu (2021), p. 5: "All five NWSs party to the NPT have concluded voluntary offer agreements with the IAEA. Three countries that are not Party to the NPT, India, Israel, and Pakistan, have item-specific safeguards agreements in force with the IAEA."

[17] Baker (2023).

[18] Jervis (2006).

[19] The Commission on the Intelligence Capabilities of the United States Regarding Weapons of Mass Destruction (2005).

[20] Kimball (2022); Arms Control Association (2023a).

[21] The treaty has had however a rocky pathway after the Trump declined to engage in negotiations to extend it, and even more so after the invasion of Ukraine. See ABC News (2023).

activities, established rules for the controlled supply of nuclear goods for its civilian nuclear program, and maintained specific targeted financial sanctions.[22] In essence, JCPOA imposed restrictions on Iran's nuclear program in exchange for sanctions relief. Key restrictions in terms of this agreement have timelines and conditions for expiry. The JCPOA has, however, been fragile since the US unilaterally withdrew from it in 2018. Its medium-term future is uncertain, but it is set to terminate on 18 October 2025 when the UNSC will conclude consideration of the Iran nuclear issue.[23]

In addition to implementing and enforcing these sanctions, many countries also adopted their own, autonomous sanctions, aspects of which may also link to non-proliferation.

Iran and the DPRK have also been countries of focus for the FATF. As a result of a lack of commitment and progress to meet the FATF standards they have been blacklisted by the FATF. This means that the FATF requires countries to apply countermeasures to protect the international financial system from ML/TF/PF risks emanating from Iran and the DPRK and, since 2022, Myanmar.[24] Countermeasures may include enhanced due diligence in relation to affected persons and transactions and a range of risk measures that may limit transactions with the country and its institutions. In practice, however, banks debanked many affected customers linked to the blacklisted countries.

In this complicated context the FATF standards were leveraged to strengthen aspects of global action on non-proliferation.

2.3 *Broadening the FATF Standards to PF*

G8 discussions on strengthening non-proliferation led to PF being referred to the FATF in 2006.[25] While some participants pressed for a broader scope of the FATF's non-proliferation measures, the eventual scope was narrowed to aspects of the UNSC's non-proliferation sanctions.

There are various reasons for the limited scope of the FATF measures. Five nuclear weapon States that are parties to the NPT (China, France, the Russian Federation, the UK, and the US) are also members of the FATF (with membership of the Russian Federation suspended in February 2023). They are also the permanent members of the UN Security Council. In addition, India, a nuclear State, and Israel, that is generally viewed as nuclear State, are not State parties to the NPT but are also

[22] Kassenova and Early (2023), p. 10. The JCPOA is set to terminate on 18 October 2025.

[23] Robinson (2023); Arms Control Association (2023b).

[24] De Koker et al. (2023).

[25] These discussions in 2006 in Paris took place against the backdrop of especially G8 calls for action in G8 (2003, 2004, 2006). They resulted in the decision to refer proliferation financing to the FATF for appropriate responses.

members of the FATF. The FATF takes decisions by consensus. It is therefore unlikely that the FATF standards would go beyond what the most conservative and protective of these States are comfortable to endorse.

In 2012 rule-based[26] PF measures were incorporated into the revised set of 2012 FATF standards.[27] They were limited however not only to UNSC sanctions but also to targeted financial sanctions (TFS) that formed part of those sanctions.[28] The key standard, Recommendation 7, reads as follows:

> Countries should implement targeted financial sanctions to comply with United Nations Security Council resolutions relating to the prevention, suppression and disruption of proliferation of weapons of mass destruction and its financing. These resolutions require countries to freeze without delay the funds or other assets of, and to ensure that no funds and other assets are made available, directly or indirectly, to or for the benefit of, any person or entity designated by, or under the authority of, the United Nations Security Council under Chapter VII of the Charter of the United Nations.

In practice, that means that the FATF PF standards are focused on support for UNSC sanctions against Iran and the DPRK. That narrow focus is however limited even further: the PF standards are restricted to the UNSC's TFS in relation to those two countries, i.e., they are limited to those sanctions levied on named entities and individuals, and do not extend to general activities that are listed as part of the UNSC's activity-based sanctions.

The FATF recognizes that PF risks range broader than its standards. In its 2021 PF guidance it described the broader risks as follows:[29]

> The broader PF risks, which are not covered in the updated Recommendation 1, refer to the risk of WMD proliferation and the risk of financing of proliferation. WMD proliferation refers to the manufacture, acquisition, possession, development, export, trans-shipment, brokering, transport, transfer, stockpiling or use of nuclear, chemical or biological weapons and their means of delivery and related materials (including both dual-use technologies and dual-use goods used for non-legitimate purposes). The financing of proliferation refers to the risk of raising, moving, or making available funds, other assets or other economic resources, or financing, in whole or in part, to persons or entities for purposes of WMD proliferation, including the proliferation of their means of delivery or related materials (including both dual-use technologies and dual-use goods for non-legitimate purposes.

While clarifying the narrow scope of the application of its provisions, the FATF also nudged countries to consider the broader scope when undertaking risk assessments and designing risk responses to meet the FATF's PF-TFS standards:[30]

---

[26] For the rule-based approach, see Goldbarsht and De Koker (2024).

[27] Financial Action Task Force (2012-2023).

[28] See Rec 7 of Financial Action Task Force (2012-2023). The FATF explicitly recognised its narrow focus on TFS and noted in Financial Action Task Force (2021a), par 14 that "United Nations Security Council Resolutions are much broader and prescribe other types of sanctions (such as travel bans) and other types of financial provisions (such as activity-based financial prohibitions, category-based sanctions and vigilance measures)."

[29] Financial Action Task Force (2021b), n. 7.

[30] Financial Action Task Force (2021b), n 7.

> An understanding of the risk of WMD proliferation and its underlying financing, which is not required under the FATF Standards, may have a positive contribution to the understanding of the risk of the breach, non-implementation or evasion of PF-TFS (i.e. the narrow definition of PF risks covered in the FATF Standards), and assist the implementation of risk-based measures and targeted financial sanctions.

The FATF standards are therefore not focused on financing of proliferation by States that are not subject to UNSC sanctions. The narrow focus on Iran and the DPRK as the countries subject to UNSC TFS leaves other relevant countries out of scope. Non-NPT States have developed nuclear capacities and other States have used chemical and biological weapons.[31] In addition, the UNSC targeted financial sanctions scheme is under pressure. Russian and Chinese companies have been implicated in DPRK sanctions breaches and Russia and China have not supported increased UNSC sanctions against the DPRK since 2017, despite the country's aggressive increase in its WMD capacity. In March 2024 a Russian UNSC veto brought the UN Panel of Experts on the DPRK and its work to an end. As noted in Sect. 2.2, the UNSC sanctions against Iran are also being terminated. The future of the UNSC's targeted financial sanctions, the very basis of the FATF's Recommendation 7, is therefore uncertain.[32] For a variety of reasons, a broader scope of the FATF PF standards would have been more supportive of non-proliferation in general.

FATF standards are minimum standards and countries may go beyond them. In addition, countries are bound under international law to implement UNSC sanctions, including those aspects that are not covered by the FATF standards. How those are implemented and aligned with FATF-related measures may differ from country to country and institution to institution.

2.4 *Introducing PF-TFS Risk Measures*

The FATF's new mandatory risk-based approach that it introduced in 2012 did not extend to its PF-TFS standards. The UNSC sanctions are rule-based and hence PF-TFS measures were excluded from the FATF's risk-based approach. In practice that meant that the standards did not compel countries to undertake national PF-TFS risk assessments. Neither were they required to compel their regulated institutions to perform PF-TFS risk assessments and adopt risk-based measures to counter identified risks. In practice regulated institutions could therefore implement PF-TFS regulations easily by scanning customer names against UNSC sanctions lists.

[31] United Nations (2023).

[32] Keatinge and Arnold (2023). In July 2023 senior Russian and Chinese joined the North Korean leader Kim Jong Un at a military parade where the DPRK's newest nuclear-capable missiles were on show. Smith and Yim (2023). This raises further questions regarding the willingness of China and Russia to pursue UNSC sanctions against the DPRK.

FATF's presidency rotates and increasingly each presidency identifies priority goals for its term. Improving the FATF's contribution to combating proliferation financing standards was a key goal of the 2018–2019 US presidency of FATF.[33] Draft amendments to Recommendation 1 relating to the risk-based approach were negotiated during the Chinese presidency of the FATF and published for public comment following the June 2020 plenary of the FATF. Public consultation ended on 31 August 2020[34] and the final texts were adopted by the FATF in October 2020, under the German presidency.

The enhanced PF standards require countries and their AML/CTF/CPF-regulated institutions to undertake PF-TFS risk assessments and to adopt enhanced control measures where higher risks were identified. As the UNSC sanctions regimes do not allow for a risk-based approach to sanctions compliance, PF-TFS measures may not be simplified where risks are assessed as lower:[35]

> Where countries identify lower risks, they should ensure that the measures applied are commensurate with the level of proliferation financing risk, while still ensuring full implementation of the targeted financial sanctions as required in Recommendation 7.

As a result of submissions during the brief consultation period the FATF did introduce a partial low risk exemption in a footnote to the interpretative note to Recommendation 1:

> Countries may decide to exempt a particular type of financial institution or DNFBP from the requirements to identify, assess, monitor, manage and mitigate proliferation financing risks, provided there is a proven low risk of proliferation financing relating to such financial institutions or DNFBPs. However, full implementation of the targeted financial sanctions as required by Recommendation 7 is mandatory in all cases.

The exemption, when granted, therefore only excludes institutions from the need to adopt PF-TFS risk management measures. They must still comply in full with Recommendation 7, for example by scanning the names of parties to transactions against UNSC sanctions lists, and taking appropriate action where name matching occurs. Further aspects of the exemption are discussed in greater detail in context in Sect. 3 below.

3 Institutional PF-TFS Challenges to Navigate

As outlined in Sect. 2.1, regulated institutions are key data collection, data analysis and reporting role players in the AML/CTF/CPF framework. The FATF standards position them as the main guardians of the integrity of the formal financial system.

[33] Financial Action Task Force (2018).

[34] Adoption followed a very brief public consultation opportunity. See Financial Action Task Force (2020). For a submission see De Koker (2020).

[35] FATF (2012-2023), Rec 1.

Proliferation financiers use tools and strategies that resemble those used by terrorist financiers and money launderers, e.g., setting up front companies, hiding beneficial ownership, channeling transactions through third countries, etc.[36] When concerns grew that the anti-proliferation strategy was faltering, it made sense to increase the crime combating role of these institutions.

In the earliest discussions of potential global measures that could be taken against PF, officials raised concerns about an increased regulatory burden on regulated institutions.[37] The FATF was also sensitive to overly burdensome expectations and to some of the limitations of regulated institutions. In their 2010 status report on policy development and consultation on combating PF, they commented as follows on the ability of regulated institutions to identify potential proliferation based on screening of goods:[38]

> [T]he evaluation of whether goods are involved in a transaction requires a large amount of technical knowledge only available to export controls experts and/or exporters. Goods lists pose a tremendous challenge even for export control enforcement and a greater one for real time screening than entity lists. Furthermore, FIs in general lack the expertise to discriminate between legitimate and proliferation-sensitive goods.[39]

The 2010 FATF report furthermore stressed that "increased awareness and effective information sharing are critical in enabling FIs to address proliferation financing risks"[40] and expressed concern that "increased awareness seems to be concentrated among anti-money laundering and compliance specialists in major international banks in the financial sector while awareness of proliferation finance risks seems more limited among small- and medium-sized FIs."

Concerns about the ability of financial institutions to play a meaningful role in relation to PF were also raised in 2011, during FATF consultations regarding Recommendation 7.[41] The International Banking Federation, for example, noted that:[42]

> For the great majority of transactions, financial institutions do not have the necessary information that would let them distinguish between a transaction involving weapons of

[36] Brewer (2017); Stewart et al. (2020).

[37] These discussions in 2006 in Paris took place against the backdrop of especially G8 calls for action in G8 (2003, 2004, 2006). They resulted in the decision to refer proliferation financing to the FATF for appropriate responses.

[38] Financial Action Task Force (2010), par 73.

[39] This concern was again aired in 2011 when the Banking Association of South Africa responded to FATF consultations on proposed revisions to the standards. See Financial Action Task Force (2011), p 167: "Sect. 22 on page 9 notes that the FATF is still considering including 'proliferation financing' within its scope. We have motivated on several occasions before that the financial sector is unable to provide any support to government's anti-proliferation efforts due to the difficulties associated with 'dual use' items. We again recommend that the FATF not engage itself or its members this impossible effort, which is based left to trained and experienced customs officials."

[40] Financial Action Task Force Force (2010), par 81.

[41] Financial Action Task Force Force (2010), par 84.

[42] Financial Action Task Force (2011).

> mass destruction and ordinary and perfectly innocent transactions. While a financial institution may be able to offer a limited supplemental and secondary role, the primary responsibility for detecting weapons of mass destruction properly rests with customs and export control officials at the border.

One participant in this study who participated in the discussions at that time mentioned that these concerns about the capacity of the private sector informed the limited, PF-TFS-focused footprint of Recommendation 7. When the FATF consulted on introducing PF-TFS risk assessments in 2020, however, the same objections were not publicly raised by regulated institutions. Large banks that participated in consultation meetings did not voice concern about their ability to comply with enhanced standards. Some stated that they were already doing so as part of their standard compliance practice. Smaller regulated institutions and designated non-financial businesses and professions, on the other hand, were largely absent from the discussions. Civil society and academia participated to a limited extent. They pointed to unintended consequences to financial inclusion and called for lower risk institutions to be excluded from the risk assessment obligation and for regulatory support for assessments and appropriate risk mitigation responses.[43] The concern resulted in the adoption of the low-risk PF-TFS exemption by the FATF, as mentioned in Sect. 2.4. In addition, the FATF issued non-binding guidance on the role of government agencies to share information with regulated institutions.[44]

This study identified a range of key challenges that institutions must navigate when implementing risk-based PF measures. These challenges can broadly be grouped as follows:

- navigating different definitions of PF;
- assessing and mitigating PF risk with limited information about PF threats and with a limited geopolitical and geoeconomic capacity to identify and mitigate threats;
- monitoring trade-related transactions effectively to prevent PF-TFS while having limited or no information about the goods involved; and
- efficiently and effectively combating PF-TFS without being allowed to simplify compliance measures where risks are lower.

These are discussed in greater detail below.

3.1 Navigating Different Definitions of PF

As discussed above, the 2020 changes to the FATF standards require countries and regulated institutions to undertake PF-TFS risk assessments. In compliance with these new standards, countries have started to undertake their national risk

[43] See e.g. De Koker (2020).

[44] Financial Action Task Force (2021a, b).

assessments. While risk assessments of some countries focus on PF-TFS, other countries adopted the broad proliferation financing definition for their assessment exercise, i.e., a definition not limited to breaches of the UNSC targeted financial sanctions. Among the countries adopting a broader definition some differences are also evident. In addition, the proliferation financing risk assessments also differ in scope and focus.

The 2022 PF risk assessment of the US provides a good example of an assessment process that adopted the FATF's broad definition as its point of departure:[45]

> To establish a baseline for a comprehensive CPF regime, the United States uses the FATF's definition from its 2021 PF Risk Assessment Guidance:
>
> The financing of proliferation refers to the risk of raising, moving, or making available funds, other assets or economic resources, or financing, in whole or in part, to persons or entities for purposes of WMD proliferation, including the proliferation of their means of delivery or related material (including both dual-use technologies and dual-use goods for non-legitimate purposes).

The 2022 PF risk assessment of Australia adopted the Royal United Services Institute's working definition, which is a more detailed, but also more extensive version, of the broader definition:[46]

> Proliferation financing is when a person: a. makes available an asset; or b. provides a financial service; or c. conducts a financial transaction; and the person [knows that, or is reckless as to whether,] the asset, financial service or financial transaction is intended to, in whole or in part, facilitate the proliferation of WMDs, regardless of whether the activity occurs or is attempted.
>
> The specified activities that comprise WMD proliferation include: a. the manufacture, production, possession, acquisition, stockpiling, storage, development, transportation, sale, supply, transfer, export, transhipment or use of: i. nuclear weapons; or ii. chemical weapons; or iii. biological weapons; or iv. materials related to nuclear weapons, chemical weapons or biological weapons that are prescribed by Regulations; or b. the provision of technical training, advice, service, brokering or assistance related to any of the activities in Paragraph (a).

Hong Kong's 2022 Money Laundering and Terrorist Financing Report, on the other hand provides an example of a risk assessment that employs FATF's narrow, TFS-focused definition:

> In the context of R.1, PF risk refers strictly and only to the potential breach, non-implementation or evasion of the TFS obligations referred to in Recommendation 7.[47]

South Africa also employs the narrow definition. It urges regulated institutions to consider the broader definition, but the regulator focuses its industry guidance only

[45] Department of the Treasury (2022).

[46] AUSTRAC (2022), p. 11.

[47] Financial Services and the Treasury Bureau (2022), par 9.1 read with 9.4.

on PF-TFS. In addition, however, it focuses its guidance only on PF-TFS in relation to the DPRK, and not also in relation to Iran.[48]

The use of different national definitions of PF, and even the use of similar definitions with different wording, combined with differences in scope and focus of the assessments, create a range of challenges for regulated institutions that operate across borders÷.

Firstly, it makes it difficult to compare and appraise the PF-TFS risk levels of different countries. What may be held to pose a standard or lower risk in one country may pose a higher risk from the perspective of a jurisdiction that uses a broader definition. Proliferation schemes generally involve a cross-border element. The lack of definitional standardisation complicates the task of compliance officers who need to consider the risks posed by the jurisdictions that are involved in a specific export transaction.

Secondly, different definitions may also bring different methodologies and typologies into play, especially where specific PF-TFS typologies relate to geopolitical features of Iran and the DPRK.

Thirdly, the use of different definitions complicates the management of compliance in global groups that operate in different countries. Standardised risk assessment and compliance practices will need to be adjusted to respond to national differences. Alternatively, a compliance approach that responds to the strictest national regime may need to be adopted groupwide. The latter may increase compliance costs and lead to over-compliance in countries with less strict approaches.[49]

The FATF standards are aimed at creating a standardised AML/CTF approach globally. This is predicated on the so-called "weakest link" view, i.e., that criminals will abuse the system of the countries and institutions that are not sufficiently compliant, thereby threatening their more compliant counterparts. In relation to proliferation, however, we are not seeing the same level of standardisation of the PF concept compared to the money laundering and terrorism financing concepts. This approach stems from the political tensions in the global proliferation space.[50] While the reason is understandable the lack of standardisation will result in a weaker PF-TFS legal and compliance framework globally. It will also add to the compliance costs of financial institutions that operate in multiple jurisdictions. This increase in costs may in turn result in de-banking of customers who cannot be served profitably.[51]

[48] Financial Intelligence Centre (2022).

[49] De Koker and Symington (2014); De Koker and Casanovas (2024).

[50] See Sect. 2.2 above.

[51] See Sect. 3.4 for a brief discussion of de-banking.

3.2 *Limited Information About Threats and Limited Geopolitical and Geoeconomic Capacity to Identify and Mitigate Threats*

To assess and manage PF-TFS risks, regulated institutions need to understand the related threats appropriately. Regulated institutions are heavily reliant on governments to provide them with appropriate information. Participants, however, pointed to concerns regarding the usefulness of the information that they receive regarding national PF-TFS threats and risks. National risk assessments are being undertaken but many are not particularly informative,[52] in some cases because sensitive information is stripped out before a sanitized version is released publicly. One FSRB representative, P1(S), commented as follows on PF-TFS national risk assessments:

> We don't think that the private sector is obtaining sufficient information for them to appreciate the risk behind proliferation financing in their respective jurisdictions. Even if you look at the report of Country X (deidentified), for example, it was set in a general way, and possibly based more on speculation than the actuality on the ground. So, this might also impact on the understanding of PF risk by the reporting entities in these kind of jurisdictions.

A global PF-TFS expert, P2(P), additionally expressed frustration that national risk assessments are not appropriately communicated to all government and private sector stakeholders:

> It is important to consider what the value of that risk assessment is to external stakeholders. How widely has it been distributed within government, or is it just staying within the FIU? Then, has that risk assessment or at least some version of it, perhaps a sanitised one, been shared with the private sector? We always say, 'If you do your risk assessment and you just park it on a shelf, that's not particularly helpful to anyone.' The idea is that you communicate, and you distribute those findings to the key stakeholders, and the private sector is on the frontline of that. That's the question that I have. To what extent has that risk assessment benefitted the private sector?

In AML/CTF increasing attention is given to public-private information-sharing partnerships.[53] These can be valuable[54] but they are restricted to the largest regulated institutions in jurisdictions and their benefit to smaller regulated institutions can be negligible. Aaron Arnold, a global PF expert, commented as follows on information-sharing challenges from a PF perspective:[55]

> Suggesting that states promote better information-sharing relationships between public and private sectors, however, has become an almost comedic mantra – often repeated, but rarely

[52] Australia's proliferation financing risk assessment contains helpful information but its threat-related information is very high level. See AUSTRAC (2022).

[53] Lyman et al. (2019).

[54] Maxwell (2019).

[55] Arnold (2022). Also see Financial Action Task Force (2021a), par 27 where the FATF acknowledges that, due to the sensitivities of first PF NRAs, their results may not be fully shared with regulated institutions but that some sharing may take place for example through closed-door briefings to discuss outcomes of the assessment. This will not be of benefit to the majority of smaller regulated institutions that are unlikely to be invited to such closed-door meetings.

> understood or followed. In some cases, sharing information may not be feasible due to security concerns; in others there may be legitimate legal or regulatory challenges. For instance, information sharing among manufacturers in the US could run afoul of antitrust legislation. In other cases, the political will to do so may just not be present.

Without appropriate information, it is unlikely that regulated institutions will be able to make a meaningful contribution to combating PF risk. Compliance measures will still be implemented. They will require time and resources, but they will be less likely to be effective.

3.2.1 Geopolitical and Geoeconomic Understanding

The FATF's PF-TFS strategy assumes that regulated institutions have a sophisticated level of knowledge regarding trade patterns and levels of industry development in countries that are disclosed as final export destinations. Controlled goods would not be exported directly to Iran and the DPRK but diverted to other countries from where they will be shipped to their final destination. Some countries are more likely to be such transit destinations, often linked to their geographical position and their political relationship with the country of final destination. Those relationships may change and some of the shifts may be rapid, as was evident after the full-scale invasion of Ukraine in 2022.

The FATF's list of *Maritime Sector Risk Indicators* in its proliferation guidance, for example, sets out several indicators that may flag proliferation activity.[56] Selected indicators and some of the knowledge required to identify and respond to those indicators are summarized in Table 1.

While indicators of PF are helpful, indicators such as these require a higher level of geopolitical knowledge and expertise than required in relation to anti-money laundering. There is no data now pointing to most regulated institutions having the required level of such knowledge. Assumptions about geopolitical knowledge should not be made lightly. In a 2017 experiment conducted at the request of the *New York Times*, only 36% of Americans, out of 1746 adults, could correctly point to the DPRK on a world map.[57] Several participants in the study agreed that many compliance officers of small, regulated institutions outside the Asia-Pacific region will face similar challenges. Instances where companies incorrectly assigned the country code for the DPRK to goods exported to South Korea and where these were reported by the countries to the UN were noted by the UN Panel of Experts.[58] These are general human errors but point to some of the challenges that will have to be navigated in this area. In essence, however, we do not have firm evidence that

---

[56] Financial Action Task Force (2021a), par 31.

[57] Quealy (2017). Fifty three percent of participants with post-graduate degrees could correctly locate North Korea.

[58] United Nations Panel of Experts (2022), par 106 and Table 5. Table 5 records that one country declared that the mistake was: "(d)ue to declarant's inability to differentiate between the Democratic People's Republic of Korea and the Republic of Korea / supplier was the Republic of Korea."

Table 1 Maritime Sector PF Indicators and Knowledge Required[a]

Indicator	Knowledge required
Shipment of goods incompatible with the technical level of the country to which it is being shipped, e.g., semiconductor manufacturing equipment being shipped to a country that has no electronics industry	Understanding the diverse uses of the goods Understanding of the current and developing state of relevant industries in the country that may use such goods
Shipment of goods is inconsistent with normal geographic trade patterns, e.g., the destination country does not normally export or import the goods listed in trade transaction documents	Understanding the normal geographic trade patterns of the destination country Understanding the state of innovation and industry development that may be relevant in the particular country
Shipment of goods is routed through a country with weak implementation of relevant UNSCR obligations and FATF Standards, export control laws or weak enforcement of export control laws	Understanding the level of current UNSCR and FATF compliance (especially challenging where regulations were amended, and practices changed since their last FATF/FSRB mutual evaluation or follow-up report) Understanding the quality of their export controls, the quality of compliance with those controls and the quality of enforcement in cases of non-compliance

[a]Source of Indicators: FATF. Source of Knowledge Required: Author

compliance officers of large and small regulated institutions have the level of knowledge to assess the geopolitical and geoeconomic elements of PF-TFS, and we do not have reasonable grounds for an assumption that that they possess that general level of knowledge.

This is however largely an informational challenge that may be addressed, at least in part, by appropriate regtech tools, provided that these tools can be informed by accurate and unbiased data. The data dilemma is considered in 4.3.4 and 4.3.5 below. Participants also pointed to information sources such as the Peddling Peril Index[59] and the Strategic Trade Atlas[60] that would be very helpful if combined with appropriate supportive technology, especially where these are made available by governments to regulated institutions. The cost barriers that small institutions face when having to obtain data or regtech solutions must not be underestimated.

In addition to Iran and the DPRK other countries may give rise to proliferation concerns. Specific countries are in the market for WMD technologies. Russia, a UNSC member, is currently posing an elevated nuclear threat. Where an institution adopts a broader view of PF risk, i.e., one going beyond Recommendation 7, compliance officers need to understand which countries pose a higher proliferation risk and how threats may present themselves.[61] Informational support for institutions that wish to combat PF and not only PF-TFS will be required. This will be an ongoing

[59] Albright et al. (2021).
[60] Versino et al. (2021).
[61] Arnold (2022).

challenge and occasional information sessions and general typologies will have limited value. A collaborative approach informed by appropriate intelligence will be required to support the effectiveness of a broader non-proliferation strategy.

3.2.2 PF-TFS Data Quality

Participants in this study identified PF-TFS case law, the King's College proliferation typologies,[62] and the reports of the UN Panel of Experts of the UNSC Sanctions Committee on the DPRK as particularly informative.[63] These reports are technical rich documents, but they are also political in nature. Some of their contents may therefore be compromised.

In 2022 an article on the impact of a US vacancy on the Panel cited Kleine-Ahlbrandt, a former expert of the UN's DPRK Panel of Experts, voicing concern that, without an American endeavour to push back against Chinese and Russian efforts to neuter key aspects of the report, the reports would be weakened:[64]

> If the U.S. isn't actively engaging with the Secretariat, China and Russia are able to use procedural and technical loopholes and other means to shorten and weaken the reports, in addition to actions within the Panel to hinder investigations," she explained.
>
> China attempted to whittle the 2020 report down from 20000 words to 8000 and the 2018 midterm report was not published as a result of a dispute between Russia and the U.S.[65]

Aaron Arnold, also a former expert of the UN Panel of Experts for DPRK, said that drafting the report sometimes sparked "heated" exchanges. Some of the points of difference may be detected in the language and footnotes. The 2022 article provided the following example:[66]

> To cite just one instance, the Panel's latest report notes how a North Korean company with ties to Pyongyang's weapons industry owns 60% of a China-based company. A footnote on the section indicates one expert pushed to remove this information, saying it needed further corroboration. Similar footnotes are typically sprinkled throughout the report, more often than not on sections that implicate China.

While the UN Panel of Experts reports are important sources of information, they do not pretend to be comprehensive, and the comprehensiveness and clarity of the information are impacted by the political nature of the Panel. To complicate matters for readers, countries that are criticized in the reports may also reject the findings of the Panel, leaving readers to judge which version they accept.[67] A further

[62] Brewer (2017).

[63] This UN Panel of Experts support supports the UNSC Sanctions Committee on North Korea.

[64] Jewell (2022).

[65] O'Carroll (2020).

[66] Jewell (2022).

[67] See for example, Republic of Namibia (2021), p. 391: "... [T]he UN suspected Namibia of having supported PF activities of the DPRK by availing certain persons access to conduct business

complication is that the reports will become increasingly dated over time. On 28 March 2024, Russia vetoed a UNSC resolution to renew the mandate of the Panel of Experts for another year. The veto brought the panel and its work to an end, unless a political solution is found.[68] Compliance officers may turn to court cases to access information about PF. There is however a limited number of reported cases.[69] Given that the relevant evidence was considered by the court, the information set out in the judgement would be of a higher quality. The judgement may however not capture the full facts of the PF scheme.

Sources such as these capture some of the information that is known about PF. The DPRK has been able to build its nuclear program despite global sanctions. This would indicate that a significant amount of proliferation and PF was not detected and may not be known. The current reports may give some indication of what is known about PF but may not reflect a significant amount of PF or, indeed, the most successful PF typologies.

The limited information on PF poses a challenge to effective PF risk management by regulated institutions. This, coupled with the limited data (small data) on PF-TF typologies, also complicates the development of reliable AI regtech tools to analyse transactions and identify potential PF-TFS breaches.[70] While technology is playing an increasing role to support risk management in AML/CTF/CPF, small data will remain a challenge in relation to effective PF-TFS transaction screening role.

3.3 *Limited Information About Goods Involved in Transactions*

Analysing financial transactions to find evidence that may point to proliferation activities is complex. As discussed above, proliferation often involve so-called controlled goods and especially dual-use goods, i.e., technology that can be abused to construct WMD or applied for civilian use, such as medical or engineering purposes. Many governments therefore maintain trade regimes that allow the export of listed technology only if the necessary permission is granted.

Exporters of such controlled goods therefore have obligations to ensure compliance with export control requirements. Export control regimes generally require an application for an export permit from the relevant government agency and the granting of the required permit. Customs authorities also have vital roles to play,

---

in the construction industry in Namibia. The Namibian Government not only denied such but went further to terminate all engagements with such persons from the DPRK and expelled them from the country."

[68] Arnold (2024).

[69] For Australia's first conviction for a breach of DPRK sanctions, see *R v Choi (No 10)* [2021] NSWSC 891.

[70] Bennett Moses and De Koker (2017).

as their officials can inspect the goods that are being exported and prevent unauthorised exports.[71]

Banks play key roles in international trade by ensuring payment for goods against their delivery. Trade finance bank instruments are designed to limit the risk of a party performing its part of the trade agreement should the other party fail to do so. As part of these processes, banks receive documents with information about the goods and the parties. This is viewed as an opportunity for banks to analyse the documents to identify potential PF.[72] The documents presented to the bank may, however, describe the goods incorrectly, whether intentionally or simply because the relevant party used different language to describe the goods. Whether the information about the goods is correctly disclosed to the bank can only be verified by those who inspect or can inspect the goods, for example customs officials.

An industry compliance expert with more than two decades experience in a range of developing countries, P3(P), raised practical questions regarding screening of transactions against national lists of dual-use goods:

> Getting to the likes of dual-use goods conceptually: There is no screening tool out there. Yeah, we've got Refinitiv and LexisNexis that may now be putting tools in place. But how do I screen against it? When do I screen them? Do I screen each and every trade against a dual-use goods list? What is my risk-based approach to dealing with that?

Dual-use goods screening tools, however, also have limitations. Proliferators often evade controlled goods processes by exporting goods that fall below the specifications of listed controlled goods but can be upgraded for WMD use when received at the final destination. Few compliance officers would have the technical expertise to identify that a trade transaction involves goods that may not be listed but may still be abused for proliferation purposes. P3(P), put it as follows:

> If we start screening for dual-use goods, that's fine, but it's almost a tick-box approach. I'm just going through the list and if this component happens to be on there and it's picked up, then yes, I've got a match, and we are not going to proceed. But there are goods that are one level down. Those guys (in trade finance) are never going to know that stuff. They are never going to know it. And that's the challenge we have.

P4(O), a leading PF-TFS expert, agreed that screening is challenging and that there is a need for advanced screening tools that can identify goods that may be susceptible to abuse:

> Once again, if you do pure screening against a list, you will only identify what's on the list. If there's a match between the invoice and the list, for example, you will only identify that. The out-of-the-box intelligence you can buy for screening applications won't give you that flexibility. That's where you need the artificial intelligence component right at the end of your screening process to identify stuff that looks very similar, but not equal to listed goods.

---

[71] Wetter (2009), p. 1: "The enforcement of export controls on dual-use goods is an important complement to the international agreements and multilateral export control regimes and dialogues aimed at limiting the proliferation of WMD. It often depends on the vigilance of individual front-line customs officers and the dedication of a few customs investigators and prosecutors."

[72] See e.g., Dall et al. (2017) p. 25.

> Q: Is that available?
>
> I don't think so, though I'm not quite sure. I don't think it's available off the shelf. It's something that needs to be developed and built over a period of time. And that's up to the institution to put that capability in place to build that kind of capability.

While a large global bank may perhaps be able to develop such systems and put them in place, that is not a feasible solution for smaller regulated institutions.

In practice, however, even well-designed trade finance PF-TFS systems will have a limited effect on PF-TFS breaches. Proliferators do not necessarily use trade finance facilities to purchase the goods. They can pay for the goods in full without relying on formal trade finance products and services. In that case the bank may receive no detailed information about the goods being purchased and exported.[73] Open account trading is trading where the parties do not rely on the trade finance services of a bank. P5(P), a senior compliance officer at a leading global bank described the issue as follows:

> There's a big focus in a lot of the literature around trade finance without necessarily always defining exactly what they mean when they say trade finance. Everything that we've looked at internally at the bank, if there is exposure it's to open account trading, not through formal trade finance products. Any potential sanctions evasion examples we've got, its always open account trading, not trade finance products. So, I find this disconnect between our reality and the literature, often written by people outside the banking sector, that says the risk is in trade finance. And what we actually see is the risk is anywhere but in trade finance.

The concerns raised in 2011 that financial institutions may not have the necessary information that would enable them to distinguish between a PF transactions and perfectly innocent transactions therefore remain relevant.[74]

Siloed approaches further limit the effectiveness of the due diligence measures of the parties that mitigate PF risks. The FATF amended Recommendation 2 in 2020 to ensure that national agencies collaborate and coordinate their AML/CTF/CPF activities. The interpretive note to Recommendation 2 specifically mentions customs and border authorities as well as import and export control authorities as examples of agencies that could be included in an inter-agency collaborative framework. The required level of inter-agency collaboration is, however, difficult to obtain in practice.

Ideally export permit application data, financial transaction data and customs data should be accessible to all the relevant parties to inform the due diligence measures of exporters, export authorities, the financial institutions and customs authorities. At the very least, the bank should be able to verify with the relevant authority that an export certificate was indeed issued, where required. That access to information may not be readily granted. A group of bank compliance official representing key banks of one country described their group's unsuccessful attempt to obtain information from the national export control authority (deidentified to "NECA" for purposes of this chapter). P6(P) put it as follows on behalf of the group:

---

[73] See Stewart et al. (2020).

[74] See Sect. 3 above.

> We have approached the NECA on a number of occasions and actually asked if they would be open to sharing names of parties who are issued with export permits so that we can then also use that, in addition to an understanding of industries, to perform the relevant checks. But unfortunately, from a NECA perspective, they have not agreed to share that information and they are citing privacy concerns.

Unless information flows improve there is a real risk that regulated institutions may implement a range of measures that increases compliance costs but have little PF risk mitigation impact.

3.3.1 The Broadening Scope of Proliferation Technologies

A narrow focus on traditional technology that may in the past have been required for WMD purposes may also limit the effect of compliance measures on WMDs in their current and future forms. Advances in technology mean that many more parts that can support WMD development are now more generally available and may fall outside the scope of controlled goods frameworks. It was found, for example, in 2022 that parts in Iranian missiles used by Russia against Ukraine were made in the US. These were components that are being used widely and that are routinely sold to overseas distributors.[75] Some may fall within the export control framework and may have been onsold by initial purchasers who were vetted. Others are simply commercial in nature and widely available. As P7(O) explained:

> You know, a lot of the things that are being found in Ukraine, for example, including Western component parts, are not military grade parts. They're things that would go into your iPhone or into games centres all over the world. The reason we are concerned about them is not because of the danger that they themselves represent, but because they're being used on the battlefield and to kill innocent civilians. And so, I think that raises the stakes considerably. I don't think that technology was intended to be utilized in this manner, how that's going to play out is, you know, definitely a consideration. There is a lot of implications for export controls.

Nuclear, chemical, and biological technology is developing and these advances also complicates the interpretation of PF-TFS obligations, especially by regulated institutions who wish to act ethically and responsibly. They also increase the already broad range of institutions that may be at risk. The UK's 2021 national proliferation risk assessment put it as follows:[76]

> Many UK industrial sectors can be procurement targets, including goods which can be used in the nuclear industry which are also used in everyday items or for use in commercial industry, such as carbon fibre, vacuum pumps, electronic components and testing equipment. Chemical weapon precursors are also considered to be dual-use items which can be vulnerable to PF actors, an example being those chemicals used as flame retardant. UK-manufactured electronic components, for example, were found in the debris of a 2012 North Korean missile test.

---

[75] United States Institute of Peace (2023).

[76] HM Treasury (2021), p. 14.

Artificial intelligence (AI) technologies are raising WMD concerns. This increases the PF-TFS scope to an extent that is probably not yet fully understood.[77] It is however important to consider how concerns regarding the development of enhanced data technologies by high-tech customers may relate to the management of PF-TFS risks by regulated institutions.

3.4 *Effectiveness and Efficiency*

Financial crime compliance costs are significant. In 2022 LexisNexis estimated the total cost of financial crime compliance across financial institutions worldwide to be USD $274.1 billion, up from USD $213.9 billion in 2020.[78] Compliance costs in turn drive de-banking of customers and business relationships that are not profitable. This is a major policy concern as de-banking undermines financial inclusion policies of governments and drive transactions into cash and informal economic sectors, weakening regulation and law enforcement.[79] PF-TFS measures will add to financial crime compliance costs, though it is not clear how much it will add. PF-related de-banking has also had a chilling impact on the work of some charities, for example those who helped to combat famine in the DPRK.[80]

As discussed in Sect. 2.4 above, the FATF in 2012 embraced a mandatory risk-based approach, requiring countries and institutions to undertake money laundering and terrorist financing risk assessments and adopt enhanced AML/CTF control measures where higher risks are identified. Where lower risks are present, countries may allow their institutions to simplify some of their AML/CTF measures.[81]

The risk-based approach was adopted to facilitate the effectiveness and efficiency of AML/CTF measures. The FATF standards, for example, put it as follows in relation to supervisory bodies:[82]

> Adopting a risk-based approach to supervising financial institutions' AML/CFT systems and controls allows supervisory authorities to shift resources to those areas that are perceived to present higher risk. As a result, supervisory authorities can use their resources more effectively.

---

[77] Dresp-Langley (2023); Gaulkin (2023).

[78] LexisNexis Risk Solutions (2022).

[79] Collin et al. (2015); Financial Action Task Force (2021b); Van Broekhoven (2020); De Koker et al. (2017); US Department of the Treasury (2023); D'Hulster et al. (2023).

[80] E.g., Zadeh-Cummings and Harris (2020), p. 9: "Fida, a Finnish NGO, withdrew from the DPRK in June 2019 after nearly two decades in the country. An official statement said the withdrawal was due to sanctions impact on the banking sector, which made 'financial services related to North Korean projects impossible".

[81] Financial Action Task Force (2021a, b); Financial Action Task Force (2017).

[82] Financial Action Task Force (2012-2023), INR 26.2.

The effectiveness and efficiency objectives are, however, only achievable when countries and institutions can identify lower risks where fewer compliance resources may be required and those that exceed the requirements can be shifted to areas of higher risk.[83]

As discussed above, that is not possible in relation to PF-TFS, as the underlying UNSC sanctions do not allow for simplified compliance. Countries must require all their AML/CTF/CPF-regulated institutions to undertake similar risk assessments unless a particular institution or type of institution is assessed as posing a lower PF-TFS risk and hence can be exempted from the risk assessment obligation. In all lower risk cases however, simplified CPF responses are not allowed: "... [F]ull implementation of the targeted financial sanctions as required by Recommendation 7 is mandatory in all cases."[84]

In response to impact concerns raised by civil society during the public consultation phase in 2020, the FATF introduced a low-risk exemption in Recommendation 1 allowing countries to elect to exempt a particular type of financial institution or DNFBP from the requirements to identify, assess, monitor, manage and mitigate PF risks, "provided there is a proven low risk of proliferation financing relating to such financial institutions or DNFBPs." They still need to ensure full implementation of the targeted financial sanctions as required by Recommendation 7, as the latter is mandatory regardless of risk profiles and levels.[85] Despite its limited scope, this exemption can increase the efficiency of national PF-TFS risk measures by only imposing PF-TFS risk management obligations on institutions at risk. Unfortunately, this exemption is unlikely to be used broadly.

The FATF describes risk as a function of three factors: threat, vulnerability, and consequence. "Consequence", the FATF advised, in the PF-TFS context is "ultimately the threat of use or the use of a weapon of mass destruction".[86] This consequence "is more severe than that of ML or other financial crimes, and is more similar to the potential loss of life associated with the consequences of TF."[87] Even where PF-TFS threat levels may be low, the severe consequences that should be ascribed to a PF-TFS event leave little scope to make an assessment that residual risk levels are low and, hence, that the conditions for a low risk exemption are met.

Some regulators have also opted not to use the exemption as they believe that exempted institutions would become targets of abuse. P8(O), a senior official of a national financial regulator, expressed the concern as follows:

[83] Celik (2021). The FATF standards allow countries to decide whether institutions may simplify some AML/CFT responses where risks are assessed as lower. Where that is not allowed, institutions cannot achieve the effectiveness and efficiency objective by shifting resources to areas of higher risk.

[84] Financial Action Task Force (2012-2023), INR1.4.

[85] Financial Action Task Force (2012-2023), n 3.

[86] Financial Action Task Force (2021a), par 22.

[87] Financial Action Task Force (2021a), par 22.

> For me, if you narrow it and you leave any of the regulated populace outside of the framework, they become immediately vulnerable for abuse. And the reason why I'm saying it, when we had the banks clamping down on proliferation, you immediately saw how other sectors then became vulnerable industries. We saw, for instance, the real estate industry, then being very subject or highly subject to abuse. We saw the legal profession highly subject to abuse for proliferation purposes. So, it was as if once you closed one door for it, the other one would open. And those involved in proliferation would try to find the weakest link in the system for abuse, you see. So, if you allow simplified due diligence based on risk for any of the sectors around proliferation, you may cause them to even be more vulnerable.

If exemptions are not applied where appropriate, the costs of PF-TFS measures will increase. Some of the negative impact may be limited where regulators embrace a risk-based approach and allow institutions that face a lower risk to implement fewer PF-TFS control measures than institutions facing a higher risk. This, however, requires a level of regulatory sophistication that has not been evident in many developing countries that would benefit most from efficient compliance.[88]

3.4.1 Customer Due Diligence to Counter PF

Effectiveness and efficiency are specifically relevant in relation to customer due diligence measures required to counter PF.

During the interviews PF experts whose work informed the drafting of the FATF's PF-TFS standards expressed the view that AML/CTF-related customer due diligence measures undertaken by regulated institutions would be sufficient to enable them to assess the PF-TFS risks posed by their customers. Participants from regulators and banks, including Wolfsberg Group banks, expressed similar views. These views became more nuanced and less emphatic when the interviewer asked questions about the assessment of risks posed by customers such as mining companies, universities,[89] engineering companies, etc.[90] These are customers that would generally not have been subject to enhanced customer due diligence for money laundering and terrorist financing purposes. In most cases they would be classified as lower risk customers for those purposes. Depending on their activities, their proliferation risk profile may, however, be much higher.

The bank participants agreed that additional customer due diligence will need to be undertaken in relation to these and other customers that may have a proliferation

[88] Celik (2021).

[89] HM Treasury (2021), pp. 27–28.

[90] FATF's customer profile risk indicators for PF-TFS include: "customer affiliated with a university or research institution is involved in the trading of dual-use goods or goods subject to export control." Financial Action Task Force (2021b), p. 18. FATF's concept of WMD proliferation includes both dual-use technologies and dual-use goods used for non-legitimate purposes but is not confined to these. In practice, the scope therefore expands beyond dual-use goods. WMD proliferation also includes development of WMDs and their means of delivery and related materials. This broadens the scope of application regarding university research that may potentially be of interest to proliferation programs.

risk profile that exceeds their money laundering and terrorist financing risk profiles. Some of the due diligence measures may be complex, for example to understand the research programs of universities to assess the quality of the proliferation risk mitigation measures they employ. Universities tend to be complex institutions with diverse departments, institutions and intra- and inter-university and industry collaborations, domestically and internationally, that can have different and changing touchpoints with nuclear, chemical, and biological WMDs. Universities increasingly have non-proliferation policies but their ability to implement these effectively may differ widely.

Additional due diligence measures in relation to these customers will need to be undertaken by all the relevant regulated institutions dealing with them. In addition to the bank of the university, the university's insurer, external lawyers, and real estate agents handling leases of property rented to the university's research departments or institutes may therefore also be required to undertake such risk assessment measures, should they be subject to PF-TFS risk assessment requirements.

Additional due diligence measures will impact on new relationships, i.e., when a bank opens an account for a university that has not been its customer before, especially where that university conducts research that may be relevant to proliferation. Initially, the main impact will, however, be on existing relationships. Due diligence processes that require extensive additional information from existing clients are generally sensitive from a customer service perspective, expensive, and time-consuming. These measures, in turn, may lead to risk-informed terminations of banking relationships and refusals to provide financial services to affected customers, as discussed in Sect. 3.4.

PF-TFS risk assessment obligations therefore pose significant effectiveness and efficiency challenges that regulators and institutions need to navigate.

4 PF-TF and Technology

Given these challenges, could appropriate technology support PF-TFS measures?

Compliance officers, especially those of smaller institutions, cannot be expected to understand the relevant technology and geopolitical risks adequately. Ideally appropriate products should be developed by government agencies and made available to the key stakeholders in public-private information-sharing partnerships. The AUSTRAC Fintel Alliance Alerting Project[91] employing homomorphic encryption may provide a model for a solution that would confidentially identify transactions of interest. Such partnerships should extend to the controlled goods stakeholders and allow for appropriate information-sharing. PF-TFS obligations of smaller, low risk institutions can be limited by applying the PF exemption, by allowing simplifications and by providing regulated businesses with technology that can support their

[91] Maxwell (2021).

compliance measures. In most cases, appropriate customer due diligence by such institutions combined with general information about PF-TFS and data tools may suffice to lower national PF-TFS risk levels.

In addition to supporting human decision-taking by filling gaps in expertise, AI technologies may fulfil a range of other helpful functions too. Schörnig investigated the use of AI as a WMD arms control tool and points to a range of additional helpful functions that AI technologies may perform, such as translation of technical texts from languages such as Russian, Farsi, Korean, Arabic and Swahili; interpretation of fast-changing rules and embedding them in Compliance by/through Design into compliance processes;[92] analysis of visual data, e.g. images of freight haulage and storage; integration of multi-modal data, e.g. communications, media and social media, etc.; and data visualisation to support human decision-taking, where required.[93]

These functions would indeed be invaluable, if not indispensable, to those who wish to combat PF. However, developers of such technologies and those who wish to rely on appropriate tools face a range of challenges, including the lack of big data—and reliable data—on actual PF-TFS breaches, as discussed in Sect. 3.2.2. above. The relatively limited data on actual breaches of UNSC sanctions, for example, will complicate the development of reliable AI tools in this context.

Some of the basic steps towards information support have not yet been taken. In 2022, Aaron Arnold pointed to challenges regarding UNSC sanctions data:[94]

> Currently, most sanctions-related data is diffuse and siloed – some is only accessible to those with the means to access it. Published designated entity lists, which are those lists that contain pertinent information about sanctioned individuals, companies and vessels, are often incomplete or difficult to integrate into IT systems.

The interviews have not identified any specific investments by international development agencies in technology that can provide such support to lower capacity countries. What has been indicated is that significant funds are now being invested in assisting countries to design appropriate export control regulatory systems and to undertake their first PF-TFS risk assessments. P3(O), who is closely involved in technical assistance to countries, expressed it as follows:

> If you take one abstract country, what you're going to spend the longest time on is the cheapest thing and that is legal regulatory development: Getting enough buy in from the host government to actually agree to draft and adopt the legislation and then all of the work that goes into the drafting and the consultations and everything else. It's low cost but, you know, it takes time. To do that, they need to know who their exporters are. We encourage them to engage in active and proactive outreach to their domestic industry to identify those that that may be involved in trade and dual-use goods and commodities. And then they need to figure out who they're trading with and highlight the risks of trading with the wrong people. And then they need to train customs officials.

[92] Casanovas et al. (2017).

[93] Schörnig (2022).

[94] Arnold (2022).

This is of course vital work that must be supported but it shows that implementation is focused on systems and people rather than technology. The development of regtech in this space seems to be largely left to the large corporate providers of AML/CTF regtech. That holds the risk that the initial products may be unaffordable for most smaller AML/CTF-regulated institutions.

Kassenova and Early suggest that distributed ledger or blockchain technology can support export controls in the PF-TFS context "as it provides information on all parties and is hard to falsify."[95] Much of the success of blockchain technology in this space would depend on the level of assurance of the data that is blockchained, i.e., that the goods and/or parties are described correctly; and the design of the solution, i.e. whether the blockchain is private or public, as that would impact on access to the data but also on the environmental footprint of the solution.[96]

Despite the promise technology holds to support trade controls and PF and other WMD and arms control measures, this is still receiving insufficient attention. An August 2023 United Nations Institute for Disarmament Research and Flemish Peace Institute paper found that there is "limited evidence of technologies being used to strengthen or enhance efforts to prevent, detect, and investigate the diversion of conventional arms, their ammunition, and parts and components."[97] Application of technology in relation to conventional arms would be an important building block of an effective system to control WMD proliferation.

5 Reflection

As set out in Sect. 3 above, the challenges faced by regulated institutions to assess the PF risks and to design and appropriately implement steps to mitigate them, can be clustered in four broad groups:

- navigating different definitions of PF;
- assessing and mitigating PF risk with limited information about PF threats and with a limited geopolitical and geo-economic capacity to identify and mitigate threats;
- monitoring trade-related transactions effectively to prevent PF-TFS while having limited or no information about the goods involved; and
- efficiently and effectively combating PF-TFS without being allowed to simplify compliance measures where risks are lower.

[95] Kassenova and Early (2023), p. 35. See also HSBC (2023) in relation to the Contour trade finance platform.

[96] Truby et al. (2022).

[97] Grand-Clément and Cops (2023), p. 1.

These challenges are heightened where PF-TFS risk assessment obligations are extended to lower capacity regulated institutions, especially small financial institutions and designated non-financial businesses and professions.

Capacity and information challenges in this space have been recognized since 2006 when additional step to counter PF were first discussed. A RUSI and ACAMS survey in 2020 confirmed that these were still posing challenges.[98] Only 20% of the respondents agreed that governments provided adequate guidance on dual-use and sensitive items. 71% of the respondents believed that sanctions evasion by proliferators is almost impossible to detect unless industry has intelligence leads and/or clear information on entities engaged in sanctions evasion. The survey however also reflected that many respondents did not actively consult information that was being published. Only 20% of the respondents regularly consulted PF reports, guidance and typologies issued by non-governmental, academic or research organisations, while 13% read the 6-monthly reports issued by the UN Panel of Experts on the DPRK. High-priority tools requested by respondents from governments, include the sharing of trends and typologies to better identify PF patterns (66%), and the sharing of intelligence including names of entities suspected of being involved in PF (58%).[99]

General levels of implementation of the 2012 PF-TFS standards by countries were, however, also low. A 2022 FATF report on the levels of compliance and effectiveness of the implementation of their standards found that levels of effectiveness with its PF-TFS standards to be largely unsatisfactory, with 52% of FATF members and 82% of FATF-style regional body members rated either low or moderate:[100]

> Most countries have not yet developed the legal framework to implement, without delay, targeted financial sanctions related to proliferation financing when they are called for by the United Nations Security Council (a requirement of the FATF Recommendations). Countries are also experiencing shortfalls in (i) identifying assets held by those acting on behalf of designated entities and (ii) communicating and enforcing clear policies related to listings/delisting/exemptions for covered private sector entities. This impacts effectiveness levels for Immediate Outcome 11, which are largely unsatisfactory, with 52% of FATF members and 82% of FATF-style regional body members rated either low or moderate. Only 34% of the 59 sampled jurisdictions transpose United Nations Security Council designations without delay.

The report also considered the understanding of PF-TFS obligations by regulated institutions and found that only 25% of financial institutions had a strong understanding (medium/varied 46%, poor 22%, not clear 7%), compared to 5% of

[98] RUSI and ACAMS (2020). The survey was conducted between 7 November 2019 and 6 January 2020 and had 366 unique survey responses. Kassenova (2018) identified a range of institutional PF-TFS challenges based on interviews in 2017–18.

[99] RUSI and ACAMS (2020), p. 32.

[100] Financial Action Task Force (2022a, b). Lack of implementation was identified earlier than this study. See e.g. Stewart et al. (2020).

designated non-financial businesses and professions (medium/varied 29%, poor 46%, not clear 7%).[101]

The FATF report concluded that countries need to improve their technical compliance with Recommendation 7 but also ensure that they communicate and enforce sanctions-related procedures; provide additional guidance to regulated institutions to improve overall risk-awareness and address vulnerabilities to PF; and provided targeted guidance to higher risk entities on the potential risks of breach or evasion of targeted financial sanctions.[102]

Given that PF-TFS effectiveness was mainly impacted by insufficient implementation of Recommendation 7 by countries, insufficient communication of relevant information to their regulated institutions, and insufficient transactional data received by regulated institutions, it is not clear why the imposition of additional risk assessment obligations on regulated institutions was viewed as the most appropriate way to strengthen the combating of financing of proliferation.[103] The respondents in the RUSI-ACAMS survey did not select the conduct of PF-TFS risk assessments as the most effective measure for implementing UN import/export provisions on the DPRK either. Only 31% were in favour of conducting a risk assessment to determine exposure to the DPRK's trade in sanctioned goods.[104]

The lack of a regulatory impact assessment process to inform FATF standard-setting, the sensitive politics around the topic and the impact of the COVID pandemic on FATF engagement may explain in part the adoption of the requirements.[105] While the new standards have raised the profile of PF-TFS measures, especially measured by the increased number of articles and training activities, it is not clear that effectiveness and efficiency were front of mind when the 2020 measures were adopted.

The study encountered a surprising absence of coherent policy about the purpose and strategic objectives of the new measures. This emerged from discussions of the study with various stakeholders who did not agree to participate formally in interviews. Officials with non-proliferation portfolios were generally reluctant to participate, because they felt that they knew too little about PF-TFS. Their remarks reflected that PF measures were not yet embedded and actively applied in national non-proliferation and disarmament strategies, frameworks and processes. There was generally an awareness of the proliferation sanctions regime but very few of the officials knew about the FATF standards or actively considered how the broader PF-TFS role of the private sector would support current strategic objectives. They often advised the researcher to rather speak to the agencies that were responsible for the implementation of AML/CTF measures if he wanted to access information about

[101] Financial Action Task Force (2022a), Table 7.5.

[102] Financial Action Task Force (2022b), p. 47.

[103] For some background see Dall et al. (2017), Brewer (2019), Stewart et al. (2020), Dolzikova and Dall (2020).

[104] RUSI and ACAMS (2020).

[105] De Koker (2022); De Koker (2023).

PF-TFS measures. This was also the case in countries that had already completed a national PF risk assessment. Among the AML/CTF officials who were interviewed there was little indication that implementation was more than a box-ticking exercise to meet FATF standards. The absence of strategic thinking around the design of PF-TFS measures and the siloed approaches were especially striking given the heightened threat of the use of WMDs in this period and the fact that a country of major concern—Russia—fell outside the scope of the FATF's PF-TFS measures.

One private sector compliance expert, P3(P), remarked as follows on their experiences of country-level commitment and the lack of a sense of urgency and importance of PF-TFS measures:

> [I]f your country has not been filed a missile at, there is going to be very little buy-in for you to stop PF. ... If it's not real, if we don't see a country like Ukraine being blown up by Russia, there will be no real buy-in. Unfortunately, ... you need to feel it before you will do it.

Given the heightened levels of WMD threats globally, the low level of knowledge about and prioritization of PF-TFS measures and how they could support the control of WMDs in general are concerning. Their appears to be a mismatch between the levels of knowledge of those who set global policy and standards and those who are responsible for their implementation at national and institutional level.

Looking back historically it is not clear that the global non-proliferation, disarmament, and conventional arms control[106] stakeholders pushed for the adoption of PF strategies to actively support non-proliferation and disarmament measures. This study did not find evidence that they have now fully embraced the use of PF risk management measures and embedded it in their strategies. The general impression is that a siloed approach was being followed where PF-TFS measures would function to support UNSC sanctions without being aligned with the overarching non-proliferation and disarmament objectives the sanctions schemes were intended to advance and without those measures being integrated with the broader measures serving those objectives.

Given that the PF-TFS measures were adopted as FATF standards, countries are bound to implement these risk management measures. This presents an important opportunity to strengthen national and international non-proliferation controls. When designing national regulation it will be important to consider the objectives of the new measures as well as the institutional challenges outlined above. It is submitted that the following may be elements of an approach aimed at supporting effective and efficient counter-PF measures by regulated institutions:

A meaningful definition of PF and a holistic approach: The FATF standards require countries to implement PF-TFS measures, but they do not prevent countries from adopting PF measures that are broader in range than the FATF standards. As discussed in Sect. 3.1, countries are adopting different definitions, also for purposes of their national PF risk assessments. It is important that countries take a considered and holistic policy decision on the definition. The drafting of the policies and

[106] Mensah et al. (2023).

regulations to implement the FATF's PF risk management standards provide governments with an important opportunity to ensure that the new financial surveillance capacity is employed effectively to support the country's WMD policies.

Ideally the definition should support the country's position on WMD non-proliferation and disarmament,[107] UNSC sanctions and potentially its conventional arms control policies,[108] and align with its WMD and export control measures as well as its capacity to support the adoption and implementation of effective and efficient control measures by regulated institutions.

Before adopting a narrowly-defined PF-TFS position the country should consider how new and expensive compliance obligations that are focused only on a sub-set of UNSC PF obligations will deliver value for the country and for global security in the future.[109] UNSC members are not equally committed to observing or enforcing the UNSC's DPRK sanctions.[110] As discussed in Sect. 2.3., the future of the UNSC's sanctions against the DPRK is currently bleak. Key UNSC sanctions and export control measures against Iran have sunset clauses in the JCPOA and while some restrictions will continue to 2041, the JCPOA and UNSC resolution 2231, which endorsed the JCPOA, are set to terminate in October 2025.[111] Fragmentation of the global financial system may furthermore allow proliferators access to financial services and products outside the scope of the current system.[112] These developments may require revised global and national strategies regarding non-proliferation and financial sanctions to ensure that measures remain fit for purpose without undue negative consequences.

---

[107] For countries such as Australia, Canada, Chile, Germany, Japan, Mexico, the Netherlands, Poland, Turkey, and the United Arab Emirates, for example, their measures could go beyond PF-TFS to reflect their disarmament position as member of the Non-Proliferation and Disarmament Initiative. See Ogilvie-White (2013). The same holds true for signatories to the TPNW.

[108] The new FATF PF risk management measures are not yet clearly part of the non-proliferation discussions globally. Much more need to be done to ensure a more holistic policy approach globally and domestically. It is telling that an August 2023 publication by United Nations Institute for Disarmament Research (UNIDIR) and the Stimson Center and Conflict Armament Research on the role of industry in responsible international transfers of conventional arms, addressed the role that financial institutions could play, and the relevance of Know Your Customer (KYC), without referencing the PF risk standards of the FATF (Mensah et al. (2023). The measures are not explicitly considered in other proliferation focused UNIDIR publications either. See e.g. Dunn (2022).

[109] See Stelzenmüller (2023) on Russia.

[110] See Sects. 2.2 and 2.4 above and Keatinge and Arnold (2023).

[111] See Sect. 2.2 above and Arms Control Association (2023b).

[112] See IMF 2023; US Department of the Treasury (2023), p. 38 (in relation to de-banking): "Loss of bank access, where it is widespread and indiscriminate enough to be considered de-risking, has the potential to push countries to seek closer relationships with geopolitical competitors and cause significant macroeconomic damage to regions of U.S. foreign policy interest. … While the U.-S. dollar is the leading currency in the international monetary system, some individuals whom Treasury interviewed expressed concern that the increased use of U.S. sanctions in the last decades has made the U.S. dollar less attractive and created demand for payment channels that do not depend on it. Although the U.S. dollar's position remains strong, unchecked de-risking could compound moves towards de-dollarization."

There is an opportunity for NPT, BTWC and CWC State parties to shape national PF measures to support more effective NPT compliance and control measures, rather than only support UNSC TFS sanctions. This, it is submitted, will ensure that the compliance investment will advance a broader and more meaningful global security objective. That broader objective will also better justify the compliance spend required for an effective PF framework. NPT breaches to date, for example, helped more countries like the DPRK to build nuclear programs.[113] The current WMD compliance framework is under pressure.[114] The 2023 NTI Nuclear Security Index records a host of troubling developments:[115]

> Among them, countries and areas with weapons-usable nuclear materials and nuclear facilities have made almost no progress since 2020 toward improving security culture and insider threat prevention; stocks of weapons-usable plutonium at civilian nuclear facilities have grown rapidly; 34% of countries and areas with nuclear facilities have no regulatory requirements in place for protecting nuclear infrastructure during a natural or human-caused disaster; in those same countries and areas, support for political and legal commitments to improve security is faltering; support for the role of the International Atomic Energy Agency (IAEA)—the world's leading agency with a mission to prevent nuclear proliferation and strengthen the global framework for nuclear safety and security—is inconsistent; and minimal progress has been made on securing radioactive sources against those who might steal them to build radioactive dirty bombs

There is therefore a real need for the shoring up of WMD compliance measures.[116] This need could be addressed in part by proportional and collaborative PF measures.

Embedding new obligations into the current AML/CTF and sanctions framework also requires thought and careful design. In Australia, for example, regulators will need to consider how best to implement PF-TFS risk measures given that Australia's existing sanctions laws do not require risk assessments to be undertaken. Australia's sanctions laws do allow bodies corporate to raise as a defence that they took reasonable precautions and exercised due diligence to avoid contravening the sanctions law. Appropriate risk management measures may arguably form part of reasonable precautions and due diligence, but this defence is not explicitly available

---

[113] Kassenova (2021-22), p. 84: "North Korea, the most sanctioned country in the world, continues to advance its nuclear and missile programs."

[114] See e.g., Schulte (2023), p. 118: "Existing multilateral global disarmament regimes, like the Biological and Toxin Weapons Convention (BTWC) or Chemical Weapons Convention (CWC), are losing the plausible prospect of enforceability in hard cases, even if they approach universal membership. There is a discouraging list of past 'cornerstones of international order,' starting perhaps with the Conventional Armed Forces in Europe Treaty (CFE), which have been undermined, abolished, or abandoned. And it is now evident that even the last surviving, rare, and reverenced bilateral nuclear treaties, like the Intermediate Range Nuclear Forces (INF) or Measures for the Further Reduction and Limitation of Strategic Offensive Arms (New START), can either be wrecked by withdrawal provoked by prolonged, defiant noncompliance, or suspended to convey political displeasure in conditions of growing global polarization."

[115] NTI (2023).

[116] Wunderlich et al. (2021).

to individuals that contravene the laws.[117] Introducing risk management measures only for PF-TFS obligations but not for any other sanctions-related financing obligations will complicate management of sanctions compliance in Australia. Broadening risk management measures to all other sanctions obligations will however create a significant compliance obligation for all affected parties. The Australian challenges in this regard will be encountered in different forms in all jurisdictions when the regulations implementing the PF-TFS standards are drafted. The correct calibration of PF-TFS obligations will therefore be challenging but is best done following an evidence-based and consultative approach that pursues clearly-identified national objectives of the relevant measures.

A phased approach: Start by focusing on higher risk institutions with capacity to design and implement PF-TFS risk management measures appropriately. That select group would generally involve banks. Building core capacity and adopting effective strategies to support the select group of regulated institutions will help to inform broader strategies when PF-TFS risk management obligations are extended beyond the select group. This approach is ideally combined with a collaborative approach.

A collaborative approach: A private-public partnership approach to planning full implementation of the new obligations will be helpful.[118] It would enable regulators to work with intelligence and law enforcement agencies, export control authorities, customs authorities, dual-use goods manufacturers, importers and exporters, financial institutions, and a select group of non-financial businesses and professions, e.g. import/export businesses, to (i) determine actual compliance capacity levels and information-sharing requirements, and (ii) inform the design and implementation of strategies to build appropriate national systems, to support public and private capacity, and to ensure appropriate information-sharing that would support effective and efficient CPF measures by agencies and regulated institutions.[119] AML/CTF/CPF regulators will need to establish intra-government information-sharing relationships with government counterparts that may not have been involved in AML/CTF collaboration before, and consider how to provide meaningful information and access to data to regulated institutions to support effective and efficient CPF measures.

The collaborative approach should go beyond current AML/CTF public-private information-sharing partnership by focusing on an effective system that supports all regulated institutions, i.e. not only a small group of large regulated institution but all

[117] See s 20 of the *Charter of the United Nations Act 1945* (Australia) and s 16 of the *Autonomous Sanctions Act 2011* (Australia).

[118] For early support for such partnerships see Kassenova (2018).

[119] The FATF support such partnerships for purposes of PF risk assessments, but ideally their scope should range beyond risk assessment. See Financial Action Task Force (2021a), pp. 46–7. See also Kassenova and Early, p. 36: "Our interviews with the government representatives in various jurisdictions revealed that there is little day-to-day coordination or information-sharing between the counterproliferation community (e.g., those dealing with export controls) and the financial crime prevention community."

regulated institutions that are required to implement CPF risk management obligations.

Appropriate use of the FATF's low risk exemption: The majority of AML/CTF/CPF-regulated institutions are small and may pose a very low risk of PF abuse. Their compliance capacity also tends to be limited. Appropriate exemption from AML/CTF/CPF risk management obligations will assist authorities to focus their support and activities on the higher risk institutions. This will, however, only be possible to do in terms of the FATF standards if the national PF risk assessment considers the PF risk profile of each of the regulated sectors and ideally also risk distribution within those sectors to identify those that pose a low risk. Risk levels may, for example, differ between remittance service providers depending on the corridors and customers they serve.[120] These institutions will still need to meet rule-based sanctions compliance obligations and they should receive the appropriate support from government agencies to meet those obligations.[121] An improved FATF risk concept will, however, be required to ensure that the nature and consequences of a PF abuse can be considered without automatically elevating all potential PF abuses, regardless of the value involved and the role of the relevant transactions, to a higher—or the highest—risk level.[122]

Support CPF compliance: Effective and efficient CPF compliance requires a higher level of information-sharing and institutional capacity than AML/CTF compliance. Many of the smaller regulated institutions, including those that may have higher PF-TFS risk level, may not have the capacity to correctly source, interpret and apply general jurisdictional threat information to their products and customers.[123] Regulators should ideally support institutions by undertaking or supporting sectoral risk assessments.[124] This would provide businesses in that sector with a generic assessment for the industry that would be easier to tailor and apply to their own context. Regulators can also assist by supporting the development and adoption of appropriate regtech tools, e.g., in relation to dual-use goods, sanctions lists, and risk levels of export destinations. In addition, credible, free initial and continuing PF compliance training support should be made available by governments, and this should be accessible to all regulated institutions that are required to comply with PF risk management obligations. Ideally, government support should include extend to name-screening support. This will limit increases in compliance costs that may otherwise result in de-banking, as discussed in Sect. 3.1.

[120] World Bank and IMF (2021). Expanding this draft risk assessment framework to PF risk would also be helpful.

[121] See Kassenova (2018) for sanction-related information challenges faced by regulated institutions.

[122] See Sect. 3.4 above.

[123] RUSI published an institutional PF risk assessment guide, that can be useful for institutions with more comprehensive compliance functions. See També (2023).

[124] See De Koker (2020), p. 19 for this suggestion during the public consultation phase that preceded the adoption of the new PF risk management measures by the FATF.

Regulated institutions that operate cross-border may also require support to navigate their risks and obligations when countries define PF differently.

The effectiveness and value of such compliance support will depend on the quality of the national coordination and collaboration among the key law enforcement, intelligence, customs, export, and regulatory agencies, as envisaged in the FATF's amended Recommendation 2. Their ability will be enhanced if government agencies and institutions can partner with PF experts, academia and think tanks operating in this space.

Governments may argue that such support is unnecessary given that it has not been provided in relation to AML/CTF. With PF measures, however, governments employ their private sector against sanctions evasion programs of foreign nations. Regulated institutions cannot be expected to be sufficiently effective against military-grade PF-TFS evasions measures if they lack appropriate support from their governments.

Tailor compliance expectations: Regulated institutions can only manage the threats that they can reasonably identify, assess, and mitigate. Where government agencies have information that is too sensitive to share with industry and publish in national risk assessments, it is important to accept—and clearly signal—that institutions may be involved in transactions that they may otherwise have been able to avoid. Regulatory as well as law enforcement agencies will need to assure that regulated institutions do not adopt a zero-tolerance approach that does not allow for reasonable failures, in order to prevent over-compliance and de-banking of customers perceived to pose a risk.[125]

Monitoring intended and unintended consequences: Much more can be done to assess and report on whether AML/CTF/CPF systems are managing to limit the risk of abuse and whether measures may have negative unintended consequences. Questions would include: Are the new measures delivering sufficient value? Can the value be increased by reforming aspects of the system? Is there evidence of unintended consequences?

Designing a review mechanism that would collect performance-related data and inform policy and law reform decisions where issues are identified, would strengthen national PF measures.

Continuing policy engagement: Non-proliferation is a multi-faceted and complex policy topic. Globally and at a domestic level PF measures may easily be siloed and boxed as part of sanctions management and mainly as the responsibility of AML/CTF stakeholders. The real value of the industry investment that PF risk measures requires lies however in the support for increased global security. In this space countries have different views on how that could best be attained, for example with nuclear weapons or without.

This debate will become more democratic when the new PF measures compel each regulated institution to reflect on its role in relation to WMD threats. While financial institutions may continue to de-bank customers with high PF risk profiles

[125] De Koker and Symington (2014).

that cannot profitably be serviced, it is also increasingly likely that some institutions may elect not to provide services to any customer in the legitimate nuclear weapons industry. Institutions like these are joining the "Don't Bank on the Bomb" initiative which is a PAX project in conjunction with the International Campaign to Abolish NuclearWeapons (ICAN n.d.). The "Don't Bank on the Bomb" group of financial institutions that support the TPNW is growing.[126]

Policymakers will need to continue to engage all stakeholders to bridge the sanctions, PF, export control and conventional arms control silos globally and at a domestic level, while developing and furthering a coherent national policy in this space. Without appropriate policy coherence and coordination, private sector PF implementation may be ineffective.

The private sector may wish to lead some of these engagements. While some regulated institutions may support a Don't Bank on the Bomb approach others may consider supporting non-proliferation and disarmament objectives by only providing services to relevant customers where they receive sufficient assurances, information, and collaboration to effectively support compliance with the NPT, BTWC and CWC. Those compliance approaches will, however, only be effective if they are supported by national policy and by public-private information- and data-sharing arrangements.

6 Conclusion

AML/CTF measures aim to minimize the risk of organized crime and terrorism globally. These are important policy objectives but arguably not as important to global security as the objectives of non-proliferation. Here the threats are dire. The task of preventing the financing of WMD in defiance of the norms of international law and the frameworks of international agreements is, however, complex. The focus is now on assisting countries to implement the standards and undertake their first risk assessments. Limited attention is being given to the dilemmas the private sector will face to implement effective and efficient compliance measures. The standards envisage that regulated institutions will play a key role in risk-informed PF-TFS. If that is to be the case regulators should do more now to understand the constraints faced by the private sector and what they would require to perform these functions effectively and efficiently, without undue disruption of business, or undue imposition of increased costs on customers and society.

FATF standards are however minimum standards and countries, and regulated institutions may elect to go beyond the standards and adopt policies, regulations and compliance practices that serve broader non-proliferation objectives. Given the current increase in WMD risks globally that approach deserves serious consideration. Increased compliance with global non-proliferation obligations is required and

[126]Muñoz (2023).

the FATF's financial surveillance framework can provide a helpful additional layer of controls.

Acknowledgements The study benefited from sabbatical support by SOAS, University of London; Wolfson College, Oxford; the Faculty of Law of the Autonomous University of Barcelon (and especially the IDT-UAB); the AI Research Institute of the Spanish National Research Council (CSIC); and La Trobe Law School. Their support and the warm support of the colleagues at those institutions are gratefully acknowledged but the views expressed in this chapter are not necessarily shared by the relevant institutions or colleagues. Thank you also to scores of anonymous interviewees who graciously shared their views. I gratefully acknowledge the thoughtful and constructive feedback received from Jonathan Brewer, Togzhan Kassenova, Bryan Early, Mark Turkington and Anton Moiseienko on earlier drafts but remain responsible for all errors.[127]

References

ABC News (2023) The new START Nuclear Treaty, and why Vladimir Putin is walking away from it. https://www.abc.net.au/news/2023-02-22/new-start-us-russia-arms-control-treaty-explainers/102008364

Albright D, Burkhard S, Faragasso S, Keenan L (2021) The Peddling Peril Index (PPI) 2021: ranking national strategic export control systems. Institute for Science and International Security

Arms Control Association (2023a) U.S.-Russian Nuclear Arms Control Agreements at a Glance. https://www.armscontrol.org/factsheets/USRussiaNuclearAgreements

Arms Control Association (2023b) The Joint Comprehensive Plan of Action (JCPOA) at a Glance. https://www.armscontrol.org/factsheets/JCPOA-at-a-glance

Arnold A (2022) The haves and have nots of sanctions implementation RUSI, 18 October 2022. https://rusi.org/explore-our-research/publications/commentary/haves-and-have-nots-sanctions-implementation

Arnold A (2024) Russia just gutted the UN Panel of Experts on North Korea – What now? RUSI, 3 April 2024 https://www.rusi.org/explore-our-research/publications/commentary/russia-just-gutted-un-panel-experts-north-korea-what-now

AUSTRAC (2022) Proliferation financing in Australia: national risk assessment. https://www.austrac.gov.au/sites/default/files/2022-12/AUSTRAC_Proliferation_Financing_in_Australia-National_Risk_%20Assessment_Web.pdf

Baker M (2023) Nuclear arms control verification and lessons for AI treaties. arXiv preprint arXiv:2304.04123

Bender B (2023) The dangerous and frightening disappearance of the nuclear expert. Politico, 28 July 2023. https://www.politico.com/news/magazine/2023/07/28/nuclear-experts-russia-war-00108438

Bennett Moses LB, De Koker L (2017) Open secrets: balancing operational secrecy and transparency in the collection and use of data by national security and law enforcement agencies. Melb Univ Law Rev 41:530

Brewer J (2017) Study of typologies of financing of WMD proliferation - final report centre for science and securities studies. King's College, London

[127] An early version of parts of this paper was delivered in October 2022 at the Artificial Intelligence, Governance, Ethics and Law seminar series hosted by the Institute of Law and Technology of the Autonomous University of Barcelona and the AI Research Institute of the Spanish National Research Council.

Brewer (2019) The financing of WMD proliferation (JCE test): conducting risk assessments centre for a new America. http://104.239.228.80/publications/reports/the-financing-of-wmd-proliferation-2

Cirincione J (2005) Enforcing compliance with the non-proliferation treaty. Carnegie endowment for international peace, 24 March 2005. https://carnegieendowment.org/2005/03/24/enforcing-compliance-with-non-proliferation-treaty-pub-16701

Casanovas P, González-Conejero J, De Koker, L (2017) Legal compliance by design (LCbD) and through design (LCtD): preliminary survey. TERECOM@JURIX. https://ceur-ws.org/Vol-2049/05paper.pdf

Celik K (2021) Impact of the FATF Recommendations and their implementation on financial inclusion World Bank. https://openknowledge.worldbank.org/entities/publication/f3c905fe-5caa-567d-beb4-bd9f9756a77e

Collin M, De Koker L, Juden M, Myers JL, Ramachandran V, Sharma A, Tata GM (2015) Unintended consequences of anti money laundering policies for poor countries: A CGD Working Group Report. Centre for Global Development. https://www.cgdev.org/sites/default/files/CGD-WG-Report-Unintended-Consequences-AML-Policies-2015.pdf

Cooper B, Ferreira M, Janse van Vuuren L (2020) Digital identity and financial inclusion: how digitising customer due diligence can strengthen providers curing COVID-19 and beyond next billion. https://nextbillion.net/digital-identity-and-financial-inclusion/

Dall E, Keatinge T, Berger A (2017) A countering proliferation finance: an introductory guide for financial institutions RUSI. https://static.rusi.org/201704_rusi_cpf_guidance_paper.1_0.pdf

De Koker L (2020) Financial action task force standards and financial inclusion: What should be done – and not done - to improve the alignment between integrity and inclusion policy objectives?. https://papers.ssrn.com/sol3/papers.cfm?abstract_id=3679779

De Koker L (2022) Editorial: regulatory impact assessment: towards a better approach for the FATF. J Money Laund Control 25(2):265–267. https://doi.org/10.1108/JMLC-05-2022-149

De Koker L (2023) Editorial: towards meaningful action against proliferation financing. J Money Laund Control 26(2):213–214. https://doi.org/10.1108/JMLC-03-2023-172

De Koker L, Howell J, Morris N (2023) Economic consequences of greylisting by the financial action task force. Risks 11(5):81

De Koker L, Singh S, Capal J (2017) Closure of bank accounts of remittance service providers: global challenges and community perspectives in Australia. Univ Queensl Law J 36:119

De Koker L, Symington J (2014) Conservative corporate compliance: reflections on a study of compliance responses by South African banks. Law Context Socio-Legal J 30:228

De Koker L, Turkington M (2016) Transnational organised crime and the anti-money laundering regime. In: Hauck P, Peterke S (eds) International law and transnational organised crime. Oxford University Press, 241–263

De Koker L, Casanovas P (2024) "De-risking", de-banking and denials of bank services: an over-compliance dilemma? In: Goldbarsht D, de Koker L (eds) Financial crime, law and governance, Ius Gentium: comparative perspectives on law and justice. Springer International Publishing, Cham

Department of the Treasury (2022) National proliferation financing risk assessment. https://home.treasury.gov/system/files/136/2022-National-Proliferation-Financing-Risk-Assessment.pdf

D'Hulster K, Morris N, Jaffer S, De Koker L (2023) The decline of correspondent banking in Pacific Island countries: state of knowledge and what can be done to fix the problems. World Bank/Pacific Island Forum Secretariat. PIF, Suva

Dolzikova D, Dall E (2020) Two steps forward, one step back: the limits of new standards on assessing WMD financing risk. https://rusi.org/explore-our-research/publications/commentary/two-steps-forward-one-step-back-limits-new-standards-assessing-wmd-financing-risk

Dresp-Langley B (2023) The weaponization of artificial intelligence: what the public needs to be aware of. Front Artif Intell 6:1154184. https://doi.org/10.3389/frai.2023.1154184

Dunn L (2022) The disarmament, arms control, and non-proliferation implications of the Russian invasion of Ukraine – and what next for reducing global nuclear dangers. UNIDIR, Geneva. https://doi.org/10.37559/WMD/22/DDAC/01

Financial Action Task Force (1991) Report 1990–1991. https://www.fatf-gafi.org/en/publications/Fatfgeneral/Fatfannualreport1990-1991.html

Financial Action Task Force (1996) The forty recommendations. https://www.fatf-gafi.org/en/publications/Fatfrecommendations/Review-and-history-of-fatf-standards.html

Financial Action Task Force (2001) FATF IX special recommendations. https://www.fatf-gafi.org/en/publications/Fatfrecommendations/Ixspecialrecommendations.html

Financial Action Task Force (2010) Combating proliferation financing – a status report on policy development and consultation. https://www.fatf-gafi.org/content/dam/fatf-gafi/reports/Status-report-proliferation-financing.pdf.coredownload.pdf

Financial Action Task Force (2011) Consultation on proposed changes to the FATF standards: compilation of responses from the financial sector. https://www.fatf-gafi.org/content/dam/fatf-gafi/public-consultation/Second%20public%20consultation%20document%20responses%20financial%20sector.pdf

Financial Action Task Force (2012) Declaration of the ministers and representatives of the Financial Action Task Force. https://www.fatf-gafi.org/en/publications/Fatfgeneral/Ministersrenewthemandateofthefinancialactiontaskforceuntil2020.html

Financial Action Task Force (2012-2023) International standards on combating money laundering and the financing of terrorism & proliferation: the FATF recommendations. https://www.fatf-gafi.org/en/publications/Fatfrecommendations/Fatf-recommendations.html#:~:text=As%20amended%20February%202023,of%20weapons%20of%20mass%20destruction

Financial Action Task Force (2017) FATF guidance on AML/CFT measures and financial inclusion, with a supplement on customer due diligence. https://www.fatf-gafi.org/media/fatf/content/images/Updated-2017-FATF-2013-Guidance.pdf

Financial Action Task Force 2018 Objectives for the FATF during the US presidency 2018–2019. https://www.fatf-gafi.org/en/publications/Fatfgeneral/Objectives-2018-2019.html

Financial Action Task Force (2020) Draft proposals for amendments to recommendation 1 and its interpretive note (for public consultation). https://www.fatf-gafi.org/content/dam/fatf-gafi/public-consultation/PF-Public-Consultation-Draft-Amendments.docx

Financial Action Task Force (2021a) Guidance on proliferation financing risk assessment and mitigation. https://www.fatf-gafi.org/en/publications/Financingofproliferation/Proliferation-financing-risk-assessment-mitigation.html#:~:text=The%20Guidance%2C%20which%20builds%20on,mitigate%20the%20risks%20they%20identify

Financial Action Task Force (2021b) High-level synopsis of the stocktake of the unintended consequences of the FATF standards http://www.fatf-gafi.org/media/fatf/documents/Unintended-Consequences.pdf

Financial Action Task Force (2022a) Report on the state of effectiveness and compliance with the FATF standards. https://www.fatf-gafi.org/en/publications/Fatfgeneral/Effectiveness-compliance-standards.html

Financial Action Task Force (2022b) Public compliance communication no 54: guidance on compliance measures aimed at combating proliferation financing. https://www.fic.gov.za/Documents/220930_PCC%2054%20Combatting%20Proliferation%20Financing%20FINAL.pdf

Financial Intelligence Centre (2022) Guidance on compliance measures aimed at combating proliferation financing. Public Compliance Communication No 54. https://www.fic.gov.za/Documents/220930_PCC%2054%20Combatting%20Proliferation%20Financing%20FINAL.pdf

Financial Services and the Treasury Bureau Bureau (2022) Hong Kong money laundering and terrorist financing report. https://www.fstb.gov.hk/fsb/aml/en/doc/2nd%20HK%20ML%20TF%20Risk%20Assessment%20Report_e.pdf

G8 (2003) Non-proliferation of weapons of mass destruction: a G8 declaration, Evian. http://www.g7.utoronto.ca/summit/2003evian/wmd_declaration_en.html

G8 (2004) G8 action plan on nonproliferation, Sea Island. http://www.g8.utoronto.ca/summit/2004seaisland/nonproliferation.html

G8 (2006) Gleneagles statement on non-proliferation. http://www.g7.utoronto.ca/summit/2005gleneagles/nonprolif.pdf

Gaulkin T (2023) What happened when WMD experts tried to make the GPT-4 AI do bad things. Bulletin of the Atomic Scientists, 30 March 2023. https://thebulletin.org/2023/03/what-happened-when-wmd-experts-tried-to-make-the-gpt-4-ai-do-bad-things/

Goldbarsht D, de Koker L (2024) Financial crime and the law: identifying and mitigating risks. In: Goldbarsht D, de Koker L (eds) Financial crime and the law. Springer

Grand-Clément S, Cops D (2023) Project D-Tect: technologies to counter the diversion of small arms and light weapons, and components of conventional weapons. United Nations Institute for Disarmament Research and Flemish Peace Institute. https://www.unidir.org/sites/default/files/2023-08/FPI_UNIDIR_Technologies_to_Counter_Diversion_of_SALW_and_Components_of_Conventional_Weapons.pdf

HM Treasury (2021) National risk assessment of proliferation financing. https://assets.publishing.service.gov.uk/government/uploads/system/uploads/attachment_data/file/1020695/National_risk_assessment_of_proliferation_financing.pdf

HSBC (2023) Introducing contour: leveraging blockchain technology to transform trade finance. https://www.business.hsbc.ae/en-gb/campaigns/blockchain/contour

ICAN (n.d.) Signature and ratification status. https://www.icanw.org/signature_and_ratification_status

IMF (2023) Financial stability report - safeguarding financial stability amid high inflation and geopolitical risks (April). https://www.imf.org/en/Publications/GFSR/Issues/2023/04/11/global-financial-stability-report-april-2023?cid=bl-com-spring2023flagships-GFSREA2023001

Jervis R (2006) Reports, politics, and intelligence failures: the case of Iraq. J Strateg Stud 29(1): 3–52

Jewell E (2022) How a key UN vacancy could undermine investigations into DPRK sanctions-busting. NK News, 3 February 2022. https://www.nknews.org/2022/02/how-a-key-un-vacancy-could-undermine-investigations-into-dprk-sanctions-busting/

Kassenova T (2018) Challenges with implementing proliferation financing controls: how export controls can help. World ECR J Export Controls Sanctions 30

Kassenova T (2021–22) Proliferation financing: revised FATF recommendations and challenges on the ground. ACAMS Today. Regulatory Initiatives, 83. https://www.acamstoday.org/proliferation-financing-revised-fatf-recommendations-and-challenges-on-the-ground/

Kassenova T, Early BR (2023) Countering the challenges of proliferation financing. The Centre for Policy Research, University of Albany

Keatinge T, Arnold A (2023) Will 2023 be the end of international sanctions? 5 January 2023. https://rusi.org/explore-our-research/publications/commentary/will-2023-be-end-international-sanctions

Kimball D (2022) U.S.-Russian nuclear arms control agreements at a glance. Arms Control Association. https://www.armscontrol.org/factsheets/USRussiaNuclearAgreements

LexisNexis Risk Solutions (2022) 2022 true cost of financial crime compliance study - global summary. https://risk.lexisnexis.com/global/en/insights-resources/research/true-cost-of-financial-crime-compliance-study-global-report

Lyman T, De Koker L, Martin Meier C, Kerse M (2019) Beyond KYC utilities: collaborative customer due diligence. Consultative Group to Assist the Poor. https://www.cgap.org/research/publication/beyond-kyc-utilities-collaborative-customer-due-diligence

Maxwell N (2019) Expanding the capability of financial information-sharing partnerships. https://www.rusi.org/publication/occasional-papers/expanding-capability-financial-information-sharing-partnerships

Maxwell N (2021) Case studies of the use of privacy preserving analysis to tackle financial crime. https://www.future-fis.com/uploads/3/7/9/4/3794525/ffis_innovation_and_discussion_paper_-_case_studies_of_the_use_of_privacy_preserving_analysis_-_v.1.3.pdf

Mensah A, Perkins R, Fletcher R (2023) The arms trade treaty: the role of industry and other private sector actors in efforts to counter the diversion of conventional arms. Issue Brief 4. United Nations Institute for Disarmament Research (UNIDIR) and the Stimson Center and Conflict Armament Research. https://unidir.org/publication/role-industry-and-other-private-sector-actors-efforts-counter-diversion-conventional

NATO Heads of State and Government (2023) Vilnius Summit Communiqué, 11 July 2023. https://www.nato.int/cps/en/natohq/official_texts_217320.htm

NTI (2023) NTI nuclear security index: falling short in a dangerous world (July). https://www.ntiindex.org/wp-content/uploads/2023/07/2023_NTI-Index_Report.pdf

O'Carroll C (2020) UN panel of experts: how cold war squabbling hinders north Korea sanctions NK PRO. https://www.nknews.org/pro/panel-of-experts-how-cold-war-squabbling-hinders-north-korea-sanctions/

Ogilvie-White T (2013) Australia and the non-proliferation and disarmament Initiative: difficult times for disarmament diplomacy. Australian Strategic Policy Institute. https://www.files.ethz.ch/isn/164836/Policy_Analysis110_NPDI.pdf

Organisation for the Prohibition of Chemical Weapons (2023) OPCW confirms: all declared chemical weapons stockpiles verified as irreversibly destroyed (7 July 2023). https://www.opcw.org/media-centre/news/2023/07/opcw-confirms-all-declared-chemical-weapons-stockpiles-verified?s=09

Muñoz A (2023) Moving away from mass destruction: 109 exclusions of nuclear weapon producers. Pax, ICAN. https://www.dontbankonthebomb.com/wp-content/uploads/2023/07/PAX_Rapport_DBotB_Moving_Away_FINAL_digi_Single_Page.pdf

Quealy K (2017) If Americans can find North Korea on a map, they're more likely to prefer diplomacy. New York Times, 5 July 2017. https://www.nytimes.com/interactive/2017/05/14/upshot/if-americans-can-find-north-korea-on-a-map-theyre-more-likely-to-prefer-diplomacy.html

Robinson K (2023) What is the Iran nuclear deal? Council on Foreign Relations. https://www.cfr.org/backgrounder/what-iran-nuclear-deal

També N (2023) Institutional proliferation finance risk assessment guide. RUSI. https://static.rusi.org/proliferation-finance-risk-assessment-special-resource.pdf

United Nations (2023). Security Council Deems Syria's Chemical Weapon's Declaration Incomplete, Urges Nation to Close Issues, Resolve Gaps, Inconsistencies, Discrepancies. https://press.un.org/en/2023/sc15220.doc.htm

United States Institute of Peace (2023) Explainer: American parts in Iranian drones. https://iranprimer.usip.org/blog/2023/mar/01/explainer-american-parts-iranian-drones

Republic of Namibia (2021) Detailed report: national money launderign, terrorist and proliferation financing risk assessment (Period Jan' 2015–Dec' 2019). https://www.fic.na/uploads/Publications/ML%20TF%20PF%20Risk%20Assessment%20Reports/2020%20NRA/Final%20Approved%20NRA%20Report%20Sept%202021.pdf

RUSI & ACAMS (2020) RUSI-ACAMS proliferation finance survey. https://www.acams.org/en/media/document/18566

Schörnig N (2022) Artificial intelligence as an arms control tool: opportunities and challenges. In: Reinhold T, Schörnig N (eds) Armament, arms control and artificial intelligence: the janus-faced nature of machine learning in the military realm, pp 57–72

Schulte P (2023) Conflicting views of a darkening strategic prospect: the opposed sensibilities and discordant perspectives of the nuclear practitioners and disarmament archipelago. In: Roberts B (ed) Morality and nuclear weapons: practitioner perspectives. Center for Global Security Research and French Commission on Atomic and Alternative Energy, 97–146. https://cgsr.llnl.gov/content/assets/docs/CGSR-Occasional_Paper_MoralityandNuclearWeapons_06302023.pdf

Science and Security Board (2023). 2023 doomsday clock statement. Bulletin of the Atomic Scientists. https://thebulletin.org/doomsday-clock/current-time/
Smith J, Yim, H (2023) Russian, Chinese officials join Kim at North Korea military parade. Reuters, 29 July 2023. https://www.reuters.com/world/asia-pacific/north-korea-shows-off-drones-ballistic-missiles-night-time-parade-2023-07-28/
Stelzenmüller C (2023) The return of the enemy: Putin's war on Ukraine and a cognitive blockage in Western security policy. Brookings. https://www.brookings.edu/articles/the-return-of-the-enemy/
Stewart IJ, Viski A, Brewer J (2020) Combating the financing of proliferation: challenges and new tools. J Financ Crime 27(4):1107–1121
Stockholm International Peace Research Institute (2023) States invest in nuclear arsenals as geopolitical relations deteriorate (12 June 2023). https://www.sipri.org/media/press-release/2023/states-invest-nuclear-arsenals-geopolitical-relations-deteriorate-new-sipri-yearbook-out-now?s=09
Suseanu I (2021) The NPT and IAEA safeguards. IAEA Bull 62(4):–4
The Commission on the Intelligence Capabilities of the United States Regarding Weapons of Mass Destruction (2005) Report to the President of the United States. https://www.govinfo.gov/content/pkg/GPO-WMD/pdf/GPO-WMD.pdf
Truby J, Brown RD, Dahdal A, Ibrahim A (2022) Blockchain, climate damage, and death: Policy interventions to reduce the carbon emissions, mortality, and net-zero implications of non-fungible tokens and Bitcoin. Energy Res Soc Sci 88:102499. https://doi.org/10.1016/j.erss.2022.102499
United Nations Panel of Experts. (2022) Final report of the Panel of Experts Submitted Pursuant to Resolution 2569 (2021) S/2022/132. https://www.un.org/securitycouncil/sanctions/1718/panel_experts/reports
US Department of the Treasury (2023) AMLA: the Department of the Treasury's de-risking strategy. https://home.treasury.gov/system/files/136/Treasury_AMLA_23_508.pdf
Van Broekhoven L (2020) Derisking and civil society: drivers, impact and solutions. Human Security Collective. https://www.hscollective.org/news/timeline/article-derisking-and-civil-society-drivers-impact-and-solutions/
Versino C, Heine PM, Carrera J (2021) Strategic trade atlas 2015–2019: country-and commodity-based views. Pacific Northwest National Lab, Richland
Wetter A (2009) Enforcing European Union law on exports of dual-use goods. Oxford University Press
Wunderlich C, Müller H, Jakob U (2021) WMD compliance and enforcement in a changing global context. UNIDIR. https://doi.org/10.37559/WMD/21/WMDCE02
World Bank & IMF. A Draft Framework for Money Laundering/Terrorist Financing Risk Assessment of a Remittance Corridor (IMF, 2021). https://www.imf.org/-/media/Files/Research/imf-and-g20/2021/g20-methodology-for-remittance-corridor-risk-assessment.ashx
Zadeh-Cummings N, Harris L (2020) Humanitarian aid in North Korea: needs, sanctions and future challenges. Centre for Humanitarian Leadership. https://centreforhumanitarianleadership.org/wp-content/uploads/2020/04/CHL_North-Korea-Report_Final.pdf

Louis de Koker LLB LLM (UFS) LLM (Cantab) LLD (UFS) FSALS, is a Professor and Associate Dean: Research and Industry Engagement at the La Trobe Law School (Australia), an Extraordinary Professor at the Faculty of Law of the University of the Western Cape (South Africa) and a Board member of the Financial Integrity Hub (FIH) at Macquarie Law School. From 2014 to 2019 he was the national program leader of the Law and Policy research program of the Australian government-funded Data to Decisions Cooperative Research Centre. Louis is an expert on anti-money laundering and counterterrorist and proliferation financing, and especially the relationship between financial integrity and financial inclusion policies and regulations. Louis has worked with the Consultative Group to Assist the Poor, the World Bank, the OECD, the Asian

Development Bank regulators and financial service providers on the design and implementation of appropriate integrity and inclusion over the past two decades. He has advised on a range of laws and regulations and his research on integrity laws and their impact on financial inclusion has been cited in publications of various international bodies including the World Bank, IMF, the Financial Action Task Force (FATF) and the Basel Committee on Banking Supervision.

Dancing in the Dark: Terrorist Financing Via the Dark Web

Doron Goldbarsht

Abstract Understanding the ways in which terrorist organisations manage their assets is critical to depleting those organisations of their funds and, ultimately, disrupting their activities. Terrorists continue to adapt to evolving technologies and communication platforms in the deployment of more obscure terrorist financing techniques. With little regulation, low barriers to entry, and numerous opportunities, the dark web appeals to terrorists seeking to securely receive large amounts of money from supporters beyond law enforcement oversight. The dark web offers a high degree of anonymity that is fortified through the use of decentralised cryptocurrencies. While cryptocurrencies are used also for legal purposes, their pseudonymity and their lack of independent regulation have made them an attractive vehicle for terrorists. This has created a jackpot for terrorist financing and, simultaneously, exposed a legal blind spot for regulators. The key objective of this paper is to shed light on the prevalent use of the dark web by terrorist organisations in furtherance of terrorist financing activities.

1 Introduction

The internet has revolutionised our lives, connecting people across the globe, providing instant access to information, and enabling new opportunities for communication, education and business. It can be divided into three basic areas: the *surface web*, the *deep web*, and the *dark web*. The surface web typically refers to the unencrypted or non-dark web. This traditional web has relatively low-base anonymity, with most websites routinely identifying users by their Internet Protocol (IP) address. The deep web refers to internet content that is not part of the surface web. This means that instead of being able to search for websites, users must visit them directly. The dark web is part of the deep web that can only be accessed by

D. Goldbarsht (✉)
Macquarie Law School, Sydney, NSW, Australia
e-mail: doron.goldbarsht@mq.edu.au

D. Goldbarsht, L. de Koker (eds.), *Financial Crime and the Law*, Ius Gentium: Comparative Perspectives on Law and Justice 115,
https://doi.org/10.1007/978-3-031-59543-1_7

specific software, configurations or authorisations, often using nonstandard communication protocols and ports. It offers users anonymity, thus paving the way for a range of illegal activities.

While governments have made some successful efforts to target terrorist financing on the dark web,[1] the high degree of anonymity has made this part of the internet a virtual safe haven for terrorists. This may incentivise terrorists to move financing efforts from the surface web to the dark web,[2] although the existing evidence of terrorist financing on the dark web is sporadic. It is unclear how widespread the use of the dark web has been in this context. In 2010, cybersecurity firm Procysive estimated that there were nearly 50,000 radical websites and more than 300 terrorist forums operating on the dark web.[3] However, due to procedural, security and logistical barriers, there is a lack of primary data available from the dark web. This has limited the ability of researchers to assess the frequency or extent to which the dark web is used in the furtherance of terrorist financing and, ultimately, in countering terrorism. To improve understanding of how terrorist organisations secure funding, this paper uses a quantitative methodology that incorporates information collection, analysis and visualisation techniques to search various web information sources and illuminate the prevalence of terrorist financing on the dark web in comparison with popular surface web social networking platforms.

To do this, a sophisticated keyword search was conducted over 3 months, from February to April 2023, to compare the nature and frequency of terrorist financing themes on the surface web and on the dark web. The initial search was conducted using standard keywords: 'terrorist finance', 'terrorist funding', 'terrorist financing with bitcoin', and 'terrorist donations'. A keyword permutation tool was used to target the search and improve the accuracy of flagged keywords. To enhance search efficiency, we used the Semantic Table of Ten (STT).[4] The table offers an empirical scheme of 10 semantic principles to consider when formulating search terms. Each 'principle' can greatly enhance the process of open-source research by developing a guided process to develop search terms that enable the identification of desired information. For each search, the table suggests possible semantics combinations, including variations in spelling, acronyms, technical jargon, relevant history, synonyms, antonyms, homonyms, languages, broader terms and narrower terms. Without limiting the results to an 'exact search', the following terms were considered: 'dark web hawala', 'hawala anonymous', 'mujahideen hawala', 'sadaqacoins', 'hawala crypto', 'terrorism finance', 'terrorist funding', 'terrorist bitcoin', 'hawala darknet', 'zakat jihad', 'crowdfunding charity', 'charities ISIS', 'hawala ISIS', and 'crypto hawala'.

---

[1] Weimann (2016b), p. 41; Maloney (2021); Rivera and Archy (2019).

[2] Macdonald et al. (2019), p. 183.

[3] McCormick (2013).

[4] Landman and Crook (2013).

Each search term was explored using Maltego, a professional software used for open-source intelligence and forensics.[5] All keywords were searched on selected surface web social media platforms—namely, Twitter, Facebook, Instagram and TikTok—and also on the dark web. It was anticipated that our keyword search would produce a significantly greater number of results in relation to the dark web when compared to social media sites. This, we suggest, reflects the ability of criminals to exploit the cryptographic protocols of the dark web, enabling them to more openly engage with terrorist financing. This is particularly the case in the current climate, which has seen the proliferation of digital payment systems that are difficult to trace.

Following this Introduction, Part 1 will explain the need to fight the financing of terrorism, particularly with regard to emerging technologies. After emphasising the risks of terrorist financing online, this part introduces the dark web and clarifies basic elements of the cryptofinance sector with regard to cyber risks. Part 2 explores how terrorists use the surface web (including social media) and the dark web, while taking advantage of cryptocurrencies to raise and transfer funds outside of law enforcement oversight. This section focuses on financing via crowdfunding and reveals that discussions concerning terrorist financing are occurring on a far greater scale on the dark web than on the selected social media sites on the surface web. Part 3 examines current counter-terrorist financing (CTF) efforts, particularly the recommendations of the Financial Action Task Force (FATF) to mitigate the risk of terrorist financing, as well as the measures implemented by large multinational social media platforms. Part 4 offers some conclusions.

It should be noted that this paper does not put forward a solution to prevent terrorist financing on the dark web. Instead, it aims to demonstrate that an understanding of the complex digital tactics used by terrorists can shed broad light on the novel challenges created by emerging technologies and new digital payments, services and products.

2 Terrorist Financing and the Dark Web

Terrorist financing has been defined by the United Nations as the unlawful and wilful provision or collection of funds with the intention that they be used to carry out a terrorist-related offence or any other act intended to cause death or serious bodily injury to a person (who is not participating in armed conflict), when the purpose of the act is to intimidate a population, or to compel a government or international organisation to do or abstain from doing any act.[6] While terrorist groups differ in

[5] Turner et al. (2020).

[6] International Convention for the Suppression of the Financing of Terrorism, 9 December 1999, entry into force 10 April 2002, 2178 UNTS 197. For the importance of adopting an agreed definition of 'terrorism', see Gibbs (1989); Shanahan (2016); Burns (2011).

their motivations,[7] they all require financial resources to operate and to carry out terrorist acts. And, like all organisations, terrorist groups require the skills to obtain, move, store and ultimately use their financial resources. As put by former US Secretary of State Colin Powell, 'money is the oxygen of terrorism'; when you cut off the oxygen, you effectively neutralise the terror cell.[8]

The direct costs of executing terrorist acts are generally quite low. The FATF—an intergovernmental body that sets standards and develops policies to combat money laundering and terrorist financing[9]—states that terrorists require only modest amounts of liquidity in order to build and maintain an effective and discreet financial infrastructure.[10] However, funding remains a significant enabler in the perpetuation of terrorist organisations.[11] The expenses involved in funding terrorism can generally be divided into two related categories.[12] The first concerns finance for the direct execution of terror activity (otherwise known as the 'military wing').[13] This includes funding for the purposes of maintaining training facilities, the cost of travel for trainers and trainees, pre-operational surveillance, and the direct costs of the operations themselves.[14] The second category concerns funding for the organisation's community (otherwise known as the 'civil wing').[15] This involves raising funds for the provision of social services, such as health care or education—a tactic used to promote ideology and loyalty in local populations.[16] Civil expenditure is significant: in some cases, 80–90% of the money raised by terrorist organisations is spent on charitable, educational and medical institutions.[17] Terrorist organisations have the ability to transfer funds from the civil wing to the military wing without public scrutiny or detection, thus allowing them to operate under a guise of legitimacy that creates challenges for authorities.[18] The civil funds perpetuate terrorism in various ways, most notably by instilling the organisation's ideals from infancy; inciting antagonism towards states that the organisation opposes; increasing fundraising potential by promoting the organisation's community activities; and providing financial support to injured or imprisoned terrorists and to the families of terrorists

[7] Cassese (1989), pp. 1–3. There is no clear-cut categorisation of the terrorism phenomenon: see Rosie (1987), pp. 22–24.

[8] Powell (2001).

[9] Goldbarsht (2017).

[10] FATF (2015b), pp. 22–24.

[11] Rudner (2006), p. 35.

[12] Goldbarsht (2020).

[13] FATF (2015b), pp. 9–13.

[14] FATF (2015b), pp. 9–13.

[15] FATF (2015b), pp. 9–13.

[16] FATF (2015b), pp. 9–13.

[17] Gunning (2008), p. 100; Brisard (2002), p. 7.

[18] *United States v Holy Land Foundation for Relief and Development*, Criminal Action No 304CR 240G (US District Court, ND Texas, 26 July 2004), at 4.

who have been killed.[19] Larger terrorist groups thus require consistent ample funding for their survival over time. Some of the more prominent organisations include the Islamic Resistance Movement (Hamas); Lashkar-e-Taiba in Pakistan; Al-Qaeda; the Taliban in Afghanistan; Hezbollah in Lebanon; Boko Haram in north-eastern Nigeria, Chad, Niger and northern Cameroon; and the Islamic State of Iraq and the Levant/Syria (ISIL or ISIS).[20]

As terrorist organisations have evolved in their size, scope and structure—in some instances attaining global reach—so too have their fundraising methods.[21] Those methods include state sponsorship, proceeds from legitimate and criminal activities, and charitable donations.[22] State-sponsored terrorism involves the provision of logistical and financial support from governments to terrorists.[23] However, since the inception of the Financial War on Terrorism, the severity of international sanctions has forced terrorists to adapt their funding models away from reliance on state sponsors.[24] Of particular concern is the combination of several separate challenges: fundraising via charitable organisations; emerging technologies and new digital payment products and services; and the increasing use of cryptocurrencies—all of which present new CTF risks.[25]

The internet has long been a popular tool for terrorists. It provides a ready means of distributing propaganda to a global audience, soliciting donations, recruiting adherents, and fostering public awareness of their causes.[26] Most terrorist organisations have at least one form of presence online, such as email, chatrooms, e-groups, forums and resources on Facebook, TikTok and Twitter.[27] Authorities have become increasingly concerned about the use of social media as a method of coordinating fundraising campaigns and disseminating terrorist propaganda.[28] Although it is difficult to identify terrorist financing online, law enforcement agencies have been more closely monitoring—and consequently shutting down—the websites and social media platforms of many terrorist organisations on the surface web.[29] Additionally, social media companies have been making significant efforts to remove and block terrorist organisations from their platforms through the use of various technological methods, including artificial intelligence.[30] These regulatory interventions have had the effect of removing terrorist content on a large, cross-platform basis.

[19] Goldbarsht (2020).

[20] Gerges (2016), p. 22.

[21] FATF (2015b).

[22] Cortright and Lopez (2007); Goldbarsht (2020).

[23] Ryder (2020), p. 670.

[24] Hardouin (2009), p. 205.

[25] FATF (2015a); FATF (2015b).

[26] Weimann (2010), p. 19.

[27] Weimann (2010), p. 19.

[28] FATF (2015b), p. 31.

[29] FATF (2015b), p. 31; Denic (2017).

[30] Macdonald et al. (2019), p. 183; van Benthem (2018).

While these efforts are far from flawless,[31] they pose a real risk to anonymity-seeking terrorists. It may be the case that much of the material removed from the surface web reemerges on the dark web as terrorist organisations migrate to more highly anonymised platforms in order to evade detection and interception by law enforcement.

2.1 What Is the Dark Web?

The three areas of the World Wide Web—the surface web, the deep web, and the dark web—have varied methods of accessibility and anonymity. To use a familiar analogy, the surface web is like the tip of the iceberg. This area is accessible by anyone with an internet connection and has relatively low-base anonymity, with most websites, including social media platforms, routinely identifying users by their IP address. The surface web has been estimated to comprise only 6–10% of the internet.[32] Below the surface is the remaining 90–94% of the iceberg, known as the deep web.[33] In a seminal paper in which he coined the term 'deep web', Michael Bergman noted that 'searching the internet today can be compared to dragging a net across the surface of the ocean. While a great deal may be caught in the net, there is still a wealth of information that is deep, and therefore, missed'.[34] The deep web is inaccessible through conventional search engines and can only be accessed with targeted queries or keywords. It is not indexed and is often protected by security mechanisms, such as login IDs, passwords, membership, registrations and codes.[35] The dark web (also referred to as the darknet or dark internet) emerged from the deep web.[36]

It is difficult to know how much of the deep web is taken up by dark web content. The content is intentionally hidden and can be accessed only through decentralised anonymised nodes on several networks, such as Tor (an acronym for 'the onion router').[37] Tor is a distributed network of computers that obscures a user's real IP address, thus concealing their identity. This is done by routing communications and transactions through multiple computers globally and concealing them through numerous layers of encryption.[38] Upon its launch in 2002, Tor was described as a method to stop people (including government agencies) from learning about a user's

[31] Macdonald et al. (2019), p. 194.

[32] Hurlburt (2017).

[33] Hurlburt (2017).

[34] Berman (2001).

[35] Weimann (2016a).

[36] Finklea (2017).

[37] Finklea (2017), p. 3.

[38] FATF (2014).

location or browsing habits.[39] While this feature would allow a forum for whistleblowers and political dissidents, Tor has been used largely to facilitate criminal transactions beyond the oversight of law enforcement.[40]

2.2 *Cryptocurrencies and Cyber Risk*

While it is often argued that organised crime still considers 'cash is king',[41] the FATF warns that decentralised currencies can provide a powerful new tool for criminals and terrorist financiers seeking to move and store illegal funds. In fact, the development of technology and cryptocurrencies in recent years has led to this question: Is cryptocurrency becoming a cybercrime currency?[42]

The global financial crisis of 2007–08 saw the systematic mismanagement of money markets, significantly undermining trust in the system of conventional centralised national economies and financial supervision.[43] This led to the emergence of an innovative concept of computerised money, known as cryptocurrency. A digital representation of value that can be traded online but does not have legal tender status, cryptocurrency is decentralised.[44] It is a math-based convertible currency that is protected by cryptography. The cryptographic functions are relevant when considering the way in which transactions are generated. Each transaction is recorded as a 'block', with added blocks forming a chain (blockchain). This means that it can be distributed with no central administrative authority and no central monitoring or oversight.[45] Cryptocurrencies thus operate outside the traditional banking system. In this regard, they resemble a shadow banking system, in which traditional financial services are carried out without banks and hence without the usual regulations.[46]

Bitcoin, which launched in 2009, was the first cryptocurrency to have presence. Like other cryptocurrencies, Bitcoins are units of account composed of unique strings of numbers and letters that constitute units of the underlying currency and have value only because individual users are willing to pay for them. They are digitally traded between users and they can be exchanged (purchased or cashed out) for traditional currencies. Cryptocurrency is considered 'pseudo anonymous'. Although details of all transactions are shared with users in a public transaction register, this is not systematically linked to an individual's identity—which remains

[39] Piazza (2017).

[40] Piazza (2017).

[41] Soudjin (2019); Weber and Kruisbergen (2019).

[42] Cyberoam (2012), cited in Brown (2016), p. 333.

[43] Brown (2016), p. 328.

[44] FATF (2021b), pp. 26–27.

[45] Ibid, 5.

[46] Goldbarsht (2018).

hidden behind a randomly generated alphanumeric code.[47] Furthermore, services such as mixers and tumblers can be used to mingle transactions, making unclear the intended recipient.[48] It is difficult for law enforcement to link specific virtual coins (addresses) to a particular transaction due to the lack of regulation and decentralisation. This has led cryptocurrency—mainly Bitcoin—to be considered the de facto currency of the dark web.[49]

3 The Dark Web Enables Terrorist Financing

This section highlights several cases in which terrorists have used both surface web social media and the dark web to further their agendas by fundraising, largely through crowdfunding. They have maintained their anonymity by embracing cryptocurrency (in particular, Bitcoin) for financial transactions. As discussed below, the secrecy afforded by these platforms enables the proliferation of radicalisation, recruitment, and the dissemination of extremist propaganda to secure funds essential for the execution of terrorist operations. Primary quantitative data illustrates the prevalence of discussions concerning terrorist financing, both on selected surface web social networking sites and, predominantly, on the dark web.

3.1 Use of Cryptocurrency for Financial Transfers by Terrorists

Evidence suggests that, in recent years, terrorist organisations have begun to use cryptocurrency to finance their activities through various fundraising methods, posing new threats to CTF efforts both globally and domestically.[50] In the same way that they use the internet to communicate anonymously and to raise funds, terrorists use cryptocurrencies to anonymise themselves and to conduct covert fundraising activities, with cryptocurrencies offering anonymity, security, usability, acceptability, reliability and volume.[51] In addition, by fundraising and completing peer-to-peer transactions online with cryptocurrencies, terrorists can evade detection by law enforcement or financial regulators in new and sophisticated ways.

Traditionally, terrorists have relied largely on informal systems of finance known variously as *hawala*, *hundi*, *fei ch'ien*, *hui* and *phoe kuan*.[52] These systems

---

[47] Brown (2016), p. 327.

[48] FATF (2021b), p. 21.

[49] Brown (2016), p. 327. Cmp, De Koker and Goldbarsht (2022), p. 310.

[50] Wang and Zhu (2021).

[51] Ibrahim (2021), p. 81.

[52] Goldbarsht (2018), p. 265; FATF (2016), p. 7; Jost and Sandhu (2000); Passas (2003), pp. 50, 56.

originated in India and Southeast Asia, but they have operated in non-Western societies for centuries. Essentially, they allow money to be moved in a way that avoids the bureaucratic administrative processes that are part of standard banking verification practices.[53] The transferor will go to an intermediary (*hawaladar*) to arrange the transfer, provide the funds, and, ultimately, have the payment made to the beneficiary by an intermediary's counterpart in the destination country. Participants are not required to provide details of their passport or visa, making it extremely difficult for authorities to investigate transactions.[54] This method is preferred by many low-income workers, as it is a cheaper way to transfer money to their home countries with a more favourable exchange rate than that offered by established financial institutions. For these reasons, it has often been abused by criminals and terrorists.[55] For example, ISIS uses hawala systems to finance itself.[56] It is interesting to note that investigations into terrorist-related offences revealed that Al-Qaeda did not use hawaladars to move money for financing the 9/11 attacks,[57] and the main financial transactions went thought US and British institutions. Recently, the FATF has stressed the need for jurisdictions to curb the criminal abuse of hawala networks.[58] However, while it is anonymous and secure, hawala lacks the immediacy of transferring funds from multiple jurisdictions—a feature available in global crowdfunding offered via cryptocurrencies.

More recently, novel financial systems, including cryptocurrency exchanges, have offered terrorists new and highly anonymous means of conducting financial transactions, particularly on the dark web. The criminal use of Bitcoin is growing rapidly, with estimates suggesting that $76 billion in illegal activity each year involves Bitcoin, representing 46 percent of all Bitcoin transactions.[59] The FATF has observed an increase in the use of cryptocurrencies, including anonymity-enhanced coins (such as Monero), for terrorist financing and the moving of funds in Africa, Europe and the Middle East, including by ISIL and Al-Qaeda.[60] Research suggests that illegal trading of this kind is most common on the dark web, with black markets adopting this form of electronic payment on a significant scale.[61] As might be expected, the proportion of Bitcoin transactions involved in criminal activity increases when mainstream interest in Bitcoin significantly declines and immediately following darknet scams or seizures by law enforcement.[62] Indeed, the multi-jurisdictional, anonymous and immediate aspects of cryptocurrency transactions

[53] Looney (2003).

[54] Looney (2003), p. 165.

[55] Teichmann (2018).

[56] Stergiou (2016).

[57] National Commission on Terrorist Attacks Upon the United States (2004); Passas (2006), p. 319.

[58] FATF (2022a), p. 44.

[59] Foley et al. (2019).

[60] FATF (2023), p. 28.

[61] Foley et al. (2019), p. 1802.

[62] Foley et al. (2019), p. 1801.

'enable fast distributions of finances into other regions, facilitate more recruitment missions, and likely make the role of middlemen—which both al-Qaeda and ISIS have historically employed—obsolete'.[63]

Terrorist organisations are increasingly shifting to Bitcoin fundraising on the internet. In particular, ISIL has posted several videos on YouTube requesting advice on the production of crypto assets.[64] There have also been instances of public promotion of Bitcoin accounts, with terrorist groups publishing Bitcoin addresses on the surface web and asking for donations.[65] In 2019, the Izz ad-Din al-Qassam Brigades (the military wing of Hamas) launched a fundraising campaign calling on supporters to donate using digital currencies.[66] It specifically asked donors to send Bitcoin to a particular digital address, later enhancing its operational security by changing the mechanism on its website to generate a new digital wallet for each transaction, thereby undermining efforts of law enforcement to 'follow the money'.[67] The website launched a 2-min video explaining, in a step-by-step guide, how to avoid the traditional financial system and provide support via Bitcoin.[68] It advised donors to use a public device so that the wallet is not linked to their IP address. Other instructional videos include advice on signing up to Twitter and Facebook without having to register a mobile phone number, as well as deactivating GPS tagging when taking or posting a photo.[69]

Bitcoin funds have also been linked to direct terrorist operations. For example, it has been alleged that Bitcoin wallets used by ISIS obtained significant transfers of money the day before the Sri Lankan bombings in 2019, which claimed the lives of more than 250 people.[70]

---

[63] Hassan et al. (2022).

[64] See, eg, Blannin (2017), p. 19; FATF (2015c), p. 25.

[65] Eisermann (2020), p. 26.

[66] Wilson and Williams (2019).

[67] Wilson and Williams (2019).

[68] Wilson and Williams (2019).

[69] Suchi and Wika (2021), p. 425. It should be noted, however beyond the scope of this chapter, that developments in technology that track the movement of crypto on the blockchain ledger have made it easier for authorities to identify those behind crypto transfers. Hamas, for example, announced on 28 April 2023 that it would stop receiving fundraising via the crypto currency Bitcoin, citing an increase in "hostile" activity against donors. See, Nidal Al-Mughrabi (2023). For further readings on how the distinct amalgamation of data gathered by Virtual Asset Service Providers in line with their AML/CFT responsibilities, coupled with blockchain analytics and supplementary intelligence, has been pivotal in law enforcement inquiries and substantially bolstered their achievements, see Wagman (2022), p. 98.

[70] Katsiri (2019).

3.2 Use of Surface Web Social Media for Terrorist Financing

Social media is a powerful tool that is widely used for terrorist fundraising. The relationship between terrorism and the media has been thoroughly explored, with terrorists communicating to a broad audience in order to multiply the effects of their violent attacks.[71] In addition, terrorist organisations such as ISIS, Boko-Haram, and the Islamic State in the West African Province continue to exploit the growing appeal of group membership inherent in social media to spread propaganda and facilitate training.[72] Terrorist groups have demonstrated a willingness to adapt to the newest communication platforms as they emerge.[73] Indeed, social networking sites offer terrorists several advantages relative to other means of communication, including interactivity, reach, frequency, usability, immediacy and permanence.[74] Concerns have been documented in various UN Security Council resolutions (UNSCRs),[75] including UNSCR 2368, which 'urges Member States to remain vigilant about the use of information and communication technology for terrorist purposes and act cooperatively to prevent terrorists from recruiting and raising funds for terrorist purposes'.[76] According to the FATF, the accessibility and relative anonymity of social media has been exploited by terrorist groups to raise funds from sympathetic individuals globally, representing a growing terrorist financing vulnerability.[77] For example, social media has notoriously been used to recruit for ISIS and to raise funds for the travel or accommodation of its members.[78] For example, investigation into the perpetrator of the 2019 terrorist attack in a Christchurch mosque revealed engagement with 'like-minded' individuals via social media, chatrooms and forums.[79]

In 2014, ISIS established the Al Hayat Media Centre outlet, a propaganda arm specifically targeting the distribution of ISIS propaganda to the West via social media platforms.[80] Between 2014 and 2015, the US Department of the Treasury imposed sanctions against financiers Al-Ajmi, Abdul Mohsen Abdullah Ibrahim al-Sharikh and Mohamed Elshinawy for operating regular social media campaigns seeking donations for Syrian fighters.[81] In March 2019, Gregory Lepsky was sentenced to 16 years' imprisonment for attempting to provide material support to

---

[71] Jenkins (1974).

[72] Suchi and Wika (2021), p. 424.

[73] Hoskins and O'Loughlin (2010); Nacos (2016); Weimann (2014).

[74] Weimann (2014), p. 2.

[75] United Nations Security Council Resolution 2178, S/RES/2178 (2014), para 7.

[76] United Nations Security Council Resolution 2368, S/RES/2368 (2017), para 23.

[77] FATF (2015b).

[78] FATF (2018), p. 22.

[79] FATF (2021a), p. 25.

[80] FATF (2015c), p. 24.

[81] US Department of the Treasury (2014).

Hamas, consisting of at least $5000 worth of Bitcoin solicited via social media.[82] Another trend within ISIS fundraising campaigns is the use of social media to facilitate the exchange of credit card numbers, prepaid card details, and account ID information.[83] ISIS groups have been known to garner support via Twitter campaigns, requiring donors to purchase international prepaid cards for disclosure to ISIS members. The card numbers are sent to ISIS members based close to an ISIS stronghold, whereupon they are sold at a lower price for cash to fund the terrorist organisation.[84]

3.2.1 Terrorist Financing via Crowdfunding

Crowdfunding—the practice of soliciting small contributions of funds from large groups of people—has been successfully exploited by terrorist organisations and others, especially online. It has become an increasingly popular method of raising funds without centralised oversight, particularly in an era in which traditional charities and donors who use formal banking systems are facing increasing global pressure.[85] While not all efforts are successful, crowdfunding websites can be easily created and advertised on social media to maximise outreach. They provide little due diligence on the legitimacy of the cause, making them vulnerable to terrorist financing efforts.[86] Indeed, the use of social media for crowdfunding has become popular partly due to the ability of donors to create fake accounts, complicating identification efforts. Crowdfunding also offers terrorists an avenue for the immediate influx of capital in preparation for a terrorist attack. For example, in the days leading up to the San Bernadino terrorist attack in 2015, the perpetrators were able to secure US$28,500 in peer-to-peer lending facilitated by Prosper Marketplace. Those funds were used in part to purchase the components for pipe bombs and ammunition.[87] Crowdfunding for terrorist organisations typically necessitates the adoption of techniques to disguise the true intent of the campaign, thus avoiding unwanted attention from the platform or from law enforcement. This may involve announcing an alternative—legitimate—target for the fundraising activity, or using keywords that signify to sympathisers the true intended use of donated funds.

In 2013, Al Sadaqah (an Al-Qaeda linked organisation) launched a fundraising campaign on Facebook. While the Facebook accounts were quickly shut down, the group continued to campaign through Twitter, asking supporters to 'donate anonymously and securely with Bitcoin'.[88] The Twitter posts contained messages that

[82] US Department of the Treasury (2019).

[83] FATF (2015b), p. 33.

[84] Planet Compliance (2021).

[85] Keatinge and Keen (2019), p. 192.

[86] Ibid (192)

[87] Davis (2020), p. 3.

[88] Malik (2018).

read, for example, 'just seen a brother with one arm going to fight the regime in Hama, what is your excuse to not help them? Keep them in your dua and message me how you can help them now financially'.[89] During 2017–18, an Al-Qaeda-linked Twitter account called for donations in Bitcoin, Monero, Dash and Verge to assist the terror campaign in Syria, urging followers to 'support the Mujihideen in Syria with your wealth 100% anonymous completely untraceable'.[90] Campaigns to finance Jihad[91] often target women, who are encouraged to donate and sponsor fighters since they are less able to join the fighting themselves.[92] This was seen in fundraising initiatives that were promoted on social media during the early stages of the Syrian conflict in 2013—particularly the Ramadan Campaign, which aimed to recruit and prepare thousands of jihadists and raised over US$350,000 in just one night.[93]

To quantify the prevalence of crowdfunding on the surface web (that is, social media platforms), our keyword search revealed, over 3 months, 536 results from Twitter, 676 results from Instagram, 730 results from TikTok, and 1788 results from Facebook. While useful in providing a benchmark against which results from the dark web can be compared, these results are limited as they do not extend to the entirety of the surface web, including encrypted messaging apps such as Threema, Signal and Telegram. Indeed, according to Europol's 2018 Internet Organised Crime Threat Assessment report, terrorist sympathisers have been pushed into using these encrypted services—which offer private and closed groups the opportunity to communicate without being detected—by the success of law enforcement takedown campaigns (Fig. 1).

3.3 Use of the Dark Web for Terrorist Financing

Social media sites are often used to direct users to sites on the dark web where they can communicate and effect transactions with a higher degree of anonymity.[94] In some cases, content is removed from the surface web and resurrected on the dark web, where it is protected from hacktivists.[95] For example, on 15 November 2015—two days after the Paris attacks—ISIS posted a message discussing its official Isdarat website. The message contained links to a hidden Tor address, indicating the move

---

[89] Ibid 42.

[90] Keatinge et al. (2018), p. 34.

[91] Jihadism can be defined as the belief that armed confrontation with political rivals is a theologically legitimate and instrumentally efficient method for socio-political change. It is used by western academics to describe violent Sunni Islamists. See BBC (2014).

[92] Keatinge and Keen (2019), p. 187.

[93] Keatinge and Keen (2019), p. 187.

[94] Keatinge and Keen (2019), p. 180; RT (2015).

[95] Weimann (2018).

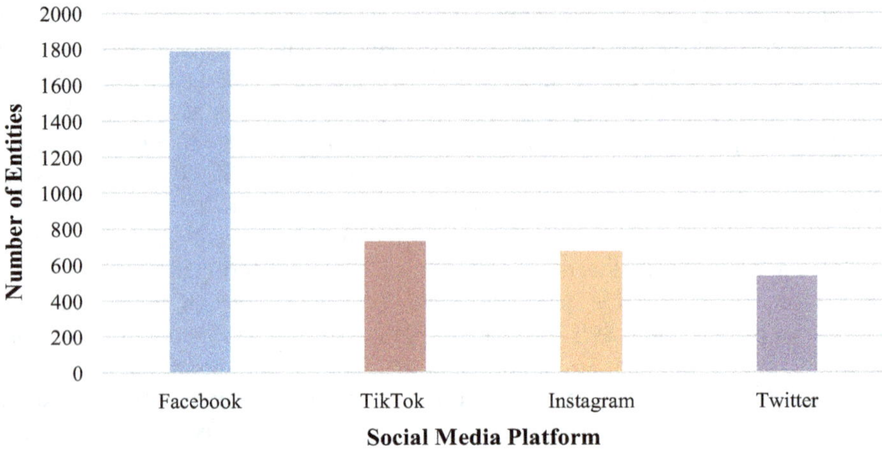

Fig. 1 Keyword Search Results from Surface Web

of the Isdarat outlet to the dark web.[96] It stated: 'Due to severe constraints imposed on the #Caliphate_Publications website, any new domain is deleted after being posted. We announce the launch of the website for "dark web".'[97] It should be noted that the dark web has not yet been used at an organisational level[98]; however, it is vulnerable to further exploitation by aspiring terrorists as it represents a medium through which activities are unlikely to be detected. In this sense, the FATF has identified that the dark web has been utilised by lone actors seeking to procure weapons in order to commit ethnically or racially motivated terror attacks.[99]

3.3.1 Terrorist Financing via Crowdfunding

In 2018, a TOR website titled SadaquaCoins was discovered on the dark web.[100] It is considered to be the first dark web crowdfunding platform. The website states that its goal is to 'support the Jihad by providing a secure platform between the funders and the project organisers'.[101] It advertises that donors can send funds in the form of Bitcoin or Monero to help pay for 4 × 4 pickup trucks, 0.50 calibre bolt action rifles and ammunition, wind readers for sniping, silencers, and even combat training for

[96] Weimann (2016b), p. 41.

[97] Ibid.

[98] Malik (2018).

[99] FATF (2021a).

[100] Maloney (2021).

[101] Maloney (2021).

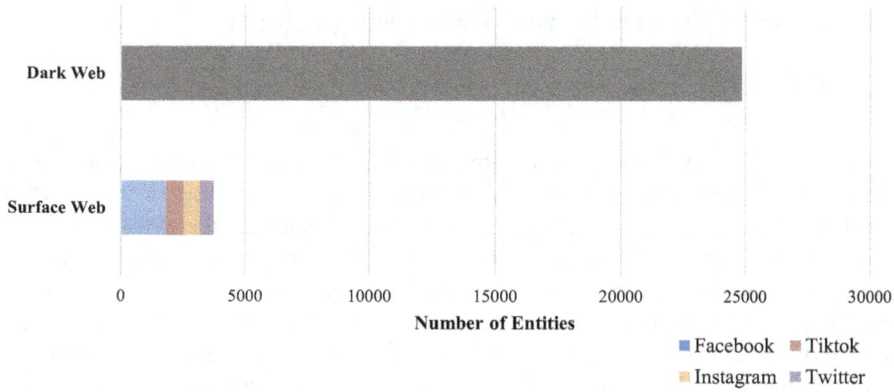

Fig. 2 Keyword Search Comparison (Dark Web vs Surface Web)

aspiring jihadists.[102] The website suggests four ways to support the project: advertising to others, purchasing cryptocurrency to donate, mining crypto for donations, and 'hustling'—a term used to describe efforts to hack or coerce cryptocurrency from non-Muslims or disbelievers by means of overpowering them. It encourages users to hack Bitcoin and redirect transactions, or to blackmail the owners of crypto databases to secure a ransom.[103] Another dark website used to transfer Bitcoins to jihadis is titled Fund the Islamic Struggle without Leaving a Trace.[104] In another instance, Israeli authorities prosecuted a man named Ahmed Sarsur for his attempt to acquire weapons, including explosives, and hire snipers on the dark web, as well as providing financial support to terrorists in Syria.[105]

To quantify the prevalence of terrorist financing via crowdfunding on the dark web, our keyword search revealed, over the same 3 months as the surface web survey, 24,849 results for the search terms. This is a significantly greater number of identified search entities when compared to the results observed on the surface web social media platforms, suggesting a willingness for terrorists and sympathisers to discuss terrorist financing activities without feeling the need for further obfuscation efforts (such as by utilising codewords or encrypted messaging applications)—a result of the anonymity inherent in the dark web (Fig. 2).

[102] Maloney (2021).

[103] Maloney (2021).

[104] Wang and Zhu (2021).

[105] Rivera and Archy (2019).

4 Current Counter-Terrorist Financing Efforts

4.1 CTF Measures: International Organisations

According to the FATF recommendations, member states are required to criminalise terrorist financing and implement targeted financial sanction regimes to comply with the United Nations Security Council resolutions regarding the prevention and suppression of terrorist financing.[106] Recommendation 16 (also known as the Travel Rule) requires jurisdictions to ensure that financial institutions include accurate originator and beneficiary information on wire transfers, and that the information remains with the wire transfer throughout the payment chain.[107] In October 2018, the FATF expanded the operation of the Travel Rule fundamentally, applying the regulatory regime to virtual assets and virtual assets service providers.[108]

Cryptocurrency service providers and financial institutions are therefore required to obtain, hold and transmit specific originator and beneficiary information immediately and securely when transferring cryptocurrencies. The updated recommendations require service providers to submit Travel Rule information in sufficient time for both parties to conduct sanctions screening, identify any designated persons or entities, and, if necessary, freeze funds before any sanctioned actor can access or dissipate the funds. Given the immediacy of cryptocurrency transactions, the updated recommendations necessitate that information be transmitted either simultaneously or before the transaction is executed.[109]

The Travel Rule is a key CTF measure aimed at prohibiting terrorists from accessing wire transfers to move cryptocurrencies across borders. Its application to the cryptocurrency context requires the implementation of a registration or licensing regime to enable the supervision and enforcement (for example, via sanctions) of CTF obligations across the cryptocurrency ecosystem at both ends of a proposed transaction. In addition, successful implementation in the private sector requires the implementation of appropriate risk identification and mitigation measures, as well as continued risk monitoring and assessment. However, as a consequence of the multi-jurisdictional nature of cryptocurrencies, the efficacy of the Travel Rule depends on its consistent global implementation and enforcement.

In June 2023, the FATF issued a targeted update on the implementation of the FATF standards on cryptocurrencies and their associated service providers.[110] The FATF confirmed that, in light of the increasing terrorist financing threats posed by cryptocurrencies, jurisdictions should take immediate action to mitigate those risks, including by ensuring full implementation of the Travel Rule.[111]

[106] FATF, Recommendations 5–6.

[107] FATF, Recommendation 16.

[108] De Koker et al. (2022).

[109] FATF (2021b), pp. 185, 187.

[110] FATF (2023).

[111] FATF (2023), p. 3.

In addition, the FATF raised several issues concerning the suitability of the Travel Rule to the transfer of cryptocurrencies. Currently, the Rule requires transmitting service providers to identify and conduct due diligence on their counterparty service provider. The lack of a uniform global approach to licensing cryptocurrency service providers undermines the ability for counterparty identification and prevents a transmitting party from determining with certainty whether a designated recipient is able to securely hold Travel Rule information or whether it is tied to a terrorist organisation or sanctioned person. The FATF has recognised that many of the private sector compliance tools implemented in response to the updated regulations fall short of the FATF Standards. It has strongly encouraged jurisdictions to maintain and publicise information on cryptocurrency service providers that are registered or licensed in their jurisdiction.

The FATF has confirmed the prevalence of cryptocurrencies being used to pay for illicit substances purchased on the dark web.[112] It emphasises that countries should ensure that the private sector is aware of the risks of dark web marketplaces and the need to take appropriate measures to deny criminals access to their business platforms and products.

4.2 CTF Measures: Social Media Sites

Social media companies regulate content that appears on their platforms according to internal policies informed by laws, regulations and community standards. These policies are often enforced via automated algorithmic systems, which have been criticised as lacking transparency and an understanding of local or culturally specific context. In this sense, algorithms targeted towards keywords or language models may lack the ability to capture the nuance inherent in informal communication, leading to the inadvertent removal of legitimate speech.

The Christchurch Call to Eliminate Terrorist and Violent Extremist Content Online was introduced in May 2019 to mobilise heads of state, international organisations, business, and digital organisations to take action against terrorist and extremist content online. It commits signatories—including more than 120 governments, as well as social media giants Facebook, Google, Twitter and YouTube—to a series of measures, including the development of tools to prevent the downloading of terrorist content, improving transparency in the detection and removal of content, and ensuring that algorithms designed and used by social media sites do not direct users towards violent extremist content. According to Facebook's internal report, 14.5 million items of content were removed from the platform in violation of its 'Dangerous Orgs: Terrorism' standard in the first quarter of 2023.[113]

[112] FATF (2022b).
[113] Meta (2023).

In 2021, the European Parliament issued Regulation (EU) 2021/784 on addressing the dissemination of terrorist content online. It established a legal framework to require Hosting Service Providers to remove terrorist content within 1 h of receiving a removal order from an authorised national authority. The regulation has the aim of preventing terrorists from using social media to propagate their ideology or to terrorise, radicalise or recruit. Platforms face sanctions if they fail to take proactive measures when they are exposed to terrorist content. Since the implementation of the regulation, the European Commission has decided to initiate infringement proceedings against 22 member states for failing to fully implement their obligations under the regulation.

In 2022, the EU adopted its Digital Services Act (DSA), aimed at preventing algorithmic systems from manipulating social media sites in order to amplify the spread of disinformation or other malicious purposes, including terrorist material. The DSA is primarily concerned with social networking and content-sharing platforms. It allows authorities to demand 'back door' access to encrypted messages on a case-by-case basis—for example, if a private Telegram group chat is suspected of being used by a terrorist group.[114] Similar measures have proved successful in limiting the effect of radicalisation efforts via social media. In 2021, ISIS spokesperson Abu Hamza al-Qurashi urged supporters to spend less time on social media and make 'more effort on high-impact attacks, jailbreaks and other operational activity'.[115] As of February 2023, the DSA obliges platforms with over 45 million users to carry out annual risk assessments.

In addition, the negative publicity surrounding algorithmic amplification has prompted certain social media services to implement measures to counter the spread of extremist content on their platforms. Facebook, Google and Microsoft have organised a Global Internet Forum to Counter Terrorism. They have also implemented a common database of 'hashes' (digital fingerprints), which restricts material removed from one site for violating community standards from being uploaded to another site. However, the commercial realities of social media sites, in which profit is click-based, encourage the use of algorithms to tailor content to individual users and to circumvent legal frameworks. Furthermore, the vast volume of material published on social media necessitates that content is screened via algorithms, to be automatically deleted or reviewed by a human moderator, or flagged via a user reporting system. This process has been criticised as lacking transparency and an understanding of local or culturally specific context, resulting in the deletion of journalism, satire, art, anti-terrorism critique, and the documentation of human rights abuses.[116]

[114]Holbrook (2022), p. 351.

[115]Burke (2021).

[116]Human Rights Watch (2020).

5 Conclusions

Given the importance of funding in supporting terrorist operations, the field of CTF aims to disrupt and seize the financial resources of terrorist actors and organisations. The FATF plays a central role in combatting terrorist financing by setting global standards for CTF, assisting jurisdictions in implementing the Security Council resolutions on terrorism and evaluating compliance for the prevention and prosecution of terrorist financing.[117] Recently, the FATF has raised concerns about the use of social media by terrorists to fundraise, highlighting the anonymity and ease with which terrorist organisations can utilise the surface web to gain sympathy and donations.[118] The FATF has also brought attention to the use of cryptocurrencies for fundraising, with some discussion of the risks posed by the dark web.[119]

Terrorists regularly adapt their methods of raising, moving and using funds to circumvent legal interception.[120] With increased regulatory efforts and CTF strategies to reduce terrorist access to fiat currencies, terrorist organisations are increasingly turning to digital cryptocurrencies to raise and transfer funds for their activities.[121] Global fundraising is enabled through the use of social media and other internet platforms to encourage or require payment in digital currencies.[122] These decentralised methods of terrorist financing create new challenges for law enforcement and CTF authorities. In light of these risks, the FATF has issued binding global standards to prevent the misuse of virtual assets. These standards have focused on guiding countries to mitigate risks by ensuring that virtual asset service providers are licensed or registered and subject to supervision or monitoring by competent national authorities.[123] The FATF recognises, however, that peer-to-peer transactions (commonly used by terrorist financiers) occur between individuals and thus are not monitored by an entity carrying out the FATF standards.[124] That is, peer-to-peer transactions are essentially unregulated and, according to the FATF, likely to increase as more jurisdictions implement FATF standards to supervise virtual asset service providers.[125]

These concerns are exacerbated when combined with the use of encryption technologies on the dark web. The emerging threat of cyberterrorism, while still in its infancy, will require the implementation of considered global countermeasures to ensure that CTF efforts to date are not undermined but strengthened. The findings of this paper highlight that terrorist financing initiatives and processes are being

117 FATF (n.d.).

118 FATF (2015b).

119 FATF (2014).

120 FATF (2019).

121 Dion-Schwarz et al. (2019).

122 FATF (2015b).

123 FATF (2021c).

124 FATF (2021c), p. 19.

125 FATF (2021c), p. 19.

considered and discussed on the dark web to a greater extent than on selected social media sites on the surface web. This is likely due to the strengthened CTF efforts by authorities and social media platforms over recent years, with criminals turning instead to the safe haven of the dark web, where anonymity and the probability of non-detection are enticing. With the growing popularity of cryptocurrency and other digital payment systems, anonymity is further protected. While terrorist financing on the dark web is not a new phenomenon, this research sheds light on the prevalence of terrorist financing on the dark web and the consequent need for global governance of this shadowy digital domain.

Acknowledgement The author wishes to thank CyberPro for granting access to their tools that operate on the dark web, which provided the unique data on which this research is based. Special thanks to Samuel Orchard and Isabelle Nicolas for their excellent research assistance, and to the anonymous reviewers for their comments on earlier drafts.

References

Al-Mughrabi N (2023) Hamas armed wing announces suspension of bitcoin fundraising, 28 April 2023. https://www.reuters.com/world/middle-east/hamas-armed-wing-announces-suspension-bitcoin-fundraising-2023-04-28/. Accessed 16 Dec 2023

BBC (2014) What is jihadism? BBC News, 11 December 2014. https://www.bbc.com/news/world-middle-east-30411519. Accessed 16 Dec 2023

Berman MK (2001) The deep web: surfacing hidden value. BrightPlanet

Blannin P (2017) Islamic State's financing: sources, methods and utilisation. CTTA 9(5):13–22

Brisard J-C (2002) Terrorism financing: roots and trends of Saudi terrorism financing. Report prepared for the president of the Security Council, United Nations. JCB Consulting

Brown SD (2016) Cryptocurrency and criminality: the bitcoin opportunity. Police J Theory Pract Principles 89(4):327–339

Burke J (2021) Islamic extremists planning 'rash of attacks' after covid curbs lifted, says UN. The Guardian, 6 February 2021. https://www.theguardian.com/world/2021/feb/05/islamic-extremists-planning-rash-of-attacks-after-covid-curbs-lifted-says-un. Accessed 16 Dec 2023

Burns L (2011) Toward a contemporary definition of terrorism. Forum Public Policy J Oxford Round Table 3(1):1–29

Cassese A (1989) Terrorism, politics, and law: the Achille Lauro affair. Polity, Cambridge

Cortright D, Lopez GA (eds) (2007) Uniting against terror: cooperative nonmilitary responses to the global terrorist threat. MIT Press, Cambridge

Davis J (2020) New technologies but old methods in terrorism financing. Research Briefing No 2, Project CRAAFT. https://static1.squarespace.com/static/5e399e8c6e9872149fc4a041/t/5f18579880818c6feb0e6a49/1595430886467/CRAAFT+Jessica+Davis.pdf. Accessed 16 Dec 2023

De Koker L, Goldbarsht D (2022) Financial technologies and financial crime: key developments and areas for future research. In: Goldbarsht D, De Koker L (eds) Financial technology and the law: combating financial crime. Springer International Publishing, Cham, pp 303–320

De Koker L, Ocal T, Casanovas P (2022) Where's Wally? FATF, virtual asset service providers, and the regulatory jurisdictional challenge. In: Goldbarsht D, De Koker L (eds) Financial technology and the law: combating financial crime. Springer International Publishing, Cham, pp 151–183

Denic N (2017) Government activities to detect, deter and disrupt threats enumerating from the dark web. Dissertation, US Army Command and General Staff College. https://apps.dtic.mil/sti/pdfs/AD1038658.pdf. Accessed 16 Dec 2023

Dion-Schwarz C, Manheim D, Johnston PB (2019) Terrorist use of cryptocurrencies: technical and organisational barriers and future threats. RAND Corporation, Santa Monica. https://www.rand.org/content/dam/rand/pubs/research_reports/RR3000/RR3026/RAND_RR3026.pdf. Accessed 16 Dec 2023

Eisermann D (2020) Cryptocurrencies as threats to public security and counter terrorism: risk analysis and regulatory challenges. In: Counter Extremism Project, Berlin Risk. https://www.counterextremism.com/sites/default/files/Cryptocurrencies%20as%20Threats%20to%20Public%20Security%20and%20Counter-Terrorism_ENG%20Translation_April%202020.pdf. Accessed 16 Dec 2023

FATF (2014) Virtual currencies: key definitions and potential AML/CFT risks. Paris

FATF (2015a) Best practices, combating the abuse of non-profit organisations (recommendation 8). Paris

FATF (2015b) Emerging terrorist financing risks. Paris

FATF (2015c) Financing of the terrorist organisation Islamic State in Iraq and the Levant (ISIL). Paris

FATF (2016) Guidance for a risk-based approach or value money transfer services. Paris

FATF (2018) Financing of recruitment for terrorist purposes. Paris

FATF (2019) Terrorist financing and risk assessment guidance. Paris

FATF (2021a) Ethnically or racially motivated terrorism financing. Paris

FATF (2021b) Updated guidance for a risk-based approach: virtual assets and virtual asset service providers. Paris

FATF (2021c) Virtual assets and virtual asset service providers. Paris

FATF (2022a) Money laundering and terrorist financing risks arising from migrant smuggling. Paris

FATF (2022b) Money laundering from fentanyl and synthetic opioids. Paris

FATF (2023) Targeted update on implementation of the FATF standards on virtual assets and virtual asset service providers. Paris

FATF (n.d.) FATF's global efforts on combating terrorist financing. https://www.fatf-gafi.org/publications/fatfgeneral/documents/terroristfinancing.html. Accessed 16 Dec 2023

Finklea K (2017) Dark web. Congressional Research Service Report. https://sgp.fas.org/crs/misc/R44101.pdf

Foley S, Karlsen J, Putniņš T (2019) Sex, drugs, and bitcoin: how much illegal activity is financed through cryptocurrencies? Rev Financ Stud 32(5):1798–1853

Gerges FA (2016) ISIS: a history. Princeton University Press, Princeton

Gibbs JP (1989) Conceptualization of terrorism. Am Sociol Rev 54(3):329–340

Goldbarsht D (2017) Who's the legislator anyway? How the Fatf's global norms reshape Australian counter terrorist financing laws. Federal Law Rev 45(1):127–151

Goldbarsht D (2018) Shedding light on shadow banking: the money or value transfer service regime in Australia and its origins. J Crim Law 82(3):264–276

Goldbarsht D (2020) Global counter-terrorist financing and soft law: multi-layered approaches. Edward Elgar Publishing, Cheltenham

Gunning J (2008) Terrorism, charities and diasporas: contrasting the fundraising practices of Hamas and Al-Qaeda among Muslims in Europe. In: Biersteker TJ, Eckert SE (eds) Countering the financing of terrorism. Routledge, London

Hardouin P (2009) Banks governance and public-private partnership in preventing and confronting organized crime, corruption and terrorism financing. J Financ Crime 16(3):199–209

Hassan A, Nafees S, Putz C (2022) Cryptocurrency and terrorist financing in Asia. The Diplomat, 4 February 2022. https://thediplomat.com/2022/02/cryptocurrency-and-terrorist-financing-in-asia/. Accessed 16 Dec 2023

Holbrook D (2022) Social media and terrorism. In: Muro D, Wilson T (eds) Contemporary terrorism studies. Oxford University Press, Oxford

Hoskins A, O'Loughlin B (2010) War on media: the emergence of diffused war. Polity, Cambridge

Human Rights Watch (2020) Joint letter to new executive director, Global Internet Forum to Counter Terrorism, 30 July 2020. https://www.hrw.org/news/2020/07/30/joint-letter-new-executive-director-global-internet-forum-counter-terrorism. Accessed 16 Dec 2023

Hurlburt G (2017) Shining light on the dark web. Computer 50(4):100–105

Ibrahim SA (2021) Decrypting the risks of cryptocurrency: money laundering, terrorism financing, and proliferation financing. Pakistan Horiz 74(1):73–89

Jenkins B (1974) International terrorism: a new kind of warfare. Rand Corporation, Santa Monica

Jost PM, Sandhu HS (2000) The hawala alternative remittance system and its role in money laundering. Interpol General Secretariat, Lyon

Katsiri R (2019) Israeli blockchain intelligence company Whitestream tells 'Globes' how ISIS used Canadian based CoinPayments platform to convert bitcoin to money. Globes, 2 May 2019. https://en.globes.co.il/en/article-exclusive-isis-funded-sri-lanka-bombings-with-bitcoin-donations-1001284276. Accessed 16 Dec 2023

Keatinge T, Keen F (2019) Social media and (counter) terrorist finance: a fund-raising and disruption tool. Stud Confl Terror 42(1–2):178–205

Keatinge T, Carlisle D, Keen F (2018) Virtual currencies and terrorist financing: assessing the risks and evaluating responses. Study for the Policy Department for Citizens' Rights and Constitutional Affairs, European Parliament

Landman T, Crook J (2013) The democratization of technology and conflict analysis. Annual convention of the International Studies Association, the politics of international diffusion: regional and global dimensions, San Francisco, 3–6 April 2013, p 6. https://papers.ssrn.com/sol3/papers.cfm?abstract_id=2236095. Accessed 16 Dec 2023

Looney R (2003) Hawala: the terrorist's informal financial mechanism. Middle East Policy 10(1): 164–167

Macdonald S, Correia SG, Watkin A-L (2019) Regulating terrorist content on social media: automation and the rule of law. Int J Law Context 15(2):183–197

Malik N (2018) Terror in the dark: how terrorists use encryption, the dark net and cryptocurrencies. Henry Jackson Society, London. https://henryjacksonsociety.org/wp-content/uploads/2018/04/Terror-in-the-Dark.pdf. Accessed 16 Dec 2023

Maloney C (2021) Crypto crowdfunding terrorists: marketplace for jihadist crowdfunding found on dark web. CNN, 4 March 2021. https://www.ccn.com/crypto-crowdfunding-terrorists-marketplace-for-jihadist-crowdfunding-found-on-dark-web/. Accessed 16 Dec 2023

McCormick T (2013) The darknet: a short history. Sydney Morning Herald, 23 December 2013. https://www.smh.com.au/technology/the-darknet-a-short-history-20131220-2zpk6.html. Accessed 16 Dec 2023

Meta (2023) Community standards enforcement report. https://transparency.fb.com/data/community-standards-enforcement/. Accessed 16 Dec 2023

Nacos B (2016) Mass-mediated terrorism: mainstream and digital media in terrorism and counterterrorism. Rowman & Littlefield, Lanham

National Commission on Terrorist Attacks Upon the United States (2004) Monograph on terrorist financing: staff report to the commission. https://www.hsdl.org/?view&did=449287. Accessed 16 Dec 2023

Passas N (2003) Hawala and other informal value transfer systems: how to regulate them? J Risk Manag 5(2):49–59

Passas N (2006) Fighting terror with error: the counter-productive regulation of informal value transfers. Crime Law Soc Chang 45(4–5):315–336

Piazza F (2017) Bitcoin in the dark web: a shadow over banking secrecy and a call for a global response. South Calif Interdiscip Law J 26(521):526–546

Planet Compliance (2021) Annual regtech report on cryptocurrencies. https://www.planetcompliance.com/fintech-regtech-and-the-role-of-compliance-report/. Accessed 16 Dec 2023

Powell C (2001) Remarks on financing aspects of terrorism, 7 November 2001. https://2001-2009.state.gov/secretary/former/powell/remarks/2001/5979.htm. Accessed 18 June 2023

Rivera J, Archy W (2019) The role of the dark web in future cyberwars to come. Small Wars Journal Blog. https://smallwarsjournal.com/jrnl/art/role-dark-web-future-cyber-wars-come. Accessed 16 Dec 2023

Rosie G (1987) The directory of international terrorism. Paragon House, New York

RT (2015) ISIS funding in US via bitcoin. RT, 30 January 2015. https://www.rt.com/usa/227703-bitcoin-isis-us-fundraising/. 18 June 2023. Accessed 16 Dec 2023

Rudner M (2006) Using financial intelligence against the funding of terrorism. Int J Intell Counterintell 19(1):32–58

Ryder N (2020) Cryptoassets, social media platforms and defence against terrorism financing suspicious activity reports: a step into the regulatory unknown. J Bus Law 8:668–693

Shanahan T (2016) The definition of terrorism. In: Jackson R (ed) Routledge handbook of critical terrorism studies. Routledge, London

Soudjin M (2019) Using police reports to monitor money laundering developments; continuity and change in 12 years of Dutch money laundering crime pattern analyses. Eur J Crim Policy Res 25(1):83–97

Stergiou D (2016) ISIS political economy: financing a terror state. J Money Laund Control 19(2): 189–207

Suchi PM, Wika PN (2021) Cybercrime and terrorism financing: Nigeria's potential vulnerabilities and policy options. Int J Inno Sci Res 5(7):425–427

Teichmann F (2018) Financing terrorism through hawala banking in Switzerland. J Financ Crime 25(2):287. https://doi.org/10.1108/JFC-06-2017-0056

Turner AB, McCombie S, Uhlmann AJ (2020) Analysis techniques for illicit bitcoin transactions. Front Comput Sci 2:600596. https://doi.org/10.3389/fcomp.2020.600596

US Department of the Treasury (2014) Treasury designates additional supporters of the Al-Nusraj Front and Al-Qaida. Press release, 22 August 2014. https://home.treasury.gov/news/press-releases/jl2613

US Department of the Treasury (2019) Under secretary Mandelker remarks at the 19th annual international conference on counterterrorism. Press release, 11 September 2019. https://home.treasury.gov/news/press-releases/sm773

van Benthem T (2018) Social media actors in the fight against terrorism: technology and its impact on human rights. Camb Int Law J 7(2):284–300

Wagman S (2022) Cryptocurrencies and national security: the case of money laundering and terrorism financing. Harv Natl Secur J 14:87

Wang S, Zhu X (2021) Evaluation of potential cryptocurrency development ability in terrorist financing. Policing 15(4):2329–2340

Weber J, Kruisbergen EW (2019) Criminal markets: the dark web, money laundering and counterstrategies – an overview of the 10th research conference on organised crime. Trends Organ Crime 22:346–356

Weimann G (2010) Terrorist Facebook: terrorists and online social networking. In: Last M, Kandel A (eds) Web intelligence and security: advances in data and text mining techniques for detecting and preventing terrorist activities on the web. IOS Press, Amsterdam

Weimann G (2014) New terrorism and new media. Wilson Centre, Washington. https://www.wilsoncenter.org/publication/new-terrorism-and-new-media. Accessed 18 June 2023

Weimann G (2016a) Going dark: terrorism on the dark web. Stud Confl Terror 39(3):195–206

Weimann G (2016b) Terrorist migration to the dark web. Perspect Terr 10(3):40–44

Weimann G (2018) Going darker? The challenge of dark net terrorism. Wilson Centre, Washington. https://www.wilsoncenter.org/sites/default/files/media/documents/publication/going_darker_challenge_of_dark_net_terrorism.pdf. Accessed 16 Dec 2023

Wilson T, Williams D (2019) Hamas shifts tactics in bitcoin fundraising, highlighting cryptorisks: research. Reuters, 26 April 2019. https://www.reuters.com/article/us-crypto-currencies-hamas-idUSKCN1S20FA. Accessed 16 Dec 2023

Doron Goldbarsht LLB, LLM (HUJI), PhD (UNSW), is the Director of the Financial Integrity Hub (FIH) and an Associate Professor at Macquarie Law School, where he teaches banking and financial crime. He is an authority on anti-money laundering and counter-terrorist financing (AML/CTF) regulations, with expertise in the related fields of compliance and financial innovation, with over 20 years of experience in the field. His recent books *Financial Crime and the Law: Identifying and Mitigating Risks* (Springer 2024, co-edited), *Financial Crime, Law and Governance: Navigating Challenges in Diverse Contexts* (Springer 2024, co-edited), *Financial Technology and the Law: Combating Financial Crime* (Springer, 2022, co-edited), and *Global Counter-Terrorist Financing and Soft Law: Multi-Layered Approaches* (Edward Elgar, 2020), as well as journal and chapter publications, focus on international AML/CTF standards and the mechanisms for their effective implementation and compliance at the national level.

Economic and Demographic Biases in FATF Mutual Evaluation Results

Charles Littrell

Abstract National anti-money laundering (AML) and countering the financing of terrorism (CFT) jurisdictional assessments are prominent in the international AML/CFT movement. These assessments are a material element in determining the extent to which any nation and its financial system can participate in the global payments system, and the terms and conditions upon which that participation will be conducted. At the extreme, badly rated countries not only lose access to the international financial system, but find it difficult to import essential food, medicines, and other supplies, even if they possess the funds to pay for them.

1 Introduction

National AML/CFT assessments are created by a number of official and private agencies. If the international AML movement relies upon legitimacy to meet its ends, then it is critical that jurisdictional AML/CFT assessments are reasonably unbiased.

This paper investigates empirically identifiable biases in the leading global jurisdictional AML risk assessment: the Financial Action Task Force's (FATF) mutual evaluation reports (MERs[1]).

Some biases are legitimate: a bias against regimes that welcome dirty money, for example, would make a great deal of sense in AML/CFT terms. Other biases would

This paper presents a personal view. Thanks to my colleagues Sharon Branch and Cindy Thompson for research support, and Marina Johnson for her assistance. A prior version of this paper was presented in Littrell (2021).

[1] FATF (n.d.-b).

C. Littrell (✉)
Central Bank of The Bahamas, Nassau, NP, Bahamas
e-mail: cwlittrell@centralbankbahamas.com

D. Goldbarsht, L. de Koker (eds.), *Financial Crime and the Law*, Ius Gentium: Comparative Perspectives on Law and Justice 115,
https://doi.org/10.1007/978-3-031-59543-1_8

be illegitimate, such as biases against (for example) poor, non-White, or small jurisdictions.

In this paper we identify four substantial and potentially illegitimate biases:

1. The FATF frameworks for both technical compliance and effectiveness standards appear punitive to poorer countries relative to richer countries;
2. FATF assessments of AML/CFT effectiveness appear heavily biased against small island states, which bias is not repeated for (among other examples) European micro-states;
3. FATF effectiveness assessments are heavily biased against Black majority countries; and
4. The FATF effectiveness assessments are remarkably biased in favour of the five White majority new world countries.

1.1 The International AML Assessment Regime

Per Littrell (2018),[2] there are several entities offering public ratings of a jurisdiction's AML effectiveness.

AML rating agencies fall into two groups: those conducting original assessments, and those building weighted indexes based upon the original assessments, plus other available databases. The FATF is the leading provider of original assessments, which at February 2023 amounted to reviews of 145 separate jurisdictions.

The FATF MERs comprise a 40-item technical compliance assessment and an 11-item effectiveness assessment. The FATF does not convert these assessments into single grades (Such as a Moody's or Fitch sovereign debt rating) but many users of FATF assessments deploy their own conversion metrics to rank countries on MER results. All users of which we are aware deploy the technical assessment results separately from the effectiveness results, and may weight these two items differently.

The FATF further delineates two lists: a "blacklist" comprising Iran, North Korea, and (recently) Myanmar, and a "grey list" of jurisdictions assessed to possess strategic deficiencies in their AML arrangements. The grey list flows from deficiencies in specified technical compliance and effectiveness findings.

[2] Littrell (2018).

2 Simple Demographic Difference Analysis in the FATF Results

The FATF has in the past decade pursued its fourth round of mutual evaluation reports (MERs).[3] The results from these MERs are published on a country-by-country basis,[4] comprising the 40 technical compliance elements and the 11 effectiveness elements. The FATF also publishes a blacklist and a grey list of jurisdictions asserted to display "strategic deficiencies",[5] with publication updated thrice yearly.

It is easily demonstrable that the FATF MERs vary across country types, with differences apparent across differing levels of national wealth, differing racial characteristics, and some differing geographic and historical characteristics. This paper quantifies these differences, and considers whether they represent justified or unjustified biases.

2.1 FATF Technical Compliance and Effectiveness Ratings

The first three rounds of FATF jurisdictional assessments focused upon technical compliance, which focuses upon legislative, regulatory, and criminal justice regimes and outcomes. From the fourth round of assessments since 2014, the FATF has included a separate rating of "effectiveness".

As a general observation, FATF technical compliance ratings are more resistant to opinion bias than are effectiveness ratings. The former are based upon detailed standards. The latter rely more upon, in the first instance, the opinions of the international MER assessment team, and in the second instance, the adjustments to the assessment team's ratings by the FATF secretariat and the FATF plenary.

For both technical compliance and effectiveness, FATF MERs follow an International Monetary Fund precedent and assign one of four descriptions. These range from "Compliant" through "Noncompliant" for technical compliance, and from High to Low effectiveness on the effectiveness assessment. We have scored the results as the square of the numbers 1 through 4, with 1 representing the best score. Jurisdictional rankings are based upon average technical compliance and effectiveness ratings.

We tested other conversion methods such as a (0, 1, 2, 3) scoring map, and linear vs. exponential weights. These produce nearly identical results, with rank correlations among the competing methods typically exceeding 0.95 and approaching 1.00.

[3] FATF (2013).

[4] FATF (2023a).

[5] FATF (2021).

Following Littrell and O'Brien (2020),[6] we have extracted the FATF's MER results as of February 2023, and ranked countries first by their aggregate technical compliance scores, and secondly by their aggregate effectiveness scores. Where relevant, we have also included macroeconomic data from the jurisdictions listed in the World Bank's database.[7] For a handful of very small and often non-country jurisdictions, we have relied upon GDP data from the United Nations.[8]

2.2 *Ethnic Classifications*

This paper initially looks at FATF MER differences by ethnicity, then delves deeper to delineate differences by jurisdictional ethnic subgroups.

Ethnic classifications are a fraught and complex topic.[9] This paper defines ethnicity as the state of belonging to a large group of people who have the same national, racial, or cultural origins, or the state of belonging to such a group.[10] The analysis draws on the dominant ethnic features of a country to classify the ethnicity of the country. To label countries the paper draws on the US government classification of racial classification: White; Black or African American; American Indian or Alaska Native; Asian; Native Hawaiian or Other Pacific Islander.[11] Those classifications are however not fully suitable to apply to countries globally, especially from a financial regulatory perspective. They are therefore augmented by religion where that is a dominant and pervasive cultural feature of a country. This is particularly the case in relation to countries with predominantly Muslim populations as the religious principles tend to impact on the law and other common features of the society, including financial services regulation and practices. As the classification is done at a global rather than a US federal level, the labels of American Indian or Alaska Native and Native Hawaiian or Other Pacific Islander are not utilised and Hispanic is added.

Determining the dominant ethnic feature of a country is not an exact science. This paper focuses on assessments made by FATF delegation officials and financial regulators. The author therefore draws on his personal experience and knowledge of such views held, to classify the countries in a manner that would reflect in his experience such classification by such officials.

In this paper we have defined the following ethnic majority groups:

---

[6] Littrell and O'Brien (2020).

[7] World Bank (n.d.).

[8] UNCTAD (n.d.).

[9] Baumann (2004); Green Elliott (2006).

[10] Cambridge Dictionary (2023).

[11] US Census Bureau (2021).

- White, mainly in Europe but including White majority ex-colonies in the new world plus Israel
- Asia and the Pacific Islands
- Black, in both sub-Saharan Africa and the Caribbean
- Hispanic/Latin American
- Moslem.

Our general approach was based upon geography, so (for example) Albania is both European and majority Moslem, but is classified as White. Israel is *sui generis*, but also classified as White. Spain and Portugal are arguably Hispanic, but are classified as White. Countries often display mixed ethnicities, but in most cases there is an obvious majority.

We have separated the North African and middle eastern Moslem majority counties (broadly, Morocco to Pakistan) into a Moslem group, while central and east Asian majority Moslem countries are included in the Asian group.

We acknowledge that there are competing ways to classify countries, and in fact this initial classification proved simplistic. The Asian, Hispanic, and Moslem groups fall broadly into the middle of the FATF classifications, and in an econometric sense offer fewer insights.[12] The Black and White jurisdictions, however, are clearly heterogeneous.

It also became clear through econometric analysis that there are probably non-racial biases in the FATF MER rankings, especially a large bias in favour of the White ex-colonies, and against small island states.

2.3 FATF MER Results by Broad Ethnic Group

We first examine the results based upon median effectiveness and technical compliance (TC) rankings across countries.[13]

The difference between technical compliance and effectiveness ranks tells us something about the overall opinion formed for a jurisdiction. Jurisdictions with large negative differences (TC rank better than effectiveness rank) are assessed to have better rules and regulations than actual performance on the ground. Jurisdictions with large positive differences are the opposite.

We consider that the differences between technical compliance and effectiveness rankings show the extent to which any MER has "forgiven" poor technical compliance with good effectiveness ratings, or vice versa. From the last column of Table 1, we see appreciable but not particularly startling outcomes. Hispanic, Moslem, and Black differences are not notably large in a practical or statistical sense, though in

[12]There are substantial differences between Asian continental and Pacific Island jurisdictions, which would reward deeper study in another paper.

[13]We also tested technical compliance and effectiveness on average rankings, but these are insignificantly different from the median comparisons.

Table 1 Summary FATF MER Results by Jurisdiction Ethnicity

Ethnicity	Count	Effectiveness Rank (Median)	Technical Compliance Rank (Median)	Rank Median Difference
White	49	35	51	18
Asia/ Pacific	30	74	83	19
Hispanic	14	60	63	(3)
Moslem	9	78	74	11
Black	43	113	111	(9)

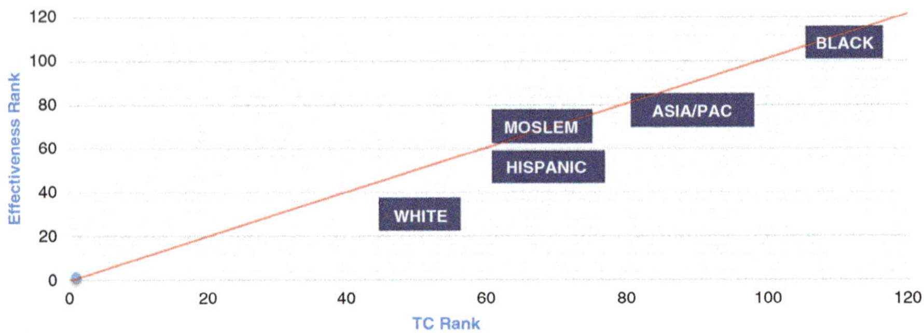

Fig. 1 Median Technical Compliance vs. Effectiveness Ranks

aggregate are negative. The White and Asian differences show a strong positive for effectiveness vs. technical compliance.

Figure 1 demonstrates a broadly linear relationship between technical compliance ranks and effectiveness ranks, across simple ethnic groups. Groups above the line are assessed with better technical compliance than effectiveness, and vice versa. The upper right of this chart is the worst quadrant, and the lower left the best.

White and Asian countries are favoured on effectiveness relative to technical compliance, but in general technical compliance is a reasonable predictor for effectiveness rank. This says nothing about whether the TC assessments are accurate, but indicates at least one strong correlation.

At the aggregate racial composition level, there are clear differences in aggregate FATF ratings, but these may be justifiable based on the reality on the ground for each group. Furthermore, there are not startling differences between technical compliance and effectiveness ratings.

At this point we have established the entirely unsurprising finding that FATF MER results vary quite a lot by jurisdictional ethnic group. This has little to say about whether such variances are legitimate, which is the subject of the rest of this paper.

When we delve below the aggregate racial categories, however, we see startling differences in jurisdictional differences between TC and effectiveness rankings.

Table 2 Five Most and Least Advantaged Jurisdictions on Effectiveness vs. Compliance

Jurisdiction	Effectiveness Rank	Technical Compliance Rank	TC Rank Minus Effectiveness Rank
Vanuatu	133	14	(119)
Mauritius	107	10	(97)
The Bahamas	103	7	(96)
Iceland	78	10	(68)
Trinidad and Tobago	98	8	(90)
United States	5	101	96
Australia	16	108	92
New Zealand	9	94	85
Uzbekistan	13	89	76
Holy See	19	91	72

Table 3 Top Ten Technical Compliance Jurisdictions

TC Rank	Jurisdiction	Effectiveness Rank	TC – Effectiveness Rank
1	Bermuda	12	(11)
2	Spain	2	–
3	United Kingdom	3	–
4	Cayman Islands	92	(88)
5	Macao	35	(30)
6	Gibraltar	78	(72)
7	The Bahamas	103	(96)
8	Iceland	98	(90)
9	Isle of Man	71	(62)
10	Trinidad and Tobago	92	(82)

From Table 2, we see that small island states of every ethnicity are often rated quite badly on effectiveness vs. technical compliance. Conversely, the White majority ex-colonies seem to be getting a very large credit for effectiveness vs. technical compliance. If we look beyond the top and bottom five on TC minus Effectiveness rank, we continue to see the pattern that mainly White, mainly rich countries are at the favoured end, and mainly non-White, often island states dominate the bottom end.

Table 3 gives a similar view, with the added emphasis that the top of the TC table is dominated by small island[14] states, which with the exception of Bermuda suffer very large reductions in their effectiveness rank relative to their TC rank. The two large, wealthy, White majority countries in the top ten, Spain and the United Kingdom, generate identical results for effectiveness.

[14] Or in the cases of Macao and Gibraltar, near-island.

Table 4 Top Ten Effectiveness Jurisdictions

Effectiveness Rank	Jurisdiction	Technical Compliance Rank	TC – Effectiveness Rank
1	France	20	19
2	Spain	2	–
3	United Kingdom	3	–
4	Israel	28	24
5	United States	101	96
6	Netherlands	40	34
7	Italy	19	12
8	Russia	71	63
9	New Zealand	94	85
10	Taiwan	52	42

It is straightforward to understand how a jurisdiction might rank well on TC but less well on effectiveness. Such jurisdictions might have a strong AML/CFT regime on paper, in the relevant laws, procedures, and regulations, but execution of that regime might be poor. Such regimes could be identified by high levels of illicit asset stocks and flows, but low levels of illicit asset recoveries, and few if any AML/CFT prosecutions and convictions. If we believe this explanation, we also need to believe that small island states of all ethnicities are good at technical compliance, but fail to follow up with effective implementation.

Alternatively, jurisdictions with good TC scores but poor effectiveness scores might be suffering from illegitimate negative bias in their effectiveness assessments for the FATF MERs.

It is less understandable how jurisdictions might rank well for effectiveness, but poorly for TC. The MER conclusion in this case is that the jurisdiction is effective despite the fact that it has failed to put in place the basic statutory and regulatory infrastructure necessary to suppress financial crime. Furthermore, it is necessary for us to believe that (most strikingly) the United States, Australia, and New Zealand are achieving remarkably good effectiveness results, despite remarkably bad TC assessments. Canada and Israel also rank high on this measure, so the White majority new world or ex-colony countries, as assessed by the FATF, are very effective in an AML sense, even though they lack the technical infrastructure to achieve that effectiveness.

Table 4 gives what is evidently the FATF conventional wisdom, that large, wealthy White majority countries are the world's most effective jurisdictions for suppressing financial crime. This is despite widely varying TC ranks.

2.4 FATF Quartile Analysis: Effectiveness

According to FATF evaluations, although four Black jurisdictions rank in the top ten of 145 jurisdictions for technical compliance, only two Black jurisdictions (Bermuda and Aruba) rank in the top half of the effectiveness quartiles, with all the remaining Black majority jurisdictions in the bottom half. Conversely, at least according to the FATF, there are no White majority countries in the fourth quartile for effectiveness, and only 6 of 49 jurisdictions in the bottom half. The other ethnic groups are more evenly distributed.

Again, we see distilled in Table 5 the FATF's aggregate assessment that when it comes to AML/CFT effectiveness assessments, White countries are much better than average, and Black countries very much worse than average.

The technical compliance Table 6 remains racially differentiated, but to a lesser degree than the effectiveness quartiles.

2.5 FATF Grey List

For many years the FATF has published a "grey list" of jurisdictions asserted to exhibit strategic deficiencies on their AML technical compliance and effectiveness MER results. Grey list presence is determined by performance on selected technical compliance and effectiveness ratings, with more practical weighting given to the effectiveness ratings. The FATF has more often than not placed jurisdictions on the

Table 5 FATF Effectiveness quartiles

Quartile	White	Black	Moslem	Hispanic	Asia-Pacific
I (best)	26	2	0	2	7
II	17	0	4	10	5
III	6	14	4	2	10
IV (worst)	0	27	1	0	8

Table 6 FATF Technical Compliance Quartiles

Quartile	White	Black	Moslem	Hispanic	Asia-Pacific
I (best)	19	7	1	5	5
II	14	4	3	6	9
III	12	8	3	3	10
IV (worst)	4	24	2	0	6

Table 7 FATF Grey List by Membership and Ethnicity, February 2023

	FATF non-Member	FATF Member
White	Albania,[a] Gibraltar	
Non-White	Barbados, Burkina Faso, Cambodia, Cayman Islands, Democratic Republic of the Congo, Ghana, Haiti, Jamaica, Jordan, Mali, Morocco, Mozambique, Nigeria, Panama, Philippines, Senegal, South Sudan, Syria, Tanzania, Uganda, United Arab Emirates, Yemen	South Africa, Turkiye

[a]Albania is ethnically European and majority Moslem

grey list; as of June 2023[15] 98 jurisdictions had spent some time on the grey list. The February 2023 grey list comprises 26 jurisdictions, distributed as per Table 7:

There are 145 global AML jurisdictions that have received a FATF MER. About one in five are currently on the FATF grey list. This grey list composition suggests that either:

(a) The world's AML/CFT non-compliance problems are nearly entirely concentrated among non-White, non-FATF member countries; or
(b) There is substantial illegitimate bias in the FATF's MER assessments and related outcomes.

2.6 Grey List Composition

The FATF has established[16] explicit standards for grey candidacy. The relevant extract from the FATF rules follows:

> The FATF reviews jurisdictions based on threats, vulnerabilities, or particular risks arising from the jurisdiction. Specifically, a jurisdiction will be reviewed when:
>
> 1. It does not participate in a FATF-style regional body (FSRB) or does not allow mutual evaluation results to be published in a timely manner; or
> 2. It is nominated by a FATF member or an FSRB. The nomination is based on specific money laundering, terrorist financing, or proliferation financing risks or threats coming to the attention of delegations; or
> 3. It has achieved poor results on its mutual evaluation, specifically:
>
>   - it has 20 or more non-Compliant (NC) or Partially Compliance (PC) ratings for technical compliance; or
>   - it is rated NC/PC on 3 or more of the following Recommendations: 3, 5, 6, 10, 11, and 20; or
>   - it has a low or moderate level of effectiveness for 9 or more of the 11 Immediate Outcomes, with a minimum of two lows; or
>   - it has a low level of effectiveness for 6 or more of the 11 Immediate Outcomes.

[15]FATF (n.d.-a).

[16]FATF (n.d.-c).

In the above context, the Immediate Outcomes are the 11 effectiveness measures. It will be evident from the above outline that a jurisdiction must perform only tolerably well on technical compliance to avoid the grey list, provided it scores reasonably well in effectiveness. Conversely, countries with poor effectiveness assessments will be grey listed even if they display perfect or near-perfect technical compliance. Here we have the essence of the problem with the grey list: it favours those countries who score well on effectiveness vs technical compliance, and the result is evident from Tables 2 through 3 above.

2.7 FATF MER Differences at the Ethnic Composition Level

It is worth emphasising that racial difference in jurisdictional MER assessments is not the same thing as racism in those assessments. The large differences shown here may reflect a reality that White countries are far more effective at AML risk management than are non-White (particularly Black) countries. This paper will test that proposition.

To better understand the composition of racial differences, the next section will delve more deeply into subgroup outcomes for White and Black majority countries.

3 Delving More Deeply into the FATF MERs

The above analyses lead to two additional questions:

1. Are the defined ethnic groups monolithic, or are there intra-group differences; and
2. Can we deploy econometric tools to determine why there are inter-group MER differences?

3.1 Better Defining White and Black Country Groups

The analysis in the previous section indicated that any racial differences are probably greatest between White and Black countries, and also that non-racial differences are in some cases important. We therefore have disaggregated our White and Black jurisdictions into segments that share common elements:

- Five White ex-colonies in the New World;[17]
- Western European countries;
- Eastern European countries;

[17] The United States, Australia, Canada, New Zealand, Israel.

Table 8 Disaggregated White and Black groups, macro inputs, and MER rankings

	TC Rank	Eff Rank	TC Rank – Eff Rank
White New World	94	8	86
Western Europe	27	19	7
Eastern Europe	71	50	17
European Micro-state	50	19	25
Africa	119	123	(7)
Caribbean	98	59	(20)

- Five European micro states;[18]
- Sub-Saharan Africa;
- The Caribbean.[19]

3.2 What Are Our Candidate Economic Explanatory Variables?

We conjectured that we would see significant differences for two economic variables:

1. GDP for a country. Broadly, large economies tend to do better than small economies; and
2. GDP per capita. Rich countries tend to do better than poor countries.

Working on this paper led to the following additional observations:

1. There is a clear difference in MER ratings between small islands and all other jurisdictions, but large (in economic and population terms) islands are indistinguishable from continental jurisdictions;
2. It might be instructive to compare the FATF treatment of small island states with its treatment of the continental European micro-states; and
3. White new world status is a major positive determinant of MER rankings for effectiveness, and/or a major negative determinant for TC rankings.

Contrasting from the aggregate racial group results, there are some extraordinary results in Table 8, which may show more readily in Fig. 2. Note that the rankings below are from the original group of 145 countries, not just the White and Black countries.

[18] Andorra, Holy See, San Marina, Monaco, Liechtenstein.

[19] Including The Bahamas and Bermuda, which are culturally if not geographically part of the Caribbean.

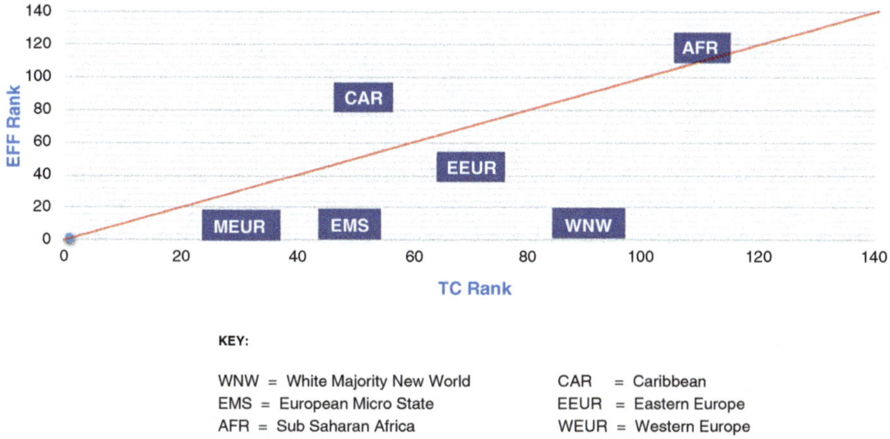

Fig. 2 MER Differences by Black and White Sub Groups

As with Fig. 1, "good" is lower left, and "bad" is upper right. We can think of "disfavoured" as above the line, and "favoured" as below the line.

We see that there are clear variances from the line of equality, notably:

(a) The Caribbean and African groups vary quite a lot on TC rank, but both are disfavoured in their "above the line" positioning.
(b) The small states of the Caribbean are about equivalent to the European micro-states (EMS) for TC, but score very much worse for effectiveness. Given the EMS concentration on financial services, which is similar to the Caribbean, this is a curious result.
(c) The three high-income White sub-groups display very different TC outcomes, but about the same effectiveness outcomes. One interpretation of this result is that from the FATF perspective, MER effectiveness outcomes are more driven by being wealthy and White, than by technical compliance in financial crime suppression.[20]
(d) The New World White outcome is difficult to explain in any satisfactory manner. The WNW countries simultaneously display near sub-Saharan technical compliance ratings and some of the world's best effectiveness rankings.
(e) Eastern European countries score about average on technical compliance, but appreciably better than average on effectiveness. This is despite the rather obvious flow of dirty money from Russia to Western countries, and increasingly persuasive reports of ineffective AML efforts.[21]

[20] There does not seem to be any difference in European regimes based upon European Community or European Union membership, which is not already explained by differences in income.

[21] Vedrenne (2023).

Table 9 Correlation (absolute value) between income and MER results

	GDP per capita	GDP
Technical Compliance Rank	0.35	0.24
Effectiveness Rank	0.46	0.23

(f) The largest difference is between Caribbean and White new world jurisdictions. The former typically score about 40 ranking places better than the latter on technical compliance, but about 80 ranking places worse on effectiveness.

3.3 *Economic Drivers for Technical Compliance and Effectiveness Ranks*

Having broken the simplistic White and Black groups into more homogenous sub-groups, we can further investigate group differences. We are seeking to answer three questions:

1. What are the determinants of technical compliance rank?
2. What are the determinants of effectiveness rank?
3. Do the answers to the above two questions vary with the racial composition of the ranked jurisdictions?

It seems clear that larger and (particularly) richer economies in general perform better on the FATF ratings, as outlined in Table 9.

3.4 *Regression Analysis: Is There a Beta for Racial Identity?*

With the insights from our previous analyses, we can deploy regression equations to directly query racial inputs into the FATF MER results. Our approach will be:

(a) To build regression equations using the two economic variables (size and income) and the two idiosyncratic variables (WNW status and small islands), and
(b) Then run the same regressions adding a new dummy variable for Black majority status.

If the regressions with a racial identity variable don't improve upon the original regression's predictive power, or generate insignificant coefficients, then this would indicate weak statistical support for explicit racial bias in our data sample. If the converse applies, this may indicate racial bias, or may indicate other variables which have not been picked up in the regression equations.

We run four regressions. The first two regressions determine coefficients for TC rank and Effectiveness rank without use of a racial identity signifier. These equations use the full data set.[22] Eqs. (3) and (4) replicate Eqs. (1) and (2), but with an additional racial signifier binary variable. Eqs. (3) and (4) only use the White and Black majority jurisdiction data.

$$\text{TCRank}_{\text{All}} = \alpha + \beta_1 \text{ LnGDP} + \beta_2 \text{ LnGDPPC} + \beta_3 \text{ WNW} + \beta_4 \text{ Island} + \beta_5 \text{EMS} + \varepsilon \tag{1}$$

$$\text{ERank}_{\text{All}} = \alpha + \beta_1 \text{ LnGDP} + \beta_2 \text{ LnGDPPC} + \beta_3 \text{ WNW} + \beta_4 \text{ Island} + \beta_5 \text{EMS} + \beta_6 \text{ TCRank} + \varepsilon \tag{2}$$

$$\text{TCRank}_{\text{BW}} = \alpha + \beta_1 \text{ LnGDP} + \beta_2 \text{ LnGDPPC} + \beta_3 \text{ WNW} + \beta_4 \text{ Island} + \beta_5 \text{EMS} + \beta_6 \text{Black} + \varepsilon \tag{3}$$

$$\text{ERank}_{\text{BW}} = \alpha + \beta_1 \text{ LnGDP} + \beta_2 \text{ LnGDPPC} + \beta_3 \text{ WNW} + \beta_4 \text{ Island} + \beta_5 \text{EMS} + \beta_6 \text{Black} + \beta_7 \text{ TCRank} + \varepsilon \tag{4}$$

We trust that most regression terms are obvious from the previous discussion. “BW” refers to the MER dataset containing the White and Black majority countries. WNW, Island, EMS, and Black are binary dummies for White New World, small island, European micro-state, and Black majority status respectively.

Negative results reflect positive outcomes: rank 1 is arithmetically lower than rank 100, for example, but is a superior result.

3.5 Regression Results

We first acknowledge that we could be fairly accused of data torture, by running six-variable regressions on a 145 or 92 item data set. Having acknowledged this, however, small data sets can be indicative if they vary appreciably.

There are at least three comparisons of interest from Table 10:

1. What drives technical compliance (Eqs. 1 and 3) vs. effectiveness (2 and 4)?
2. Does Black majority status have any effect on technical compliance (1 vs. 3)?
3. Does Black majority status have any effect on effectiveness (2 vs. 4)?

[22] We also ran Eqs (1) and (2) on the White and Black country dataset, and achieved near identical results.

Table 10 Regression results (Betas shown with T and P-values, with 5% significant values shown in bold)

Dependent Variable	B_1 Ln GDP	β_2 Ln GDPPC	B_3 WNW	B_4 Small Island	B_5 EMS	B_6 Black	B_7 TC Rank	R-Squared
1: TCRank$_{All}$	−1.19 −0.71 0.48	−15.99 **−6.15** **0.00**	42.14 **−2.49** **0.01**	−6.31 −0.61 0.54	23.14 1.13 0.26	N/A	N/A	0.32
2: ERank$_{ALL}$	−1.09 −0.86 0.38	−14.38 **−6.54** **0.00**	−25.03 **−1.95** **0.05**	28.80 **3.70** **0.003**	−5.45 −0.35 0.72	N/A	0.24 **3.70** **0.003**	0.60
3: TCRank$_{BW}$	−2.88 −1.71 0.09	−12.24 **−3.22** **0.002**	40.46 **2.37** **0.02**	−24.69 **−2.03** **0.05**	N/A[a]	14.32 1.15 0.25	N/A	0.44
4: ERank$_{BW}$	−1.63 −1.51 0.13	−9.81 **−3.87** **0.002**	−21.77 **−1.96** **0.05**	18.64 **2.37** **0.02**	N/A	29.29 **3.70** **.0004**	0.24 **3.49** **.0008**	0.78

[a]We also ran Eqs. (3) and (4) including the Beta for European micro-states, which produced no appreciable change in the results

3.5.1 Technical Compliance and Effectiveness Drivers

National income per capita levels (β_2) are strongly significant across the board. Economic size (β_1) is mildly associated with better rankings, but with low coefficients and little statistical significance. This is unsurprising, given we know many small states score better than larger states on technical compliance. WNW membership is surprisingly powerful given the small group size. There is an estimated 42 technical compliance negative ranking variance from what would otherwise be predicted by economic size and wealth. Neither small island nor European micro-state status is statistically significant for technical compliance.

The resultant R^2 result at 0.32 in Eq. (1) indicates that the model accounts for around one third of the variance in technical compliance national rankings, with the remainder flowing from idiosyncratic issues associated with each country or perhaps each group of countries. Alternatively, we are missing something useful in the regression equation.

As for effectiveness (Eq. 2), we receive a substantial head start by adding the technical compliance ranks. Unsurprisingly the R^2 is appreciably higher at 0.60. National income per capita remains the strongest predictor, remembering that this is also a large factor in the technical compliance result. It may be the case that national income per capita is double-counted in the overall FATF effectiveness assessments.

Unlike TC, small island status becomes important, with a 29-place effectiveness ranking penalty, and strong statistical significance. European Micro-State status remains statistically insignificant. This reinforces a puzzle: if FATF MERs routinely and massively mark down small island states for effectiveness relative to technical compliance, why don't they do the same thing for the European micro-states? One candidate answer is that the EMS are White and wealthy, while the micro-states are typically non-White and considerably less wealthy.

If we don't consider racial composition, then effectiveness rank is reasonably well determined by technical compliance rank, per capita income, White new world, and small island status.

3.5.2 Black Majority Status vs. Technical Compliance

The reader is invited to compare the Beta coefficients, t-values, and R^2 results for Eqs. 1 vs. 3. The Black majority status indicator (β_6 in Eq. 3) estimates a large decrement but is statistically insignificant. What does change is the econometric contribution of small island status, with a statistically significant estimate of a 25-place improvement in ranking. Considering the Black vs. White countries vs. the full dataset improves the R^2 result to 0.44—but there is no strong indication here that the FATF TC assessments are driven by Black majority status. It is worth remembering, however, that nearly all the small island states in this sample are Black majority.

One reasonable inference to draw from Eqs. (1) and (3) is that the FATF technical compliance MER assessment *process* is not significantly biased, in a racial composition sense. The underlying *framework*, however, consistently favours rich countries over poor countries, and Black countries, particularly the African countries, are the poorest group in the world.

3.5.3 Black Majority Status vs. Effectiveness

The reader is invited to compare Eqs. (2) and (4).

We see the shift in Eqs. (2) and (4): small islands rank penalties drop from 29 to 19, with more statistical variance. One inference that can be drawn from this is that the effectiveness ranking penalty for small islands is relatively heavier on Black majority islands, hence the drop in size and significance of this item from Eqs. (2) to (4).

What then are we to make of β_6 in Eq. (4)? The estimate is that Black majority status worsens effectiveness rank in the 145 country pool by 29 places on average—a substantial difference. Black majority small islands, nearly all Caribbean, suffer a 48 rank drop for effectiveness—a very substantial penalty. These differences arise even after taking into account the two economic variables, two idiosyncratic variables, and the technical compliance rank of all the MER-rated jurisdictions.

We also see that Eq. (4) explains 78% of the effectiveness variance in its data sample, a quite high result for panel data. One troubling implication from this specification is that under the MER process, jurisdictions vary relatively little in their rank based upon their idiosyncratic features—but they vary a lot based upon their income levels, small island, White new world, and Black majority status.

β_6 is a measure of direct racial differentiation in MER ranking. It looks not unlike zero in the regression equations for technical compliance—and a lot like a large and highly significant number in the regression equations for effectiveness.

To give an idea for the magnitude of bias in the effectiveness rankings, let us consider two countries with identical economic data and identical technical compliance scores. Furthermore, these variables rank them at the median of the 145 jurisdiction sample, in 73rd place. Let us further assume that Country A is a White new world jurisdiction, and Country B is a Caribbean island. Eq. (4) indicates that Country A's starting position for effectiveness rank will be 73–22 = 51rst place. Country B's starting position will be 73 + 19 + 30 = 122nd place. These are very large differences, which to demonstrate legitimacy would require equally compelling evidence that Black majority and small island states are much less effective in AML/CFT terms than theWWhite new world jurisdictions, and White jurisdictions more broadly.

Our conclusion here is that, whatever the biases built into the FATF's underlying methodology, the practice of MER evaluation shows unpersuasive evidence of racial bias for technical compliance assessment, but persuasive evidence of strong bias for effectiveness assessments.

FATF grey list status is a semi-automatic mapping from technical compliance and effectiveness assessments. The distilled result in bias terms is depicted in Table 7.

Having demonstrated racial bias in FATF MER effectiveness assessments and grey listings, we repeat an essential reminder: racial difference, even racial bias, is not the same thing as racism. The conclusions in this section of the paper, however, make it clear that FATF MER legitimacy regarding these demonstrable biases should be matched by equally demonstrable facts. Those facts should include, most relevantly:

(a) Poor countries are more of an AML/CFT effectiveness problem than rich countries;
(b) White countries are less of a problem than non-White countries in AML/CFT terms; and
(c) The WNW countries are particularly good, and small island states particularly bad, at AML/CFT risk management.

If all three of these conditions do not hold, or can't be demonstrated, then the FATF will need to consider whether the obvious and large biases in their MERs are illegitimate.

4 Where Is the World's Money?

Are the demonstrable biases in AML ratings supported by equally demonstrable money laundering problems in disfavoured jurisdictions?

It may first be helpful to remind ourselves where the world keeps its money, and to review the limited evidence for where the world manages or welcomes dirty money.

4.1 *Managed Investments*

At the end of 2018, the world's 500 largest asset managers[23] controlled over $90 trillion in assets.

An estimated 57% of these assets were controlled by American firms, and 31% by European (including UK) firms, and 5% by Japanese firms. Investment managers in the rest of the world, including the major Asian countries and Australasia, controlled 7% of the group's assets. The largest entity outside the U.S./European/Japanese triad was Banco do Brasil, ranking 79th out of 500. The largest entity from a Black majority country, South Africa's Old Mutual, ranked 255th.

4.2 *Stock Exchanges*

The world's ten largest stock exchanges[24] are also worth about $90 trillion, with the two major American exchanges accounting for half the value, and various European and Asian exchanges accounting for the rest. The five largest American tech stocks, in aggregate worth more than $5 trillion, would constitute the world's sixth largest exchange.

4.3 *Banks*

Measured by assets, 37 of the world's 100 largest banks[25] are headquartered in western and northern Europe. 37 are headquartered in Asia, of which 19 including the largest 5 are Chinese. There are 16 North American banks on the list, with four each from Australia and Brasil. The remaining two banks are Russian (60th on the list) and Qatari (96th).

[23] Thinking Ahead Institute (2019).

[24] Ali (2020a).

[25] Ali (2020b).

4.4 Real Estate

Real estate is a valuable but difficult to measure market. International broker Savills[26] estimated global value as of December 2017 at $281 trillion, of which $221 trillion was residential, and the remainder commercial and agricultural. Savills further estimated that North America and Europe each held 22% of the market, with Asia holding 48% of the global value, of which China represented over half. This left about 8% of value for the rest of the world put together.

There are competing estimates, but all support the propositions that the global real estate market is very large, and concentrated by value in Asia, Europe, and North America.

4.5 Currency

Currency notes are a relatively small asset class, but may be particularly problematic as facilitators for financial crime. The Bank for International Settlements[27] published a comparison in 2017, concluding that member countries of the Committee on Payments and Market Infrastructures (CPMI) had $4.7 trillion in currency notes outstanding. The United States ($1.5 trillion), Europe ($1.2 trillion), and Japan ($0.9 trillion) accounted for over three quarters of aggregate note issuance by value. This data excludes China, which we understand has on the order of $1 trillion in currency notes outstanding, and crypto-assets, which in aggregate are valued at more than $1 trillion. In terms of currency-based financial crime, the United States is a remarkable outlier for issuing more USD 100 denominated notes than USD 1 denominated notes.

4.6 Total Wealth by Country

Credit Suisse[28] annually estimates the world's wealth by country. The 2022 estimate had global wealth at $464 trillion, of which over 90% was held in the United States, Canada, Europe, China, and Japan. The rest of the world accounted for around 7% of total wealth.

---

[26] Tostevin (2018).

[27] Bank for International Settlements (2017).

[28] Credit Suisse Research Institute (2022).

4.7 Summary: Where Are the World's Assets?

Based upon the data summarized above, over 90% of the world's financial and property assets are resident in the United States, Western Europe, China, and Japan. Other countries control less than 10% of the world's assets.

This result sits very badly with the implicit FATF proposition that the same countries that control over 90% of the world's wealth are in MER terms seldom a money laundering problem.

5 Where Is the World's Dirty Money?

Ideally, we could compare the world's AML jurisdictional ratings with authoritative estimates of the world's stocks and flows of dirty money. Unfortunately, such authoritative estimates don't exist.

On the other hand, we possess a great many data sources that allow inferences about the origination, throughput, and final homes of the world's dirty money. We will deploy some of these data sources in this paper.

5.1 What Does the Research Say?

Several academic researchers have examined the degree to which various countries can be characterized as more or less open to dirty money flows and investment. Findley, Nielson, and Sharman (FNS) are among the most prominent of these researchers, having spent the last decade conducting tens of thousands of shadow shopping exercises on the world's banks and corporate services firms. Their work suggests[29] that professional money launderers have many avenues to incorporate shell companies.[30] Furthermore, their shadow shopping results suggest that the OECD jurisdictions are the most open to illicit company and bank account formation, and that smaller countries, particularly island nations with international financial centres, are among the most resistant to illicit company and bank account formation.

In recent work, FNS conducted shadow shopping exercises on every bank in the world with a SWIFT address, including multiple propositions signaling more or less money laundering or terrorist financing risk. The responses from this exercise were classified as "compliant" (the bank required reasonably full and correct documentation to open an account), "non-responsive" (which may include banks deciding not

[29] Allred et al. (2017).

[30] Findley et al. (2014).

Table 11 Perfectly compliant and non-compliant jurisdictions

Jurisdictions with zero non-compliant responses	Jurisdictions with zero compliant responses
The Bahamas	Mexico
Latvia	Montenegro
Liechtenstein	Italy
	Cayman Islands
	France
	The Netherlands
	Japan
	Colombia

Table 12 Quartiles by National Ethnicity for 87 FNS Countries

	White	Non-White	Black countries within the non-White total
First (best)	15	6	1
Second	9	13	4
Third	10	12	8
Fourth (worst)	9	13	1
Total	43	44	14
Reference Quartile	10.75	11	3.5

to engage with suspect proposals), and "non-compliant", which indicated a willingness to open accounts without proper documentation.

Among other things, this FNS exercise has been aggregated at the national jurisdiction level, with the following responses.[31]

Table 12 is ranked upon the proportion of total queries that generated non-compliant responses, so is calculated on a different basis from Table 7a, which ignores non-responses.

Tables 11 and 12 may be usefully compared with the FATF quartiles at Tables 5 and 6. In broad terms, the FNS quartiles are nothing like as White-positive and Black-negative as the FATF quartiles. They do reflect a view that on average, White countries are perhaps slightly better than average, and non-White countries slightly worse, but any differences are small. Among other things, the FNS results suggest that the FATF MER assertion that there are no White countries in the bottom quartile of the effectiveness rankings is insupportable.

In 2023, FNS via its consulting arm Evaluasi conducted a shadow shopping exercise on all 50 internationally active Bahamian banks and trust companies, on behalf of the Central Bank of The Bahamas.[32] This exercise generated zero noncompliant results across the entire industry, which is consistent with the Bahamian technical compliance ranking (7th) but highly inconsistent with the Bahamian effectiveness ranking (103rd).

[31] The author thanks FNS for this material, which has been provided ahead of planned publication.

[32] Evaluasi (2023).

5.2 Other AML Jurisdictional Ranking Research

FNS has provided the most data-intensive insights via their decade of shadow shopping exercises. Several other researchers have also examined AML national assessment systems. Littrell and O'Brien (2020) demonstrated that among the competing AML jurisdiction rankings there are low and sometimes negative correlations. This result is inconsistent with more than one AML ratings provider (and probably zero providers) possessing any predictive validity.

Aziani, Ferwerda, and Riccardi (2020) deployed a database comprising 29 million shareholders across 41 European countries to determine that there is a high concentration of ownership in countries that are non-transparent or which possess attractive tax regimes. On the other hand, there is also an over-concentration of ownership in countries with strong reputations for transparency and low corruption. This research is consistent with broader findings that criminals prefer, all things being equal, to place their money in low risk and low corruption countries.

Jofre, Riccardi, Bosisio, and Guastamacchia (2021) recently issued a study of European corporate ownership, which among other things found a heavy concentration of ownership in several suspect jurisdictions—notably the United Kingdom, Malta, and the Netherlands. Riccardi produced a companion piece deploying a gravity model, which has been a well-known technique since the 1990s, to assess Italian exposure to money laundering in other countries. The candidate model was tested using a large dataset of cross-border Italian AML prosecutions. Riccardi concluded that jurisdictional AML risk is relative to the country from which the risk is being viewed. In the Italian case, this means that the riskiest countries (in order) in his model are San Marino, Luxembourg, the Netherlands, Austria, and Switzerland, with White-majority and mainly European countries occupying the top 18 positions. To quote from Riccardi's summary:

> The popular perception is that secrecy countries are often small, exotic, and offshore, located somewhere in the Caribbean or the Pacific sea. They pop up regularly in high-profile media leaks like the Panama Papers or Paradise Papers. The (novel) measures of corporate opacity used in this thesis, and employed for the construction of the indicator, demonstrate instead that certain European (and even EU) countries have a level of secrecy that is equal, or even greater, than Caribbean countries and other offshore jurisdictions. In particular, European countries have the highest volume of firms with anomalous complexity of their corporate structure and with the lowest information on their beneficial owners. Most notably, the Netherlands, Luxembourg, Malta, Ireland, Liechtenstein, Austria and, to a lesser extent, the UK are the highest ranked at the global level. While these countries performed badly with respect to actual corporate opacity, they perform well in terms of statutory measures of transparency (hence, why they have pretty good scores in, e.g., the FATF ratings or the FSI's Secrecy Score). The gap between actual opacity and lack of compliance with transparency requirements is something which current official AML blacklists are not able to bridge.

Using a database of crypto-asset trading across exchanges in many countries, Nershi (2020) concluded that many exchanges display suspicious activity grouped just below required trading volumes. The United States is an upside outlier, in that minimal suspicious activity is detected. To quote Nershi, however:

> Finally, my results suggest that – contrary to widely held views in some academic and policy circles– enforcing due diligence laws poses a significant challenge for developed countries. My analysis shows significant levels of suspicious activity across countries, including developed countries like Japan and the United Kingdom. Indeed, this finding fits with a wealth of evidence from recent events that show significant failures in the enforcement of customer due diligence laws by wealthy, industrialized countries.

Here again we see the result that most of the financial activity is in the more developed, richer, and in AML terms well-rated countries—and most of the suspicious activity is concentrated in these countries too.

It is not this paper's purpose to conduct an extensive literature review. It would be fair to observe, however, that the near-unanimous consensus in the AML research community differs from the FATF aggregate MER rankings. That is: there is plenty of illicit activity, and very likely a substantial majority of illicit activity, in the large, rich, White-majority countries that are held out and hold themselves out as exemplars for AML ratings purposes.

5.3 *The Panama and Paradise Papers*

The Panama Papers[33] are a trove of several million documents stolen from Panamanian law firm Mossack Fonseca, and shared with the world's investigative journalists. These papers revealed a global network of shell companies, which were formed for more or less legitimate purposes by a great many people in a great many countries. Implicated persons, for example, included former prime ministers in the United Kingdom and Iceland.

The Paradise Papers[34] are a similar trove of data on shell companies held globally. As a general rule, the Paradise Papers exposed relatively few illegal arrangements, compared to the Panama Papers.

In both cases and with some other leaks, there has been broad attention to the fact that the documents were held in non-European countries such as Panama. Over time, however, interested observers have noted that a substantial proportion of the arrangements revealed people and firms in traditionally well rated countries in Europe, North America, and elsewhere.

[33] Panama Papers (n.d.).

[34] Paradis Papers (n.d.).

5.4 Other Journalism

British journalist Oliver Bullough's books[35] and articles[36] argue the case that there is a small but efficient global group of lawyers and other money laundering enablers. This group often has access to useful jurisdictions in western countries who are willing to write legislation to order to facilitate anonymous funds, for example via trusts. This work is facilitated by the American non-participation on an outbound basis in FATCA or CRS international tax reporting. Bullough has also noted the extreme complexity and ineffectiveness of the AML regime in his home country.

Other books on money laundering scandals tend to follow the theme of major crimes facilitated by major western financial institutions, such as Goldman Sachs and the Malaysian 1MDB matter, HSBC in Mexico, and the like. There have also been large scandals involving Russian anonymous money, such as the Danske Bank matter in Estonia.

Leaving aside the general purpose press, several firms provide AML aggregation services for media articles and public sector press releases. As this paper was being drafted in May 2021, for example, RiskScreen's (an AML consulting firm) KYC360 weekly roundup headlined seven articles:

- "DNB to be fined $48 million for AML Inadequacies"
- "The Posh London Address 4000 Companies Call Home"
- "Inside the High-Stakes World of NFTs"
- "Malta: Cash Payments over EUR 10,000 for Gold, Cars, Boats, and Property no Longer Possible"
- "Former Ukrainian President Poroshenko Secretly Controlled Offshore Firms That Banked at Austria's Raiffeisen"
- "Germany Orders Deutsche Bank to do More to Prevent Money Laundering"
- "London School of Economics Accepted Risky Cash Years After Donations Warning"

We do not pretend that these seven articles are statistically comprehensive or compelling—but they are typical. It is notable that every article refers at least in part to a White majority country or countries, more often than not one of the countries constituting the original FATF 15.

One could argue that the large number of AML media articles on White majority country institutions indicates their efficacy in finding dirty money, or perhaps the intensity of their media coverage. This argument would be more persuasive if the same pattern hadn't been in place for many years, and likely will remain in place for many years to come. A nation consistently reporting large numbers of AML prosecutions and fines may in FATF terms be demonstrating effectiveness, but in economic terms it is demonstrating that the country is awash in dirty money.

[35] Bullough (2018). More recently, Bullough (2022).

[36] Bullough (2019).

5.5 Which Countries Are Generating AML Financial Institution Penalties?

The absence of an official league table of annual financial sanctions is among the many data shortcomings in the global AML movement. From the informal efforts that have been published, however, we can see that the bulk of sanctions fall upon purportedly legitimate major institutions in White countries:

- Fenergo's 2020 summary[37] noted that fines fell most heavily upon American, Swedish, German, and Israeli firms;
- A payments industry newsletter[38] listed 2019 fines in 14 countries, of which most accrued in the United States, with a French firm paying the largest single fine, and the United Kingdom and Belgium third and fourth on the list.
- Another newsletter's[39] 2020 AML fine list had the United States in first place, followed by Australia, the Netherlands, Israel, and Sweden.

It is notable when reviewing the many data sources in this area that they don't necessarily agree upon their definitions and data, but the general conclusion is inescapable. Fines and similar sanctions fall most heavily upon financial institutions in White majority countries, often but not always for facilitating irregular financial dealings in non-White majority countries. There is also the consideration that the United States will likely always feature towards the top of any such list, given that country's public sector predilection for issuing large fines.

This raises the obvious question: if fines and similar sanctions are heavily concentrated among the leading financial institutions in White majority countries, why are these countries given the most favourable effectiveness ratings from the FATF?

5.6 Summary: Where is the World's Dirty Money?

Much of the material in this section relies upon anecdotal or other narrow and inconsistent data sources. All this material, however, consistently suggests that:

(a) Dirty money destinations are similar to clean money destinations. The great majority flows to the United States, the United Kingdom, western Europe, and to a lesser extent Asia; and
(b) Too many private sector institutions in wealthy countries often seem happy to facilitate these illicit flows.

---

37 Bhattacharya (2020).

38 Rolfe (2020).

39 Corporate Compliance Insights (2021).

In other words, there is nothing in the research or media reports to suggest that the large racial differences in the FATF MER rankings are backed by facts. The rather unsatisfactory facts available to us suggest that if anything the opposite is true:

(c) Dirty money in aggregate is much more of a problem in wealthy White majority countries and for major financial institutions in those countries, than in non-White countries; but
(d) The proportion of illicit financial stocks and flows in non-White countries, often facilitated by financial institutions from White countries, is possibly larger than in White majority countries. If this is the case, however, these stocks and flows will often move to White majority countries, facilitated by financial institutions and other agents in White majority countries.

6 How Did We Get Here?

This paper has demonstrated that the FATF needs to consider whether it has lapsed into illegitimate biases in its MER assessments, particularly of effectiveness. These biases may flow from the way in which the technical and effectiveness standards are conducted, and/or they may flow from the way in which mutual evaluations are conducted. The result is that Black majority countries and small islands states are very likely marked down more than they should be for effectiveness, and large, wealthy White majority countries, particularly in the new world, are given a de facto free pass on their effectiveness evaluations.

The question naturally arises, if we accept the above premises on illegitimacy: how did we get here? We provide some admittedly speculative explanations in this section.

6.1 The FATF's Foundation

The FATF's foundation documents make two things clear:

1. The FATF was founded by the world's White countries, to impose their views on the rest of the world; and
2. The AML problem was couched primarily in terms of drug money, and the relevant flows were ascribed to Latin America (cocaine), Asia (Heroin), and Marijuana (everywhere, but with a focus on Latin America).

The FATF's foundations date back to a 1989 G7 meeting, which resulted in the following foundation members in 1990, listed in the order given in the initial report: United States, Germany, Japan, France, United Kingdom, Italy, Canada, European Commission, Sweden, Netherlands, Belgium, Luxembourg, Switzerland, Austria, Spain, and Australia.

This grouping is in essence the world's large, rich, White majority countries, plus Japan and the European Commission, the latter also a club for rich White countries. Although the FATF membership is more demographically diverse today, its foundation and early years were as a group of nearly entirely White and entirely rich countries. To paraphrase Lincoln, the FATF was the AML governance body of all the world's countries, by the world's White countries, for the world's White countries.

The foundation membership's initial report made clear that the global AML problem was couched mainly in terms of how other countries insisted not only upon supplying illicit services and products to the member nations, but then upon spending and investing the proceeds of those sales. The focus was much less on the raising and spending of money by residents of rich White countries to purchase those illicit substances and products.

Is it any surprise that a self-appointed body comprising the world's rich White nations, would to this day be organized to favour such nations?

6.2 *Power vs. Race*

There is an increasing stream of thought leaking into the public domain[40] that the FATF's MER ratings are based upon power politics among the leading FATF member countries, not upon an objective assessment of AML compliance and effectiveness. If this were so, then the relatively poor ratings for Black majority countries might reflect their relative powerlessness, not their ethnic composition.

This paper lacks the data to test such a claim.

It is worth noting, however, that if national power were a strong determining factor, then the European micro-states are not notably more powerful than Black majority or other micro-states. Yet the European micro-states suffer no decrement in their FATF ratings. The fact that they are wealthy and White seems to count for much more than any idea that they possess little power.

It is also the case that the FATF has suspended the membership of a powerful nation, Russia.[41]

All in all, and as with any multilateral organisation, relative member power doubtless plays a role, but that does not on its face appear to be a determining factor for the FATF's MER ratings.

[40] See, for example, Karnitschnig (2023).

[41] FATF (2023b).

6.3 *Anti-terrorism*

From 2001, the FATF's mission expanded to include a focus on anti-terrorism. This gave another impetus to the idea that small, poor, and non-White states are threatening large, wealthy, White majority countries, and this concept may also have leaked into the FATF MER ratings. As with the power issue above, however, we currently lack the data to assess this proposition.

7 Where Are the Biases in National AML Assessments?

The most positive outcome in this paper is that there is weak to nonexistent evidence that the FATF technical compliance assessment process is materially biased in racial terms.

On the other hand, both the FATF technical compliance ranks and the effectiveness ranks are strongly driven by the per capita wealth of assessed jurisdictions. The FATF might usefully consider whether a more proportionate AML standards framework, offering a simpler technical compliance regime for poor countries, would be an improvement over current arrangements. This is the proportionality path favoured by (among others) the IMF and the Basel Committee on Banking Supervision.

Pro-wealth and anti-poverty bias is a particularly compelling issue in that many wealthy countries, starting with the United States, are a long way from full compliance with the FATF's 40 technical standards. But unlike poor and non-White countries, they pay no penalty for this in their effectiveness assessments.

The FATF effectiveness vs. technical compliance assessments display a large bias in favour of White majority new world countries, for which there is no non-problematic explanation. Perhaps the FATF's 11 effectiveness measures are not fit for purpose, and don't truly assess the economic effectiveness of a jurisdiction's AML/CFT efforts. They may instead simply measure how similar a jurisdiction is to the United States, a test that the United States will always win.

There is a strong bias against small island states, which are mainly non-White, but no such bias against European micro-states, which follow similar business practices but are all White majority. Given that there is no evidence that small island states are more problematic in AML/CFT terms than are larger (or smaller) wealthy states, this looks like a bad faith element in the FATF's MER framework.

There is a large and statistically significant bias in the FATF effectiveness MER assessments against Black majority countries, relative to White majority countries. As in the previous point, there is no evidence that this bias is supported by facts, and in fact strong evidence that White majority countries are far more of a global AML problem than are Black majority countries. One is hesitant to accuse the FATF of racism, but the MER ratings look like they have lapsed into systemic anti-Black racism across the assessment pool.

The FATF's grey list is a mechanical exercise based upon technical assurance and effectiveness assessments. To the extent that these assessments are biased, the FATF grey list will distill these biases. The historic very heavy weight of list membership away from FATF members and White majority countries suggests that this distillation and resultant illegitimate bias is material. The fact that one of the two FATF members currently on the grey list is also the only Black majority FATF member is anecdotal, but consistent with an anti-Black bias in the FATF's evaluation process.

The most positive implication we can draw from this is: The FATF cannot persuasively argue, much less prove, that their national assessment biases are legitimate.

A more negative implication, which we consider this paper suggests but does not prove, is that the current FATF MER system is strongly biased in favour of large, rich, White countries, particularly the new world White ex-colonies, and strongly biased against small island states and Black majority states.

It is worth observing at this point that although the FATF mimics the IMF Financial Sector Assessment Program[42] on the form of its MERs, it does not invest anything like the IMF's effort in its MER quality assurance processes. Creating an effective quality assurance framework would likely lead to less comfortable MER outcomes for FATF members, but those outcomes would become more demonstrably fair than is the current case.

7.1 Legitimacy vs. Subjectivity

It is clear that the FATF's MER ratings for both technical compliance and effectiveness contain elements of objectivity and subjectivity. As noted earlier in this paper, and more generally in the AML community, the technical compliance standards are more objectively based, as the FATF ratings can usually be independently verified against public documents such as legislation or regulations. The effectiveness rankings, however, are highly subjective, and rely on expert opinion at several levels of the MER process.

Subjective ratings are not of themselves illegitimate, but are more open to a drift to illegitimacy. In this paper we have attempted to quantify the biases in the FATF ratings using standard econometric tools. We have then tested these biases against sometimes incomplete but known findings from the international AML research community, journalism community, and relevant public data.

Our general findings are first, that the FATF's technical compliance ratings are not demonstrably biased in any illegitimate way, but we are concerned that the foundation for these ratings is unduly harsh on poor countries.

Our second general finding is that the FATF's effectiveness ratings are biased in several ways that are obviously illegitimate, unless there is clear evidence regarding

[42] IMF (n.d.).

illicit stocks and flows to support these biases. The weight of evidence, furthermore, is incomplete, but overwhelmingly supports a view opposite to that implicit in the current effectiveness ratings. It is not the case that poor, Black, and island states are the major problems in global illicit finance, but that rich, White, and continental states are the originators, repositories, and conduits for the vast majority of the world's dirty money.

Accordingly, we wish to make clear that we do not regard the FATF's MER effectiveness biases as illegitimate because they are subjective. Rather, we regard them as illegitimate because:

(a) They are clearly and materially demonstrable in the econometric analysis; and
(b) The incomplete, uncertain, but overwhelming weight of objective evidence strongly suggests that the FATF's effectiveness biases are wrong in fact.

8 Conclusion

After 30 years of effort, the world has largely put in place the legislative and regulatory tools necessary to combat financial crime. We are now moving to the even more difficult task, not yet close to achievement, of recovering a material share of the world's illicit funds, and reducing the crimes supported by dirty money.[43,44]

If the world's AML efforts are to become more effective, they must also become more legitimate. This paper has demonstrated a potential source of illegitimacy: unjustified biases in the current arrangements for the FATF's mutual evaluation reports.

To close on a happier note: there is no reason why the world couldn't move to more legitimate jurisdictional AML assessments. Ideally, the FATF will take the lead in this effort. Whatever their current MER flaws, they are the multilateral agency tasked with moving forward on the global AML effort.

References

Ali A (2020a) The world's 10 largest stock markets. Visual Capitalist, 29 October 2020. https://www.visualcapitalist.com/the-worlds-10-largest-stock-markets/. Accessed 16 Dec 2023

Ali Z (2020b) The world's 100 largest banks, 2020. S&P Global Market Intelligence, 7 April 2020. https://www.spglobal.com/marketintelligence/en/news-insights/latest-news-headlines/the-world-s-100-largest-banks-2020-57854079. Accessed 16 Dec 2023

Allred BB et al (2017) Anonymous shell companies: a global audit study and field experiment in 176 countries. J Int Bus 48(5):596–619

[43] Economist (2021).

[44] Couvée (2023).

Aziani, A, Ferwerda J, Riccardi, M (2020) Who are our Owners? Exploring the cross-border ownership links of European businesses to assess the risk of illicit financial flows, https://bahamasamlconference.centralbankbahamas.com/documents/2024-03-26-16-43-11-Estimating-Cross-Border-Corporate-Ownership-Aziani-Riccardi-and-Ferwerda.pdf, N/A .

Bank for International Settlements (2017) Committee on Payments and Market Infrastructures: statistics on payment, clearing and settlement systems in the CPMI countries – figures for 2016, CPMI Papers No 172. https://www.bis.org/cpmi/publ/d172.htm. Accessed 16 Dec 2023

Baumann T (2004) Defining ethnicity. SAA Archaeol Record 4(4):12–14

Bhattacharya M (2020) Fenergo's study reveals increase in AML, KYC and sanctions fines for global financial institutions. IBS Intelligence, 18 August 2020. https://ibsintelligence.com/fenergos-study-reveals-increase-in-aml-kyc-and-sanctions-fines-for-global-financial-institutions/. Accessed 16 Dec 2023

Bullough O (2018) Moneyland: why thieves and crooks now rule the world and how to take it back. Profile Books, London

Bullough O (2019) The great American tax haven: why the super-rich love South Dakota. The Guardian, 14 November 2019. https://www.theguardian.com/world/2019/nov/14/the-great-american-tax-haven-why-the-super-rich-love-south-dakota-trust-laws. Accessed 16 Dec 2023

Bullough O (2022) Butler to the world: the book the oligarchs don't want you to read – how Britain helps the world's worst people launder money, commit crimes, and get away with anything. St Martin's Press, London

Cambridge Dictionary (2023) Ethnicity https://dictionary.cambridge.org/dictionary/english/ethnicity

Corporate Compliance Insights (2021) Banks worldwide amass $15b in fines in 2020, U.S. banks account for 73%. https://www.corporatecomplianceinsights.com/banks-15b-in-fines-in-2020/. Accessed 16 Dec 2023

Couvée K (2023) Global AML framework rests far too heavily on prevention, authors claim. ACAMS moneylaundering.com, 5 June 2023. https://www.moneylaundering.com/news/global-aml-framework-rests-far-too-heavily-on-prevention-authors-claim/?source=Keyword%20Alert%20-%20Daily. Accessed 16 Dec 2023

Credit Suisse Research Institute (2022) Global wealth report 2022: leading perspectives to navigate the future

Economist (2021) The war against money-laundering is being lost, 12 April 2021. https://www.economist.com/finance-and-economics/2021/04/12/the-war-against-money-laundering-is-being-lost

Evaluasi (2023) Bahamas shadow shopping: public report. https://www.centralbankbahamas.com/viewPDF/documents/2023-05-17-13-29-49-Evaluasi-Bahamas-Report%2D%2D%2D%2DPublic-Version-1.pdf. Accessed 16 Dec 2023

FATF (2013) FATF issues new mechanism to strengthen money laundering and terrorist financing compliance. https://www.fatf-gafi.org/publications/fatfrecommendations/documents/fatfissuesnewmechanismtostrengthenmoneylaunderingandterroristfinancingcompliance.html. Accessed 16 Dec 2023

FATF (2021) Jurisdictions under increased monitoring – February 2021. http://www.fatf-gafi.org/publications/high-risk-and-other-monitored-jurisdictions/documents/increased-monitoring-february-2021.html. Accessed 16 Dec 2023

FATF (2023a) 4th round ratings. https://www.fatf-gafi.org/media/fatf/documents/4th-Round-Ratings.pdf. Accessed 16 Dec 2023

FATF (2023b) FATF statement on the Russian Federation, 24 February 2023. https://www.fatf-gafi.org/en/publications/Fatfgeneral/fatf-statement-russian-federation.html

FATF (n.d.-a) 'Black and grey' lists. https://www.fatf-gafi.org/en/countries/black-and-grey-lists.html. Accessed 16 Dec 2023

FATF (n.d.-b) Countries. https://www.fatf-gafi.org/countries/. Accessed 16 Dec 2023

FATF (n.d.-c) High-risk and other monitored jurisdictions. https://www.fatf-gafi.org/en/topics/high-risk-and-other-monitored-jurisdictions.html. Accessed 16 Dec 2023

Findley M, Nielson F, Sharman J (2014) Global shell games: experiments in transnational relations, crime, and terrorism. Cambridge University Press, Cambridge

Green Elliott D (2006) Redefining ethnicity 47th Annual International Studies Association Convention (March) San Diego, CA https://personal.lse.ac.uk/greened/isa.pdf

IMF (n.d.) Financial Sector Assessment Program (FSAP) https://www.imf.org/en/About/Factsheets/Sheets/2023/financial-sector-assessment-program-FSAP

Jofre M Bosisio A Riccardi M Guastamaccia S (2021) Money Laundering and the Detection of Bad Companies: a Machine Learning Approach for the Assessment of Opaque Ownership Structures, https://bahamasamlconference.centralbankbahamas.com/documents/2024-03-26-15-46-37-Money-Laundering-and-the-Detection-of-Bad-Entities-A-Machine-Learning-Approach-Jofre-et-al.pdf, N/A.

Karnitschnig M (2023) West wants to look the other way on UAE money laundering. Politico, 21 June 2023. https://www.politico.eu/article/united-arab-emirates-eu-france-ergmany-uswest-wants-to-look-the-other-way-on-uae-money-laundering/. Accessed 16 Dec 2023

Littrell C (2018) A field guide to the AML sovereign risk rating agencies. ACAMS Today, 20 December 2018

Littrell C (2021) Biases in national AML risk assessments. Paper presented at the 2022 International Research Conference on Empirical Approaches to Anti-Money Laundering, Bahamas, 20—21 January 2022. https://bahamasamlconference.centralbankbahamas.com/2022. Accessed 16 Dec 2023

Littrell C, O'Brien D (2020) Comparing sovereign debt ratings to sovereign AML ratings. https://bahamasamlconference.centralbankbahamas.com/2020. Accessed 16 Dec 2023

Nershi K (2020) How Strong are Anti-Money Laundering Regulations in Practice? Evidence from Crypto-Currency Transactions, https://bahamasamlconference.centralbankbahamas.com/documents/2024-03-26-15-45-42-How-Strong-are-AML-Regulations-in-Practice-Evidence-From-Crypto-Currency-Nershi.pdf, N/A

Panama Papers (n.d.) Wikipedia. https://en.wikipedia.org/wiki/Panama_Papers. Accessed 16 Dec 2023

Paradise Papers (n.d.) Wikipedia. https://en.wikipedia.org/wiki/Paradise_Papers. Accessed 16 Dec 2023

Rolfe A (2020) $8.14 billion of AML fines handed out in 2019 – USA and UK top the list. Payments Cards and Mobile, 13 January 2020. https://www.paymentscardsandmobile.com/8-14-billion-of-aml-fines-handed-out-in-2019-usa-and-uk-top-the-list/. Accessed 16 Dec 2023

Thinking Ahead Institute (2019) The world's largest fund managers – 2019. https://www.thinkingaheadinstitute.org/research-papers/the-worlds-largest-fund-managers-2019/. Accessed 16 Dec 2023

Tostevin P (2018) 8 things to know about global real estate value. Savills. https://www.savills.com/impacts/market-trends/8-things-you-need-to-know-about-the-value-of-global-real-estate.html. Accessed 16 Dec 2023

UNCTAD (n.d.) Statistics. https://unctad.org/statistics

US Census Bureau (2021). Measuring Racial and Ethnic Diversity for the 2020 Census https://www.census.gov/newsroom/blogs/random-samplings/2021/08/measuring-racial-ethnic-diversity-2020-census.html

Vedrenne G (2023) AML oversight ineffective, sometimes non-existent, in smaller European nations. ACAMS moneylaundering.com, 20 June 2023. https://www.moneylaundering.com/news/aml-oversight-ineffective-sometimes-non-existent-in-smaller-european-nations/?source=Keyword%20Alert%20-%20Daily. Accessed 16 Dec 2023

World Bank (n.d.) Countries and economies. https://data.worldbank.org/country. Accessed 16 Dec 2023

Charles Littrell has spent over 40 years in banking and financial regulation. He is currently a senior advisor to the Central Bank of The Bahamas, having served as head of bank supervision in The Bahamas from 2017 to 2022. From 2002 to 2017, Charles was a senior executive at the Australian Prudential Regulation Authority (APRA). While at APRA, Charles was a member of the Basel Committee on Banking Supervision. Charles is a consultant to a number of organisations, including the International Monetary Fund. In addition to his regulatory duties, Charles founded the International Research Conference on Empirical Approaches to Anti-Money Laundering and Financial Crime. This conference has become the leading event of its type in the world.

Combatting Money Laundering in Southeast Asian and Australian Casinos

John Langdale

Abstract Money laundering in Southeast Asian and Australian casinos is examined in the context of the East Asian transnational crime system. Transnational crime is growing rapidly in the region, particularly in the weakly-governed Mekong region (Myanmar, Cambodia and Laos). Casinos facilitate the operation of this crime system. A key difficulty in combatting money laundering in casinos in the region is that governments are conflicted between their desire to reduce crime and money laundering with their economic strategy of maximising employment, international tourism and taxation associated with casinos. National and state governments need to prioritise the control of money laundering and transnational crime over their economic development goals. Failure to follow this step is likely to lead to a growing spiral of crime in the Asia-Pacific region.

1 Introduction

This paper considers two issues associated with money laundering in casinos in Southeast Asia and Australia. Firstly, money laundering in casinos is examined in the context of the East Asian transnational crime system. Casinos play a significant role in facilitating this crime system's operation by laundering illicit profits.

Secondly, the paper considers a key difficulty in combatting money laundering in casinos: governments in Australia and Southeast Asia are conflicted between their desire on the one hand to reduce crime and money laundering. On the other hand, government have pursued an economic strategy which maximises employment, international tourism and taxation associated with casinos. This conflict in government's goals is at the heart of regulatory difficulties associated with combatting crime in the region's casinos.

J. Langdale (✉)
Department of Security Studies and Criminology, Macquarie University, Sydney, NSW, Australia
e-mail: john.langdale@mq.edu.au

D. Goldbarsht, L. de Koker (eds.), *Financial Crime and the Law*, Ius Gentium: Comparative Perspectives on Law and Justice 115,
https://doi.org/10.1007/978-3-031-59543-1_9

Money laundering in Southeast Asian and Australian casinos is set in the context of facilitating the operation of the East Asian transnational crime system. The nature of this transnational crime system is poorly understood, but transnational criminal groups use casinos to launder the proceeds of illegal drug sales.[1] A parallel situation was found to occur in British Columbia, Canada, where casinos were used as one means of laundering the proceeds of illegal drug sales in the province.[2]

Illegal drug proceeds in Southeast Asia and Australia are either spent locally or are often moved to Hong Kong/Macau, where the money is used to pay "investors" in crime syndicates or to purchase precursor chemicals for manufacturing methamphetamines in Myanmar and thus continue the operation of the transnational crime system.[3]

Government regulation of money laundering in Australian and Southeast Asian casinos has been poor. State government inquiries into money laundering in Australian casinos found that casino operators failed to properly regulate their casinos and were unfit to hold their licenses.[4] Australian casino operators largely ignored criminal activity taking place in their casinos. This activity was particularly apparent in the VIP gaming market oriented to Chinese gamblers, a market largely controlled by Macau-based junket operators many of whom were associated with Chinese criminal groups.[5]

Crime problems are even greater in the Southeast Asian casino market, with large-scale money laundering taking place in casinos, particularly in the VIP gambling market. While Singapore has reduced the problem by banning junkets, casinos in many other Southeast Asian countries are caught in a cycle of money laundering and transnational crime.[6] Casinos are a major means of laundering the proceeds of this criminal activity.[7]

Combatting money laundering in the Asia-Pacific is critical to current and future regional stability. The rapid expansion of transnational crime in the weakly-governed states in the Mekong region of Southeast Asia (Myanmar, Cambodia and Laos) is causing great concern on the part of governments throughout the Asia-Pacific region. A particular concern is the potential for money laundering and transnational crime to destabilise surrounding countries in Southeast Asia and elsewhere in the Asia-Pacific region in a complex set of spillover effects.[8]

China is concerned about the use of casinos to facilitate capital flight out of China.[9] It is difficult to determine whether the money fleeing China is licit or illicitly

---

[1] UNODC (2019), p. 177.

[2] German (2018), pp. 33–37.

[3] Langdale (2022).

[4] Bergin (2021); Finkelstein (2021); Bell (2022), Gotterson (2022), Western Australia (2022).

[5] Bergin (2021), pp. 298–306.

[6] UNODC (2019, 2022a, 2023).

[7] Douglas (2022).

[8] Wantakan Arcado (2022).

[9] China's ban on gambling is a cash gift to the rest of Asia (2022); Master (2020).

earned, but it violates Chinese government restrictions on Chinese citizens moving money overseas. Australian casinos have been used to facilitate Chinese capital flight[10] and it is likely to be undertaken in Southeast Asian physical and online casinos as well although little evidence is publicly available.

Transnational criminal groups use a variety of techniques to launder the proceeds of transnational crime, particularly trade-based money laundering (TBML) and underground banking.[11] However, casinos are an important means of money laundering in poor Southeast Asian countries, since the banking and financial systems of these countries are weakly developed.[12] Casinos often function as quasi-financial institutions in these countries and are used to bypass AML regulations imposed on the formal banking and financial system.

More generally, casinos undertake various financial activities which expose them to money laundering. They accept funds on account, conduct money exchange, money transfers, foreign currency exchange, stored value services, debit card cashing facilities and cheque cashing.[13] Austrac has argued that Crown Casino provided more than just gaming services to customers; it provided financial services that facilitate the movement of money into and out of the casino, including across international borders. These financial services are high value and high volume.[14]

The nature of transnational crime in the East Asian transnational crime system, as well as the role of money laundering in casinos in facilitating its operation is examined in Sect. 2. Section 3 considers means of combatting money laundering in casinos in Australia and Southeast Asia. Finally, in Sect. 4 some possible futures for casinos in the region are outlined.

2 Transnational Crime and Money Laundering in Southeast Asia

Rapid growth has taken place in transnational crime in the East Asian region, particularly in illegal drugs centred on Southeast Asia.[15] The Mekong region countries of Myanmar, Laos and Cambodia are of particular concern in Southeast Asia, although the Philippines, Vietnam and Thailand are impacted by transnational crime in casinos as well. Methamphetamines production grew rapidly from 2013, as China cracked down on illicit drugs production in China. In addition, opium

[10] Bell (2022), p. 205.

[11] Financial Action Task Force (2018), pp. 30–34.

[12] U.S. Department of State (2022).

[13] Financial Action Task Force (2009), p. 25.

[14] Austrac (2022), p. 1.

[15] UNODC (2019, 2022a).

production in the Golden Triangle has grown recently as well, reflecting the political unrest in Myanmar following the military coup in 2021.[16]

2.1 Transnational Crime and Money Laundering as an Interlocking System

Transnational crime and money laundering in the East Asian region is an interlocking system, with changes in one country having flow-on impacts on other countries. Money laundering networks in the region are a key component of East Asian transnational crime networks and allow criminal groups to pay expenses to suppliers, distributors and corrupt government officials. In addition, money laundering networks allow the proceeds of crime to be remitted to "investors" in criminal syndicates, often located in Hong Kong and Macau.[17] The inability or unwillingness of governments in the region to effectively control the rapidly growing casino industry provides criminal groups with a convenient way to launder huge amounts of money into the formal economy.[18]

2.2 Displacement Effects

A systems perspective is important in understanding the nature of displacement effects operating in transnational crime. The crackdown on methamphetamines production in China pushed production out of China to weakly-regulated Southeast Asian countries, particularly Mekong region countries of Myanmar, Laos and Cambodia.[19]

The displacement effect has reshaped the illegal drug and wildlife trafficking industries in the region, with methamphetamines production skyrocketing in Shan State in Myanmar and more illegal wildlife trafficking and marketing taking place in Southeast Asia.[20] The displacement effect has had major flow-on effects on the demand for money laundering in the region, since a significant percentage of the proceeds of these crimes is recycled through the region's rapidly-expanding network of physical and online casinos.[21]

[16] UNODC (2023); Doyle (2023).

[17] UNODC (2019), p. 177; CNN (2018).

[18] Douglas (2019).

[19] Douglas (2019); UNODC (2019); Farrelly et al. (2022), p. 10.

[20] Beech and Saw (2020).

[21] Douglas (2019, 2022).

2.3 Spillover Effects

A systems perspective is also important in spillover effects from transnational crime in the Mekong region, which is affecting surrounding countries in Southeast Asia, as well as the rest of the Asia-Pacific region. These spillover effects are likely to contribute to the growth of corruption and crime and over time destabilise the region by weakening government institutions.

2.4 Thailand Case Study

Thailand and other Southeast Asian countries face major crime overspill problems stemming from the rise of transnational crime in the Mekong countries of Myanmar, Laos and Cambodia. In particular, the overspill of crime into Thailand from Myanmar is creating significant problems.[22] Casinos are banned in Thailand, but illegal casinos operated by Chinese criminal groups are being used to launder money from illegal drug trafficking and other illicit activities..[23] While the Thai government has closed illegal online gambling operators, new groups are continually springing up.[24]

A major scandal in Thailand emerged in 2022 which has exposed extensive corruption on the part of senior police officers and politicians. Chinese criminal groups have been involved in trafficking illegal drugs from Myanmar through Thailand, as well as being involved in illegal migration of Chinese to Thailand, property development and money laundering.[25] illegal casinos were used in laundering the proceeds of these crimes.[26] although other means of money laundering are utilised such as TBML.[27] The Thai case study illustrates the overspill of crime from adjacent Mekong countries and the displacement effect of China's crackdown on transnational crime, which has pushed crime into corrupt Southeast Asian countries.

2.5 High Levels of Corruption and Crime in the Mekong Region

The difficulties of transnational crime and money laundering in the Mekong region are huge, since the countries have very high levels of corruption and crime. The

[22] Anthony (2023b).

[23] Gibbs (2022).

[24] Gamblers and hosts at illegal gambling dens are being jailed as massive crackdown proceeds apace (2021).

[25] Ngamkham (2023); Gibbs (2022).

[26] Anthony (2023a); Officials squirm amid Chuvit's Triad expose (2023).

[27] Sivasomboon (2020).

Corruption Perceptions Index for 2022 showed the Mekong countries as being highly corrupt: out of 180 countries, Laos was the least corrupt of the three countries, with a ranking of 126, Cambodia next with 150 and Myanmar, the most corrupt, at 157.[28] Money laundering rankings show a similar pattern, with Myanmar ranked the third worst and Cambodia the seventh worst of all countries in the survey.[29] Furthermore, money laundering prosecutions in these countries are very low.

2.6 *Money Laundering in Southeast Asian Casinos*

Casinos play a major role in laundering the massive profits from transnational crime in the Mekong region, the surrounding Southeast Asian region and in the broader Asia-Pacific region. A rapid growth in the number of casinos in Southeast Asia has occurred, with 340 operating in 2022,[30] although this number does not include illegal casinos operating in the region.

In particular, casinos in Special Economic Zones (SEZs) in the border regions of Mekong countries facilitate money laundering.[31] Autonomous special regions run by regional militias in Myanmar have concentrations of casinos in the Kokang, Mongla and Wa territories.[32] The casinos are central players in illicit gambling and money laundering, but also for racketeering, illegal drug trafficking, human trafficking and wildlife smuggling,[33]

The Kings Romans casino in Laos, part of the Golden Triangle SEZ and operated by the Zhao Wei criminal syndicate, has been identified by the U.S. Treasury as a major transnational crime syndicate trafficking in illegal drugs, endangered wildlife, human trafficking and prostitution.[34] Ostensibly, the SEZ facilitates economic growth in the Golden Triangle region, but it functions as a "one-stop shop" for transnational crime.[35] The SEZ has a diverse range of criminal activities, ranging from illegal drugs, wildlife and human trafficking and child prostitution. Illegal online gambling and online scamming activities are also prominent activities.[36] The Kings Romans casino occupies a key role in laundering the proceeds of these criminal activities.

---

[28] Transparency International (2023).

[29] Basel Institute of Governance (2022).

[30] Douglas (2022).

[31] UNODC (2019), p. 16; Douglas (2022).

[32] Sai (2019); Gao et al. (2019).

[33] Clapp and Tower (2023); International Crisis Group (2019), p. 15; Douglas (2022).

[34] U.S. Department of Treasury (2018).

[35] Langdale (2023).

[36] Strangio (2021); van Uhm and Wong (2021).

Sihanoukville in Cambodia has a SEZ, which is part of China's Belt and Road Initiative.[37] It attracted numerous Chinese physical and online casinos, but the banning of online casinos in 2019 by the Cambodian government and the impact of Covid-19 decimated Chinese gambling tourism and led to the exodus of thousands of Chinese workers. The ban led to the growth of online scamming centres in Sihanoukville, with online gaming continuing in an underground manner.[38] Sihanoukville is a major money laundering centre for illegal drugs and other illicit activity.[39] These casinos operate in both a physical and online manner and in recent years have become major online scamming centres with thousands of workers imprisoned in walled compounds.[40]

3 Money Laundering in Australian Casinos

Australian casinos are linked to the East Asian transnational crime system. The casinos are involved in other areas of money laundering, but these aspects are not considered in this paper.

A number of Australian state governments commissioned inquiries into money laundering taking place in their respective states.[41] The inquiries concluded that Australia's two largest casinos, Crown Casino and Star Entertainment, were unfit to hold a casino license. However, the inquiries did not terminate the companies' casino licenses; they were fined and special supervisors appointed for a number of years to ensure their performance satisfied the respective state government casino regulatory authorities. In addition, the use of China's UnionPay cards to facilitate Chinese capital flight has been banned.

The government inquiries effectively found that the casinos were "too big to fail". Governments were loath to close them down, because they employ large numbers of people, contribute to taxation revenue and are significant attractions for foreign tourists. The inquiries did not explore the failures of regulation at a state level. Similarly, at a Federal level Austrac did little to investigate the money laundering practices of Crown or Star casinos prior to press reports by investigative journalists in 2019.[42]

The government inquiries into money laundering in casinos found that their targeting of the VIP market exposed them to the crime-ridden junket operations bringing wealthy Chinese gamblers to Australia. As a result, these junket operators have been banned in Australia, but it is likely that the politically-well connected

[37] Devonshire-Ellis (2022).

[38] Farrelly et al. (2022), p. 7.

[39] Macan-Markar (2019).

[40] Kennedy and Southern (2022); Samean (2022); Tan (2022).

[41] Bergin (2021); Finkelstein (2021); Bell (2022), Gotterson (2022), Western Australia (2022).

[42] Bashan (2022).

casino companies will lobby state governments for these bans to be watered-down or eliminated over time. The Bell Inquiry found that despite publicly saying that it had ended the junket program, Star Entertainment was exploring the use of Third-Party Referral arrangements. These arrangements involved existing customers or individuals previously employed by junkets who could introduce a potential customer to the sales team.[43]

Australia is faced with growing transnational crime and money laundering problems associated with Chinese and other criminal organisations A major demand for money laundering resulted from transnational illegal drug trafficking and casinos provided a means of laundering the proceeds of this crime. Furthermore, wealthy Chinese wanted to transfer large amounts of money to Australia despite such transfers violating strict Chinese laws on capital flight. Australian casinos were used to facilitate Chinese capital flight.[44]

Money laundering problems in Australian casinos emerged for a variety of reasons. One was that regulators shifted to a self-regulation model for casinos and largely abandoned close monitoring of casino transactions.[45] Secondly, state and Federal regulators failed to appreciate that Australia's transnational crime and associated money laundering had shifted to a much larger scale. Criminals were looking for "weak links" to launder large sums of illicitly-earned money and found that casinos were loosely regulated in Australia.

Australian casinos face growing competition from Southeast Asian casinos, which have a key advantage of proximity to the Chinese market compared to those in Australia.[46] New Integrated Resort casinos have been built in Southeast Asian countries that provide high-quality holiday resorts as well as gaming facilities. Casinos in the Mekong region (e.g., Shwe Kokko in Myanmar and Kings Romans casino in Laos) are notorious hubs for transnational crime and money laundering.[47] A number of Mekong countries are corrupt and crime-ridden and transnational criminals are already laundering massive sums though these casinos.[48] As a result, Australian casinos will struggle to attract Asian gaming tourists and are likely to pressure their respective state governments to "water down" AML restrictions on their operations to match Southeast Asian casino competitors.

[43] Bell (2022), p. 144.

[44] Langdale (2022).

[45] Bergin (2021), pp. 37–43; Hatch (2022).

[46] Langdale (2022).

[47] Kennedy and Southern (2022); Langdale (2023).

[48] Douglas (2019); van Uhm and Wong (2021).

4 Combatting Money Laundering in Casinos

This section outlines a fundamental dilemma for governments in Southeast Asia and Australia in combatting money laundering in casinos. Many are conflicted in their policies in this area: on the one hand, they recognise that unless casinos are strictly regulated crime will flourish. On the other hand, they want to promote economic benefits from casinos: namely, expand international tourism and employment as well as gaining taxation revenue. Governments have followed a "pot of gold" casino strategy, neglecting money laundering and crime associated with the sector.

We considered in Sect. 2 the role of money laundering in casinos in Southeast Asia and Australia in the context of the East Asian transnational crime system. This crime system and the associated money laundering in casinos is growing rapidly. Unfortunately, most law enforcement operations are national in scope and, while they may disrupt the transnational crime system and associated money laundering briefly, they have little impact on the overall criminal activity in the region. National intervention in crime and anti-corruption policies may simply displace criminal activity to other countries.

The head of the UNODC in Southeast Asia, Jeremy Douglas, argues that the law enforcement strategy of focusing on illegal drug interdiction has not worked and its focus needs to shift to prevention of demand.[49] This proposed shift in strategy meshes in with the move away from purely law enforcement supply strategies towards the use of public health measures to reduce demand.[50] Furthermore, Douglas argues that the overall transnational crime system has to be attacked by law enforcement agencies by disrupting illicit banking networks, precursor chemical supply chains, as well as intermediaries in illicit networks, such as bankers, accountants and lawyers that facilitate money laundering networks.[51]

Unfortunately, governments in the region have not adopted such a systems approach to combat transnational crime and money laundering. The transnational crime networks in the region need to be outlined and "weak links" identified for law enforcement action. At the same time, it must be recognised that these crime networks change rapidly. What are the likely future changes in the East Asian transnational crime system?

Transnational criminal groups utilise a wide variety of money laundering approaches, with major ones being TBML and underground banking techniques.[52] Virtually no aggregate information exists on the overall size of different means of money laundering, but anecdotal evidence suggests that TBML and underground banking methods are the major means. However, casinos are an important means of money laundering in Southeast Asia, and have played a significant role in Australia.

[49] Doyle (2023).

[50] Johnson et al. (2022).

[51] Doyle (2023).

[52] Financial Action Task Force (2018), pp. 30–34.

They represent a "weak link" in preventing money laundering. Governments need to recognise the vulnerability of their societies to money laundering in casinos.

5 Southeast Asia

We have seen that Southeast Asian casinos have proliferated partly to service the large demand from physical and online Chinese gamblers, but also to launder the proceeds of transnational crime. The massive profits from transnational crime in Southeast Asia allow criminal groups to bribe government and law enforcement officials. It is very difficult to overcome corruption in the region[53] Furthermore, demand for illicit products, particularly illegal drugs, is rising globally. Consumption of illegal drugs in wealthy countries is large and few initiatives to reduce consumption are working. As a result, transnational crime and associated money laundering networks are well developed. Casinos are an ideal means of laundering the proceeds of crime.

5.1 Combatting Money Laundering and Corruption

The UNODC and other international agencies have instituted training programs to improve governance, reduce bribery and corruption in Mekong region countries[54] While these programs have had some success, transnational crime is still spiralling out of control in the region.

5.2 Myanmar

Myanmar has a particular problem in combatting money laundering in its casinos, given the lawlessness in many regions. The military junta is corrupt and the army (Tatmadaw) is heavily involved in businesses, many of which are illicit[55] Furthermore, even if the military junta wanted to crack down on transnational crime and money laundering, it does not have control over many border regions.[56] Regional ethnic militia groups are closely involved in the criminal economy;[57] the trends

[53] Lintner (2022).

[54] UNODC (2022b).

[55] United Nations. Human Rights Council (2019); Global Witness (2021).

[56] Clapp and Tower (2023).

[57] International Crisis Group (2019).

indicate that the problems are worsening.[58] Chinese transnational criminal groups control much of this criminal activity.[59] Most of the profits from transnational crime are reinvested in local businesses, but a significant amount is laundered through casinos into regional financial centres such as Hong Kong.[60] Numerous physical and online casinos are located in these conflict zones.[61]

5.3 *Laos*

The country suffers from high levels of corruption. Bokeo province is a key illegal drug trafficking route, particularly for methamphetamines.[62] The Kings Roman casino in the Golden Triangle SEZ is a "one-stop shop" for transnational crime and is ideally situated in the province to launder profits from the diverse range of illicit activities.[63] A key difficulty in controlling money laundering in the casino is that the Laotian government is a 30% owner of the Golden Triangle SEZ. The Zhao Wei group, the owner of the Kings Romans casino, has high-level links to the Laotian government. The government has ceded security to this group in return for economic rents and is unlikely to combat money laundering in the casino. In fact, the Laotian government is allowing Zhao Wei to expand his activities in other parts of Laos.[64]

5.4 *Cambodia*

Combatting money laundering in Cambodia's casinos is difficult given the endemic corruption at national, provincial and local scales.[65] Cambodia is ranked seventh worst in the world in 2022 for money laundering.[66] Cambodia has passed AML legislation and it has been removed from the FATF's grey list of countries in need of increased monitoring.[67] Cambodia has responded to international criticism over the human rights abuses in its illegal casinos and shut down many of them.[68] However,

---

[58] UNODC (2023).

[59] Tower and Clapp (2021).

[60] Sai (2019).

[61] International Crisis Group (2019).

[62] Strangio (2022).

[63] Langdale (2023).

[64] Zsombor (2022).

[65] Hutt (2019).

[66] Basel Institute of Governance (2022).

[67] Basel Institute of Governance (2023).

[68] Gibbs (2023).

despite these improvements, the country suffers from major crime and corruption problems and Cambodia's casinos are heavily involved in money laundering.

5.5 Role of Hong Kong and Macau

Hong Kong and Macau play an important role in facilitating money laundering in casinos throughout the Asia-Pacific region.[69] Government regulation of the casino industry in Macau has been tightened, particularly in the crime-ridden junket industry catering to VIP gamblers from China. China has imprisoned executives from Suncity, formerly the world's largest junket operator, for illegal online gambling.[70] In addition, Levo Chan, head of a major junket operator Tak Chun, has been imprisoned for illegal gambling and money laundering.[71]

However, much more needs to be done. Regulations covering shell companies in Hong Kong need to be tightened and their operations limited to genuine companies to prevent criminal groups using them.[72] Business and financial intermediaries facilitate the international operations of transnational crime and money laundering groups. Furthermore, little law enforcement activity has been directed at senior members of Triad societies, whereas regular sweeps are conducted to arrest low-level members of these societies.[73]

5.6 China's Role

China is a key player in combatting money laundering in Southeast Asia's casinos. China has been upset about the extent of illegal online gambling in Southeast Asia targeting Chinese citizens and has pressured Cambodia and the Philippines to halt such activities.[74] However, Cambodia has limited ability to control underground online casinos (e.g., Sihanoukville). The Philippines government is resistant to China's pressure although China has threatened Southeast Asian countries that it will ban Chinese tourism if they do not halt online illegal gambling.[75]

China's growing linkages in Southeast Asia raises complex geopolitical and economic issues. Its concerns about casinos facilitating Chinese capital flight, money laundering and transnational crime needs to be balanced against its other

[69] CNN (2018); Douglas (2019).

[70] Hung (2023).

[71] Chan (2023).

[72] Lo (2022).

[73] Lo (2023).

[74] Conneller (2021).

[75] Cohen (2023); Ramos-Araneta and Lopez (2022).

economic and geopolitical goals in the region. The situation is particularly complex in Myanmar given China's delicate relations with regional warlords in border regions and its overall relations with the central military government.[76]

5.7 The Philippines

The Philippines government has vacillated in its casino policies.[77] On the one hand, it has promoted itself as a regional gambling hub, particularly for Chinese gamblers, but also for gamblers in the Asia-Pacific region. On the other hand, this policy has contributed to a rise in transnational crime and money laundering.

The Philippines, like other countries in the Asia-Pacific region, recognised the opportunities in the casino industry that emerged with China's crackdown on corruption in Macau.[78] Initially, the Philippines exempted its casinos from money laundering legislation in order to maximise its casino revenue. The government's goal was to grow employment, taxation revenue and international tourism.

The Philippines Offshore Gaming Operations (POGOs) have been controversial given the crime associated with many of them.[79] Furthermore, they have targeted the online Chinese gambling market, even though it is illegal to gamble online in China. The POGOs attracted mainland Chinese workers, often working illegally in the Philippines, as well as a wide range of criminal activity, such as scams, extortion, prostitution and kidnapping.[80] The Chinese government has warned the Philippines not to target the online Chinese gambling market since it is illegal for Chinese citizens to participate in it. More recently China has threatened to cut off Chinese tourism to the Philippines is it does not act.[81]

One of the consequences of the exemption of casinos from money laundering legislation was that casinos were used to launder the proceeds of the Bangladesh Bank cyberheist.[82] Money laundering regulations have been tightened following the Bangladesh Bank cyberheist, but the U.S. Department of State[83] has criticised the money laundering regulations for having a high single-transaction reporting threshold of US$100,000 and junket operators being excluded from reporting requirements. Furthermore, the Philippines government has been criticised for continuing

[76] Clapp and Tower (2023).

[77] Romero (2023).

[78] Kritz (2016).

[79] Anti-Money Laundering Council (2020), p. 2.

[80] Specter (2022); Stradbrooke (2021).

[81] Cohen (2023); Ramos-Araneta and Lopez (2022).

[82] Katz and Fan (2017).

[83] U.S. Department of State (2019), p. 157.

the strict bank secrecy law, one that makes the Philippines an attractive location for money laundering.[84]

While the Philippines government would like to be removed from the FATF's grey list of uncooperative jurisdictions, at the same time it wants to maximise revenue from physical and online casinos with as few AML requirements as possible. The Philippines remains on FATF's "grey list" in 2023 with serious money laundering deficiencies.[85]

6 Combatting Money Laundering in Casinos: Australia

We saw in Sect. 2 that Australian casinos were involved in the laundering of illegal drug proceeds and thus facilitated the operation of the East Asian transnational crime system. Even though junkets are now banned in Australian casinos, money laundering threats from transnational crime are likely to pose even greater problems in the future. The expansion of the size and sophistication of transnational criminal organisations in Mekong countries (Laos, Myanmar and Cambodia) are creating huge spillover impacts in the region. Additional countries in Southeast Asia, particularly, Thailand and Vietnam, are under growing threats from transnational crime and money laundering. This money laundering and transnational crime system poses long-term threats to Australian society.

State government inquiries into money laundering in casinos in Australia focused on domestic issues associated with criminal activity. Transnational crime issues were considered, but the inquiries were circumscribed by their limited resources and strict time limits. While the time and resource constraints faced by the inquiries are understandable, their failure to examine Asia-Pacific transnational crime and money laundering issues facing Australian casinos meant that their findings were limited in scope.

Clearly, the casino regulatory jurisdiction of state governments is limited to their particular state. However, regulation needs to be set in the context of the international competitive environment facing casinos and the transnational crime situation. Casinos operate in a fiercely competitive international environment for the premium mass and VIP markets. Many premium mass and VIP gamblers come from overseas, particularly China; often, these gamblers are offered inducements to gamble in different Asia-Pacific casinos.

State-based regulators are ill-equipped to monitor and evaluate money laundering threats that are emerging in their respective casinos. It is unrealistic to expect that each state regulator would undertake such a review. A move towards a national casino regulator would require the states to cede regulatory control of their casino industries to the Federal government. A move to a national casino regulator would

[84] Economist Intelligence Unit (2017).

[85] Financial Action Task Force (2023).

overcome the inherent regulatory weakness of state governments in that a significant percentage of their income comes from gambling taxes and fees.[86]

A key difficulty in combatting money laundering in casinos in Australia is that they are seen by state governments as a "pot of gold". State governments view casinos as contributing to the growth of international tourism, employment and taxation revenue. In contrast, transnational crime issues are seen as a problem for law enforcement agencies. Unfortunately, few states in Australia prioritise law enforcement despite their political rhetoric. As a result, little political will exists to strictly regulate casino operations. Furthermore, casinos have politically well-connected boards who lobby their respective governments very effectively.

7 Possible Futures in Combatting Money Laundering in Casinos

7.1 Future Importance of Online Gambling

A looming difficulty in combatting money laundering in casinos is the growing importance of online gambling. It is unknown how important this trend will be once the impact of the Covid-19 travel restrictions are lifted. However, it is likely that unregulated international online gambling from offshore gambling havens will pose a significant threat to physical casinos.

A Hong Kong case study found that a major increase in online betting occurred during the Covid-19 epidemic, particularly for alternative sports (e.g., e-sports and virtual sports). In addition, illegal online betting on horse racing and other sports in Hong Kong rose significantly. Macau junket operators expanded into online betting and gambling and given their linkages to organised crime, this trend is likely to lead to more criminal involvement in the illegal online betting market.[87]

The growing importance of international online gambling makes the role of governments in regulating gambling more difficult. Most governments in the region are oblivious to the threats from online gambling to their "pot of gold" strategy and their long-term revenue streams associated with physical casinos. While governments have banned many of these online gambling ventures, new technologies make it easier for illicit entrepreneurs to bypass these regulations and allow gamblers access to their global betting systems. New technologies are likely to make the international online gaming market more global in nature, since it will difficult to recognise where the service is being provided. Global money laundering hubs will be utilised to disguise the illicit financial flows.[88]

---

[86] Ziffer (2021).

[87] Asian Racing Federation (2021), p. 2.

[88] Purbrick (2023).

7.1.1 Trends in Transnational Crime and Money Laundering

We have focused on one component of transnational crime and money laundering in the East Asian region, namely the role of Chinese criminal groups. However, other transnational criminal groups such as Mexican and other Latin American cocaine cartels have entered the Asia-Pacific region, either on their own or in strategic alliances with Asian criminal groups.[89] It is likely that these Latin American groups will become even more significant regional operators in the future, attracted by rising incomes in many countries throughout the region, as well as the presence of "weak links" in corrupt countries. Furthermore, other transnational criminal groups (e.g., Nigerian and European) are active in the region, and these might be expected to expand their existing criminal activities.

The entry of new transnational criminal groups and rising standards of living in the region will lead to more sophisticated transnational crime and money laundering networks connecting the region to global criminal networks. For example, Chinese suppliers of precursor chemicals and Chinese money launderers have developed a sophisticated illicit trafficking network linking China, Mexico and North America.[90] Chinese criminals operating these money laundering networks provide their services to any criminal group and make use of casinos and other means of laundering the money. These complex transnational illicit networks will make combatting money laundering in casinos more difficult, since criminals utilise multiple means to disguise the proceeds of crime.

Unfortunately, little understanding of the long-term challenges facing casinos exists amongst Australian state casino regulators or those in Southeast Asia. A similar conclusion emerges from government inquiries into money laundering in British Columbia, Canada. Despite reports to the British Columbia government[91] which warned of the threats from Chinese transnational criminal groups and money launderers, the report of the Commission of Inquiry[92] neglected the role of these criminal groups arguing that it was beyond its limited resources and strict time limits. The co-lead counsel, Brock Martland, of the Cullen Inquiry explained that they did not have the time and mandate to explore the transnational crime aspects of casino-based crime in Vancouver.[93]

[89] Felbab-Brown (2022).

[90] Langdale (2021).

[91] German (2018, 2019).

[92] Cullen (2022).

[93] Wood (2022).

7.2 Southeast Asia

We have seen that transnational crime and money laundering in the East Asian region has been growing rapidly and that casinos play a significant role in this growth. It is difficult to see government anti-crime policies being successful in combatting the future growth of transnational crime.

It is unrealistic to expect comprehensive policies associated with AML legislation and enforcement in poorer Southeast Asian countries in the Mekong region (Myanmar, Laos and Cambodia). A more viable option would be to reduce demand for illegal drugs and other illicit activities in developed countries (such as Australia) than to expect many initiatives from poorer countries. Such an approach would reduce the demand for illegal drugs in developed countries and thus lower prices and profitability for transnational criminal groups.

However, it is important to encourage poorer Southeast Asian countries to enact policies to reduce transnational crime and prosecute criminals using casinos. Pressure from the FATF has led to some Southeast Asian countries passing legislation covering money laundering in casinos and Cambodia has been removed from FATF's "grey list" of countries subject to increased monitoring.[94] However, few Mekong region countries have prosecuted criminals and it is unlikely that much will be done for the foreseeable future.

Myanmar is the most extreme case of the breakdown of law and order in Southeast Asia.[95] The underlying security situation in Myanmar is getting worse and the central government has little control in many border regions. In addition, Myanmar's government is highly corrupt and shows little signs of improvement. Similarly, corruption needs to be brought under control in all regions of Laos and Cambodia, something that is unlikely for the foreseeable future.

The most likely outcome is that transnational crime and money laundering through casinos in the Mekong region countries will continue. Even if one country did manage to crackdown on crime and money laundering, it is likely that a displacement effect will occur and criminals will find other "weak link" countries in order to continue their operations.

7.3 Australia

A key difficulty in combatting money laundering in Australian casinos is that state governments compete amongst themselves to expand casino turnover in their jurisdictions. It is likely that there will be pressure in the future to loosen AML regulation covering casinos. Any loosening of AML regulation by one state is likely to be matched by other states, especially as the memory of state government inquiries into

[94] Cambodia removed from international money laundering "grey list" (2023).

[95] UNODC (2023).

money laundering fades. We have already seen that Australian casinos will be facing growing competition from loosely-regulated casinos in some Southeast Asian countries.

The future threats to Australian casinos from Southeast Asian and online gaming platforms make it important that Australia establishes a national gaming regulator. A key component of the role of such a regulator would be to examine trends in gaming, ranging from physical casinos and gambling ventures to new online gaming. Such a gaming regulator would identify the social and economic impacts of these new gaming ventures. Far too often Australian gambling regulators are too slow in reacting to looming money laundering and transnational crime threats.

Unfortunately, it is unlikely that states will cede regulatory control over their casinos to the Federal government. Most states view casinos as a key part of their broader economic strategy of promoting international gambling tourism and see themselves competing with other states for tourist income. Casinos are an important employment generator and contribute significantly to state taxation revenue.

It is difficult to be optimistic about the future success of law enforcement agencies in Southeast Asia and Australia in combatting money laundering in casinos. An important first step would be for national and state governments to prioritise the control of money laundering and transnational crime over their economic development goals. Failure to follow this step is likely to lead to a growing spiral of crime, which will worsen social and economic development throughout the region.

References

Anthony J (2023a) Charges brought against Chinese mafia kingpin as Chuwit warns witnesses are put under pressure. Thai Examiner, 20 Jan

Anthony J (2023b) Rising anger at Myanmar's regime is leading to scrutiny of its clandestine business links with Thailand. Thai Examiner, 18 Apr

Anti-Money Laundering Council (2020) Understanding the internet-based casino sector in the Philippines: a risk assessment. Republic of the Philippines, Manila

Asian Racing Federation (2021) A report of illegal betting growth during the Covid-19 pandemic. Council on Anti-Illegal Betting and Related Financial Crime, Hong Kong

AUSTRAC (2022) Concise statement. Federal Court of Australia, Sydney

Basel Institute of Governance (2022) Basel money laundering index. Basel Institute of Governance, Basel

Basel Institute on Governance (2023) Country briefing: Cambodia. Basel Institute of Governance, Basel

Bashan Y (2022) Austrac blind to Star's breaches. The Australian, 26 Mar, p 24

Beech H, Saw N (2020) Record raids in Myanmar point to shifting drug trade. The New York Times, 20 May 17

Bell A (2022) Review of The Star Pty Ltd, 31 Aug, Sydney, Vol 1

Bergin P (2021) Report. Inquiry under Section 143 of the Casino Control Act 1992 (NSW). Sydney. Vol 1

Cambodia removed from international money laundering "grey list" (2023) Inside Asian Gaming, 27 Feb

Chan P (2023) Former Tak Chun CEO Levo Chan sentenced to 14 years in prison. Inside Asian Gaming, 21 April

China's ban on gambling is a cash gift to the rest of Asia (2022) The Economist, 5 Dec

Clapp P, Tower J (2023) A criminal cancer spreads in Southeast Asia. U.S. Institute of Peace

CNN (2018) Asia's meth boom

Cohen M (2023) Philippine POGOs stick with Chinese betting, tempting Beijing's wrath. IGaming Business

Conneller P (2021) Beijing expands gambling travel blacklist to 'safeguard lives and property'. Casino.org

Cullen Commission (2022) Commission of inquiry into money laundering in British Columbia. Final Report, Vancouver

Devonshire-Ellis C (2022) Foreign investment opportunities in Cambodia. ASEAN Briefing

Douglas J (2019) Asian organized crime doubles down on casinos. CNN Wire

Douglas J (2022) How the Covid-19 pandemic forced Southeast Asia's casino criminals to bet on tech – and win. South China Morning Post, 7 Aug

Doyle K (2023) Q&A: The opium surge in Southeast Asia's 'Golden Triangle'. Al Jazeera, 18 Feb

Economist Intelligence Unit (2017) No major clean-up of dirty money. ViewsWire

Farrelly N, Dawkins A, Deegan P (2022) Sihanoukville: a hub of environmental crime convergence. Geneva, Global initiative against transnational crime

Felbab-Brown V (2022) The foreign policies of the Sinaloa Cartel and CJNG – Part II: The Asia-Pacific. Brookings Institution, Washington, DC

Financial Action Task Force (2009) Vulnerabilities of casinos and gaming sector (With the Asia/Pacific Group on Money Laundering). FATF Report, Asia/Pacific Group on Money Laundering, Paris

Financial Action Task Force (2018) Professional money laundering, Paris

Financial Action Task Force (2023) Jurisdictions under increased monitoring, Paris

Finkelstein Inquiry (2021) Report of the Royal Commission into the Casino operator and licence, vol 1, Melbourne

Gamblers and hosts at illegal gambling dens are being jailed as massive crackdown proceeds apace (2021) Thai Examiner, 9 Jan.

Gao J et al (2019) Tourism border-making: a political economy of China's border tourism. Ann Tour Res 76:1–13

German PM (2018) Dirty money: an independent review of money laundering in lower mainland casinos conducted for the Attorney General of British Columbia, 31 Mar

German P (2019) Dirty Money - Part 2 Turning the Tide - An Independent Review of Money Laundering in B.C. Real Estate, Luxury Vehicle Sales & Horse Racing. Conducted for the Attorney General of British Columbia

Gibbs E (2022) Thailand political corruption and illegal gambling becoming the new norm. Casino.org, 4 Nov

Gibbs E (2023) Cambodia's efforts to rid country of illegal casinos are paying off. Casino.org, 3 Jan

Global Witness (2021) Jade and conflict: Myanmar's vicious circle, London

Gotterson Inquiry (2022) External review of the Queensland operations of the star entertainment group limited. Brisbane

Hatch P (2022) 'The deceit, the crime, the destroyed lives': How Australia lost its gamble on casinos. Sydney Morning Herald, 1 Apr

Hung E (2023) 18 years' jail for 'junket king'. Chau South China Morning Post, 19 Jan. A3

Hutt D (2019) The truth about Cambodia's so-called corruption crackdown. The Diplomat, 28 Aug

International Crisis Group (2019) Fire and ice: conflict and Drugs in Myanmar's Shan State. Asia Report No. 299

Johnson K et al (2022) The global movement towards a public health approach to substance use disorders. Ann Med 54(1):1797–1808

Katz A, Fan W (2017) Baccarat binge helped launder the world's biggest cyberheist. Bloomberg, 4 Aug

Kennedy L, Southern N (2022) Inside Southeast Asia's casino scam archipelago. The Diplomat, 2 Aug
Kritz B (2016) PH casinos playing a dangerous game. The Manila Times, 19 Oct
Langdale J (2021) Chinese money laundering in North America. Eur Rev Org Crime 6(1):10–37
Langdale J (2022) Money laundering in Australian casinos. J Money Laund Control 26(7):26–109
Langdale J (2023) Transnational crime, money laundering and illegal online betting in Southeast Asia. Asian Racing Federation. Council on Anti-Illegal Betting and Related Financial Crime Bulletin
Lintner B (2022) Guide to investigating organized crime in the golden triangle: chapter 3 - Money laundering. Global Investigative Journalism Network
Lo C (2022) Hong Kong police arrest 13 linked to syndicate behind laundering of HK$1.4 billion in suspected crime proceeds. South China Morning Post, 5 Aug
Lo C (2023) Hong Kong police arrest more than 230 people in triad crackdown and seize drugs, illegal cigarettes, gambling chips, weapons and cars. South China Morning Post, 24 Feb
Macan-Markar M (2019) Cambodia and Laos casinos targeted for drug-trade money laundering. Nikkei Asian Review, 30 July
Master F (2020) Macau VIP casino industry out of luck as China cracks down on capital flows. Reuters News, 18 Aug
Ngamkham W (2023) 'We're on the triads' trail'. Bangkok Post, 2 Feb
Officials squirm amid Chuvit's Triad expose (2023) Bangkok Post, 9 Jan
Purbrick M (2023) The displacement of illegal betting and transnational organised crime. Asian Racing Federation Bulletin Council on Anti-Illegal Betting and Financial Crime, Quarterly Bulletin
Ramos-Araneta M, Lopez V (2022) China 'blacklists' PH as tourist site due to POGOs. Manila Standard, 12 Oct
Romero A (2023) Marcos wants good reason to ban POGOs. The Philippine Star, 22 Jan
Sai W (2019) Myanmar struggles to deal with money laundering and related crime. Mizzima
Samean L (2022) Sar Kheng, Chinese envoy discuss transnational crime. Phnom Penh Post, 28 Sept
Sivasomboon B (2020) Thai police say they have busted major money-laundering ring. Associated Press, 5 June
Specter H (2022) Philippine gaming operators involved in prostitution ring. Gambling News, 25 Feb
Stradbrooke S (2021) Philippine online gambling ranks shrink while kidnappings rise. Calvin.Ayre.com, 12 Jan
Strangio S (2021) Chinese casino magnate's empire set to expand in Laos. The Diplomat, 8 Apr
Strangio S (2022) Lao authorities seize another huge shipment of methamphetamine. The Diplomat, 26 Sept
Tan HY (2022) Remaking Sihanoukville. The Straits Times, 25 June
Tower J, Clapp P (2021) Chaos sparked by Myanmar coup fuels Chinese cross-border crime. United States Institute of Peace, 21 Apr
Transparency International (2023) Corruption perceptions index. Berlin
U.S. Department of State (2019) International narcotics control strategy report. Vol 2, Money laundering. Washington
U.S. Department of State (2022) Laos. Investment climate statements, custom report excerpts. Washington, D.C.
U.S. Department of Treasury (2018) Treasury sanctions the Zhao Wei transnational criminal organization. Washington, DC
United Nations. Human Rights Council (2019) The economic interests of the Myanmar Military. Independent International Fact-Finding Mission on Myanmar
UNODC (2019) Transnational organized crime in Southeast Asia: evolution, growth and impact. United Nations Office of Drugs and Crime, Bangkok
UNODC (2022a) Synthetic drugs in East and Southeast Asia: latest developments and challenges. Bangkok

UNODC (2022b) Southeast Asia anti-corruption newsletter. United Nations Office of Drugs and Crime, Bangkok

UNODC (2023) Myanmar Opium Survey 2022: cultivation, production, and implications. United Nations Office of Drugs and Crime, Bangkok

van Uhm D, Wong R (2021) Chinese organized crime and the illegal wildlife trade: diversification and outsourcing in the Golden Triangle. Trends in Organized Crime 24:486–505

Wantakan Arcado N (2022) Ice and instability: illicit financial flows along Thailand's borders. Center for Strategic and International Studies, Washington, D.C., p 22

Western Australia (2022) Perth Casino Royal Commission, Final Report. Perth, Western Australia

Wood G (2022) What B.C.'s money laundering inquiry missed. Burnaby Now, 26 May

Ziffer D (2021) Crown shows why casino regulation should go national, experts argue after Bergin report. Australian Broadcasting Corporation

Zsombor P (2022) UN warns of growing criminal threat from Mekong region casinos, SEZs. Voice of America News, 26 Sept

John Langdale is an Honorary Research Fellow at the Department of Security Studies and Criminology at Macquarie University in Sydney. His current research interests are in money laundering and transnational crime in the Asia-Pacific region. Recent research has examined the role of Chinese money laundering groups in North America, with a particular focus on the Vancouver Model of money laundering. He has also published on money laundering in Australian casinos, again focusing on the role of Chinese criminal groups. His current research focus is on the role of transnational crime and money laundering in Southeast Asia and gives particular attention to the role of casinos (physical and online) in facilitating criminal activity in the region.

FATF's Risk-Based Approach: Has the Pendulum Swung too Far?

Louis de Koker and Doron Goldbarsht

Abstract The introduction of the mandatory risk-based approach in the FATF standards in 2012 was revolutionary. It promised to free institutions from a general rule-based approach to empower them to manage their risks individually. This approach has however not delivered as much benefit as was promised. It burdens institutions, especially smaller institutions, which may not have sufficient resources to undertake appropriate financial crime risk assessments. It also leads to perverse unintended consequences that regulators are unable to effectively prevent. This chapter considers some of the questions regarding the risk-based approach in practice and concludes with suggestions for further research.

1 Introduction

The development of the risk-based approach of the Financial Action Task Force (FATF) is discussed in Chap. 1 of this collection[1] and the contributions to this collection highlight various aspects relating to the application of the risk-based approach to money laundering (ML), terrorist financing (TF) and proliferation financing (PF).

The risk-based approach, rooted in a proactive assessment of vulnerabilities and threats and identification of appropriate risk mitigation measures, allows regulated entities to allocate their resources and efforts more effectively by focusing on areas of higher risk.[2] It replaced the rule-based approach which became unfairly associated

[1] Goldbarsht and De Koker (2024), p. 1.

[2] FATF (2012–2023), p. 31.

L. de Koker (✉)
La Trobe Law School, Bundoora, VIC, Australia
e-mail: l.dekoker@latrobe.edu.au

D. Goldbarsht
Macquarie Law School, Sydney, NSW, Australia

D. Goldbarsht, L. de Koker (eds.), *Financial Crime and the Law*, Ius Gentium: Comparative Perspectives on Law and Justice 115,
https://doi.org/10.1007/978-3-031-59543-1_10

with a one one-size-fits-all approach. Rules, of course, do have an element of generalisation but they do not need to lack sophistication to distinguish between different sectors and different types of providers and customers within a sector. The risk-based approach was however attractive to regulators as they believed that regulated entities are better able than regulators to assess and mitigate their risks. That view was however not informed by extensive evidence when the FATF adopted it as a mandatory element of its standards. In fact, the Global Financial Crisis pointed emphatically to the risk assessment and risk mitigation weaknesses of the regulated financial entities. The risk-based approach did however hold the benefit of absolving regulators from political responsibility when institutional risk assessments turned out to be wrong.

Despite advice[3] in that regard the FATF did not adopt a specific definition of risk when it embraced the risk-based approach. It rather opted to describe it in general terms: "Risk can be seen as a function of three factors: threat, vulnerability and consequence."[4] In the terrorist financing methodology of the IMF staff, for example, the risk level is formally defined as "the likelihood of successful terrorist financing events in a jurisdiction multiplied by the consequences of the events."[5] The FATF itself however does not venture far beyond their general description when they discuss the concept of risk and even questioned their own description by indicating that countries in their national risk assessments may pay devote less time and attention to the "consequence" factor:[6]

> Given the challenges in determining or estimating the consequences of ML and TF it is accepted that incorporating consequence into risk assessments may not involve particularly sophisticated approaches, and that countries may instead opt to focus primarily on achieving a comprehensive understanding of their threats and vulnerabilities.

The risk lens tends to restrict discussions about the best ways to prevent ML/TF/PF. The anti-money laundering "follow the money" strategy that was embedded in the Vienna Convention, and underpinned the first set of FATF Forty Recommendations, was driven by a sense of opportunity rather than risk. A novel strategy was developed to access and leverage information and financial institutions to combat drug trafficking. Has the focus on risk mitigation since 2012 blinded policymakers and institutions to alternative approaches and opportunities to combat organised crime? Telecommunications data has proved quite powerful in the combating of crime. May that be a better—and more efficient approach—than the current level of reliance on financial services to combat crime?

Furthermore, institutional risk management can easily confuse regulatory and criminal enforcement and reputational risk for non-compliance with AML/CTF/CPF with actual risks of processing transactions involving crime or the financing of terrorism or proliferation.

---

[3] De Koker (2011), p. 379.

[4] FATF (2013), par 10.

[5] El Khoury (2023), p. 10.

[6] FATF (2013), par 10.

Given these concerns, are national and institutional risk-based anti-money laundering and counter terrorist and proliferation financing (AML/CTF/CPF) measure actually more effective than rule-based measures? Has the pendulum perhaps swung too far? This question together with research required to deepen our understanding of the risk-based approach and its alternatives, is explored in this chapter.

2 Financial Crime Risk Assessment Challenges

2.1 *Biased Assessments?*

Crime risk assessment is not an exact science. The FATF recognises that ML/TF/PF assessments are judgment-based processes.[7] In addition, the FATF, as quoted above, allows assessors to incorporate key elements of the risks assessment process—the consequences of abuse—without following "particularly sophisticated" or a "scientific"[8] approaches. In that regard it allows, if not encourages, assessors to assume that consequences are severe and amend their views if they identify data to alter that conclusion.[9] This approach primes the process for the overly conservative assessment of risk.[10]

Participants in ML/TF/PF risk assessment exercises at a national and institutional level may furthermore not have objective, disinterested views on risks. As subject-matter experts they may hold siloed views on the relevant risks that may overestimate the relevance of the threats or the extent of the vulnerabilities.[11] Risk assessment conclusions often inform budget decisions and that may also impact on views that key participants contribute.

Careful design of the risk assessment methodology, especially the way in which expert opinion is elicited in risk assessment processes, can mitigate the risks of reliance on subjective views. Leading examples of ML/TF/PF risk assessments by large economies have however been found to use questionable methodologies.[12] National risk assessments in turn inform institutional risk assessments. These are undertaken with fewer resources but generally with equally flawed methodologies. A number of academic studies have suggested improved approaches and methodologies,[13] but these have not resulted in changes in FATF risk assessment guidance or general practices.

---

[7] See FATF (2013) 7–8.

[8] FATF (2013), par 10.

[9] FATF 2019, pp. 8–9.

[10] De Koker and Casanovas (2024).

[11] Ferwerda and Kleemans (2019), p. 46. See also Hopkins and Shelton (2019), p. 64.

[12] Ferwerda and Reuter (2022), p. 5. See also Ferwerda and Reuter (2019).

[13] See Celik (2023), p. 22. E.g. Unger and Van Waarden (2013); Savona and Riccardi (2017); Ferwerda and Kleemans (2019); Hopkins and Shelton (2019).

Apart from the often thin and potentially biased data that may inform financial crime risk assessments, they also suffer from a lack of understanding of the problem as a whole. In Rumsfeldian terms, they reflect the "known knowns".[14] Our understanding of financial crime is, however, limited. Fraud, for example, is not always identified by victims or by law enforcement. Corruption is another example of a type of crime that may also escape notice. Unlike with offences of violence there are no bodies or blood, and physical evidence may be challenging to uncover and interpret. As mentioned in the introduction, certain effects of money laundering can paradoxically be experienced as advantageous to the overall operation of an organisation. Significant risks may therefore not feature or feature correctly in the assessments. This is of course often appreciated by risk assessors. Concerns about "unknown knowns" and "unknown unknowns" may, however, lead assessors to err on the side of caution. In those cases some risks may perhaps be assessed as higher than they actually are.

Financial crime risk assessments, it is submitted, care therefore often less helpful than believed.[15]

2.2 Resources and Expertise

Risk assessments processes require resources. Relevant data should be collected and made available. Appropriate expertise is also required, ranging from crime risk management expertise to data analysis to ensure appropriate synthesis of the information. It is understood that lower capacity countries do not have sufficient resources to perform appropriate national risk assessments. Technical assistance is therefore provided by a range of bodies. The World Bank, for example, developed a national money laundering risk assessment methodology and tools to assist such jurisdictions.[16] There is furthermore a small body of global experts that inform and facilitate these national processes.

National ML/TF/PF risk assessments are important elements of the FATF's risk-based approach. Institutional risk assessments are, however, as important, and arguably more important to the general effectiveness of a country's AML/CTF/CPF system. Regulated institutions and designated businesses and professions are at the cutting edge of preventive action. It is important that they can access and interpret national crime threat information correctly and apply that information to their own products, services and customer to assess institutional risk and design appropriate risk mitigation measures.

Despite the importance of their role, little attention is given to the risk management resources of these institutions. When the FATF adopted the risk-based

[14] See Alles (2009); Hampton et al. (2012).

[15] See Southworth and Levi (2024).

[16] See World Bank (2023).

approach in 2012 it was believed that regulated institutions are better able to understand and assess the money laundering and terrorist financing risks posed by their products, services and customers, than their regulators and supervisors were. That view was not backed by evidence. In fact, the Global Financial Crisis in 2008 showed that the world's largest banks and even insurance companies were not good at assessing major credit risks. Unlike crime risks, credit risk assessment lies at the heart of modern banking. The failure of large, resource-rich financial institutions to identify and manage such a key financial risk should not have inspired confidence about their ability to manage crime risks. The large fines for AML/CTF/CPF contraventions by large global banks also point to major weaknesses. The assumption that regulated institutions can identify crime risks and design better risk mitigation measures than their regulators is even more problematic in relation to small AML/CTF/CPF-regulated businesses and professions, like real estate agents and lawyers.

Failures in institutional financial risk assessments are however not only attributable to the institutions. In theory, the national risk assessment should provide the regulated institutions with sufficient information about crime threats at a national level to support institutional risk assessment processes. Governments often release general high-level sanitised versions of their national risk assessments. The sanitised public version may not be sufficiently informative to support accurate threat identification and assessment by institutions.

The design of crime risk control measures by institutions also receives little attention. The assumption is that an institution that identified criminal threats and vulnerabilities is able to identify, design and implement the most effective and efficient measures to mitigate the identified risks. While that assumption may hold for some large financial institutions the bulk of AML/CTF/CPF-regulated institutions are small and there is no obvious reason why many designated non-financial businesses and professions could be assumed to have such expertise. Even for large financial institutions, there is little evidence that this assumption is reasonable or evidence-based.

Westpac, one of Australia's four big banks, provides a good example. In 2014 Westpac became the last of Australia's big banks to de-bank money remitters, due to their concerns about the risks posed by these customers.[17] Westpac was subsequently charged and fined for risk management failures and reporting lapses relating to its own post-2014 remittance services, including processing repeated suspicious payments to the Philippines where money transfers matched known child-exploitation transaction patterns.[18]

[17] Eyers (2014).

[18] Goldbarsht and Sheedy (2024).

Westpac incurred a fine of A$ 1.3 billion for its compliance lapses,[19] many of which included risk management governance failures. An independent review report to its board put it as follows:[20]

> While Westpac carried out regular preliminary risk assessments and due diligence assessments of the correspondent banks identified in the AUSTRAC Claim, the assessments:
> - did not sufficiently assess some of the AML/CTF risks posed by those banks; and
> - did not sufficiently assess certain matters relating to the relevant correspondent banks that were required to be regularly assessed under the AML/CTF Rules.
>
> These issues were caused by limitations in the design of Westpac's processes and procedures, and in a small number of cases, by a failure to follow our established processes and procedures. In addition, reliance was placed on a particular operational team to perform functions that were critical to the due diligence process when that role would have been better suited to those with particular financial crime expertise.
>
> Aspects of the assurance obligations for all three lines of defence were not clear enough. Westpac should have had a more robust assurance process to detect the deficiencies.

In this regard the report concluded "Westpac's AML/CTF risk culture was immature and reactive."[21] This is just one example of many globally where poor risk management of large, well-resourced financial institutions led to AML/CTF/CPF fines.[22]

In most cases these flaws go unnoticed for extended periods. The majority of regulated institutions adopt ML/TF/PF risk assessments as a box-ticking exercise. Institutional risk assessments of supervised institutions are not generally reviewed by supervisory bodies. Flaws are generally only noticed when supervisors disagree with the application of simplified or standard due diligence measures where they believe enhanced due diligence is appropriate. It is uncommon for supervisors to find that institutional control measures are overdesigned and should be simplified. Flaws are of course also identified when institutions contravene AML/CTF laws and the contravention reflects a flawed appreciation of risk and risk control measures. These cases are however rare. In most cases supervisors defer to the institutions and view their risk assessment decisions as private commercial decisions.

Given the lack of government information-sharing about threats, regulated institutions turn to commercial and not for profit providers of information. Institutions tend to rely on indices such as Transparency International's Corruption Perceptions Index and the Basel AML Index of the Basel Institute for Governance for geographic risk data on ML/TF/PF risks posed by jurisdictions. In these cases, institutions often lack an in-depth understanding of the methodologies that inform these indices and

---

[19] See *Chief Executive Officer of the Australian Transaction Reports and Analysis Centre v Westpac Banking Corporation* [2020] FCA 1538 par 191. A$300 million for lapses relating to its correspondent banking relationships.

[20] Westpac (2020), par 4.2.3.

[21] Westpac (2020), par 4.1.

[22] See e.g. Prudential Inquiry into the Commonwealth Bank of Australia (2018), p.3 noting flaws in the bank such as inadequate oversight and challenge by the Board and its gatekeeper committees of emerging non-financial risks and an operational risk management framework that worked better on paper than in practice, supported by an immature and under-resourced compliance function.

how best to draw on them, for example the extent to which Transparency International Index highlight the bribe-paying countries compared to the jurisdictions of the bribe-takers, and how threats relating to the proceeds of corruption of the bribe-payers compare to threats relating to the proceeds of corruption of the bribe-takers.[23]

National and institutional responses to FATF-produced information further confirm concerns about the quality of risk assessment processes. Responses to the FATF's grey listing processes and to the FATF's changes regarding NPOs illustrate these responses.

3 FATF Greylisting

Commencing with the public listing of Non-Cooperative Countries and Territories ('NCCTs') in 2000, the FATF has been using peer review processes of country compliance with the FATF standards, combined with a public listing of jurisdictions that failed to make the grade.[24] The listing has however undergone various changes over the years.[25] From 2016, the FATF publishes two listing statements at the end of its three plenary meetings per year:

- *High-Risk Jurisdictions subject to a FATF Call for Action* (generally known as its blacklist): these high-risk jurisdictions have significant strategic deficiencies in their AML/CTF/CPF regimes and FATF calls on all jurisdictions to implement "counter-measures" against these countries to mitigate the risks they pose.
- *Jurisdictions under Increased Monitoring* (generally known as the greylist): these jurisdictions are actively working with the FATF to address the identified strategic deficiencies in their AML/CTF/CPF regimes. They have committed to swiftly resolving these within agreed timeframes.

The listing process was initially adopted to put economic pressure on governments of countries that were not ensuring appropriate compliance with the FATF standards. This is still very much the purpose of the blacklist. The greylist however changed in nature in 2016. The countries that are added to this list have FATF-identified strategic deficiencies, have committed to an action plan to address those deficiencies and are working with the FATF to implement that plan expeditiously. The greylisting statement was amended to reflect the change in nature of the listing. Since 2019, for example, it advises other countries to consider the information in the

[23] Transparency International had a Bribe-Payers Index but discontinued it in 2011. Transparency International (2011). See Cassin (2020): "Companies from the five highest-ranking "very clean" countries on the 2019 CPI (Denmark, New Zealand, Finland, Singapore, Sweden) have collectively paid $2.49 billion in FCPA (US Foreign Corrupt Practices Act) penalties since FCPA enforcement began. . . . There have not been any FCPA settlements involving companies from the bottom ten countries on the CPI."

[24] FATF (2000); Stessens (2001), p. 205; Goldbarsht (2020), p. 70.

[25] See De Koker et al. (2023).

statement but explicitly states that the FATF does not call for enhanced due diligence in relation to transactions and business linked to these countries. That is a very clear indication that the FATF does not view the listed countries as inherently higher risk jurisdictions.

In 2016, the European Union (EU), in response to the EU Fourth AML Directive,[26] adopted a list of AML/CTF-related high-risk third countries.[27] In essence, the EU list includes countries that are on the FATF greylist,[28] unless those countries are EU or European Economic Area members or EU-defined "least-developed countries" that do not pose a threat to the EU financial system or are designated as offshore financial centers.[29] In addition, it adds a small number of non greylisted jurisdictions too. Once added, greylisted countries may remain on the EU list even after FATF de-listed them.

When a country is listed on the EU list, EU institutions are obligated to implement enhanced due diligence measures. This, as explained above, is contrary to the FATF's position regarding greylisted countries.[30] The rationale behind the EU list and the required enhanced due diligence are based on the AML/CTF risks posed by these jurisdictions to the EU[31] and the need for a consistent EU response. However, these risks are usually highest during the country's assessment for FATF compliance. Many countries work to improve their assessed compliance levels in an attempt to avoid greylisting. As a result, the risks they pose, as evaluated by the FATF mutual evaluation processes, tend to be lower by the time they are greylisted, compared to the initial assessment period.[32]

South Africa provides a good case in point. FATF assessors visited the country from 22 October to 12 November 2019. Their mutual evaluation report was adopted by the FATF at its June 2021 Plenary meeting and published in October 2021.[33] The FATF identified 67 recommended actions that South Africa had to complete to align its AML/CTF/CPF framework with the international standards.[34] South Africa

[26] The measures envisaged by the EU Fourth Directive (2015), par 30 are extensive: "Member States should at least provide for enhanced customer due diligence measures to be applied by the obliged entities when dealing with natural persons or legal entities established in high-risk third countries identified by the Commission. Reliance on third parties established in such high-risk third countries should also be prohibited."

[27] Amended in 2020. See Unger (2023).

[28] The Commission's own processes allow for autonomous assessment of FATF greylisted countries but these assessments have hardly resulted in the non-listing of an EU-eligible FATF greylisted jurisdiction. European Commission (2020), p. 12.

[29] European Commission (2020); European Commission (2022).

[30] EU Fourth Directive (2015), par 30.

[31] See e.g. European Commission (2023): "Considering the level of financial systems' integration, the Single Market would be exposed to serious risks of money laundering and terrorist financing if the EU were not to consider adding jurisdictions identified by the FATF to the EU list."

[32] In relation to the EU list and FATF greylisting, see De Koker et al. (2023).

[33] FATF (2021).

[34] South African National Treasury (2023a).

began to address the deficiencies and by February 2023, when it was greylisted by the FATF, only 8 strategic deficiencies remained. When it greylisted South Africa, the FATF acknowledged the improvements made since 2021:[35]

> Since the adoption of its MER in June 2021, South Africa has made significant progress on many of the MER's recommended actions to improve its system including by developing national AML/CTF policies to address higher risks and newly amending the legal framework for TF and TFS, among others.

On 17 May 2023 the European Commission, responded to the FATF greylisting of South Africa, by adding South Africa to the EU list.[36]

While the EU should protect its financial system against risks poses by other jurisdictions the question is why they failed to act against the risk when it is first identified or at least when the mutual evaluation report was published. In South Africa's case the risk level clearly changed between 2019 and 2023 and the risks it posed to the EU were much lower in May 2023 than before. Listing South Africa based on the risks it poses to the EU system at time when those risks are lower than they were, does not reflect sound risk management principles.

This listing approach is even more absurd in the case of the United Kingdom. The UK maintains a similar list of high-risk third countries in terms of the Money Laundering, Terrorist Financing and Transfer of Funds (Information on the Payer) Regulations 2017. The UK listed South Africa on that list on 5 December 2023 when the Money Laundering and Terrorist Financing (High-Risk Countries) (Amendment) (No.2) Regulations 2023 took effect. Ironically this happened just after the FATF in October 2023 re-rated South Africa's compliance levels with 18 of the initial 20 deficiencies. Of these, 14 were upgraded to compliant or largely compliant, while one standard was found not be applicable:[37]

> Following these re-ratings, South Africa is now deemed to be fully or largely compliant (or not deficient) in 35 of the 40 FATF Recommendations, including in 5 of the 6 core FATF Recommendations. This means that South Africa is left with 5 deficiencies in technical compliance (including 3 of the 18 which were upgraded from non-compliant to partially compliant), and 2 which remain as partially compliant since 2021).

By the time the UK listed South Africa as a high-risk third jurisdiction, its FATF compliance levels compared well with most of the FATF members.

Risk management measures should be designed to respond to available risk information. Using FATF greylisting as a trigger rather than the publication of the initial mutual evaluation report is flawed risk management. The failure to respond to actual risks timeously is a fundamental flaw in this risk assessment and risk

---

[35] FATF 2023.

[36] European Commission (2023).

[37] South African National Treasury (2023b).

mitigation measure of the EU.[38] By following the EU but failing to respond to the FATF's own re-rating of a country the UK reflected an even weaker risk management foundation for its listing process.

4 The FATF Signaling Regarding NPOs

Country and institutional responses to FATF signaling about risk levels of Not-for-Profits (NPOs) raise further questions about the quality of country and institutional risk information processing abilities.

The FATF first extended its standards to NPOs in October 2001, when FATF when it adopted its eight Special Recommendations. This set included a standard on terrorist financing through the non-profit sector (Recommendation 8, previously Special Recommendation (SR) VIII).[39] Although Special Recommendation VIII merely called on participating states to review the non-profit sector in view of concerns about terrorist financing, it identified NPOs as 'particularly vulnerable' to abuse for the financing of terrorism.

For purposes of this standard, NPO was defined as "a legal entity or organisation that primarily engages in raising or disbursing funds for purposes such as charitable, religious, cultural, educational, social or fraternal purposes, or for the carrying out of other types of 'good works'".[40]

The NPO definition was important: It limited the scope of VIII to NPOs that raised or disbursed funds. When countries implemented measures responding to the Recommendation, many went beyond the FATF's scope and imposed more general NPO regulation to mitigate terrorist financing risks. This has had significant negative consequences for international development and global governance agendas as it impacted on donations to NPOs, their relationships with stakeholders and their cross-border activities.[41]

In June 2016, following ongoing efforts and calls by NPO advocates, the FATF revised Recommendation 8,[42] removing the blanket statement about NPO vulnerability and emphasising a focused, proportional and risk-based approach to NPO

[38] The same argument holds in relation to the UK's approach in terms of The Money Laundering, Terrorist Financing and Transfer of Funds (Information on the Payer) Regulations 2017.

[39] Romaniuk and Keatinge (2018), p. 267; Hayes (2012), p. 21–22.

[40] FATF (2010), INRVIII par 4.

[41] Romaniuk and Keatinge (2018), p. 269; Van der Does de Willebois (2010) 11–12.

[42] Romaniuk and Keatinge (2018).

regulation.[43] A revised interpretive note to Recommendation 8 reiterated the importance of proportionality in the application of Recommendation 8.[44]

As in 2001 many countries and institutions continued to ignore the FATF's risk guidance when implementing the FATF standards. A 2021 FATF review report on unintended consequences of the FATF standards found "... there continue to be countries that incorrectly implement the Standards and justify restrictive legal measures to NPOs in the name of "FATF compliance", both unintentionally and, in some cases, intentionally,"[45] and continued:[46]

> The FATF's assessment on the global implementation of the RBA in relation to R.8 indicates that most countries are not yet conducting adequate risk assessments of their NPO sector, and fewer are conducting risk-based outreach and monitoring.

In addition, banks have responded to the FATF standards by terminating or restricting services to NPOs.[47] In 2023 FATF revisited it standards and guidance hoping to influence risk management responses to its standards.[48]

The pre-2023 experiences, however, do not build confidence in the ability of countries or institutions to correctly interpret and apply the FATF's NPO standards and guidance or to appropriately assess and proportionally mitigate NPO risks. The 2023 amendments and guidance are furthermore limited to terrorist financing risk of NPOs and do not extend to their money laundering or proliferation financing risk. This restricts their ability to influence more holistic institutional risk assessments of NPOs.

5 Future Research

The risk-based approach is clearly far from perfect. Despite the tensions and strains inherent in the approach, increasing weight is being placed on it in the FATF standards, especially after it was extended in part to proliferation financing in 2020.[49] It is highly unlikely that the FATF will abandon the risk-based approach.

---

[43] Financial Action Task Force, *International Standards on Combating Money Laundering and The Financing of Terrorism & Proliferation: The FATF Recommendations* (FATF, 2012–2023) 11.

[44] The interpretive note uses language such as 'focused measures', 'identified threats' and 'flexibility'. The note clearly states that measures 'should not disrupt or discourage legitimate charitable activities': Financial Action Task Force, *International Standards on Combating Money Laundering and The Financing of Terrorism & Proliferation: The FATF Recommendations* (FATF, 2012–2019) 52–53.

[45] FATF (2021a), p. 5.

[46] FATF (2021a), p. 5.

[47] FATF (2023a), par 109.

[48] FATF (2023b, 2023c); Van Broekhoven et al. (2023).

[49] De Koker (2024).

There is therefore a clear need for research and evidence on current approaches to inform potential improvements to the current approach.

Are there for example instances where elements of the rule-based approach may deliver more effective and efficient results than the risk-based approach? Can the key definitions of risk used globally be aligned? Can more be done by governments to support industry or sectoral risk assessments that can provide more meaningful information to inform risk assessments by smaller institutions in regulated sectors?[50] Would sectors with fewer resources and more limited AML/CTF/CPF experience be better supported by industry risk assessments led by a public private partnership between the AML/CTF regulator and the sector's representative body?

While the risk-based approach leads to individualised approaches in each sector and institution, there may be benefit in standardising some aspects of the approach to ensure more consistent AML/CTF/CPF measures in a jurisdiction, e.g. to adopt consistent terminology and consistent best practice methodologies to effectively identify, assess and mitigate ML/TF/PF risks.

Institutional risk assessments can be used to mask bias and even anti-competitive behaviour. Can more be done to ensure a measure of oversight and independent review of institutional risk assessments, especially where these lead to financial exclusion? Should supervisory bodies assess the quality of institutional risk assessments and intervene where they are overly conservative?

Is there perhaps space for a hybrid approach? One where the regulator defines a set of AML/CTF/CPF rules for smaller institutions while larger institutions with the appetite and resources may implement a risk-based approach?

How can technology be used to provide all regulated institutions with appropriate real-time access to data to inform their risk management practices?[51]

We are still in an early phase of the transition from a rule-based approach to a risk-based approach. Acknowledging the challenges inherent in crime risk assessment and risk mitigation and researching current and alternative approaches will help support better implementation and identification of appropriate regulatory options to be employed in diverse contexts (Southworth and Levi 2024).

References

Alles M (2009) Governance in the age of unknown unknowns. Int J Discl Gov 6(2):85–88

Cassin H (2020) Is the CPI upside down? FCPA Blog. 24 January 2020. https://fcpablog.com/2020/01/24/is-the-cpi-upside-down/

Celik K (2023) Lessons learned from the first generation of national risk assessments. Draft report. EFI insight-finance. World Bank, Washington, DC

[50] Unger and Van Waarden (2013), p. 957.

[51] De Koker and Goldbarsht (2022), pp. 313–14.

De Koker L (2011) Aligning anti-money laundering, combating of financing of terror and financial inclusion: questions to consider when FATF standards are clarified. J Financ Crime 18(4): 361–386. https://doi.org/10.1108/13590791111173704

De Koker L (2024) Chapter 6: The FATF's combating of financing of proliferation standards: private sector implementation challenges. In: Goldbarsht D, de Koker L (eds) Financial crime and the law, Ius Gentium: comparative perspectives on law and justice. Springer, Cham

De Koker L, Casanovas P (2024) Chapter 3: De-risking, de-banking and denials of bank services: an over-compliance dilemma? In: De Koker L, Goldbarsht D (eds) Financial crime, law and governance, Ius Gentium: comparative perspectives on law and justice. Springer, Cham

De Koker L, Goldbarsht D (2022) Financial technologies and financial crime: key developments and areas for future research. In: De Koker L, Goldbarsht D (eds) Financial technology and the law: combating financial crime. Springer International Publishing, Cham, 303–320

De Koker L, Howell J, Morris N (2023) Economic consequences of greylisting by the Financial Action Task Force. Risks 11(5):81–113. https://doi.org/10.3390/risks11050081

El Khoury C (ed) (2023) Countering the financing of terrorism: good practices to enhance effectiveness. IMF, Washington DC. https://www.elibrary.imf.org/display/book/9798400204654/9798400204654.xml

EU Fourth AML Directive (2015) Directive (EU) 2015/849 of the European Parliament and of the Council of 20 May 2015 on the Prevention of the Use of the Financial System for the Purposes of Money Laundering or Terrorist Financing, Amending Regulation (EU) No 648/2012 of the European Parliament and of the Council, and Repealing Directive 2005/60/EC of the European Parliament and of the Council and Commission Directive 2006/70/EC. Off J Eur Union L 141: 73–117

European Commission (2020) Methodology for Identifying high-risk third countries under directive (EU) 2015/849. Commission Staff Working Document SWD(2020) 99. https://ec.europa.eu/info/sites/default/files/business_economy_euro/banking_and_finance/documents/200507-anti-money-laundering-terrorism-financing-action-plan-methodology_en.pdf

European Commission (2022) EU policy on high-risk third countries. https://ec.europa.eu/info/business-economy-euro/banking-and-finance/financial-supervision-and-risk-management/anti-money-laundering-and-countering-financing-terrorism/eu-policy-high-risk-third-countries_en#objectives

European Commission (2023) Anti-money laundering: European Commission updates list of high-risk third-country jurisdictions. Daily News 17.5.2023. https://ec.europa.eu/commission/presscorner/detail/en/mex_23_2805

Eyers (2014) Westpac closes door on money transfer operators as terror laws bite. The Sydney Morning Herald. 18 November 2014. https://www.smh.com.au/business/banking-and-finance/westpac-closes-door-on-money-transfer-operators-as-terror-laws-bite-20141118-11p75z.html

FATF (2000) Annual Report 1999–2000. FATF, Paris. https://www.fatf-gafi.org/en/publications/Fatfgeneral/Fatfannualreport1999-2000.html

FATF (2010) In: FATF (ed) FATF IX special recommendations, Paris. https://www.fatf-gafi.org/content/dam/fatf-gafi/recommendations/FATF%20Standards%20-%20IX%20Special%20Recommendations%20and%20IN%20rc.pdf.coredownload.pdf

FATF (2012-2023) International standards on combating money laundering and the financing of terrorism & proliferation – the FATF recommendations. FATF, Paris

FATF (2013) Guidance: national money laundering and terrorist financing risk assessment. FATF, Paris. https://www.fatf-gafi.org/en/publications/Methodsandtrends/Nationalmoneylaunderingandterroristfinancingriskassessment.html

FATF (2019) Terrorist financing risk assessment guidance. FATF, Paris. https://www.fatf-gafi.org/en/publications/Methodsandtrends/Terrorist-financing-risk-assessment-guidance.html

FATF (2021) Anti-money laundering and counter-terrorist financing measures - South Africa: mutual evaluation report. FATF, Paris. https://www.fatf-gafi.org/en/publications/Mutualevaluations/Mer-south-africa-2021.html

FATF (2021a) High-level synopsis of the stocktake of the unintended consequences of the FATF standards. FATF, Paris. https://www.fatf-gafi.org/en/publications/Financialinclusionandnpoissues/Unintended-consequences-project.html

FATF (2023) Jurisdictions under increased monitoring. FATF, Paris. 24 February 2023. https://www.fatf-gafi.org/en/publications/High-risk-and-other-monitored-jurisdictions/Increased-monitoring-february-2023.html

FATF (2023a) Public consultation on the FATF best practice paper to combat the abuse of NPOs. Annex A: best practices paper on combating the abuse of non-profit organisations (Recommendation 8). https://www.fatf-gafi.org/en/publications/Fatfrecommendations/FATF-BPP-Combat-Abuse-NPOs-Public-Consultation.html

FATF (2023b) Protecting non-profits from abuse for terrorist financing through the risk-based implementation of revised. FATF Recommendation 8. 16 November 2023. https://www.fatf-gafi.org/en/publications/Fatfrecommendations/protecting-non-profits-abuse-implementation-R8.html#:~:text=Paris%2C%2016%20November%202023%20%2D%20The,%2DProfit%20Organisations%20(NPOs)

FATF (2023c) Best practices paper: combating the terrorist financing abuse of non-profit organisation. www.fatf-gafi.org/en/publications/Financialinclusionandnpoissues/Bpp-combating-abuse-npo.html

Ferwerda J, Kleemans ER (2019) Estimating money laundering risks: an application to business sectors in the Netherlands. Eur J Crim Policy Res 25:45–62. https://doi.org/10.1007/s10610-018-9391-4

Ferwerda J, Reuter P (2019) Learning from money laundering national risk assessments: the case of Italy and Switzerland. Eur J Crim Policy Res 25:5–20. https://doi.org/10.1007/s10610-018-9395-0

Ferwerda J, Reuter P (2022) National assessments of money laundering risks: learning from eight advanced countries. NRAs. https://openknowledge.worldbank.org/server/api/core/bitstreams/b860c956-659e-5005-93c9-4f06993c37ab/content

Goldbarsht D (2020) Global counter-terrorist financing and soft law. Edward Elgar, Cheltenham

Goldbarsht D, De Koker L (2024) Chapter 1: Financial crime and the law: identifying and mitigation risks. In: Goldbarsht D, de Koker L (eds) Financial crime and the law, Ius Gentium: comparative perspectives on law and justice. Springer, Cham

Goldbarsht D, Sheedy E (2024) Money laundering and the risk in the risk-based approach: the Australian context. Monash Univ Law Rev 50(1)

Hampton JA, Aina B, Andersson JM, Mirza HZ, Parmar S (2012) The Rumsfeld effect: the unknown unknown. J Exp Psychol Learn Mem Cogn 38(2):340–355. https://doi.org/10.1037/a0025376

Hayes B (2012) Counter-terrorism, "policy laundering," and the FATF: legalizing surveillance, regulating civil society. International Journal of Not-for-Profit Law 14(1–2):21–22

Hopkins M, Shelton N (2019) Identifying money laundering risk in the United Kingdom: observations from national risk assessments and a proposed alternative methodology. Eur J Crim Policy Res 25:63–82. https://doi.org/10.1007/s10610-018-9390-5

Prudential Inquiry into the Commonwealth Bank of Australia (2018) Australian Prudential Authority https://www.apra.gov.au/sites/default/files/CBA-Prudential-Inquiry_Final-Report_30042018.pdf

Romaniuk P, Keatinge T (2018) Protecting charities from terrorists ... and counterterrorists: FATF and the global effort to prevent terrorist financing through the non-profit sector. Interdiscipl J 69(2):265

Savona EU, Riccardi M (eds) (2017) Assessing the risk of money laundering in Europe: final report of project IARM. Transcrime, Università Cattolica del Sacro Cuore, Milan. www.transcrime.it/iarm

South African National Treasury (2023a) Fact sheet: what does FATF greylisting mean for a country? https://www.treasury.gov.za/comm_media/press/2023/2023022501%20FATF%20Grey%20Listing%20Fact%20Sheet.pdf

South African National Treasury (2023b) National Treasury welcomes latest Financial Action Task Force progress report (press statement, 29 November 2023) https://www.gov.za/news/media-statements/national-treasury-welcomes-latest-financial-action-task-force-progress-report#:~:text=On%2027%20October%202023%2C%20the,2021%20mutual%20evaluation%20(MER)

Southworth R, Levi, M (2024) Chapter 5: Application of the risk-based approach (RBA) for financial crime risk management by banks. In: Goldbarsht D, de Koker L (eds) Financial crime and the law, Ius Gentium: comparative perspectives on law and justice. Springer, Cham

Stessens G (2001) The FATF black list of non-cooperative countries or territories. Leiden J Int Law 1:199, 205–06

Transparency International (2011) Bribe payers index. https://www.transparency.org/en/publications/bribe-payers-index-2011

Unger B (2023) Reforming EU blacklisting. How to increase the effectiveness and avoid politicisation of the EU list of high-risk jurisdictions for anti-money laundering and counter-terrorism financing: US experience and considerations for EU reform. Publication for the Committee on Economic and Monetary Affairs (ECON), Policy Department for Economic, Scientific and Quality of Life Policies, European Parliament, Luxembourg. https://www.europarl.europa.eu/RegData/etudes/STUD/2023/740091/IPOL_STU(2023)740091_EN.pdf

Unger B, Van Waarden F (2013) How to dodge drowning in data? Rule- and risk-based anti-money laundering policies compared. In: Unger B, der Linde V (eds) Research handbook on money laundering. Edward Elgar, 399–425

Van Broekhoven L, Goswami S, Malmberg T, Knoote F (2023) The future of FATF Recommendation 8: a foresight piece. Human Security Collective. https://fatfplatform.org/assets/Final_R8-Foresight_pdf

Van der Does de Willebois E (2010) Nonprofit organizations and the combating of terrorism financing: a proportionate response. Working Paper No 208, The World Bank, Washington DC. https://openknowledge.worldbank.org/handle/10986/5926

Westpac (2020) Westpac releases findings into AUSTRAC Statement of Claim issues. 14 June 2020. https://www.westpac.com.au/about-westpac/media/media-releases/2020/4-june/

World Bank (2023) National money laundering and terrorist financing risk assessment toolkit https://www.worldbank.org/en/topic/financialmarketintegrity/brief/national-money-laundering-and-terrorist-financing-risk-assessment-toolkit-disclaimer-and-terms-of-use

Louis de Koker LLB LLM (UFS) LLM (Cantab) LLD (UFS) FSALS, is a Professor and Associate Dean: Research and Industry Engagement at the La Trobe Law School (Australia), an Extraordinary Professor at the Faculty of Law of the University of the Western Cape (South Africa) and a Board member of the Financial Integrity Hub (FIH) at Macquarie Law School. From 2014 to 2019 he was the national program leader of the Law and Policy research program of the Australian government-funded Data to Decisions Cooperative Research Centre. Louis is an expert on anti-money laundering and counterterrorist and proliferation financing, and especially the relationship between financial integrity and financial inclusion policies and regulations. Louis has worked with the Consultative Group to Assist the Poor, the World Bank, the OECD, the Asian Development Bank regulators and financial service providers on the design and implementation of appropriate integrity and inclusion over the past two decades. He has advised on a range of laws and regulations and his research on integrity laws and their impact on financial inclusion has been cited in publications of various international bodies including the World Bank, IMF, the Financial Action Task Force (FATF) and the Basel Committee on Banking Supervision.

Doron Goldbarsht LLB, LLM (HUJI), PhD (UNSW), is the Director of the Financial Integrity Hub (FIH) and an Associate Professor at Macquarie Law School, where he teaches banking and financial crime. He is an authority on anti-money laundering and counter-terrorist financing (AML/CTF) regulations, with expertise in the related fields of compliance and financial innovation, with over 20 years of experience in the field. His recent books *Financial Crime and the Law:*

Identifying and Mitigating Risks (Springer 2024, co-edited), *Financial Crime, Law and Governance: Navigating Challenges in Diverse Contexts* (Springer 2024, co-edited), *Financial Technology and the Law: Combating Financial Crime* (Springer, 2022 co-edited), and *Global Counter-Terrorist Financing and Soft Law: Multi-Layered Approaches* (Edward Elgar, 2020), as well as journal and chapter publications, focus on international AML/CTF standards and the mechanisms for their effective implementation and compliance at the national level.

Printed in the USA
CPSIA information can be obtained
at www.ICGtesting.com
CBHW071411030724
11078CB00003B/25

9 783031 595424